Creating Effective
Learning Environments

First Edition

Creating Effective Learning Environments

Ingrid Crowther
Athabasca University

THOMSON

NELSON

Australia   Canada   Mexico   Singapore   Spain   United Kingdom   United States

Creating Effective Learning Environments
First Edition

by Ingrid Crowther

Editorial Director and Publisher:
Evelyn Veitch

Executive Editor:
Joanna Cotton

Marketing Manager:
Chantal Lanning

Publisher's Representative:
Peter Jackson

Developmental Editor:
Joanne Sutherland

Production Editor:
Julie van Veen

Production Coordinator:
Hedy Sellers

Copy Editor/Proofreader:
Kelli Howey

Creative Director:
Angela Cluer

Interior Design:
Sonya V. Thursby/Opus House

Cover Design:
Pedro Gaudenz Pereira

Cover and Interior Images:
Ingrid Crowther

Compositor:
Carol Magee

Printer:
Webcom

National Library of Canada Cataloguing in Publication Data

Crowther, Ingrid, 1944–
Creating effective learning environments/Ingrid Crowther.

Includes bibliographical references and index.
ISBN 0-17-616978-4

1. Classroom environment.
2. Education, Preschool.
I. Title

LB1140.4.C76 2002   372.21
C2002-901054-3

Table of Contents

Chapter **7** Quiet Play 139

Chapter **8** Dramatic Play 161

Chapter **9** Creative Arts 181

Chapter **10** Manipulative Experiences 205

Preface

▶ Why Was This Book Written?

Many books have been published that discuss the subject of curricula for young children. Most of these texts, however, either have a strong focus on early childhood curriculum theories or focus on the application of those theories. Furthermore, the applications discussed are often prescriptive, as specific methodologies and materials are suggested for groups of children.

Regardless of which philosophical approach is embraced in the teaching of young children, there is one fundamental truth. Curriculum needs to be based on the strengths and needs of children. This information is gathered through careful observation and documentation and is one of the cornerstones of curriculum development (figure P-1).

The purpose of this text is to take curriculum development to another level: to fill the gap between theory and practice. This text will help students to look at curriculum from the child's perspective and to understand how that perspective is linked to learning and theory. The centre of any curriculum is the child. Therefore, it is critical to start not with general theories or applications that are suitable for many, but with each individual child.

▶ Philosophy

Children, families, early childhood educators, and other adults are seen as partners in creating learning experiences for children. All partners in this process continually evolve and learn from each other. Thus, curriculum is a fluid process that continually changes and evolves with changing needs, interests, and learning. Curriculum starts with the learner—the child. Curriculum emerges from each child's interests, experiences, and abilities.

This book is a documentation of individuals and groups of children learning over time. Each curriculum discussion starts with the *real* experiences that children have had. From these experiences, pertinent theory is woven in, explained,

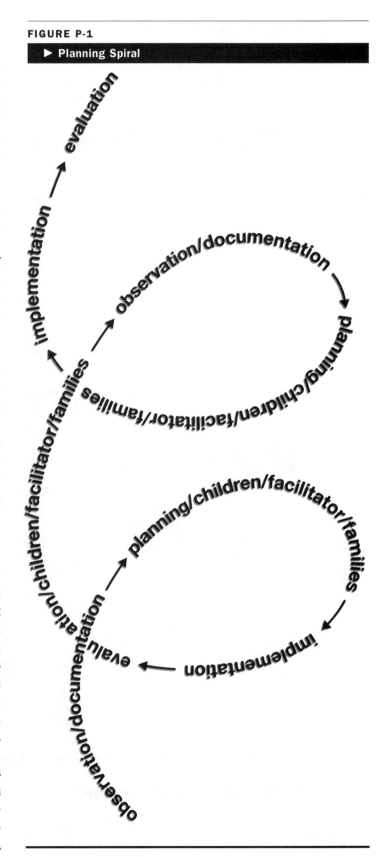

FIGURE P-1

▶ Planning Spiral

and expanded. Aspects of the learning environment and facilitator interactions are also woven around these experiences and explained or expanded.

Curriculum is treated as an integrated unit that includes a child as the centre of that unit with all other aspects supporting the growth and development of that child (figure P-2).

FIGURE P-2

▶ **Interactive Learning Cycle**

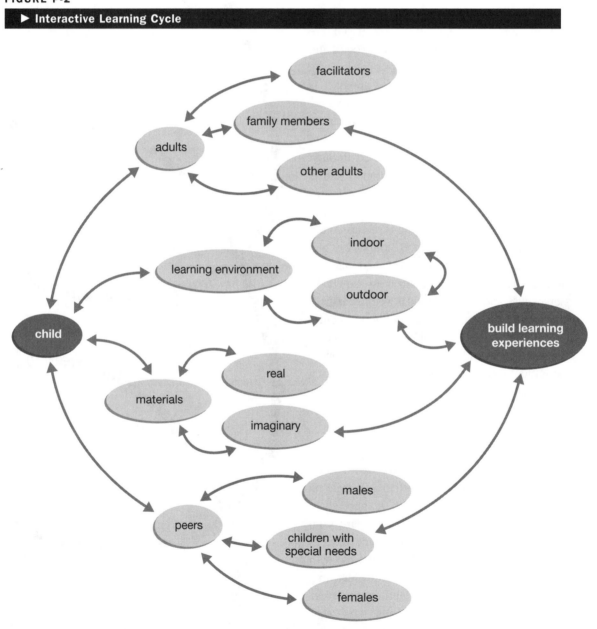

▶ The Learning Environment

It is impossible to separate the learning that occurs within various environments—home, community, indoor environments, and outdoor environments. All parts of the learning environment are equally important and there should be uninhibited flow from one environment to another. Experiences from home are part of the experiences in the daily lives of children. All activities that occur indoors can also occur outdoors. In order for learning to be transferred from one setting to another, children's experiences must be maximized in all environments.

The children involved in the experiences documented in the text are an inclusive group. They are from a variety of cultural and ethnic backgrounds including Native, Chinese, Japanese, black, and white. Some of the children also have special needs. The environment was set up to encourage the skills of all of these children. The children played an active part in making decisions, helping set up the learning environment, and evaluating their experiences. Families participated in helping in the learning environment, evaluating the children's learning experiences, and making suggestions in the planning process.

The facilitator's role in this environment was to coordinate all activities, document the children's learning and experiences, and provide an environment that empowered all individuals to become active partners in learning.

▶ Organization of the Text

The first two chapters lay the foundations of the text. The focus of Chapter 1 is the relationship of play and learning for young children, whereas the focus of Chapter 2 centres around how to effectively set up learning spaces that encourage play as a means of learning.

The remaining ten chapters each discuss a specific learning environment. These learning environments are based on curricular areas that are essential components of all quality learning environments for young children. A glossary is included at the end of the text. Key terms are highlighted in the text as they first appear and defined in the glossary.

Each chapter opens with learning outcomes. The body of the text includes:
- learning experiences of the children described through scenarios and supported by photographs,
- theoretical aspects of the learning experiences,
- value of the learning experiences,
- the role of the facilitator,
- appropriate storage and labelling systems, considerations for setting up specific learning areas,
- observation and documentation techniques,
- international considerations,
- listings of equipment and materials, and
- ages and stages of development specific to the specified learning setting.

Key points summarize the content of each chapter. Student activities at the end of the chapter provide opportunities for independent study or group discussion during class times. References and some additional resources conclude each chapter.

▶ Key Features

The text is based on children's real experiences. The theory and methodology is integrated around these experiences. The children's experiences are documented both in picture format and in actual written scenarios. This allows students in the field of early childhood studies to acquire learning that is more practical and to make the connections to theory more readily.

The information is presented in a logical flow. The activities of the child are described; theoretical aspects are discussed; and discussions about facilitator interactions, the value of the experiences, environmental experiences, and documentation techniques are provided based on the activities.

The reader is presented with an approach that embraces current philosophies about integration, play, bias, and learning practices. Additionally, each chapter ends with an international component that is a reflection of practices in other parts of the world.

Integrated technology supports online courses, research studies, and independent learning, and enriches classroom activities. This technology includes:

- CD-ROM—contains interactive exercises linked to content of the text. This CD-ROM is free with each new book.
- Web links related to each of the curricular areas can also be found on the Nelson ECE Resource Centre Web site at www.ece.nelson.com.

► Acknowledgements

I would like to sincerely thank the children who so actively participated in the program at the Loyalist College Curriculum Lab. Without the children's interactions this text would not have been possible. Additionally, I would like to acknowledge the consistent interest, support, and help of the children's families.

A special acknowledgement is extended to Dewey's Independent Grocer in Belleville, Ontario for the consistent support to produce photographs of excellent quality, in a very timely fashion, and at a discount.

I would also like to thank the following individuals for their valuable input throughout the writing process: Lynn Wilson, George Brown College; Ann Stone, Langara College; Mabel F. Higgins, Lambton College; Marian Warwick, Fanshawe College; Louisa Dyck, Conestoga College; Joanne Baxter, Mount Royal College; Donna Mese, Cambrian College; Dale Long, Seneca College; Lorrie Baird, Fleming College; Judith Boyd, New Brunswick Community College; Pauline Camuti, Centennial College; and Anna MacDonell, The Institute for Early Childhood Education and Developmental Studies.

► About the Author

Ingrid Crowther holds a Doctor of Education in Early Childhood and the Middle Years. Her teaching background is diverse and includes teaching in early childhood, elementary school, high school, college, and university programs. She has taught in Alberta, Ontario, Newfoundland, and Great Britain.

Ingrid believes that learning should a pleasurable activity that is initiated by children and by adults. Both children and adults learn best when the learning is pleasurable and meaningful. Consequently, much of Ingrid's learning and research has focused on how individuals learn best. She has been published in a number of journals and has completed the first Canadian edition of *Infants and Toddlers.*

Ingrid is currently conducting research, funded by Human Resource Development Canada, at Athabasca University into the effects of various types of educational practices on long-term learning.

CHAPTER 1

Introduction to Play

Play is an activity. It does not necessarily result in a product. It may involve one child or a group of children. It may be built around toys and tools or may involve nothing more than the child's imagination. A play period may last a few minutes or go on for days.

—M. Mayasky, Creative Activities for Young Children

Chapter Outline

▶ Historical Perspectives on Children's Play
▶ Stages of Play: Social and Cognitive
▶ Developmentally Appropriate Practices and Play
▶ Learning and Play
▶ Emergent Curriculum and Play
▶ The Role of the Environment in Learning and Play
▶ International Considerations
▶ Key Points
▶ Student Activities
▶ References

Learning Outcomes

After reading this chapter the reader will:

1. Discuss the historical development of play
2. Discuss modern theory as it applies to play
3. Define and give examples of stages of social play
4. Define and give examples of cognitive play
5. Identify the relationship between play and learning
6. Discuss how play supports the concept of emergent curriculum
7. Identify aspects of indoor and outdoor learning environments that support learning through play

Interactive Learning Exercises

 Remember, the CD-ROM that came with this text contains interactive exercises that relate to the topics in this chapter, as well as other valuable resources.

▶ Historical Perspectives on Children's Play

Play as a learning activity is not a new concept. The roots of play can be traced throughout the ages and are a reflection of how children learn based on particular societal values held at that time. Learning environments in turn have reflected the current philosophical viewpoints of particular time periods.

Early roots of play as a best practice for early learning were already documented by Plato, a Greek philosopher, who insisted that play should be considered a natural activity of childhood. "Leave young children to themselves and you will discover that they soon find plenty of activities which will delight them; they will, in fact, invent their own games" (Curtis and Boultwood, 1963, p. 24). The focus was on creating learning environments that stimulated children to enjoy learning in surroundings that emphasized beauty, fostered imagination and imitation, and contained materials that provided children with practice in the skills that would prepare them for adulthood.

During Roman times, play was also acknowledged as a valuable learning activity for young children. Quintilian, a Roman philosopher, stated that the child's first instruction should be through play. The emphasis was to provide the child with early learning materials that would be necessary for later experiences. For example, activities could include ivory letters to play with and grooved boards carved with letters and words to encourage the child to trace them. These play activities were thought to prepare for later reading and writing. Additionally, Quintilian recognized that young children were capable of a tremendous amount of learning. Quintilian advocated that the best learning was encouraged through many repetitions and subsequent memorization.

John Amos Comenius (1592–1670) was a bishop in Moravia and Czechoslovakia. Comenius emphasized the importance of active learning, hands-on experiences, and parental involvement as critical aspects of early learning. In 1658, Comenius published what is believed to be the first picture book for young children, *Orbis Pictus.*

John Locke (1632–1704) advocated that children's play be free and unrestrained. Locke emphasized the need to make early learning a pleasurable experience. He also recognized the need to observe play to determine the children's interests. Locke advocated that early learning experiences should be encouraged through good modelling activities by sensitive adults and through carefully set up experiences within the learning environment.

Jean Jacques Rousseau (1712–1778) was the first to argue that children should be allowed to be children. He recognized the powerful effect a poor learning environment had on the child's later abilities. He advocated that learning for the young child should be based on the child's abilities, interests, and needs and be sensitive to his or her developmental levels. Early learning environments were to be informal settings that encouraged the child to explore using his or her senses and motor abilities.

Johann Heinrich Pestalozzi (1746–1827) also focused on the right of the child to learn through pleasant, free exploration. Pestalozzi argued that children develop through self-activity. Learning was seen as normative, passing through a hierarchy of developmental stages. Therefore, learning environments were structured in such a way as to encourage children to learn through trial and error, active participation, observation, imitation, and with opportunities for lots of repetition.

Friedrich Froebel (1782–1852) believed that children learned best by manipulation of real materials, guided by adults. It was the teacher's task to organize learning activities and guide behaviours through play activities.

In summary, early theorists supported the following key points about play and the young child:

- play was seen as a natural activity of early learning;
- the role of the adult was to set up learning environments and activities that encouraged active exploration; and
- the role of the adult was to guide children within these learning environments.

Subsequent modern theories of teaching young children have been influenced by past practices and have incorporated aspects of learning through play. Table 1.1 is a synopsis of the modern theories and philosophies.

Current philosophies and research support the right of the child to learn through play. In the *Early Years Study* sponsored in 1999 by the government of Ontario, McCain and Mustard identified that, during the **critical periods** within the first six years of life, "Critical or sensitive periods are stages of development for particular parts or functions of the brain. They are windows of opportunity in early life when a child's brain is exquisitely primed to receive sensory input and develop more advanced neural systems, through the wiring and sculpting process" (McCain and Mustard, 1999, p. 29). Children develop neural networks that establish patterns for later learning, behaviour, and health. It is through quality interactions in the early

TABLE 1.1

▶ Play and Theoretical Approaches

Theorist/Approach	Description
John Dewey (1859–1952)	Active learning based on real experiences
Child-centred approach	Learning based on children's interests
Margaret McMillan (1860–1931)	Playground within which children could flow from the indoor to the outdoor environment
Play-oriented, open-air nursery school garden	Play-based creative program with emphasis on clay, blocks, movement, drawing
Maria Montessori (1870–1952)	Children learn differently from adults
Prepared environment	Unique characteristic of children's tremendous amount of learning in the early years (absorbent mind)
	Sensitive periods during which children are most receptive to new learning
	Match between appropriate materials and children's abilities
	Use of self-correcting materials to explore and learn
Lev Vygotsky (1896–1934)	Culture is shared through social interactions
Sociohistoric theory	Children learn through shared experiences between peers and adults
	Adults guide children in the process of learning
	Adults scaffold children's learning by adjusting the learning activities to allow the child to succeed
Jean Piaget (1896–1980)	Children progress through stages of cognitive development by constructing own knowledge
Constructivist theory	Children learn about three types of knowledge: physical, logico-mathematical, and social
	Physical: child manipulates objects in order to learn about the properties of the object—size, shape, weight, colour
	Logico-mathematical: child manipulates objects to discover relationship between objects
	Social: child engages in social play activities to learn about rules, values, and morals
Loris Malaguzzi (1920–1994)	Children are active participants in their construction of learning
Emergent curriculum	Children, families, and teachers are equal partners in learning
	Emphasis on the visual arts and an aesthetically pleasing environment
	Documentation and dialogue of children's efforts to build curriculum
	Children participate in creation of project-based learning

TABLE 1.1 PLAY AND THEORETICAL APPROACHES (continued)

Theorist/Approach	Description
Erik Erikson (1902–1994) Psycho-social theory	Developed a developmental sequence of social interactions that identifies the needs of children at various ages Each stage identifies tasks to be accomplished These tasks are best accomplished through play activities
Howard Gardiner (1943–) Theory of **multiple intelligences**	Intelligence develops through interaction with the learning environment and abilities that child was born with Seven intelligences—linguistic, logical/mathematical, spatial, musical, bodily/kinesthetic, interpersonal, and intrapersonal—are distinct from each other, relate to various learning types, and identify the best way a child will learn

years that these patterns evolve. "Learning in the early years must be based on quality, developmentally attuned interactions with primary caregivers and opportunities for play-based problem solving with other children that stimulates brain development" (McCain and Mustard, 1999, p. 7).

Play evolves through a predictable sequence. The sequence of social play was described by Mildred Parten in 1932. Jean Piaget in 1962 described various categories of cognitive development through play. Sara Smilansky in 1968 adapted these stages of play. Although play develops in a predictable order, as outlined later in table 1.2, it is important to recognize that various types of play will be used throughout the child's life. This depends on the child's experiences, the type of activity engaged in, how the environment is set up, and what the child wishes to be involved in.

▶ Stages of Play

1. Stages of Social Play (Parten, 1932)

Solitary Play

Scenario: Two tables were set up with the following materials. There were rolling pins; plastic knives; green play dough; a container of short pieces of straws, wood, and twigs; and a container of flour.

Mikel had been moulding and shaping the play dough using a rolling pin, his hands, and plastic forks and spoons (photo 1.1). At one point, he left the area to get some dinosaurs and a paper plate. Mikel returned and began to mould the play dough onto the plate. He then stuck the dinosaurs into the play dough. He indicated that the dinosaurs were stuck in

PHOTO 1.1

the mud and could not get out. He got some flour and sprinkled it over the dinosaurs. He said that it was snowing. Mikel was playing by himself without interacting with any of the children around him.

Parallel Play

Reghan came over to the area, picked up some green play dough, and sat at a table next to Mikel and proceeded to shape the dough (photo 1.2). She poked her fingers into the dough. Next, Reghan rolled out the dough with a rolling pin. She re-shaped the dough into a ball. Then Reghan stuck various coloured pieces of straw and sticks into her creation.

PHOTO 1.2

PHOTO 1.3

Both Mikel and Reghan continued to shape and decorate the dough. Each one concentrated on his or her own creation. Each one used the materials in similar ways. Each child shaped the dough, used rolling pins to roll out the dough, and stuck objects into the dough. Reghan left the area, but Mikel continued to add dinosaurs to his creation.

Reghan is a toddler. She was attracted to the activity that Mikel was engaged in. Since Mikel was concentrating on his activity, no dialogue or sharing of materials occurred between the two children. This is an appropriate stage of development for Reghan. For Mikel, it is also developmentally appropriate. It was his choice to work alone. He was working on something of interest to him.

Associative Play

Mikel called over Sarah, his teacher, to look at his dinosaurs in the mud and in the snow. As Sarah walked over, several other children followed her. Sarah asked Mikel to explain to the children what he had been doing. Mikel pointed to his dinosaurs and again explained that the dinosaurs were in the mud and that it was snowing. Two of the children, Liesl and Benjamin, immediately asked where the plates were. Mikel pointed to where they were stored. Each child got his or her own play dough and dinosaurs, and Benjamin also got some dinosaur moulds. As Liesl and Benjamin started to create the mud for their dinosaurs, an active dialogue among the children developed (photo 1.3). The children named their dinosaurs and compared the number of dinosaurs,

the size of the dinosaurs, and the amount of snow falling in their respective creations. Benjamin informed Liesl and Mikel that he had "lying-down dinosaurs." He had created them by pressing dinosaur moulds into the dough. Liesl immediately asked if she could use one of the moulds. Benjamin readily agreed. Each child was involved in a similar activity: dinosaurs in the mud and snow. The children talked to each other about what they were doing and also shared materials, but each child continued to concentrate on his or her own efforts.

When the opportunity arose to share his discoveries with others, Mikel was very keen to interact with the other children. He helped the other children by directing them to where he had found materials and by explaining why he was engaged in this particular activity. He was also interested in what the other children were doing, but continued to do his own thing; when Benjamin announced that his dinosaurs were lying down, Mikel looked at what Benjamin had created although he continued with his own activity.

Cooperative Play

Two of the older children, Jacob and Ben, were attracted to the activity. The two boys looked at what the children were doing. Jacob asked Ben if he would like to go to play in the sand. Ben agreed. As they walked over to the sandbox, Ben explained that he had been to the zoo in Toronto. Jacob said, "Cool! So have I. Let's make a zoo." They discussed what materials were needed. Each boy collected the materials and brought them back to the sandbox. As they looked through the storage area containing the animals, they noticed that there were a number of dinosaurs left in one container. Jacob said, "Let's make it a dinosaur

PHOTO 1.4

PHOTO 1.5

zoo instead." Ben agreed and both boys decided what task each would do. Ben decided that they should both make the mud. They also decided that this would become Jurassic Park. Jacob wanted to go outside to collect some branches and rocks to add to their park. Ben decided that he would collect more dinosaurs, tracks, and fences. When the boys had completed their park (photo 1.4), they decided that Jacob would be the "dinosaur actor." Ben would operate the cars driving through the park. The boys also decided that the fences would be too high and strong for the dinosaurs to break down. The boys planned their activity, assigned tasks to each other to complete their activity, decided on some simple rules for their play, and decided what roles each would play.

Onlooker Behaviour

The noise level and activity in the sandbox attracted Jenna. Jenna watched the boys play (photo 1.5). She offered no comments, nor did she indicate that she wished to join their play. She watched for about 10 minutes and then left the area to go to the manipulative area to create a necklace. Jenna could well have tried to become involved in the activity. It was her choice to watch and decide whether she would like to participate or not.

2. Stages of Cognitive Play (Piaget, 1962; Smilansky, 1968)

Functional Play

Reghan (see photo 1.2) repeatedly manipulated the dough. She poked it with her fingers, rolled it out, and re-shaped it several times. Reghan engaged in these activities because she enjoyed the sensory activity of moulding the dough and because she could practise various techniques to shape the dough. She repeatedly used those techniques enjoyable to her—poking, rolling, and forming the dough into a ball. This type of play is also referred to as *repetitive play* or *practice play*.

Symbolic Play

1. Constructive Play

Mikel (photo 1.1), Liesl, and Benjamin (photo 1.3) each verbalized what their particular play dough scene was. Mikel decided it represented dinosaurs stuck in the mud. Each of the children went along with Mikel's idea of creating snow by sprinkling flour on the dinosaurs. Each child was using the play dough, dinosaurs, and flour to represent the scene he or she had made.

2. Dramatic Play

Jacob and Ben were involved in active role-play upon completion of their dinosaur park. Ben got a hat from the drama centre and loaded his toy people onto the train. He drove his train down the track. Jacob marched his animals or dinosaurs around in the enclosure that they had created. He pretended to let the dinosaurs eat the branches and grass that he had collected outside, and let them drink from the "pond." When the train came near the fence, he rushed the animals or dinosaurs to the fence and roared. Ben let out continual shrieks. He said, "Some of the people are scared. They're yelling." Dylon heard the shrieks. He came over to investigate. He asked if he could play. Both boys said yes. They explained that this was a dinosaur zoo. They also explained the rules. Ben said, "You can walk the peoples around." The three boys continued to act out their roles. At various times they would switch roles.

Ben and Jacob had both visited the zoo in Toronto. Each boy had experience with what a zoo looked like, and how people behaved in a zoo. The boys had heard about the movie *Jurassic Park,* but neither boy had actually seen the movie. Thus, the structure that they had created and the dramatic play that evolved

related to their personal experiences and perceptions of those experiences.

3. Games with Rules

When Dylon joined Ben and Jacob in their Jurassic Park zoo, Ben and Jacob carefully explained the rules that they were using. They told him that he had to keep the people on the roads, that the people could not get close to the fences, and that the noise of the animals and dinosaurs would scare the people. Dylon played along, but decided to let one of his people climb over the fence. Both Ben and Jacob told him that this was not allowed and that the person would be kicked out of the zoo. Dylon decided to play by the rules that Ben and Jacob had set.

TABLE 1.2

▶ Comparison of Ages and Stages of Social and Cognitive Play	
Infants	
Solitary Play	Play by themselves
	Initially play involves using hands, feet, and mouths
	As infants mature, infants grasp and manipulate toys
Onlooker Behaviour	Watch other individuals in their environment
	Focus on objects near them
Parallel Play	Older, more mobile infants will play close to each other, using similar materials and engaging in similar activities
Functional Play	Play involves much repetition
	Infants engage in manipulation of objects—poking, prodding, pushing, pulling, turning, and twisting
	Older infants will start to use realistic objects as intended—cups to drink, spoons to feed
Toddlers	
Onlooker Behaviour	Attention easily attracted by activity of other toddlers
	Toddlers will leave own activity to see what is happening elsewhere
Solitary Play	If interested in the activity, will continue to play by self for long periods of time
Parallel Play	Often plays beside other individuals, without interactions, using similar toys and engaging in similar activities
Functional Play	Engage in repetitive play, especially if the play experience is a new one
	Engage in activities that focus on emptying, filling, taking apart, stacking, and knocking down

TABLE 1.2 COMPARISON OF AGES AND STAGES OF SOCIAL AND COGNITIVE PLAY (continued)

Symbolic Play	Start to use one object to represent another object
	Play is rich in symbolic actions
Preschoolers	
Onlooker Behaviour	May watch new experiences to see if they wish to participate
	May watch play, if unsure of self or situation
Solitary Play	Will play by self by choice to explore new situations or simply to be alone for a while
Parallel Play	May play side by side if child becomes absorbed in what he or she is doing
Associative Play	Often play along with others, sharing toys and ideas but continuing to do own thing
Functional Play	May resort to functional play to explore unknown situations or activities
Constructive Play	Readily uses available materials to substitute materials not available
	Engages in many symbolic actions—raising hand for stop, shrugging shoulders to indicate uncertainty
Dramatic Play	Often becomes involved in role play and/or imaginative play without props
School Age	
Will engage in all types of play depending on interest, mood, inclination, setting, and materials	
Cooperative Play	Start to play with peers to organize play activities
	Activities include working toward a common goal, planning and assigning roles to reach the goal
Competitive Play	Children become increasingly competitive
	Play includes winning and losing
Games with Rules	Children may set own rules for their play
	Engage in activities that have increasingly complex sets of rules—team sports, board games

▶ Developmentally Appropriate Practices and Play

Developmentally appropriate practices can best be described as:

- "taking into account everything we know about how children develop and learn, and matching it to the content and strategies planned for them in early childhood programs," "treating children as individuals, not as a cohort group," and

- "treating children with respect by recognizing their changing capabilities, and viewing them in the context of their family, culture, and community, and their past experiences and circumstances" (Kostelnik, 1993, p. 1).

The National Association for the Education of Young Children (NAEYC) has identified a set of principles within its **position statement**. These principles provide a foundation of learning in the early childhood years. One of the principles stresses the importance of play. "Play is an important vehicle for children's social, emotional, and cognitive development, as well as a reflection of their development" (Gestwicki, 1999, p. 10). Each of these principles has been adapted from Gestwicki, 1999 in order to explore the relationship of play to these principles.

1. **Physical, social, emotional, language, and cognitive development are closely related and development in any one area is influenced by the other areas of development.** Mikel, when he was using the play dough and dinosaurs (photo 1.1), is a good example of the above principle:
   - He had developed the fine motor control to shape the play dough (physical development).
   - He was able to make use of the materials in a symbolic way, using the flour to represent snow (cognitive development).
   - He varied his social play accordingly; solitary play changed to **associative play** as other children decided to join the play (social development).
   - He had the self-confidence in own abilities to create, and continue to create, his own scenarios (emotional development).
   - He discussed his ideas with other children and the **facilitator** (language development).

2. **There is an orderly sequence by which later skills, abilities, and knowledge is built.** As indicated in table 1.2, play activities appear in a logical sequence and build upon each other.

3. **Development occurs at varying rates and is uneven in different areas of development for each child.** Reghan (photo 1.2) was involved in solitary play, moulding and shaping the play dough continuously. Reghan's behaviour is expected for her age group. Toddlers tend to manipulate objects and tend to be involved in both parallel and repetitive play. However, when her mother picked her up later, Reghan said, "I made a cake for you. I stuck in candles. Blow them out." The language she used was advanced for her particular age.

4. **Children's early experiences are cumulative and may have delaying effects on children's development.** In each of the children's play scenarios discussed earlier, it is easy to see that each child was building upon what he or she already knew and the skills that had already been developed:
   - Mikel was able to relate back to something he had seen in a book to build his dinosaur creation.
   - Jacob and Ben were able to relate to past experiences of a trip to the zoo to create their Jurassic Park zoo.
   - All children built upon previously developed motor skills and social skills.

Unfortunately, it is also possible to delay any one of the areas of development. These delays may be caused by many factors. Specific delays may be caused by illness, lack of stimulation, abuse, or through genetic disorders. "Negative experiences in the early years have long-lasting effects that can be difficult to overcome later" (McCain and Mustard, 1999, p. 26). For children in these kinds of circumstances, it is even more critical to provide an environment that provides a range of opportunities to reinforce, practise, and gain new skills.

5. **Development is predictable and moves from easiest to more complex and from concrete experiences to abstract thought.** The type of play that the children were engaged in (photos 1.1 and 1.4) showed the progression from simple to more complex activities and from concrete to abstract thought. The younger children, such as Reghan, were engaged in repetitive manipulation of the materials to practise emergent skills. The preschool children tended to use more symbolized interactions—using flour to create snow; using toy dinosaurs and impressions of dinosaurs in their play (abstract thought).

6. **Learning occurs in many social and cultural settings.** It is easy to see how the children's play was influenced both by what each child had experienced within the family context (a trip to the zoo) and by the interactions of others within the environment (Benjamin and Liesl's decisions to also use dinosaurs in the dough). Interactions are also influenced by the cultural setting that the children are exposed to. Two of the children, Jennifer and Brad, had just attended a Native celebration. The children brought back pictures of their experiences. These pictures were developed into a book that all the children could look at. Jennifer mentioned that her father had played the drums. When Jennifer's father picked her up, some of the children gathered around him and asked him to play the drums for them. He not only played the drums for the children, but also brought in a variety of drums for the children to use and play on the next day. This activity continued over many weeks, with many visitations and demonstrations from Jennifer's father.

7. **Children are active learners. During their play the children demonstrate their knowledge of the world around them.** Reghan was able to relate her experiences of a recent birthday in her creation of a birthday cake for her mother. Jacob and Ben were able to recall their experiences from the zoo to recreate a zoo in the sandbox. They knew that animals were kept in enclosures, that people used vehicles or walked through the zoo, and that there are rules that one must abide by when visiting the zoo.

8. **Development is an interaction between biological maturation and the environment.** "Biological maturation is in fact a prerequisite of learning. But a child's interrelationship with the environment determines just what learning takes place" (Gestwicki, 1999, p. 10). All the children within the play activities described were able to actively construct their own learning by using the materials in ways that supported their individual growth and development. Materials were provided to facilitate this process.

9. **Children need opportunities to practise skills in an environment that provides opportunities and challenges.** As the children manipulated their dough and built their structures in the sand, they could use materials from various areas in the room—dinosaurs; paper plates; rocks, flowers, and twigs from outside; tracks; and cars. This encouraged each child to practise those skills that were relevant to that child—symbolized play for Liesl, Benjamin, and Mikel; role play for Dylon, Jacob, and Ben.

10. **Children present what they know in different ways.** Sarah, the facilitator, at all times acknowledged the children's efforts. She supported their need to get materials, even going outside to collect materials for the zoo. Sarah was sensitive to the developmental levels of the children's play and to the choices each had made. She made no attempt to coax children into a different form of play. She observed the children and empowered each child to make his or her own choices.

▶ Learning and Play

WHAT IS PLAY?

Stephanie had decided to make her own play dough (photo 1.6). She found the ingredients, found the picture recipe to follow, and proceeded to create the play dough.

Through observation of the activity that Stephanie is engaged in, the following definitions of play could evolve:

- *Play involves symbolized activities.* At one point during her activity, Stephanie said that what she was doing was like making bread. She then proceeded to knead the dough.
- *Play is **process-oriented**.* Stephanie was involved in a process: measuring quantities, mixing materials, changing the consistency of the dough, and verbalizing what the process felt like.

Piaget would describe the experiences that Stephanie had in the play dough making as follows. First, through the process of *assimilation* (using information that is already known, without changing it), Stephanie was able to use her past experiences in baking and making play dough to create her own play dough. As she creates her play dough, she needs to adapt her thinking. For example, if the dough she has created is too sticky or too dry, she needs to think about what she needs to do in order to change the consistency of the dough. Should she add more water or add more flour? This process is called **accommodation** (taking new information—more water or more flour?—and adding it to an existing knowledge base: making dough). Thus, Stephanie was able to integrate old knowledge with new knowledge to continue to learn about consistency in making mixtures.

Vygotsky, on the other hand, would describe Stephanie's learning through a process he referred to as **scaffolding**. Scaffolding is a method used to help children achieve a goal they might otherwise not be able to achieve. In order for Stephanie to make play dough, she needed a recipe. This recipe was provided in a picture format accompanied by simple words. The adult simplified the process by:

- providing visual and written clues to help make the dough,
- limiting quantities to ensure success (each container had enough materials in it to provide opportunity to measure, but limited the quantity of the materials to ensure success; that is, if the child dumped all the materials from each container in a bowl, the activity would still be successful), and
- providing encouragement as needed.

Through the use of these strategies, Stephanie was able to sustain the activity and learn how to make her own play dough.

Braelyn had discovered toothbrushes when she was looking for a paintbrush. She used the toothbrush to paint with. Later, at the water table, children had taken dinosaurs to that area to give them a drink. Braelyn watched this play for a few minutes. Finally,

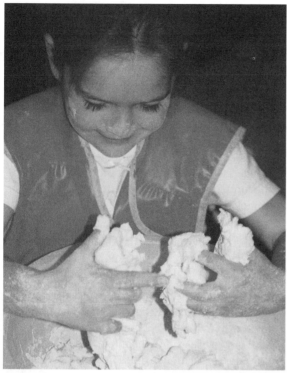

PHOTO 1.6

PHOTO 1.7

she went back to the brushes, picked out one tooth-brush, and brought it back to the water table. She picked up one of the dinosaurs and proceeded to brush the dinosaur's teeth (photo 1.7). When they were clean she took the dinosaur over to the sandbox, explaining that "He's hungry." She pretended to feed the dinosaur. When she was finished, she held up the dinosaur to the facilitator and said, "Look, his teeth are dirty. I have to brush his teeth again." Braelyn has developed the following skills during this play episode:

- thinking with greater flexibility: she was able to use the toothbrush for more than one purpose;
- thinking divergently: she was able to create a situation that required her to think in different ways. She used a familiar experience of brushing your teeth, applied that knowledge to creating a need to brush the dinosaur's teeth, and created a situation that allowed her to follow through with her actions;
- using materials in her environment in an innovative way; and
- learning to solve her own problems: she was able to find all the materials she needed in order to create her play opportunity (adapted from Stone, 1995).

During this pretend play episode, Braelyn was very imaginative and showed great **creativity**. Her activity

attracted other children to the water centre. Soon other children were feeding the dinosaurs, brushing their teeth, and giving them a drink. As children played together, they talked about what they were doing and made suggestions about their play.

Braelyn: "My dinosaur has no cavities."

Benjamin: "Mine does, lots and lots"

Stephanie: "He'll have to go to the dentist."

Braelyn: "That won't hurt. He'll get a needle. Then the dentist will fix the cavity."

Jacob: "My dinosaur is bigger than yours."

Braelyn: "Mine is a great, big one! He's huge." She held her dinosaur up to Jacob's to compare the two dinosaurs, and said, "It's the same."

Jacob: "No mine is more bigger."

Braelyn (looking at Jacob's dinosaur): "His tail is longer."

Children learn language best in social settings (Morrow, 1993). This play activity provided wonderful opportunities to expand and increase:

- language—building vocabulary, learning correct forms of speech;
- negotiating skills—creating and maintaining roles, settling differences of opinion;
- memory skills—talking about experiences (Newman, 1990).

Children were also able to:

- form, test, and modify concepts;
- become aware of their own feelings and the feelings of others; and

- develop motor skills (hand–eye coordination and control over body movements).

In summary, play offers children rich learning experiences that enhance all levels of development. "Playing is a fundamental process of creative thinking, allowing the child to construct and reconstruct the imagery of rich, early experiences, and thus to grow and develop" (Frost, 1986 in Puckett and Diffily, 1999, p. 249). "Play:

- Enables children to make sense of their world.
- Develops social and cultural understandings.
- Allows children to express their thoughts and feelings.
- Fosters flexible and **divergent thinking**.
- Provides opportunities to meet and solve real problems.
- Develops language and **literacy** skills and concepts." (Packer Isenberg and Jalongo, 2001, p. 59)

▶ Emergent Curriculum and Play

Josh has been pouring water into the experimental water wheel using various materials (photo 1.8). He started out by using a large bowl-shaped container.

PHOTO 1.8

As he poured the water into the funnel, most of the water spilled over the edge of the funnel. The water wheels did not turn. He said, "Oh no!" Sarah noticed that Josh needed help.

Sarah: "I see you have a problem. Your water is flowing over the top of the funnel!"

Josh: "Yes!"

Sarah: "How could you solve this problem?"

Josh looked around. He picked up a pail that was beside the water table and poured the water into the funnel. The water poured over the side of the funnel. "Oh no!" Josh threw the pail into the water.

Sarah: "Let's look to see what else we can find to pour with." She and Josh walked over to the storage container that held various pouring utensils.

Josh looked at the containers. He picked up a watering can and a measuring cup and brought them over to the table. He used the measuring cup to pour water into the funnel. The water flowed into the funnel. "Look, look!" Josh looked down at the wheels turning.

Sarah: "I see. You have poured the water into the funnel. The water is turning the wheels."

Josh (with a big smile): "Yes!"

"An **emergent curriculum** evolves through continuous dialogue and documentation, frames learning as children devise and engage in projects" (Essa et al., 1998, p. 80). Sarah, the facilitator, observed and recorded Josh's activity at the water table. She noticed that Josh was interested in pouring water and interested in the cause and effect relationship between the flow of the water and the turning of the wheels. This activity serves as a building block to maintain the interest and to expand learning over time, and it also helps the facilitator decide what range of materials and experiences are needed.

As a child interacts in the environment, with the materials in that environment, and with the adults and other children, the curriculum for that child or group of children unfolds. The facilitator must observe and record:

- what materials the children use—Josh used the containers to pour water into the experimental water wheel;
- how these materials are used—Josh found it difficult to pour with a container that had no spout: he needed a container with a spout;
- what skills the children use—Josh's motor skills to pour, observation skills to watch what had hap-

pened, and communication skills to indicate his feelings and draw attention to what he had observed; and

- how the children interact with each other and the adults (facilitators and family members)—Josh interacted with Sarah in order to help him solve his problem of finding an appropriate container to pour with, to share his discovery, and to indicate his sense of pride in his accomplishment.

Once the children's experiences have been documented, the facilitator must then plan for the following:

- how to involve the other partners—family members, community members;
- what additional materials are needed;
- what experiences can be provided to expand the learning activity;
- what other skills the children need to continue to build upon the experiences; and
- how best to organize the environment.

The best-known program that follows the emergent curriculum approach to educating young children is in Reggio Emilia, Italy. The approach can best be summarized by the following points (adapted from Cadwell, 1997, p. 4, and Fraser, 2000, p. 8):

- **The child as a protagonist.** The child is the chief player to make things happen; the child is seen as competent and inventive. Both Stephanie and Josh initiated their own activity, decided what they would play with, how they would use the materials, and when they had completed what they had done.
- **The child as a collaborator.** The child works together with other children and with the adults within that child's community. Both Josh and Stephanie **collaborated** with their facilitator to accomplish their goals. Each child shared their success of what had happened with family members. Josh showed his father what he had done, and Stephanie bagged her dough to take home with her so that she could continue to use it at home.
- **The child as a communicator.** Children communicate in a variety of symbolic ways: words, actions, drawing, painting, building, sculpting, shadow play, collage, dramatic play, and music. In the previous examples, children represented their ideas in various forms—through moulding and creating their dinosaur scenes, through dramatic play in the Jurassic Park zoo, verbally at the water centre while brushing the dinosaur's teeth, and physically by throwing the container into the water to express frustration with the experimental water wheel.

- **The environment as a third teacher.** The physical space needs to be designed to empower children to interact with each other and the materials within the environment. "Every corner of the space has an identity and a purpose, is rich in potential to engage and to communicate, and is valued and cared for by the children and adults" (Cadwell, 1997, p. 5). (Refer to the discussion in the next section, The Role of the Environment.)
- **The facilitator as a partner, nurturer, and guide.** Sarah was able to be a partner in the children's learning by providing appropriate materials to reinforce the children's choice of activities. She nurtured and guided Josh when she realized that he was getting frustrated by guiding him to get alternative materials that would enhance his success.
- **The facilitator as a researcher.** Facilitators need to work together with each other and with the children in order to provide a continued rich environment based on the children's interests.
- **The documentation as a communication.** Facilitators carefully document the children's experiences through transcriptions of the children's words and actions (see the example of Josh) and through photographs. These are carefully put together as panels or books to record and show the children's activities.
- **The families as partners.** Family participation is critical. Families enrich any program through their ideas, skills, and enthusiasm for their children, and need to take an active part in their children's learning.

▶ The Role of the Environment in Learning and Play

A number of assumptions can be made about the learning environment for young children. Young children learn through play best in environments that:

- are safe from physical harm;
- create a sense of wonder and awe;
- promote all activities in both the indoor and outdoor environments;
- are **inclusive settings**—according to Salisbury (1991, p. 146–155), the underlying theme in inclusive programs is that all children will occupy the same space they would if they did not have a disability and that all stakeholders (facilitators, families, administrators) define the culture for the program to include children from diverse backgrounds, abilities, and contributions;

- promote the use of materials and equipment in a number of ways and in a variety of settings—books outdoors to identify birds and planes; books in the block, carpentry, or sand area to refer to for ideas on building various structures;
- encourage children to make decisions and solve problems;
- encourage children to take safe risks; and
- empower children to actively participate.

Thus, the environment becomes a critical part in planning programs for young children. The facilitator must consider:

- the learning areas to be included;
- the relationship of learning areas to each other;
- the organization of each learning area;
- the materials to include; and
- the effective use of storage.

Learning Areas

The Early Childhood Environmental Rating Scale (ECERS) (Harms, Clifford, and Cryer, 1998) is a good start to identify the learning areas that all quality children's programs should include. This is a rating scale that identifies core areas to include and gives the facilitator a tool to measure the effectiveness of the overall environment and program. The core areas identified include books and pictures; fine motor; art; music and movement; blocks; sand and water; dramatic play; nature/science; math and numbers; use of TV, video, and computers; and promoting acceptance of diversity.

Relationship of Learning Areas to Each Other

As previously discussed, all learning areas should have value to both the children and the adults and should have a purpose. Guidelines that lead to more effective locations for various learning areas are outlined in ECERS (Harms, Clifford, Cryer, 1998). These include:

- separation of noisy and quiet areas—for example, the quiet area (includes books and other quiet activities) should be separated from other more noisy areas such as blocks, sand, creative arts, and water;
- placement of noisy or messy areas on appropriate surfaces—blocks on a rug to absorb the sound, creative arts on a tile floor to allow for easier cleanup;
- proximity to water—creative art and water should be close to a sink to facilitate setup and cleanup;

- easy supervision of all areas—it should be easy to observe all the children at all times;
- defined space to maximize active participation of children and minimize interruption due to traffic flow—this might be accomplished by careful placement of low shelves or tables;
- safety considerations—space where it is easy to wipe up spills; clear areas around doors/gates; confinement of areas through use of furniture (such as carpentry area or riding areas); enough space to play safely (for example, block play); protective devices over outlets and furniture placed over or in front of electrical cords; sturdy furniture/equipment; equipment and furniture that is in good repair; clear areas in which to run, jump, ride, and climb; protection from sun and wind; and
- space that may be used for larger group interactions.

Another consideration for the placement of learning areas is the relationship of learning areas to each other. The following points are just some of the suggestions that might be considered when adjoining play areas:

- Dramatic play and block play. This could encourage children to build props for their dramatic play. For example, Jordan has built a car (photo 1.9). He had been involved in a dramatic play episode that included a store. He indicated that he was driving to the store.
- Sand and water play. Many of the activities children are involved in include creating mixtures: how to create mud, what happens to sand in water, differences between wet and dry sand, creating natural scenarios in sand (lakes or ponds or rivers). For example, Benjamin is creating a pond (photo 1.10). The pond was needed for the farm animals he then added to the sand area.
- Carpentry and creative arts. When children complete their carpentry projects, they can finish them by decorating them or painting them (photo 1.11). Children finish their projects from the carpentry area by painting them.
- Math and manipulative materials. Many of the fine motor materials also lend themselves to math activities, one-to-one correspondence, counting, pre-measurement, matching, and seriation. Braelyn had built a horizontal structure using small cubes (photo 1.12). She then placed small bears on the cubes. She was careful to place only one bear on one block (one-to-one correspon-

PHOTO 1.9

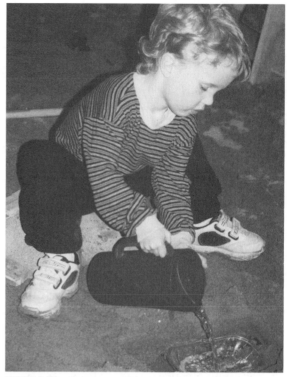

PHOTO 1.10

dence). She continued this activity until all the bears had been used up.

Organization of Learning Areas

The primary consideration for the organization should be based on the developmental level of the child. The younger the child, the more realistic the setting should be. Younger children view the world from their own perspective; they are influenced by what

they see and tend to react appropriately. Leaving fake food out for toddlers in the housekeeping area will probably encourage the toddler to eat these foods. This could be potentially dangerous for the child. It also presents the child with a problem that is difficult to solve: the items look like food, therefore I should be able to eat them.

PHOTO 1.11

PHOTO 1.12

Younger children are easily distracted. Offering too many choices may cause the activity level of the child to become disrupted. The child may quickly move from one activity to another, or might use materials inappropriately. Too many materials left in containers on a shelf could well result in a lot of dumping activities. This not only leaves an untidy environment, but also it poses a danger of tripping to other children. Since we know that toddlers like to dump, it is important to create opportunities for this to happen by providing appropriate containers to dump out of or into: large bowls, pails, or plastic containers. Older children, however, need more choices and more materials to maintain learning activities over longer periods of time.

Another consideration is that materials need to be accessible to the children, thereby encouraging them to become independent in making choices and engaging in activities that are of interest to them. Items should be clearly visible, easy to reach, and clearly labelled by picture and word.

Some learning areas such as blocks need to have a larger play area to extend the play. Shipley (2002, pp. 92–95) identifies various sizes of play areas: *simple, complex,* and *super* units based on the complexity of the task the child is involved in. Simple units are the type of activities that a child engages in that are solitary activities such as painting at the easel and using a toy camera. Small group work usually occurs in complex units. During this type of play, children usually combine materials from several simple units— creating a doctor's office by using a phone, note pad, pencil or crayons, and a doctor's kit. A super unit is formed when there are at least three types of play materials used at the same time. For example, a small group of children created a garden in the sandbox. They used the materials from the science area (dried plants), materials from the water centre (squirt bottles and watering cans), tools from the sand area (shovels and rakes), and blocks from the block area to create fences.

In order to decide on the size of an area, the following measure can be used:

- simple unit: 1 play space
- complex unit: 4 play spaces
- super units: 8 play spaces (Shipley, 2002, p. 95).

Areas such as blocks and drama usually involve super units, whereas areas such as water, sand, carpentry, and music involve complex units. Areas such as painting at the easel, reading a book, or **working** with puzzles are usually simple units.

Some units may be transformed from simple to complex or even super units. Children in the creative arts may start to work with large boxes, decorating these boxes with play and other materials. These boxes may then become buildings and dramatic play may occur.

Materials

There are some basic principles to consider when placing learning materials or equipment into an area. Some materials seem to logically belong in certain areas: shovels, rakes, or sieves would be suitable in the sand area; musical instruments seem to be best placed in the music area. There are, however, a great many materials that could be placed in more than one area. Vehicles and animals could be used in the sand, with the blocks, and with fine motor materials such as small blocks and interlocking road tracks. Many of our science and math materials would equally fit in the fine-motor area or in the sand or water areas— magnifying glasses, scales, and stacking cups, for example. Materials that can be used in more than one area could be placed in more central locations to encourage children to use them in more than one place and for more than one purpose. A scale, for example, could be used to compare weights of the counting bears in the fine motor area, containers of sand in the sand area, and containers of water in the water centre.

There are a great number of **open-ended accessories** that can be used in a variety of activities. Children should have access to these materials and be able to use them where and when they wish. Table 1.3 provides a list of materials along with some purposes each might be useful for.

When purchasing materials you should consider how useful the items are. Can the items be used for more than one area? Avoid cheap plastic imitations: these often tend to be too small to be of real use. For example, small plastic dishes are too small to hold sufficient quantities for small hands to manipulate, are not useful to engage in mixing and pouring activities, and do not encourage careful handling. They look like toys and are often treated that way. Real items can be purchased cheaply at flea markets and yard sales. Children learn to handle these items with care and respect.

Storage

All materials should be stored so that independent use of the items is encouraged. Materials should be:

TABLE 1.3

▶ Open-ended Accessories and Possible Uses

Materials	Possible Uses
Cardboard tubes of various sizes	Sand, to fill and empty
	Blocks, to add to structures
	Fine motor area, to roll small balls or cars down them
	Creative area, to decorate and paint
Real props such as steering wheels, car parts	Block play, dramatic play
Drawing/blueprints	Block play and carpentry, to give ideas to build
Real dishes, cutlery, and pots and pans (these are much more aesthetically pleasing than cheap plastic imitations)	Housekeeping area, to encourage cooking and baking activities and gentle handling
Wooden planks	Block area, to cover enclosures or build ramps
	Sand area, to cover holes, create roads and ramps
Scrap materials	Cut or glue in creative area
	Substitute for sand
Clear plastic bottles	Cut to provide storage containers
	Containers for filling and emptying
Large blankets, sheets, quilts	Create covers for large block play
	Light and shadow play
	Curtains for dress-up corner or a stage
	Private areas to sit in
	Paint or draw on fabric to hang to display
Pillows	Create cozy area to lie or sit in
Cardboard boxes of various sizes	May be used as building blocks
	Create and decorate to make buildings or vehicles
Tires	Used for obstacle courses to walk/crawl/jump into and out of
	Used in sand to fill or plant in
	Roll outside
Small logs, branches cut into rounds	Add realism to block or sand area
	Use in water to float: small plastic animals can be placed on the logs and they continue to float
Large logs	Outside, suitable for balancing activities
Various sizes of plastic tubing	Ideal for experimenting with flow of materials in water and sand

- accessible—children can easily get them by themselves,
- visible—stored on open shelves, or in clear containers, and
- labelled—by picture and word or outline; children need to know where to find things and where to return them.

▶ International Considerations

Although there are cross-cultural variations in children's play, children in all societies engage in play (Mead, 1975). The variations in children's play may be summarized as follows:

- types of pretend play vary and are dependent upon the interactions of the children and caregivers;
- types of play materials are dependent on culture and on economic resources;
- pretend play varies from social routines to fantasy play around children's movies, books, and related play materials;
- areas with a lack of economic resources show more work-related play;
- differing levels of value are given to play as a means of learning; and
- some areas see increased pressures to prepare children for the next stage of education.

▶ KEY POINTS

Types of Social Play

- onlooker—observing others play;
- solitary—play alone without interactions with others;
- parallel—play beside each other with similar materials and similar activity without interacting with each other;
- associative—play with others, sharing materials and ideas, but continuing with own activity;
- cooperative—work toward a common goal, define and assign roles to reach goal; and
- competitive—play that results in winners and losers.

Types of Cognitive Play

- functional or repetitive—repeated practise of skills through interaction with objects, people, and communication;
- symbolic—using one object to represent another object;
- constructive—use of materials or objects to make other things; and
- dramatic—creation of imaginary roles to act out situations or create events.

Developmentally Appropriate Practices

1. Physical, social, emotional, language, and cognitive development are closely related and development in any one area is influenced by the other areas of development.
2. There is an orderly sequence by which later skills, abilities, and knowledge is built.
3. Development occurs at varying rates and is uneven in different areas of development for each child.
4. Children's early experiences are cumulative and may have delaying effects on children's development.
5. Development is predictable and moves from easiest to more complex and from concrete experiences to abstract thought.
6. Learning occurs in all social and cultural settings.
7. Children are active learners. During their play the children demonstrate their knowledge of the world around them.
8. Development is an interaction between biological maturation and the environment.
9. Children need opportunities to practise skills in an environment that provides opportunities and challenges.
10. Children represent what they know in different ways.
11. Children learn best in environments that are safe, and where their attempts are valued.

Play Is:

- enjoyable and pleasurable
- self-initiated
- active participation

▶ KEY POINTS (continued)

Play Is (continued)

- spontaneous
- free from direction
- integration of experiences
- symbolized activity
- process oriented

Value of Play:

- flexible thinking
- divergent thinking
- learning to use materials in new ways
- learning to solve problems
- build language
- form and test concepts
- develop social skills
- develop awareness of feelings
- develop motor skills

Student Activities

1. Compare the various philosophies of play throughout history.
2. How does play through learning support the new research on brain development?
3. Using the table provided, observe the children's play in a practical setting.

Types of Play	Age of Child	Evidence
Onlooker play		
Solitary play		
Parallel play		
Associative play		
Cooperative play		
Competitive play		
Functional play		
Symbolic play		
Dramatic play		

4. For each of the principles of developmentally appropriate practices listed, find an example of how a child care program meets that principle.
5. Using the chart provided, identify aspects of play such as bathing a baby doll, mixing sand and water, or digging in the sand. For each aspect, discuss and record why this is a valuable activity to the child.

Aspect of Play	Value of the Activity

6. List the values of play
7. Define *emergent curriculum*. How does emergent curriculum support the notion of learning through play?
8. What is the role of the facilitator to initiate an emergent curriculum program?

9. Using photo 1.2, Reghan at play manipulating the play dough, describe how a facilitator might interact with Reghan to expand Reghan's activity and what the facilitator might do to encourage this activity over several days. In your discussion, consider communication that might be used, materials that might be provided, and interaction strategies for the facilitator.

10. In this chapter we discuss the relationships among various learning areas. What other learning areas could be placed close to each other? Explain your reasons.

11. What considerations need to be made to:
   a) organize the learning areas?
   b) select and organize materials in the learning areas?

▶ References

Cadwell, L. (1997). *Bringing Reggio Emilia Home.* New York, NY: Teachers College Press.

Curtis, S., & Boultwood, M. (1963). *A Short History of Educational Ideas.* London, UK: University Tutorial Press Ltd.

Essa, E., Young, R., & Lehne, L. (1998). *Introduction to Early Childhood Education.* (2nd Canadian ed.). Scarborough, ON: ITP Nelson.

Fraser, S. (2000). *Authentic Childhood: Experiencing Reggio Emilia in the Classroom.* Scarborough, ON: ITP Nelson.

Gestwicki, C. (1999). *Developmentally Appropriate Practice: Curriculum and Development in Early Childhood Education.* (2nd ed.). Toronto, ON: Nelson Canada.

Harms, T., Clifford, R., & Cryer, D. (1998). *Early Childhood Environmental Rating Scale.* (Revised ed.). New York, NY: Teachers College Press.

Kostelnik, M. (1993). Developmentally Appropriate Programs. *Eric Digest.* ericeece@uiuc.edu.

Mayasky, M. (1998). *Creative activities for young children.* Toronto, ON: ITP Nelson.

McCain, M., & Mustard, F. (1999). *Reversing the Real Brain Drain: Early Years Study Final Report.* Toronto, ON: Publications Ontario.

Mead, M. (1975). Children's play style: Potentialities and limitations of its use as a cultural indicator. *Anthropological Quarterly 48,* 157–181.

Morrow, L. (1993). *Literacy development in the early years: Helping children read and write.* Boston, MA: Allyn and Bacon.

Newman, L. (1990). Intentional versus unintentional memory in young children: remembering versus playing. *Journal of Experimental Child Psychology 50,* 243–258.

Packer Isenberg, J., & Jalongo, M. (2001). *Creative Expression and Play in Early Childhood.* Upper Saddle River, NJ: Merrill Prentice Hall.

Parten, M. (1932). Social participation among preschool children. *Journal of Abnormal and Social Psychology 27,* 243–269.

Piaget, J. (1962). *Play, dreams, and imitation in children.* New York, NY: Norton.

Puckett, M., & Diffily, D. (1999). *Teaching Young Children and Introduction to the Early Childhood Field.* Orlando, FL: Harcourt Brace and Company.

Salisbury, C. (1991). Mainstreaming during the early childhood years. *Exceptional Children, 58,* 146–155.

Shipley, D. (2002). *Empowering Children: Play-Based Curriculum for Lifelong Learning.* (3rd ed.). Scarborough, ON: Nelson.

Smilansky, S. (1968). *The effects of sociodramatic play on disadvantaged preschool children.* New York, NY: Wiley.

Stone, S. (1995, September). Wanted: advocates for play in the primary grades. *Young Children, 50*(6), 45–5.

CHAPTER 2

The Learning Environment

Every aspect of the physical environment from the general arrangement of furnishings to the smaller details of colour and texture communicates something to the children using that space.

—Bowers, in Puckett and Diffily, Teaching Young Children: An Introduction to the Early Childhood Profession

Chapter Outline

- ▶ Introduction
- ▶ Designing the Learning Environment: Functional Aspects of Space
- ▶ Lighting
- ▶ Colour
- ▶ Noise
- ▶ Maximizing Learning Spaces

- ▶ Aesthetics
- ▶ Role of the Facilitator
- ▶ Planning Learning Experiences
- ▶ Cultural Aspects
- ▶ Key Points
- ▶ Student Activities
- ▶ References

Learning Outcomes

After reading this chapter the reader will:

1. Discuss how young children learn best
2. Discuss and list the principles of effective organization
3. Compare the similarities and differences between indoor spaces for various age groups—infants, toddlers, preschool, and school-age
4. Compare the similarities and differences between outdoor spaces for various age groups—infants, toddlers, preschool, and school-age
5. Identify appropriate outdoor space and materials
6. Describe potential hazards in indoor and outdoor environments
7. Discuss the importance of appropriate lighting in relation to children's learning
8. Discuss the impact of various colour schemes on children's learning
9. Discuss the effects of noise on children's learning
10. Identify various ways to maximize learning spaces
11. Discuss the importance of aesthetics within the learning environment
12. Identify aspects of the role of the facilitator
13. Compare the effectiveness of various types of planning techniques
14. Identify critical cultural aspects in a learning environment

Interactive Learning Exercises

 Remember, the CD-ROM that came with this text contains interactive exercises that relate to the topics in this chapter, as well as other valuable resources.

▶ Introduction

Before discussing the learning environment, it is important to consider how young children learn best. "Children are naturally curious and playful. They learn when they

- explore and play
- involve their senses
- manipulate a wide range of real objects
- work together with adults and children
- make meaningful plans and decisions
- see the result of their actions
- build upon what they already know

Children learn best when they deal with the real world—people, natural materials, problems to solve, their own creations" (Holt, Kamii, and Seefeldt, 1984, p. 20).

Most of the approaches to educating young children embody the above principles. The High/Scope preschool curriculum describes learning as **active learning**: "Active learning is defined as learning in which the child, by acting on objects and interacting with people, ideas, and events, constructs new understanding.... Active learning stands for four critical elements: (1) direct action on objects, (2) reflections on actions, (3) intrinsic motivation, invention, and generativity, and (4) problem solving" (Hohmann and Weikart, 1995, p. 17).

Loris Malaguzzi identified children's learning in the Reggio Emilia approach this way: "What children learn does not follow as an automatic result from what is taught. Rather, it is in a large part due to the children's own doing as a consequence of their activities and our resources.... In any context, children do not wait to pose questions to themselves and from strategies of thought, or principles, or feelings. Always and everywhere children take an active role in the construction and acquisition of learning and understanding. To learn is a satisfying experience. But also, as the psychologist Nelson Goodman tells us, 'to understand is to experience desire, drama and conquest' " (Edwards, Gandini, and Forman, 1998, p. 67).

The position statement of the National Association for the Education of Young Children (NAEYC) addresses quality programs through developmentally appropriate practices. A cornerstone of this statement is that "Children of all ages need uninterrupted periods of time to become involved, investigate, select, and persist at activities" (Bredekamp, 1987, p. 7).

The Canadian Association for Young Children (CAYC) supports play as a means of learning in its mission statement and expands that statement by indicating that play is natural, essential, fun, open-ended, creative, spontaneous, complex, stimulating, and non-judgmental. Play is a process that encourages children to make choices and decisions, and pose questions (CAYC, 1996).

In summary, young children learn through play. Play is enjoyable, may be social, is controlled by the children involved, provides learning without pressure, is intrinsically motivating, is free from rules set by adults, and provides opportunities for children to express themselves in a multitude of ways (see photo 2.1). "The children's use of many media is not a separate part of the curriculum but an inseparable, integral part of the whole cognitive/symbolic expression involved in the whole process of learning" (Hendrick, 1997, p. 21).

▶ Designing the Learning Environment: Functional Aspects of Space

1. General Principles

In order to encourage children to use the environment effectively it is important to ensure that there are designated areas for certain types of play. These designated areas are usually referred to as **learning areas** or **interest centres**. These areas should represent the core elements of the learning environment.

Learning areas are set up to encourage children to:

- become curious;
- make choices about what activities they wish to become engaged in;
- work alone or with others;
- solve problems by themselves or with others;
- work creatively alone or with others;
- organize time;
- progress at their own rate;
- learn social behaviours;

PHOTO 2.1

- gain communication skills, cognitive skills, and physical skills; and
- use materials and equipment creatively (see photo 2.2).

Effective organization makes use of the principles outlined in table 2.1 (see also photos 2.3 and 2.4).

2. Indoor Space

Each indoor space is a reflection of the age group within that space. To maximize the space, "The circulation between entrance and exits should be as directed as possible. Adjacent to circulation, it is appropriate to position tables and work surfaces—more crowded functions while retaining corners and floor areas for more protected and nurturing activities" (U.S. General Services Administration, 1998, p. 7–7).

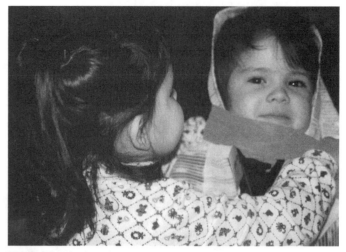

PHOTO 2.2

TABLE 2.1

▶ Principles of Effective Organization

Principle	Definition	Strategies
Display space	Area to display a variety of children's efforts at child's level	Flat—walls, bulletin boards, back of shelves
		Three-dimensional—tables, shelves
Traffic flow or circulation patterns		Block off areas that need more privacy (reading, quiet, writing areas) or need closer supervision (carpentry)—low shelves, low dividers
		Exits safely secured from unknown visitors and children wanting to leave
		Spill-out areas provided for play that may extend boundaries
		Large open area to use as a gathering spot for larger groups
		Infants and toddlers need area free from clutter
		Easily visible for children (encourages making choices) and adults (appropriate supervision, observation)
		Clear emergency exit
		Clear flow from area to area—drama to blocks to washroom
Separation of noisy and quiet areas	Noisy areas—blocks, carpentry, music, drama	Separation by distance—reading in one corner of the room, blocks in the opposite far corner
	Quiet areas—reading, writing, some manipulatives such as puzzles, concentration games	Providing sound-absorbent materials—blocks on rug surface, hard foam on carpentry bench to absorb pounding of hammer
		Sound barriers—low sturdy shelves, cushions to sit on or lie against—absorb sound

TABLE 2.1 PRINCIPLES OF EFFECTIVE ORGANIZATION (continued)

Principle	Definition	Strategies
Extension of play over more than one day	Block play, projects	Materials and equipment stay in place over more than one day; protect from main traffic flow
Separation of spaces	Acoustic, visual, physical	Solid or Plexiglas partitions (partial or full height), doors, cabinets, shelves, panels, railings, curtains (must be fire-proofed) Easy visibility for supervision and view for children
Messy areas	Messy, easily spilled materials, harder to clean after play Areas: water, sand, carpentry, creative arts	On tiled floor Near water source On tarp taped down with slip-proof materials attached to tarp Cleaning of area becomes part of children's play Cleaning materials—child-sized brooms, dusting pans, squirt bottles, sponges, pails, garbage cans—provided in each area Smocks to protect child's clothing
Specialized areas	Space for large group activities and space to be alone	Large clear carpeted area Protected quiet area—playhouse, decorated large boxes with windows and doors, hanging see-through fabric in a corner of the room Protection from intrusions—rule and sign
Storage	Where and how materials and equipment are displayed to maximize independent use by children	Clear storage containers—easy to see items in containers Mobile units for items used in more than one area—storage containers on wheels, caddies to move from place to place, centralized unit—accessible from more than one location Labelling system—picture and word, recognizable symbol—stop sign, outlines of objects on shelves Low shelves accessible to all children Storage by type to prevent dumping and easy to find—all red round beads in one container
Visibility	Ease with which adults and children can see various areas	Supervision of children; easy for children to see areas

As adults and children interact within the environment, it will be adapted to accommodate changing interests and needs. It is, therefore, extremely important to create an environment that can be modified readily. Larger, heavier units that cannot be easily moved should be placed around the periphery of the room. Smaller, wheeled units should be used to maximize opportunities for children to help in creating

PHOTO 2.3

PHOTO 2.4

and adapting their environment. Shelves and dividers may be used to partition off various areas, but these must be securely anchored.

Variety can be added to the environment by varying such things as:

- The height of the ceiling—differential ceiling height and wall colour lead to greater cooperative behaviour in preschoolers (Read, Sugawara, and Brant, 1999). This is an important design feature when first creating an environment. Other techniques that can be used include draping material (note that the material needs fireproofing) or suspending structures from the ceiling (e.g., grids to hang pots and pans on in housekeeping area, framed pictures over creative art area, hanging plants).
- Various levels of play—lofts, climbers, platforms, sunken areas. For security reasons these are usually permanent structures. These can also become more mobile if anchors are provided in the walls or the floors that allow for removing or changing the equipment.
- Configuration of wall spaces—flat walls can be changed by adding texture and dimension with curved dividers or partitions. These structures can be covered with material (burlap, felt, satin, netting) to add a softer space to a room or to provide interesting ways to display materials.

Various age groups have differing needs. These needs are clearly reflected in how each environment is set up. The environment should as much as possible reflect children's home environments; for example, by adding furniture like easy chairs and couches and taking care to represent cultural values in food preparation.

Infant Environment

- toileting needs—diapering area and storage cubbies within diapering area;

- nursing area—comfortable, quiet area appropriate for nursing mothers and for bottle-fed infants;
- eating area—high chairs, low tables and chairs for older infants;
- sleeping area—separate sleep room with cribs; and
- play areas—open activity area for mobile infants, protected area for non-mobile infants; low shelves that are sturdy enough to pull oneself up provide accessibility of materials and are highly adaptable to meet the changing developmental levels of infants.

Toddler Environment

- toileting needs—diapering area adjacent to toddler area, including storage cubbies, small toilets and sinks, personal grooming items (toothbrushes, facecloth, toothpaste, comb);
- nursing area—comfortable, quiet area appropriate for nursing mothers and for bottle-fed toddlers;
- eating area—low tables and chairs;
- sleeping area—easily accessible cots that can be retrieved easily to accommodate toddlers' sleeping patterns;
- play areas—open activity area; low, sturdy, open shelves provide accessibility of materials; dramatic play, block play, sand, water, music, pre-carpentry, manipulatives, quiet, books, creative arts, science/math; and
- open unrestricted area—gross motor activities.

Preschool Environment

- toileting needs—adjacent to preschool area; storage for personal grooming items (toothbrushes, facecloth, toothpaste, comb); small toilets and sinks;
- eating area—low tables and chairs, small groupings of tables and chairs;
- sleeping area—easily accessible cots that can be retrieved easily;

- quiet area for non-sleepers and early risers;
- play areas—open activity area; low, open shelves to provide accessibility of materials; dramatic play, block play, sand, water, music, carpentry, manipulatives, quiet, books, writing, creative arts, science/math, mobile storage units; and
- open unrestricted area—gathering area.

School-Aged Environment

- toileting needs—private male and female washrooms;
- eating area—tables and chairs for small groupings;
- quiet area—area to relax;
- play areas—open activity area; sturdy, open shelves to provide accessibility of materials; dramatic play, block play, sand, water, music, carpentry, manipulatives, reading, writing, creative arts, science, math, places to do homework; and
- open unrestricted area—gathering area.

3. Outdoor Space

The outdoor play area should be a natural extension of the indoor play space, encouraging children to transfer skills from one setting to another. Outdoor play spaces should reflect what is happening indoors (see photos 2.5 and 2.6). All areas of play should therefore be planned for and implemented outdoors. "Play yards should serve as extensions of classroom spaces, especially where temperate climate allows for easy flow of children and staff into the exterior space on a regular basis. Play yards should be integrated, to the greatest extent possible, into the overall design of the center. Within a central play yard, separate play areas are recommended for each age group of children" (U.S. General Services Administration, 1998, p. 6–3).

"Circulation within the play yard should branch throughout the various play areas, moving through the play yard. Dedicated pathways and routes should be provided for play with wheeled toys. The circulation pathway is the primary element that can tie the entire play yard together" (U.S. General Services Administration, 1998, p. 6–3).

Some of the areas that should be represented outside are listed in table 2.2. As outdoor play should be an extension of indoor play, all the materials and equipment available indoors should also be available outdoors; therefore, only additional materials and equipment that are not generally used or brought indoors are listed in table 2.2. Learning areas such as manipulatives, creative arts, carpentry, blocks, music, and reading and writing can be implemented with very few changes outdoors: it is simply a matter of encouraging children to bring out what they need for play (see photo 2.7). Mobile containers such as cotton bags, carry totes, baskets, and units with wheels on them facilitate this process and encourage children to

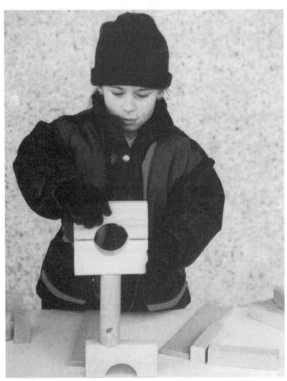

PHOTO 2.5

PHOTO 2.6

TABLE 2.2

▶ Outdoor Learning Areas

Learning Area	Skills	Additional Materials (all materials as listed in appropriate chapters plus....)
Sand/soil Water	Discover and compare similarities and differences in colour, texture, composition, temperatures Create real scenarios—plant a flower garden or vegetable garden and care for it Combine sand and water to create mixtures Use water to add reality—moats, rivers, ponds Discover properties of water added to sand or soil—absorbent, waterlogged, porous, contained, flow/current, dammed Discover properties of water—collection in puddles, force, flow, runoff, speed, move objects, displacement, temperature, changes in state	Gardening tools—spades, forks, shovels, wheelbarrows Plants (see table 2.3 for non-poisonous plants) Edible plants, use variety to indicate various types of growth patterns (underground, vine) and familiar food for children: tomatoes, sweet peas, pumpkins, carrots, radishes (others as reflected by culture) Hoses, wading pools, stones, small logs, watering cans, sieves, jars to collect rainfall, graduated jars with holes in them to create waterfalls when stacked (use cut plastic bottles of various sizes) Provide opportunities to explore outside during rain/snow and after rainfall/snowfall Fountains for drinking
Dramatic Play	Opportunity to dramatize using real materials—planting, water, wheeled toys Cooperate and share—wheeled toys, pathways, planting Creative thinking—use various levels of play space (ground level, climbing equipment) as part of dramatizations Develop gross motor abilities—coordination, balance, moving around obstacles Develop awareness of different spaces and how to effectively use these Problem solving—how to use space, materials, equipment	Playhouse structure along with appropriate furnishings Natural elements to use as props—boards, lumber, large rocks, logs, tree stumps Props—tarpaulins, banners, signs, tires, large boxes, riding toys Landscaping—small hills, shaded areas, trees with low hanging branches to wing self from, concrete large pipes to crawl through Accessible taps, working hose
Quiet area	Activities for concentration: sorting, matching, one-to-one correspondence, memory Reading, writing (photo 2.7)	Natural elements for concentration activities: stones, shells, twigs, leaves Work area/relaxed area: benches, blankets, pillows, small tables and chairs in the shade, under a tree, under a canopy Reading—book bags to bring books outside Writing—clipboards, caddies to hold writing tools: crayons, scissors, pencils, rulers
Science and math	Observing animals, insects, bugs, birds, reptiles, amphibians Counting, comparing, measuring, collecting—sorting, matching, categorizing	Camera to take pictures of interest Magnifying glasses, collecting baskets, paper, pencils, clipboards, crayons, markers, tape, glue, scissors, clippers Measuring—scales, measuring tapes, metre/yard sticks, unit blocks/cubes, string, wood Use natural materials in the environment—stones, sand, twigs, leaves, trees Take field trips to zoos, natural environments, conservation areas, parks

TABLE 2.2 OUTDOOR LEARNING AREAS (continued)

Learning Area	Skills	Additional Materials (all materials as listed in appropriate chapters plus....)
Large-muscle play	Climbing (photo 2.8), riding, running, jumping, balancing, sliding Building strength, endurance, coordination, rhythm	Various levels of difficulty in materials and equipment: riding toys (push with feet, pedal), climbing equipment (more than one way to reach top, come down), stairs, ladder, rope ladder, ramp Connect with nature: obstacle courses (logs, hills, stumps, trees, bushes, pathways) Large pipes to crawl into, ride through Various levels of difficulty, connect with nature, obstacle courses (logs, small hills, stumps, trees, bushes) Jump/balance (tires, logs, low walls, beams)

return the things they took outside, thus teaching responsibility for property. Additionally, appropriate storage is needed outside.

Storage

"Storage facilities should be easily discernible and have a unique, easily understood symbol indicating its content. Storage facilities provide an opportunity for children to learn organization and cooperation skills. Children acquire a sense of responsibility by learning to return toys and tools under the direction of the caregiver, to the correct storage areas when they are finished playing" (U.S. General Services Administration, 1998, p. 6–6).

Storage outside needs to be in an area that can be locked. Locks must be on the outside of the unit to avoid the possibility that a child may be trapped inside the unit. The storage units need to be in central locations close to the relevant activities for easy access and supervision.

PHOTO 2.7

PHOTO 2.8

TABLE 2.3

▶ Poisonous and Non-poisonous Plants

Non-poisonous Plants		Poisonous Plants	
African violet	Jade plant	Amaryllis	Hyacinth
Christmas cactus	Lilac	Arrowhead	Hydrangea
Coleus	Marigold	Azalea	Iris
Corn plant	Mulberry	Barberry	Jersusalem
Crocus	Norfolk pine tree	Black lotus	cherry
Dandelion	Peperomia	Boxwood	Jimsonweed
Dogwood	Petunia	Caladium	Lily-of-the-
Dracaena	Prayer plant	Castor bean	valley
Easter lily	Rose	Chinaberry	Mistletoe
Fern	Rubber tree plant	Chinese evergreen	Mountain laurel
Firethorn	Snake plant	Chrysanthemum	Narcissus
Forsythia	Spider plant	Crown of thorns	Nightshade
Fuchsia	Swedish ivy	Daffodil	family
Geranium	Wandering Jew	Dieffenbachia	Oak acorns
Hibiscus	Wax plant	English ivy	Peony
Honeysuckle	Wild strawberry	Euonymous privet	Philodendron
Impatiens	Zebra plants	Four o'clock	family
		Fruit pits or seeds	Poison oak/ivy
		Gladiola	Poison sumac
		Holly	Pokeweed
			Rhododendron
			Water hemlock
			Wysteria
			Yew

Note: The sap of the following plants may be irritating—ficus, poinsettia, scheffiera, and tulip (adapted from U.S. General Services Administration, 1998, pp. B–1, B–2).

Safety

"To provide a safe environment that still allows gross motor activity, the movement of the children themselves rather than the equipment is key. In addition, the following items are not to be used in GSA playgrounds as they have been found to be unsafe in group settings" (U.S. General Services Administration, 1998, p. 6–3):

- metal slides—cause burning during hot days;
- enclosed tunnels—are difficult to supervise, children may get stuck, children may hit other children when they slide down;
- seesaws—if one child jumps off, the other child drops rapidly; children too close may get hit;
- spring-mounted, rocking toys—children may overextend the swing and catapult off or may pinch fingers on springs; and

- surfaces under slides, swings, climbers—pre-engineered wood chips, wood or bark chips, processed wood fibres, pre-formed rubber matting, poured in place rubberized surfaces—may cause cuts or abrasions.

It is important to check with the ministry in your jurisdiction to make sure that the appropriate guidelines are met. Table 2.4 lists additional hazards that must be checked regularly, as identified by the Canadian Safety Association (CSA, 1998).

Separation of Space

Infants' outdoor spaces should have an area that is securely separated from other areas. Ideally this should be near the toddler area to allow visual and communicative contact between the two age groups and a smoother transition from infancy to toddlerhood. Care

TABLE 2.4

► Potential Hazards

Hazard	Areas to Check
Missing, broken, or loose parts Warping, decay	Equipment with rungs, steps, planks, splintering wood, hand holds, seats, fences, supports, bolts, metal (rust), wood (decay), foundations, guardrails, hardware (nails, nuts, bolts, clamps), protective pieces
Drainage	Drain holes; hollow equipment such as tires; under swings and slide exit areas
Squeaky or noisy action, jammed parts, constrained or excessive motion	Swings, gates, props (wheels), clatter bridges, pumps, ropes, cables
Dangerous items in area	Needles, debris, animal excrement, nails, glass, sharp objects, pooling water, litter

must be taken to ensure that there are appropriate surfaces such as grass, sand, or mats for crawling and soft comfortable areas for sitting—small cube chairs, soft foam chairs, blankets, and pillows. Care should be taken to ensure that colour is used appropriately; colours should blend into the environment. In addition, harsh, bright primary colours on bright days cause glare, which is hard on the eye and very distracting. Colour can also be used to draw attention to different activities. For example, green areas (grass, blankets, mats) can indicate crawling activities, brown areas climbing activities (climbing equipment), and grey areas pushing/pulling activities (using pushcarts or pull toys on a paved area). "Soft surfaces should have different textures and (not garish) colours denoting changes in activities and challenges" (U.S. General Services Administration, 1998, p. 6–9).

Toddlers need a space that will allow them to actively explore the environment. This space should also be enclosed and protected from the slower infants and the more skilled preschoolers. The ideal placement of this area would be between the infant and the preschool areas, encouraging ease of transition to the preschool age group and communication with both age groups.

Toddlers need movement to stimulate their senses. The space for toddlers needs to be varied to accommodate these needs, and should include:

- resilient surfaces—to dig or jump in, such as sand;
- open grassy areas—to run through, roll in, jump around in;

- pavement—to ride on, push and pull wagons to transport objects;
- hilly places—to run up and down, roll down; and
- curved paths—to navigate riding toys around.

The preschool environment needs to be multidimensional to capture the preschoolers' interest and ability in dramatic play, **constructive play,** and creative play. Preschoolers need to have both activity and quiet represented in their play yard, along with plenty of opportunities to explore the natural environment—trees, flowers, animals, insects, effects of weather patterns, and seasonal changes.

Ideally, the preschool playground should be separated between the toddlers and the school-aged children, for many of the same reasons stated for separating the infant and toddler age groups.

School-aged children need a lot of room to explore and to practise their more advanced skills. School-aged children play cooperatively and competitively; the play space must accommodate both. There needs to be allowance for games—hopscotch, skipping, dramatic play—and places to practise and engage in sports activities—soccer, baseball, basketball, and gymnastics.

► Lighting

A number of studies have addressed the importance of appropriate lighting within learning environments. Poor lighting and/or fluorescent lighting have been linked to hyperactivity, decreased productivity, and poorer health (Harmon, 1951; Ott, 1976; and Liberman, 1991). Hathaway (1994) conducted a study in which **full-spectrum fluorescent lighting** with ultraviolet enhancement (which produces the closest match to solar light) was used within the classroom setting. He found a decrease in cavities, absenteeism, and an increase in growth and development. Lexington (1989) found that student productivity increased with better lighting.

Hollwich and Dieckhues (1980) found that sitting under strong non–full-spectrum light causes an increase in two metabolic hormones that are linked to stress. "Since their activity increases under stress, and since both these hormones also function as growth inhibitors, this may account for the observation that persistent stress stunts bodily growth in children" (in Liberman, 1991, p. 60). As a result of the research on non–full-spectrum light, cool white fluorescent bulbs (deficient in red and blue-violet light) have been banned from hospitals and medical facilities in Germany.

Seasonal affective disorder (SAD) is characterized by depression during fall and winter, when there are shorter days. The depression spontaneously disappears during spring and summer. The condition is well-documented in adult populations, but until recently few studies have been concerned with SAD in children. Swedo, Allen, and Glod (1997) found that 28 children suffering from SAD were treated effectively with light therapy. It is estimated that as many as one million children in the United States may be suffering from SAD, with many more cases undiagnosed (Giedd, 1998).

Lighting requirements in many jurisdictions recognize the need for natural light within the child-care settings, but regulations are not in place to change the type of lighting that is used in most day-care centres. The Illuminating Engineering Society (SDPL) recommends that a window should take up at least 20 percent of a wall's space (Hawkins and Lilley, 1992).

Given some of the strong evidence that lighting does play a critical role in the child-care setting, the following are a few suggestions that can be implemented:

- having outdoor play for at least one hour a day, irrespective of weather;
- having children sit near an unshielded closed or open window while indoors;
- using individually controlled incandescent lights (this light is preferable to fluorescent lighting, but

is deficient in the blue end of the spectrum and contains no ultraviolet light);
- placing mirrors opposite windows; and
- using full-spectrum fluorescent lighting.

▶ Colour

"Colour appears to describe life itself, evoking inner feelings, memories, and responses. It has a power and language of its own, which when communicated as energy, can excite, sedate, balance, motivate, inspire, enhance learning, and even lure us into buying things we may not need" (Liberman, 1991, p. 37).

Interior decorators have long used colour for many of the "powers" listed above. The variety of purposes for the use of colour are identified in table 2.5.

According to Harrington and Mackie (1993), colour also affects all individuals at two levels: behavioural response and learned response. A **behavioural response** is a response that "is automatic and inherited and unaffected by sex, age, income, culture or environment" (1993, p. 28). This type of response occurs naturally; the individual is not aware of making a response. For example, using bright, intense colours, such as red, to decorate an infant's room can prevent the infant from sleeping well (Chiazzari, 1998, p. 154). This is not a surprising response, as the colour red has been shown to elevate blood pressure (Liberman, 1991).

A **learned response** is exactly the opposite. A learned response involves the assimilation of knowledge and is dependent "on sex, age, income level, cultural background and so on" (Harrington and Mackie, 1993, p. 28). An example of a learned response might be the response to red. In our culture, red has become associated with "stop"; when a preschooler stops at the street corner at a red light, he or she has learned that red means stop.

In a Canadian study in Edmonton, Wohlfarth and Wohlfarth (1982) combined full-spectrum lighting and colour within a school for handicapped children. Walls were painted warm light yellow and warm light blue. Results included:

- reduced systolic pressure;
- reduced aggression;
- decreased stress levels;
- less moodiness;
- quieter classroom;
- less illness;
- increased academic achievement; and
- increased IQ levels.

TABLE 2.5

▶ Interior Design and Impact of Colour		
Impact	**Colour**	**Desired Effect**
Short-term calming effect	Pink	Sweetness, innocence, helps muscles relax
Stimulate, excite	Red	Desire to touch, strong feelings, draw attention
Exuberance, refreshing	Orange	Release of emotions, association with thirst
Enlightenment	Yellow	Stimulate memory, expression of thought, anticipation, discernment, discrimination, clear thinking, philosophical attitude
Relaxing, comforting, quieting	Green (easiest colour for the eye to see)	Encourage concentration, relaxation, empathy
Cooling, calming	Turquoise	Heightens communication, sensitivity, creativity
Soothing, calm, non-threatening	Blue	Sense of coolness, dependability, longevity, calmness, protection Inspires mental control, creativity, clarity
Calm, pacify	Purple, indigo, violet	Quell internal dialogue, pacify individuals with mental, nervous disorders
Non-commitment, set mood, power, mystery, dignity	Black	Rouse curiosity; role play controlling situations, individuals
Cleanliness, purity, innocence	White	Alleviate emotional shock, cleanse emotions, reflect
Sense of discipline	Grey	Plan actions, deliberate, self-controlled, self-reliant
Warmth, comfort, reliability	Brown	Nurture, supportive, retreating

(Harrington and Mackie, 1993; Chiazzari, 1998)

In summary, colour is an important consideration in any learning environment. Early childhood educators cannot make assumptions based on casual observations of children's likes and dislikes. Bright primary colours serve to stimulate and excite. Pale, warm colours cause the opposite effect—they are calming, soothing, relaxing. A child-care environment needs to emulate both components. It is also important to remember that children's creative efforts are often bright and colourful. Displaying these creative efforts in an environment that is already highly stimulating in terms of the use of colour can cause a very unsettling, overwhelming effect. "The overuse of strong colour schemes should be avoided, as this may result in over-stimulated, excited behaviour" (U.S. General Services Administration, 1998, p. 6–9).

▶ Noise

Young children's play areas are often noisy places to be. Children express their exuberance in active play, which also includes active dialogue. For example, Jenna was trying to blow a bubble. When she was successful, her joy erupted into a loud yell followed by shouting: "Look, look, look! I did it!" Jenna's excitement was natural, spontaneous, and should not be discouraged. However, if the noise level in the environment starts to escalate, there is a danger of disrupting the concentration of other children engaged in quiet activities. In one daycare centre, children were engaged in boisterous dramatic play. The children started to shout to each other; this had a ripple effect around the room. In order to communicate, other groups of children also raised their voices. One child crawled under a table and held his ears, and another child stopped her play and watched the room with wide, startled eyes. This is a noise level that has become disruptive to the children's play and the general tone of the room.

Abundant research documents hearing damage: the above example does not fall into this category. Centres that are near airports, major roadways, railroads, or other noise sources would be in more danger of causing damage to children's hearing. However, there is a growing concern about nonauditory effects. **Nonauditory effects** can be described as noise that does not damage the child's hearing but can be shown to have a negative effect in any one or all of the following categories: physiological, motivational, and cognitive.

> Chronic exposure to noise has been shown harmful to children of various ages; it can have especially detrimental effects on younger children when language and discrimination skills are forming. Sometimes major noise sources are not under the control of teachers or designers.... Sometimes the noise source is the design of spaces. Designers should keep in mind the use of the space they are creating. In child care centers, spaces must allow for the fact that children need to make noise but the subsequent noise levels should not be harmful to them or others in the centre. (Maxwell and Evans, 2001, p. 3)

In any environment there are a variety of things that can be done to decrease noise levels:
- using sound-absorbing materials—carpets under blocks, foam surfaces on carpentry benches, mats in gross motor areas;
- using sound barriers—carpets, upholstered furniture, grass in outdoor areas, upholstered dividers, acoustic tiles;
- separating noisy and quiet areas;
- encouraging and modelling appropriate voice volume; and
- using music to calm: "The music of Mozart invariably calmed listeners, improved spatial perception, and allowed them to express themselves more clearly" (Campbell, 1997, p. 27).

In the example above, where the noise levels escalated to inappropriate levels, the teachers in the program tried two techniques. One teacher quickly put on a CD that combined the music of Mozart with nature sounds, while the other teacher walked over to the children who were most noisy and started to interact with them on a quiet level. In a quiet voice, she asked them what was happening. The combined soothing sounds of the music and the interactions of the teacher soon brought the tone of the room back to a normal level.

▶ Maximizing Learning Spaces

An important consideration in any child-care setting is the physical arrangement of space. There are always so many learning-area possibilities, but only so much space. One way to maximize space is by placing centres that are linked closer together so that the space and many of the materials can be shared effectively. The same principles apply for both indoor and outdoor spaces. Many of the ideas listed for more mobile storage have the added advantage of being easily carried outside as needed. Some suggestions for combining centres are:
- sand area and water area—This is a natural and familiar combination. The children are encouraged to explore other concepts (creating mixtures, what happens to sand in water, how much water the sand will hold until saturated, and how to change the consistency of the sand). Many of the toys can be shared in both areas: containers for moulding or pouring; scoops and funnels to transfer; measuring cups, scales, spoons; containers of various sizes. Materials may be compared using containers of the same size but different shapes.
- carpentry area and creative area—This is an excellent combination, as children can learn more about various ways of attaching materials (glue, tape, nails, screws, nuts and bolts, staples, a needle and thread). Since most carpentry projects involve a finishing process, the materials are readily available (paint, crayons, markers, and decorative items such as ribbons, shells, and paper).
- reading area and writing area—This combination encourages a whole language approach. It encourages exploration of print through reading and writing of symbols.
- dramatic area and block play area—Blocks lend themselves to dramatic play (building cars, houses, extensions to an existing structure—the possibilities are unlimited) (photo 2.9).

PHOTO 2.9

- music area and writing area—Both music and writing require a formal process of recording.
- science area and math area—These two areas share many prerequisite skills (comparing, measuring, counting, sorting, matching, formulating, observing, and, in later years, patterning, seriating, **classifying,** and operations).
- manipulatives area and blocks area—Many of the materials can be shared (small and large blocks, and accessories including people, vehicles, animals).
- music area and movement area—Many of the skills in gross motor can be enhanced through music (marching, moving creatively, using props to move to music).

A second way to use space effectively is to maximize the gathering area(s) for more than one purpose. Activities that need spill-out space, such as blocks, should be placed near the gathering area. Music and movement needs more space and should also be placed adjacent to this area.

A third way is to create **mobile storage** units that children can transport from one area to another. For example:

- caddies—can be used to carry writing materials (paper, pens, glue, markers, crayons, pencils, pencil sharpeners, scissors, clipboards) and to transport paint and brushes;
- clear plastic boxes—can be used to sort animals, people, plants, vehicles;

- vehicle tote boxes;
- clear sewing organizer boxes—can hold beads, sewing materials, decorative materials;
- tool boxes—can hold hammers, nails, pencils, tape measures, screws, drills, screwdrivers; and
- baskets—can be used by children to collect the items they need and to move them to where they are needed.

These storage units can be placed in a central storage area. Children can get them as needed and return them when finished. Children can also become responsible for re-stocking items that are missing or that no longer work.

A fourth idea is to keep storage units that contain materials that can be used in more than one area in a central location. These units could be shelves open on two sides containing clear plastic containers; clear drawer units; stackable open plastic containers; and low hanging baskets. Materials suitable for these areas include paper, writing utensils, animals, people, vehicles, decorative materials (shells, stones, feathers, scraps, material, straws, play dough), attachment materials (glue, nails, nuts and bolts, screws, needles and thread, wire), containers, dress-up clothes, dramatic props (steering wheels, bells, gloves, umbrellas, scarves), and musical instruments.

A related idea is the rotation of materials to avoid clutter. Children should know where these materials are, so that they can be empowered to retrieve them personally or ask an adult to help them. Materials should be well organized, so that adults and children alike can easily retrieve items as needed.

Finally, storage units themselves can be mobile—stackable drawers on wheels, open stackable plastic containers on wheels, crates on wheels that can be pulled. Mobility encourages children to move units to where they are needed.

▶ Aesthetics

When individuals talk about aesthetic experiences, they often refer to aesthetics as it refers to appreciation of art. Aesthetics is so much more. It is an expression and appreciation of beauty through using all our senses. Beauty is culturally determined and literally "in the eye of the beholder." Children must learn to appreciate beauty and learn to express it in a variety of different ways—literature, music, nature, art, writing, sculpting. It is the expression of beauty that the Reggio Emilia approach expresses so well in terms of *The Hundred Languages of Children*, the title of the text describing this approach.

"**Aesthetics** refers to an appreciation for the beauty and feeling of wonder. It is a sensibility that uses imagination as well as the five senses. It is seeing beauty in a sunset, hearing rhythm in a rainfall, and loving the expression on a person's face. Each person has an individual personal sense of what is or is not pleasing" (Mayesky, 1997, p. 26).

Aesthetic feeling—the full, rich, thick presence of feeling, is not present to our normal every day waking consciousness. "Aesthetic feeling is special. ...We come to aesthetic feeling when we allow feeling to take command of our full attention. Aesthetic feeling, because it completely floods consciousness, increases the intensity of feeling. It is feeling with the volume turned up. It does not lead to practical, efficient, or productive end in and of itself. It is its own end." (Flannery, 1977, p. 22).

"What are the beginnings of **aesthetic response**? First of all, children need to know that an aesthetic response is something people do and secondly they need the raw materials of aesthetic response—conscious awareness of aesthetic qualities and the language for the expression of their responses" (Sharp, 1976, p. 26).

Mature aesthetic sensitivity does not simply come with age. It cannot be assumed that a developed aesthetic sensitivity comes about spontaneously or independently of environmental conditions (Tauton, 1982, p. 104).

How does the educator of young children create an environment that encourages beauty? Some suggestions for increasing the aesthetic appeal in the environment are through the use of (Mayesky, 1997, p. 30; Feeney and Moravcik, 1997, p. 11):

- colour—Emphasis should be on warm, light shades. Children should feel welcomed, not overwhelmed. (Refer to the section on colour above.)
- light—Maximize natural light. Replace fluorescent lighting with full-spectrum fluorescent lighting. (Refer to the section on lighting above.)
- furnishings—"Group similar furniture together. Keep colours natural and neutral to focus children's attention on the learning materials on the shelves. When choosing furniture, select natural wood rather than metal or plastic. If the furniture must be painted, use one neutral colour for everything so that there is a greater flexibility in moving it from space to space. Periodically give children brushes and warm soapy water and let them scrub the furniture" (Mayesky, 1997, p. 30).
- storage—Storage should display learning materials clearly and attractively. Avoid clutter. Children should be attracted to the materials, know where they are, and be able to return the

materials appropriately. (Refer to the section on storage above.)
- decoration—Children need to feel that what they accomplish is valued. One way to do this is to display their creative efforts. As in an art gallery, paintings should be mounted and hung. Sculptures should be displayed on a shelf, so that the piece can be admired from various angles. Other creative efforts can be displayed through a series of photographs that are mounted on panels or within books.
- awareness and appreciation of beauty—Children need to be surrounded by beauty in order to appreciate beauty. Adults need to point out the beauty that is around children; this can be done by pointing out the beauty in everyday occurrences and asking open-ended questions about what is happening or by describing what has happened: "When I see a rainbow, I study it and watch it change, knowing that the intensity of colors and the width of the stripes of color depend on the size of the raindrops. As the size changes, the rainbow changes too. The rainbow is a story in the sky waiting to be read, and it takes some time to read and appreciate the story" (Murphy and Doherty, 1996, p. 16).
- outdoors—"Design or arrange play structures as extensions of nature rather than intrusions upon it. If possible, use natural materials like wood and hemp instead of painted metal, plastic, or fiberglass. Provide adequate storage, to help maintain materials. Involve children, parents, and staff in keeping outdoor areas free of litter. Add small details like a garden or a rock arrangement to show that the outdoors also deserves attention and care" (Mayesky, 1997, p. 30).

In summary, aesthetic experiences need to be developed over time. They are closely linked to a child's development. For example, an infant will express joy in sensory activities (such as lying on a blanket that has a soft, fluffy texture) through body movement or a smile. The toddler will actively choose the blanket that he likes the best—texture, pattern, or colour—and the preschooler will tell you why he or she likes this particular blanket. School-aged children are more discerning and might well research which blanket is the best before deciding on one particular type.

▶ Role of the Facilitator

Research often proves common sense to be correct. It stands to reason that when a baby or young child is with a sensitive and responsive caregiver or teacher for many hours a day over a long period of time, an emotional bond will develop. One would guess that this happy, reliable relationship would make the infant or young child feel more secure, confident, and eager to learn. Now research says it's so (Elicker and Fortner-Wood, 1995, p. 70).

In a Canadian study on the aspects of quality care, Doherty-Derkowski (1995, pp. 25–33) shows that caregiver interactions are one of the critical components leading to quality care. She identifies the following interactions as critical:

- using developmentally appropriate practices—what is appropriate to expect of a child and what is appropriate based on abilities, needs, background, and interests;
- being responsive to children—reacting to children appropriately and immediately, listening to them with attention and respect, initiating a variety of activities based on their abilities and interests, and being sensitive to the child's mood and situation;
- using positive adult interactions—showing interest in what the child is doing, getting actively involved with the child, and encouraging the child's efforts (see photo 2.10);
- engaging in high appropriate verbal exchanges—two-way communication between adult and child, such as discussing a picture in a book while reading the book;
- providing an environment that is rich in a variety of things to explore; and

PHOTO 2.10

- providing an atmosphere that encourages and supports the child.

Elicker and Fortner-Wood further identify the following aspects as critical to the facilitator's role to develop:

- an attachment relationship with each child;
- a special time with each child; and
- a positive relationship with family members.

Most current approaches to caring for young children recognize and use many of the research findings above. The adults in a High/Scope setting support the children by:

- organizing environments and routines for active learning
- establishing a climate for positive social interactions
- encouraging children's intentional actions, problem solving, and verbal reflection
- observing and interpreting the actions of each child in terms of the developmental principles embodied in the High/Scope **key experiences**
- planning experiences that build on the child's actions and interests. (Hohmann and Weikart, 1995, p. 17)

The adult's role in the position statement of the NAEYC is to "provide opportunities for children to choose from a variety of activities, materials, and equipment; and time to explore through active exploration. Adults facilitate children's engagement with materials and activities and extend the child's learning by asking stimulating questions or making suggestions that stimulate children's thinking" (in Bredekamp, 1987, p. 7).

The Reggio Emilia approach focuses on the partnership among children, families, and teachers. According to Malaguzi, "Our goal is to build an amiable school, where children, teachers, and families feel at home. Such a school requires careful thinking and planning concerning procedures, motivation, and interests. It must embody ways of getting along together, of intensifying relationships among the three central protagonists, of assuring complete attention to the problem of education, and of activating participation and research" (Edwards, Gandini, and Forman, 1998, pp. 64–65).

In addition, the facilitator must know when to step in and when to let the play continue without interference. The following are some guidelines that help the facilitator to make that decision. The facilitator should observe without interference when:

- children are gainfully employed;
- children are interacting with each other and the materials and equipment provided;

- children are solving their own problems;
- play extends over a long period of time; and
- materials and equipment are used appropriately.

The facilitator should always step in when:

- the play becomes harmful either to the child or to other children;
- the play becomes destructive of the materials or equipment;
- the children ask for help, or it seems evident that they need help;
- arguments among children erupt;
- the noise level starts to escalate;
- children exhibit signs of stress—raised voices, tense body language, tears;
- opportunities to extend play occur;
- children interfere with each other's creativity; and
- children seem to flit from one activity to another.

Adults in any program should focus on making the learning experience and environment a positive experience for all children. Careful observation of children's interactions, the type of materials used, the type of play occurring, and the skills children are using give guidelines on how to extend children's play.

▶ Planning Learning Experiences

Many textbooks on the market today offer quick solutions to planning for children. These texts offer the educator ideas on what to provide to the children, how to provide it, and, often, how to evaluate the experiences. What all of these texts fail to do is to consider *the individual child.* Planning is based on what the adult perceives as interesting, instead of observing the children to note what new materials are needed, what additional experiences should be provided to enhance the learning, what adaptations should be made, and what learning has already taken place.

Terminology for planning is varied and confusing. Terms such as *activity plans, lesson plans, unit plans, themes, individual plans,* and *projects* are commonly used. The planning terminology is often used interchangeably to mean the same thing. The concept of each planning tool, however, is quite different.

PLANNING FOR INDIVIDUAL ACTIVITIES

Planning for individual activities usually focuses on one activity. Once this activity has been implemented, the plan is completed. **Activity plans, lesson plans,** and **individual plans** fit into this category. The plan usually has an objective or a purpose that can be very specific: "Paint a girl in a garden holding a watering can" (Libby,

2000, p. 178), or very general: "Spark creative thinking and inspire budding artists with a repeating poem" (Miller, 1991, p. 58). Each then lists the materials needed, the process used to reach the objective of purpose, and strategies such as questioning techniques and process techniques. If the basic premise of planning is planning for children, then these types of plans are inappropriate. In each case, the plan is more of a blueprint for the adult. The focus on the child—interests, abilities, uniqueness—is totally missing.

Some of these types of activity plans tend to compensate for this by adding developmental norms: "15 to 18 months. Your toddler is at the perfect age for exposure to the sounds of other languages" (Silberg, 2000, p. 38). Some planning formats add information to base the plan on the children—usually a blank space that is filled in as children are observed, prior to planning. This is an attempt to base the planning process on the child.

This type of planning is usually a one-time activity. It does not nurture children's learning over time, nor does it involve children in making decisions, solving problems, or making choices.

PLANNING FOR THE WHOLE LEARNING ENVIRONMENT

Another type of planning tool, *unit plans* or *theme-based plans,* involves a process of planning the learning environment over time. The purpose can be very specific ("water flows"), or very general ("Magnificent Me") (Jackman, 2001, p. 42). This approach requires adults to set up the environment based on one topic at a time. A theme is generally a concept for the whole learning environment ("Magnificent Me") or one specific area (water flows, the water centre). The intent of this type of planning is "to introduce children to activities that require active exploration, problem solving, and acquisition of a specific concept or skill" (Jackman, p. 42). The process that is involved is as follows:

> Developing a list of themes is usually the first phase. This is useful as you move toward developing a lesson plan and the activities that fit within this plan. Remember to remain flexible and responsive to the children, including being adaptable to the varying developmental stages and experiences within the group. Your theme planning should merge play with child-directed and teacher-initiated experiences. (Jackman, p. 42)

As clearly indicated, the primary force of the learning is the adult. The adult is responsible for planning and shaping the learning environment. Within this environment, children can make choices, solve problems, and make decisions. What is missing is the children's involvement in the learning process. The assumption is that all children will benefit and will be interested. It does not empower children to become part of the planning process, nor does it acknowledge each child's uniqueness.

Much of the **theme-based planning** and unit-based planning is developed in a web planning format. An example is provided in figure 2.1. The web-based plan attempts to integrate various planning units within the learning environment. The webbing is a visual process that gives some degree of flexibility to the adult and the children. New ideas and concepts can be added at any time. Children can be involved in the brainstorming and the documenting process.

One of the problems associated with a planning web is that it does not take into account the whole planning environment. Certain critical learning areas are often left out. For example, in the web shown in figure 2.1 it is hard to link in sand, water, carpentry, blocks, and manipulative play without a considerable stretch of the imagination. As a result, these critical learning areas are often ignored or the area may be closed. The **web-based planning** still tends to be teacher-initiated, based on a perceived group approach. The uniqueness of individual children is still largely ignored.

The last approach discussed is the **project approach**. This approach "refers to a way of teaching and learning, as well as to the content of what is taught and learned. This approach emphasizes the teacher's role in encouraging children to interact with people, objects, and the environment in ways that have personal meaning to them" (Katz and Chard, 1991, p. 3). The aim of this approach is to "cultivate the life of the young child's mind. In its fullest sense, the

FIGURE 2.1

▶Planning Web

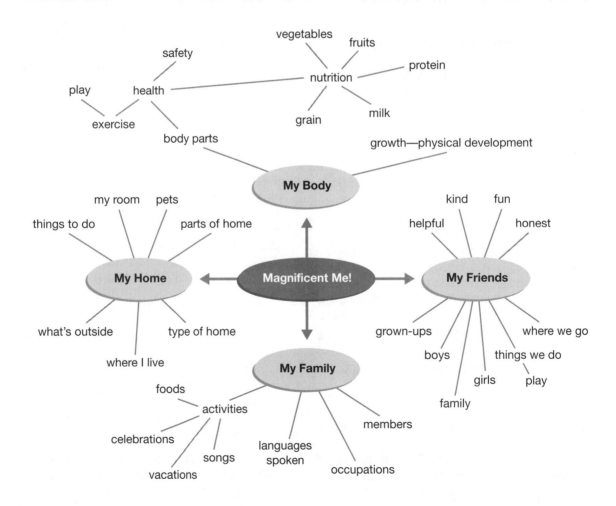

term *mind* includes not only knowledge and skills, but also emotional, moral, and aesthetic sensibilities" (Katz and Chard, p. 3).

The project approach is based on the children's interests and involvement. They are instrumental in deciding on a project, become the experts on that project, and share the accountability of learning with the adults (Katz and Chard).

The advantages of this approach are that it actively involves the children, it requires activity over time, and it encourages cooperative efforts between children and adults. An example of such a project would be one conducted by the children of the Reggio Emilia program, about a lion. In brief, the children became interested in lions. The teachers provided opportunities to view lions in various ways—sculptures, videos, books, pictures. The children engaged in various activities concerning lions—pictures, paintings, clay models, costumes, dramatic play. The development of the project, the implementation of the project, and the display of children's efforts continued over many weeks. The video *To Make a Portrait of a Lion* is a wonderful documentation of this process.

In summary, a variety of planning formats can be used. It is important to keep several questions in mind for any format used:

- Is the process developmentally appropriate? For example, a theme-based curriculum is not developmentally appropriate for infants or toddlers.
- Is the process inclusive? Are the strengths, needs, interests, and cultural values of all children and families represented?
- Is the learning experience based on the observations of children's interests and abilities?
- Are the children empowered to initiate activities, adapt materials/equipment, and work on activities over time?
- Is the planning multidimensional, involving all partners—families, children, community members?
- Is planning supportive of smooth expansion of play by providing daily opportunities in both indoor and outdoor environments?
- Is the planning flexible and easy to adapt based on the changing needs and interests of the children?

▶ Cultural Aspects

According to Stoecklin, "As child care centers are being built around the world, it is important that during schematic design phase, we create children's environments which reflect values and traditions of the country or area where they are located" (2001, p. 1). Stoecklin further identified 12 factors that have a direct influence on how one sets up the environment—gestures, language, nature, history/heritage, childrearing practices, family structure, territory, colours, textures, shapes, spatial styles, and architectural styles (p. 2).

Although many cultures of the world embrace the fundamental learning units in their child-care settings, changes are made based on the cultures. Some cultures (for example, some Arabic cultures) require separate washrooms for the male and female children. Many cultures value that children meet and talk during certain times of the day; in Tokyo, for example, one of the daycares had its classrooms surround a large central open area. In Sweden, children of various ages attend daycare at various times of the day. It is believed that this model is more like the home setting and more welcoming to the children. In Finland, infants nap outside all year long. "A unique feature of the infant/toddler space is the outdoor portion, facing south and built for naptime" (Swiniarski, Breitborde, and Murphy, 1999, p. 51).

In multicultural settings, it is important to adapt the environment as much as possible. Print-based materials can be displayed from the various language bases. Families can bring books written in their native language to the centre and read to the children. Washroom time can be split to accommodate the need for separating males and females. Family pictures can be attractively hung to represent both traditional and everyday dress and customs. Drama centres can include cultural dress and eating utensils. Meal times can include a variety of different foods. Adults should research the various cultures represented in their learning environments and involve the families to create a more culturally friendly place for the children.

▶ KEY POINTS

Children learn best when they:

- explore freely;
- use all their senses;
- manipulate real objects;
- work with children and adults;
- see the results of their actions; and
- build upon past knowledge and experiences.

► KEY POINTS (continued)

Principles of setting up the environments are to provide:

- appropriate display spaces;
- traffic patterns that encourage appropriate circulation;
- separation of noisy and quiet areas;
- space to encourage play that extends over time;
- separation of learning areas;
- proximity of linked learning areas, accommodating specific needs and specialized uses of learning areas; and
- appropriate storage of learning materials.

Indoor environments should:

- be adaptable to children's changing interests and needs;
- be versatile in adding variety to the physical environment; and
- provide separate, individualized spaces for infants, toddlers, preschool, and school-aged children that are based on physical and developmental needs.

Outdoor environments should:

- be natural extensions of indoor spaces with similar learning areas represented;
- reflect regional safety standards of equipment, providing appropriate, safe surfaces and ensuring general equipment safety;
- have appropriate surfaces for a variety of activities; and
- have appropriate separation of space for various age groups.

Lighting considerations should include:

- natural light: at least 20 percent of wall space and at least one hour outside irrespective of weather;
- alternative lighting (full-spectrum fluorescent lighting) to decrease effects of poor health, decreased productivity, and hyperactivity.

Colour considerations should include:

- using colour effectively to stimulate, calm, refresh, or set mood; and
- effects of colour—behavioural response (automatic) and learned response (dependent on experience, culture, and gender).

Noise considerations should include:

- knowledge of auditory effects (damage to hearing system);
- knowledge of nonauditory effects (damage to physiological, motivational, and cognitive functions); and
- ways to decrease noise levels by using absorbent materials, sound barriers, separation of space (quiet and noisy), modelling techniques, and masking sounds using music.

Learning spaces can be maximized by:

- placing learning areas near other learning areas in order to share materials and equipment;
- sharing spaces among learning areas; and
- creating mobile or centralized storage of children's materials and equipment.

Aesthetic considerations include:

- creating beauty in the environment to stimulate an appreciation of beauty;
- recognizing and facilitating individual feelings about aesthetics;
- providing opportunities to gain aesthetic experiences through the use of colour, light, furnishings, storage, and decorations; and
- recognizing that aesthetic appreciation is developed over time.

The role of the facilitator is to:

- provide developmentally appropriate materials, equipment, and experiences;
- be responsive to children;
- maintain positive interactions with children and families;
- maintain high verbal exchanges with children and families;
- provide an environment that is rich in opportunities to explore;
- develop an atmosphere that is encouraging and supportive to each child;
- observe and document children's interactions;
- develop and maintain positive relations with families;
- be aware when to interact in situations and when to allow play to continue without interruption; and
- provide an inclusive environment.

Appropriate planning is that which:

- focuses on the children's strengths, needs, abilities, and interests;

▶ KEY POINTS (continued)

Appropriate planning (continued)

- is developmentally appropriate;
- involves the whole child;
- involves all aspects of the environment;
- involves children in the planning process;
- involves families in the planning process;
- is inclusive;

- involves learning activities that evolve over time;
- is flexible; and
- offers a flow from indoor to outdoor activities.

Cultural aspects should reflect:

- language systems (print, gestures, songs);
- physical space (colour, shape of learning spaces);
- architectural aspects;
- special arrangement of space;
- child-rearing practices; and
- the heritage of the individual children in the program.

Student Activities

1. Using the chart provided, find examples within a child-care environment that demonstrate how a child learns best.

Child's Learning	Documentation of Learning
Exploring	
Involving the senses	
Manipulating objects	
Working with children	
Working with adults	
Seeing results of actions	
Building upon knowledge and experiences	

2. Compare various approaches to educating young children and identify what the approaches have in common and/or how they are different.
3. Visit a child-care centre. Identify how the centre encourages the following aspects in young children—curiosity, making choices, playing alone, playing in groups, solving problems, and being creative in a variety of learning situations.
4. Develop an indoor floor plan of a daycare setting for one specified age group. Use the principles of setting up an environment (table 2.1) and indicate how your floor plan meets all of the criteria.
5. All of the equipment has been removed from your outdoor play space because it does not meet current guidelines. Remaining is a covered sandbox, a large grass area, a small rectangular paved area, and an outdoor faucet. You have enough money in the budget to buy only one permanent structure, one large tree, and a paved bike path. Develop a plan for the outdoor space. Indicate what you will purchase and what other materials you could use.
6. You are within a preschool setting. The children have been very interested in the feeding, bathing, and sleeping routines of babies. A large portion of the dramatic area has been dedicated to this activity. The activity is still very popular with the younger children. You have a small group of children who have decided that they would like to have a fire station in the room. What adaptations could you make to accommodate both scenarios?
7. What are some ways that you could use colour in the environment in order to offer a place for children to be creative, to relax, to concentrate, and to calm down?
8. Research how much it would cost to change the lighting in one area to full-spectrum fluorescent lighting. How might you raise awareness and funds to proceed with this project?
9. Using the chart below, identify various materials/equipment that could be used to lessen the noise within the environment.

Noise-Reducing Agent	Possible Materials/Equipment
Absorbent materials	
Sound barriers	
Impact of noise	

10. You have a large number of children of Muslim descent within your learning environment. Research the kinds of changes you would need to make to provide a more aesthetically pleasing environment for this group.

11. Discuss the role of the facilitator in a small group. Decide on three specific aspects of that role. Develop specific strategies on how the facilitator might meet the criteria you have selected.

12. In a small group, plan a developmentally appropriate environment that reflects a major event of interest within your community.

13. Research one of the minority groups in your area. What adjustments would need to be made in the learning environment to accommodate this culture?

▶ References

Bredekamp, S. (1987). *Developmentally Appropriate Practice in Early Childhood Programs Serving Children from Birth to Age 8.* Washington, DC: National Association for the Education of Young Children.

Campbell, D. (1997). *The Mozart Effect.* New York, NY: Avon Books.

Canadian Association for Young Children. (1996). *Play: Young Children Have the Right to Learn Through Play.*

Chiazzari, S. (1998). *The complete book of colour.* Boston, MA: Element Books, Inc.

Doherty-Derkowski, G. (1995). *Quality Matters: Excellence in Early Childhood Programs.* Don Mills, ON: Addison Wesley.

Edwards, C., Gandini, L., & Forman, G. (1998). *The Hundred Languages of Children.* (2nd ed.). Greenwich, CT: Ablex Publishing Corporation.

Elicker, J., & Fortner-Wood, C. (1995, November). Adult–Child Relationships in Early Childhood Programs: Research in Review. *Young Children, 51*(1), 69–78.

Feeney, S., & Moravcik, E. (1997, September). A Thing of Beauty: Aesthetic Development in Young Children. *Young Children.*

Flannery, M. (1977). Art Education. *The Journal of the National Art Education Association.* Volume 30, Number 1.

Giedd, J. (1998, February). Pediatric seasonal affective disorder: A follow-up report. *Journal of the American Academy of Child and Adolescent Psychiatry.*

Harmon, D. (1951). *The Coordinated Classroom.* Grand Rapids, MI: American Seating Company.

Harrington, L., & Mackie, J. (1993). Mississauga, ON: B&E Publications Inc.

Hathaway, W. (1994). Non-visual effects of classroom lighting on children. *Educational Facility Planner, 23*(3), 12–16.

Hawkins, W., & Lilley, H. (1992). *CEFPI's guide for school facility appraisal.* Columbus, OH: The Council of Educational Facility Planners International.

Hendrick, J. (1997). *First Steps Toward Teaching the Reggio Way.* Upper Saddle River, NJ: Merrill, Prentice Hall.

Hohmann, M., & Weikart, D. (1995). *Educating Young Children.* Ypsilanti, MI: High/Scope Press.

Hollwich, F., & Dieckhues, B. (1980). "The Effect of Natural and Artificial Light Via the Eye on the Hormonal and Metabolic Balance of Animal and Man." *Ophthalmologica.* No. 4, 188–197.

Holt, B., Kamii, C., & Seefeldt, C. (1984, November). Ideas That Work with Young Children. *Young Children.*

Jackman, H. (2001). *Early Education Curriculum: A Child's Connection to the World.* (2nd ed.). Albany, NY: Delmar.

Katz, L., & Chard, S. (1991). *Engaging Children's Minds: The Project Approach.* Norwood, NJ: Ablex Publishing Corporation.

Lexington, A. (1989). Healthy offices: Hard to define but we need them. *The Office.* 73–75.

Libby, W. (2000). *Using Art to Make Art Creative Activities Using Masterpieces.* Albany, NY: Delmar.

Liberman, J. (1991). *Light Medicine of the Future.* Santa Fe, NM: Bear & Company Publishing.

Maxwell, L., & Evans, G. (2001). *Design of Child Care Centers and Effects of Noise on Young Children.* http://www.designshare.com.

Mayesky, M. (1997). *Creative activities for young children.* Scarborough, ON: Delmar.

Miller, S. (1991). *Learning Through Play: Language.* New York, NY: Scholastic.

Murphy, P., & Doherty, P. (1996). *The Colour of Nature.* Vancouver, BC: Raincoast Books.

Ott, J. (1976). *Health & Light.* New York, NY: Pocket Books.

Puckett, M., & Diffily, D. (1999). *Teaching Young Children: An Introduction to the Early Childhood Profession.* Orlando, FL: Harcourt Brace & Company.

Read, M., Sugawara, A., & Brandt, J. (1999, May). Impact of Space and Color in the Physical Environment of Preschool Children's Cooperative Behavior. *Environment and Behavior,* Vol. 31, No. 3, 413–428.

Reggio Children USA. (1987). *To Make a Portrait of a Lion.* Washington, DC.

Sharp, P. (1976, September). Aesthetic Responses in Early Education. *Journal of the National Art Education Association.* Volume 29/Number 5.

Stoecklin, V. (2001). Role of Culture in Designing Child Care Facilities. www.whitehutchinson.com/children/articles/childcarefacilities.shtml.

Swedo, S., Allen, A., & Glod, C. (1997). A controlled trial of light therapy for the treatment of pediatric seasonal affective disorder. *J Am Acad Child Adolescent Psychiatry 36,* 816–821.

Swiniarski, L., Breitborde, M., & Murphy, J. (1999). *Educating in the Global Village.* Toronto, ON: Prentice Hall.

Tauton, M. (1982). Aesthetic Response of Young Children to the Visual Arts: A Review of the Literature. *Journal of Aesthetic Education,* Volume 16, Number 3.

U.S. General Services Administration (GSA). (1998, June). *Child Care Center Design Guide.* Washington, DC: Public Building Service, Child Care Center of Expertise PBS 3425-13.

Wohlfarth, H., & Wohlfarth, S. (1982). The Effect of the Color Psychodynamic Environmental Modification Upon Psychophysical and Behavioural Reactions of Severely Handicapped Children. *The International Journal of Biosocial Research 3,* No. 1, 12–19.

CHAPTER 3

Sand Play

Sand is a versatile medium which allows for the development of creative abilities, imagination and appreciation and awareness of a natural material. The nature of sand encourages exploration and experimentation leading to concept formation. Equipment and materials provide opportunities for children to dramatize, dig, tunnel, scoop, mould, fill, pour, carry, load and move.

—*Hogben & Wasley,* Learning in Early Childhood: What Does It Mean in Practice?

Chapter Outline

▶ Sand Play to Encourage Learning
▶ Child Development:
   Developmental Skills of Sand Play
▶ Value of Sand Play
▶ Role of the Facilitator
▶ Effective Storage Systems
▶ Effective Labelling Systems
▶ Considerations for Setting Up a
   Sand Area

▶ Observation and Documentation
   Techniques
▶ International Considerations
▶ Sand Materials
▶ Ages and Stages of Sand Play
▶ Key Points
▶ Student Activities
▶ References
▶ Resources

Learning Outcomes

After studying this chapter, the reader will:

1. Identify the various levels of sand play
2. Explain the value of sand play
3. Discuss the role of the facilitator in sand play
4. Identify and discuss various aspects of setting up a sand play area in indoor and outdoor environments—physical space, storage of materials, labelling
5. Identify and discuss how to observe and record various aspects of sand play
6. Identify strategies for outdoor sand play
7. Identify alternative sand play activities in both indoor and outdoor environments

Interactive Learning Exercises

 Remember, the CD-ROM that came with this text contains interactive exercises that relate to the topics in this chapter, as well as other valuable resources.

▶ Sand Play to Encourage Learning

The children were on a field trip to a local beach in the early spring. Kai was fascinated by the sand. He had found a bucket and filled it using his hands. He took great care to fill the bucket to the top and then would carefully pat down the sand. He dumped out the sand, looked into the empty bucket, and repeated this activity many times. Braelyn, a four-year-old, watched him. Finally she went over and said, "Do you want to make a mould with me?" Kai nodded. Braelyn carefully filled a bucket, using a small plastic container. She made sure to pat down the sand in the bucket periodically. When she had filled the bucket, she got up and found a clear spot. She squatted down and quickly turned the bucket over. It was a perfect mould. Kai looked at the sand mould. A huge smile appeared on his face. "Do you want to try to make one?" He nodded again. After a few attempts, and with encouragement from Braelyn, he was successful. Kai continued to make many sand moulds. Each time, before he turned the bucket over he would beam in anticipation (photo 3.1). The two children continued to make sand moulds with their buckets. They would refer to each other about the perfection and placement of their moulds. Words used included *perfect, super, lots,*

PHOTO 3.1

in a row, beside. The placement of the moulds was more in consideration of empty space than any pattern or recognizable structure.

Kai and Braelyn clearly exhibited many of the powerful learning aspects of sand play. Sand play is:

- non-threatening—Kai and Braelyn each were able to create what they wanted. There was no expectation of a final product.
- enjoyable—Kai's facial expression and body language clearly indicated his enjoyment of this activity.
- explorative—Kai learned to make a mould by using wet sand. Both Kai and Braelyn explored using a large space to place their moulds.
- developmental—Both children were engaged in physical and social activities. Physical aspects included filling, emptying, firming, moulding, and placing sand. Social activities included solitary play (Kai in initial sand play), functional play (both children), and associative play (both children). Both were involved in social language activities.
- sensory—Kai initially explored the sand with his hands.

Sand is a familiar play medium for children. Sand activities encourage free, open exploration and promote all areas of development—social, emotional, cognitive, physical, and language:

- social development—Kai and Braelyn engaged in various play types, solitary and associative; Kai moved from solitary play to associative play. Both children showed respect for each other's creations. They were very careful to create moulds in new spots without the destruction of previous efforts. Both children gained skills in cooperating with each other. Braelyn guided Kai through the process of building a mould.
- emotional development—Both children could pursue their interest without adult interference; Kai showed pride in accomplishment when he made his first mould; Braelyn showed awareness of her peer, Kai, and a willingness to help him to accomplish a task. She gained satisfaction from a successful interaction. Thus, both children were able to further develop their self-esteem.
- cognitive development—Sand provides for a variety of opportunities to develop skills in mathematics, creativity, and science. Both children were engaged in pre-measurement skills: empty/full, heavy/light. They were able to compare their structures and identify some as "perfect" or "super" structures. They learned to use a large space effectively and were able to discuss the

placement of their creations—"beside," "in a row." Kai was able to discover how to make moulds effectively.

- physical development—Both children were able to balance themselves as they created their structures. They both had to coordinate various skills—holding the bucket, turning it over quickly to prevent spilling, and at the same time squatting to be close enough to the ground.
- language development—The children talked about what they were doing. Braelyn was able to give specific instructions for Kai to follow. Kai listened to the instructions and was able to follow them. They each labelled their structures ("perfect," "super," and so on).

▶ Child Development: Developmental Skills of Sand Play

FUNCTIONAL, SENSORY PLAY

Dillon was engrossed in the sand play area (photo 3.2). He lay down in the sand on his stomach and wriggled his body around. He stopped moving when he seemed to feel comfortable. He smiled and started to run his fingers through the sand. He repeated his actions over and over again. As he ran his fingers through the sand, his hand would disappear below

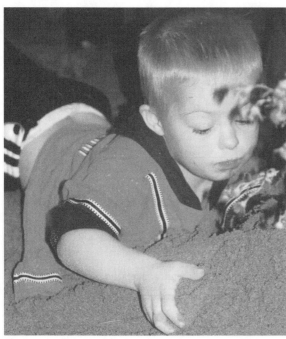

PHOTO 3.2

the sand. Deanna, his teacher, noticed Dillon's fascination. She sat down near him and watched him for a while. As Dillon's hand disappeared under the sand, he looked up at Deanna and smiled. Deanna smiled back and said, "Your hand has disappeared! Where is it?" Dillon smiled and pulled out his hand to show Deanna. He then put his hand down on the sand and used the other hand to trickle sand on it. As he gradually covered his hand with sand, Deanna noted, "Look, your middle finger is disappearing. Now the back of your hand is gone. Oh no, your hand is gone again!" Dillon smiled as Deanna continued to describe how his hand was disappearing. Each time he would pull out his hand to show Deanna that it was still there, and then bury it again.

Dillon was involved in solitary, functional, sensory, and **repetitive play.** During this type of play the child explores the various aspects of sand. It is functional play, because Dillon did not have a specific aim in mind. He was learning about the properties of sand—texture, dryness, and how sand can be manipulated. He was involved in sensory play, because he explored using his fingers, hands, and whole body to touch, feel, and manipulate the sand. He was listening to his teacher as she described the effect of his actions. As Dillon explored the various aspects of sand, he repeated his actions over and over again. As Dillon was engaged in repetitive play, he practised a variety of skills. When Dillon covered his hand, he was involved in learning about cause and effect: *When I cover my hand with sand, it will disappear.* He explored various ways of covering his hands and through these actions discovered various properties of sand by:

- trickling sand over his hand, and thus learning that sand flows;
- pushing his hands and fingers under the sand, discovering that sand is very pliable and mobile;
- pushing his body into the sand to form a mould for his body to be comfortable in; and
- listening to Deanna describe his actions and responding to her words by repeating the actions that corresponded to the words, making his fingers and hands disappear and reappear.

As Dillon was interacting with Deanna and the sand in the sandbox, other children became attracted to the activity. Benjamin and Damon walked over to the sandbox. They watched Dillon play for a few minutes. Dillon got up and left the area. Benjamin and Damon immediately got into the sandbox. Both boys lay down on their stomachs in the sand and began to smooth the sand with their hands and bury their hands in the sand (photo 3.3). Neither boy spoke to the other; both were intent on continuing to smooth

PHOTO 3.3

the sand in front of them. The boys were involved in sensory, parallel, functional play.

As Benjamin and Damon continued to play, they noticed what was happening to the other's hands and they started to talk about their play. As they started to talk about what they were doing, their play changed to associative play.

Benjamin: "My hand is gone. Now I have only one hand!"

Damon: "Both *my* hands are gone! I can make them disappear."

Benjamin: "So can I!"

During functional sand play, children learn many of the properties of sand (see table 3.1). Tools may not be needed during this stage of play, as children will explore using their senses—touching, smelling, listening, and observing. Although this is the first stage of sand play, children will use this stage repeatedly during their development. Every time a child is engaged in learning new skills, similar actions may be observed. Often, when children need a relaxing, soothing activity, they will return to this sensory mode of exploration.

During adulthood, sensory, functional play is also observed. It is interesting to watch adults engage in sand activities on any beach in the world. On the beaches in St. Martin, I have observed this type of play. A solitary male adult sat in the sand sipping a drink. He continually scooped up sand with one hand, slowly letting it trickle out. He let the sand trickle over his raised knee and down his leg. This action was repeated until he finished his drink, about 20 minutes later.

FUNCTIONAL PLAY WITH TOOLS

Reghan visited the sandbox daily. She liked to use various shovels to fill and empty containers of various sizes. She would retrieve items that she wished to use from the storage shelf. She would also collect at least one container. Reghan liked to get right into the sand (photo 3.4). She noticed that Jordaine was near the

TABLE 3.1

▶ Properties of Sand	
Property	**Child's Behaviour**
Texture	Using hands and fingers to sift the sand continuously
	Trickling sand through the fingers
	Patting, smoothing by running hands/fingers over surface of sand
	Digging with hands/fingers
	Poking fingers into sand
	Shaping by forming wet sand with hands and fingers
	Lying in sand to feel sand mould against body
Dry sand	Scooping sand with hands, letting it trickle through fingers
	Covering body parts with sand
	Pushing hands/fingers into sand
	Moving sand by moving hands or fingers to push and/or pile sand
	Creating piles of sand by scooping and dropping sand in one spot
	Running fingers through sand to create lines and geometric shapes such as circles, squares

TABLE 3.1 PROPERTIES OF SAND (continued)

Property	Child's Behaviour
Wet sand	Using two hands to shape sand into balls, squeezing sand in hand to retain shape of closed hand
	Shaping sand by creating structures in sand—piles, walls, rows
	Running fingers through sand to create lines and geometric shapes such circles, squares
	Picking sand up and dropping it
	Poking holes in the sand with fingers
	Moving sand by pushing it with hands and fingers
	Smoothing sand by patting, rubbing
Can be manipulated	Fine motor control through sifting through fingers, scooping with hand, transferring sand from hand to hand, burying body parts, shaping sand
	Exploring cause and effect properties of wet and dry sand such as shaping, weight, texture, temperature
Is sensory	Soothing media to work with
	Open-endedness allowing child to shape and reshape sand in a variety of ways
	Pleasurable sensation of sand running through fingers, shaping wet sand
Encourages language development	Modelling of terms by facilitator—*smooth, wet, dry, soft, appear, disappear, trickle, tickles your hand*
Encourages observation skills	Seeing the result of their actions directly, for example seeing objects disappear and reappear
	Comparing activities engaged in, such as differences in the properties between dry and wet sand

sandbox, and called Jordaine over. "Look what I am doing Jordaine!" Jordaine walked over and said, "I notice that the sand is flowing over the sides of the bucket. It is overflowing." Reghan emptied the bucket. She filled it again to the point of overflowing. She added one more scoop and said, "Look, it's overflowing."

Reghan was engaged in functional, repetitive, and solitary play using a variety of tools (see table 3.2). Reghan did not have a specific goal in mind. She practised the skills of filling and emptying, which she did over and over again. Reghan had also learned that she could use a variety of tools to fill her container. This gave her experience with different tools to eventually make the connection between the tool and effective filling of a container. Reghan had listened to Jordaine describe what she was doing. She learned a new word and applied it correctly to the situation. Reghan had also learned that dry sand reacts differently than wet sand. She continued to fill only the dry sand to overflowing.

PHOTO 3.4

TABLE 3.2

►Properties of Sand Using a Variety of Tools	
Property	**Child's Behaviour**
Manipulated to fill and empty	Using tools such as spoons, shovels, or scoops to empty and fill containers
	Emptying containers by dumping, pouring sand out, removing sand with sand tools
	Digging to fill containers
Dry sand	Scooping sand with tools, letting it trickle out slowly by tilting the tool
	Creating piles of sand by dumping sand from containers, or by scooping sand with sand tools and emptying these in one pile
	Moving sand by using tools to push and/or pile sand
	Running tools through sand to create lines and geometric shapes such as circles, squares
Wet sand	Using containers to create sand moulds
	Shaping sand by creating structures in sand—piles, walls, rows
	Running tools through sand to create lines and geometric shapes such circles, squares
	Picking up sand with a tool and dropping it
	Poking holes in the sand with a variety of objects, such as sticks, handles of sand tools, or other thin-tipped objects
	Moving sand by pushing sand with sand tools
	Smoothing sand by patting or rubbing using tools such as trowels, shovels, or spatulas
Can be manipulated	Fine motor control using a variety of tools through scooping and digging activities
	Exploring cause and effect properties of wet and dry sand such as shaping, weight, texture, temperature; sifting sand to separate items
	Gross motor skills through controlling emptying, moulding activities
Encourages language development	Modelling of terms by facilitator—*empty, full, slowly, fast, heavy, light, smooth, overflow*
Encourages development of observation skills	Seeing the result of their actions directly, such as observing when a container is full or empty
	Comparing activities engaged in, such as differences between the properties of wet and dry sand
	Noting how quickly a container can be filled using different tools

Josh and Iorahkote filled a cement truck and a dump truck using shovels (photo 3.5). When the trucks were full, each boy would dump out the sand. This activity was repeated a number of times. This is an example of functional parallel play with tools.

Braelyn and Alicia (photo 3.6) repeatedly poured the dry coloured sand into the sand wheel. Each used her own materials to scoop sand into the wheel and to try to catch the sand as it poured out. They talked about how much sand they caught and how fast the wheel was spinning. The girls were involved in associative, functional play with tools.

PHOTO 3.5

PHOTO 3.6

SYMBOLIC SAND PLAY

Aaron lay down in the sandbox (photo 3.7). He had a Lego car in one hand. He drove his car around the sand for a while, making repeated "brmmm brmmm" noises. He noticed that there was sand on his other hand. Aaron stopped driving his little car around. He started to move his other hand through the sand. Eventually, he curved his fingers and scooped up the sand with one hand. He said "brmmm, brmmm!" He repeated this activity over and over again. Benjamin came over to the area. He asked Aaron what he was doing. Aaron said, "Digger."

Aaron is involved in sensory, solitary, symbolic, and repetitive play. He is involved in sensory play because he is using his hands to dig and scoop sand. He is involved in **symbolic play** because he is using his hand to represent a real object, a digger. During symbolic play, children also often make the appropriate noises to represent the object that they are pretending to use, as Aaron did.

As Aaron continued to play, Benjamin joined him in the sandbox. He picked up a piece of pink foam and proceeded to smooth the sand in front of him (photo 3.8). "I am smoothing the sand with a grader. Watch me." Aaron tried to grab the foam. Benjamin shouted, "No! There's more pink stuff on the shelf." Aaron got the foam and the two boys smoothed the sand, each making machine-like sounds. Occasionally they would talk to each other about what they were doing: "My sand is very smooth." "Mine too."

When Benjamin joined the play, the play changed from solitary, symbolic play to associative, symbolic play with tools. Each boy shared his ideas and watched the other's actions and results. However, each boy continued to play using his own space and his own piece of foam.

Liam had been creating moulds in the sandbox. He noticed what Benjamin and Aaron were doing. He picked up a trowel and began smoothing the sand

PHOTO 3.7

PHOTO 3.8

PHOTO 3.9

and making machine-like sounds (photo 3.9). Liam never spoke to either Aaron or Benjamin. He continued to play in the same space and used similar actions. Liam was involved in symbolic, parallel play, both at a sensory level and by using sand tools.

During and before this stage of play it is important to make a variety of experiences available to the children so that they can form the mental representations or memories of the real world that can later be symbolically represented. Such experiences could include:

- taking field trips to observe vehicles and machinery in operation—construction sites, road repair or building new roads, farms during harvest time, gravel pits, and transportation depots;

PHOTO 3.10

- watching short videos that show construction machinery in operation (see the suggested videos at the end of this chapter);
- looking at books and pictures about construction vehicles (see the suggested books at the end of this chapter); and
- looking at photographs posted in the sand area of construction vehicles that children have observed (see the CD for a series of pictures).

Symbolic sand play is important as it helps the child:

- build mental representations—According to Piaget, children form mental pictures of events that they have seen or experienced. For example, Aaron and Benjamin represented their previous experiences: Aaron by using his hand as a digger, and both boys by using the pink foam as graders.
- build memories—By forming mental representations and later representing these images in play activities, Aaron and Benjamin are developing memory skills not only through recall of known experiences, but also through direct experience to help them accommodate new information. Each boy knew what a grader was and what its purpose was. By using the foam, they were able to discover that grading activities, in this case smoothing the sand, could be achieved by using different methods.
- observe cause and effect—Through the smoothing and digging activities the boys were involved in, they could directly see the result of their actions: smoothing the sand.
- experience the properties of dry and wet sand (as listed in tables 3.1 and 3.2).
- dramatize previous experiences—digger and graders.

REPRESENTATIONAL SAND PLAY

Miako was playing in the sand at a man-made beach park in Brisbane, Australia (photo 3.10). She was engaged in representational, solitary sand play at a sensory level. Miako named her structure a "big house." She continually went to the water to retrieve wet sand with her hands. She dribbled the wet sand

PHOTO 3.11

PHOTO 3.12

PHOTO 3.13

on top of her building and then used her hands to smooth the sides of her structure.

This type of sand play is **representational play,** because at this stage the child makes structures that represent real objects and labels the structures made. Also note that Miako had to have had previous experiences with sand. She knew that wet sand was easier to mould than dry sand. She also knew how to shape and smooth the sand effectively. These types of structures become increasingly more complex with age, ability, and experience (photo 3.11).

Yasmine and Emily used the sandbox to create a garden (photos 3.12 and 3.13). Both girls used similar materials in similar ways, but created their own garden with little dialogue between them. Each girl

articulated to her teacher that she had made a garden. Yasmine identified her creation as a great garden with flowers. Emily identified her garden as a flower garden. She was able to name some of the flowers she had used and asked for the names of others. Her teacher brought over a book on flowers. Jenna looked through the book to find her flowers, then asked her teacher to read their names. As Emily repeated the names of flowers, Yasmine pointed to her flowers and quietly repeated their names. The girls were engaged in parallel representational sand play.

Billie and Colin were both using various containers in the sand to create moulds (photos 3.14 and 3.15). They both talked about the moulds they were creating. As each child created a mould, they talked

PHOTO 3.14

PHOTO 3.15

PHOTO 3.16

PHOTO 3.17

about the sizes and shapes of their moulds. Each enjoyed destroying his or her own moulds. They shared materials and allowed each other to destroy their moulds. The children were involved in representational, associative play.

During a field trip to a beach, Danika, Michelle, and Stephanie decided to build a ladybug (photo 3.16). They first made a plan of the bug in the sand, decided how big it would be, and discussed what materials they could use for the legs, eyes, and spots. Danika decided to make the outline of the bug. Michelle decided to collect stones, shells, and twigs for the eyes, legs, and spots. Stephanie collected all the big and little shovels and pails that were needed. All three girls worked together to build the ladybug and to decorate it. The girls were involved in cooperative, representational sand play.

As demonstrated in the examples above, representational sand play encourages the development of many skills:

- imagination and creativity—The building of the ladybug required the girls to use alternative items to create the spots, legs, and eyes. They used the items that were available in their immediate environment.
- shaping and moulding of sand—Miako shaped her house by using wet sand and using her hands to smooth the structure after every application.
- problem-solving—Benjamin used the pink foam to smooth the sand, and Yasmine and Emily solved the problem of how to balance flowers upright in the sand.
- experimenting to create balance—Yasmine and Emily both experimented in planting flowers; they had to balance the flowers to stand upright. They solved the problem by adding water to the sand to

make it easier to stick the flowers in and by creating a mound of sand around the base of each flower.

- memory—In order to build the ladybug, the girls had to remember what a ladybug looked like, and also remember the specific features of a ladybug.
- language—Yasmine and Emily each learned new vocabulary when they built their flower gardens. Emily used pre-reading and research skills when she found the pictures of the flowers in the book and asked her teacher to read the words.

Children can enjoy these activities in both indoor and outdoor play spaces. Winter can provide excellent opportunities to use similar techniques outdoors (photo 3.17). Construction toys that require children to empty, fill, dig, and transfer snow are ideal opportunities to transfer knowledge from one situation to another.

Field trips to sandy beaches allow children to become creative in their use of space. When children have the opportunity to explore (that is, when not limited by space) they can explore concepts to a greater extent than is possible inside. Christopher dug a hole large enough that he could fit into it (photo 3.18), and the ladybug (photo 3.16) was created using a much larger scale, a longer time, and a cooperative effort.

▶ Value of Sand Play

Sand play encourages children to use a variety of skills and offers many varied experiences. Sand play is also a very **therapeutic** activity. It is non-threatening, does not necessarily have an end

PHOTO 3.18

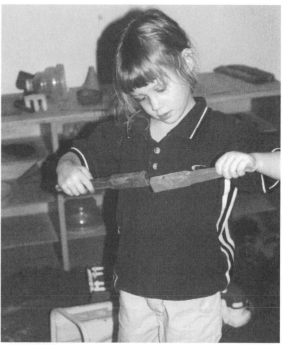

PHOTO 3.19

product, and is a very sensory experience. Through sand play children learn to:

- **perform simple experiments**—Benjamin had found a magnet in the sandbox. He noticed that the magnet was dirty at the bottom. He tried to rub off the "dirt," but it would not come off easily. He brought it over to Michael, his teacher, and said "I can't get the dirt off." Liesl heard the conversation and tried to get the dirt off with another magnet (photo 3.19). In discussion with Michael, the children learned that there are certain elements in the sand that will stick to a magnet. The children collected these grains with magnets, discovered that you could brush them off with your hands, and decided to collect the grains in a clear container.

  This activity led Michael to hide some metal objects in the sand. The children became very excited when they found objects in the sand as they were using their magnets. This soon became a popular activity: to hide various objects in the sand and try to find them with your magnet.

  Children can also discover that dry sand can be used to turn a wheel at various speeds depending on how much sand you add (photo 3.20) (adapted from Jackman, 2001, p. 194).

- **measure**—Children use many different techniques to measure size, weight, or quantity. At a field trip to a local beach in early spring, Braelyn (photo 3.21) was constructing a snowperson out of sand. She held out her hands around the ball she had created and said "It needs to be this much bigger!"

Children may compare the weights of two buckets of sand while they are holding them, or they can be encouraged to weigh the sand if scales are available. Providing different containers of various sizes encourages them to more accurately weigh two different containers. Filling these containers may lead to **measurement** of quantity by counting. Dillon was counting how many scoops it took to fill two containers. He was able to identify

PHOTO 3.20

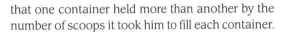

PHOTO 3.21

PHOTO 3.22

that one container held more than another by the number of scoops it took him to fill each container.

- **compare**—Winter is a great time to explore similar aspects outside: digging, scooping, tunnelling, building, emptying, filling, and so on. This activity encourages children to compare the experiences they have had with sand to a similar medium—snow. When Miranda (photo 3.22) had the opportunity to fill and empty a bucket outside in the winter, she seemed surprised. She would fill her scoop and then look at it. Jennifer, the facilitator, asked her, "You look puzzled. How can I help you?" Miranda responded, "It's light!" Jennifer responded, "You mean it is lighter than the sand you were using indoors?" Miranda nodded and continued to fill and empty her bucket. As she was trying to dump out the snow, she said, "It's more sticky. It won't come out!"
- **problem-solve**—Providing children with a variety of different materials encourages them to solve interesting problems. Taylor had been filling and emptying plastic jugs in the water centre. The facilitator decided to provide similar jugs in the sand area. Taylor noticed the jugs in the sand area. She tried to fill one using a scoop. She found it difficult because the sand kept trickling over the side as she tried to pour it in. Ann noticed her difficulty. She asked Taylor how she could make the job easier. Taylor thought for a minute and said she could use a spoon. She got a spoon from the kitchen area and started to fill her jug. This proved more effective. She stopped after a while and looked around the room. She got up and went to the block area and brought back various plastic cones (yarn spools). She tried them until she found

one that fit the neck of the jar. She again continued to fill her jar (photo 3.23).

- **play creatively**—Examples of creative play have been evident in many of the children's activities—Braelyn with the dinosaurs (see Chapter 1), Emily and Yasmine with their flower garden.
- **develop new vocabulary**—As Emily and Yasmine created their flower garden, each learned the new words associated with the flowers that they had planted. New words can be introduced as the facilitator notices children engaged in interesting activities or as the children request information about the activity engaged in or the names

PHOTO 3.23

of the items that they are using. Possible vocabulary that could be introduced includes words and phrases such as *tunneling, half full, completely empty, separating, sifting, pouring, packing, moulding,* and so on.

- **demonstrate new concepts**—that dry sand can be poured, that wet sand can be moulded into the shape of a container.

▶ Role of the Facilitator

The facilitator sets the stage for effective sand play. Critical aspects of the facilitator's role are to:

- observe the children—Ann observed that Taylor had difficulty in pouring the sand into the jug. She immediately walked over and helped Taylor solve the problem. In this way she not only prevented a possible frustrating experience for Taylor, but also created an opportunity for Taylor to do her own problem solving.
- set up the sand area—The facilitator needs to ensure that the area is set up to provide both challenging and safe activities for the children. The criteria for the activities within the sand area should always be based on the children's interests and abilities. As Ann noticed Taylor pouring water into various containers, she realized the potential learning that could occur if the same materials were set up in the sand area.
- provide materials—materials for sand should encourage a variety of skills: pouring, tunnelling, digging, emptying, smoothing, creating, dramatizing, moulding, carrying, moving, and provide the diversity to encourage use by children of various abilities. Michael added magnetic materials to the sandbox to extend the children's play.
- label, ask questions, and clarify—Jennifer noticed that Miranda looked puzzled. She labelled Miranda's feeling ("I see you look puzzled") and asked Miranda to clarify her problem by using an open-ended question ("How can I help you?"); this clarified Miranda's puzzlement that the snow was lighter than the sand.
- take cues from the children—The facilitator noted that the children were involved in many moulding experiences indoors. Thus a field trip to a local beach was arranged so that children could practise these skills outdoors in a natural setting.
- give credibility to the importance of the sand area—The facilitator needs to interact with the children within the sand area to show his or her enthusiasm and be able to share in the children's

discoveries. Deanna was able to share in the excitement of Dillon's activity, burying his hand.
- model appropriate behaviours—It is important that the sand area remain clear of toys. When all the toys are in the sand, play becomes very limited. The facilitator should model fun cleanup activities. When sand is on the floor, sweeping up needs to be modelled. Usually this is an activity that children enjoy and will readily participate in.

▶ Effective Storage Systems

Storage of materials is critical to the success of the sand area. Too often, materials are stored within the sandbox itself or are left there by children after their play. This causes problems including:

- a lack of space to create in—this limits the creativity of the children and the number of children who can participate;
- mixed concepts—it is hard to develop a concept, such as comparing the weights of various containers, if the area is cluttered with items suitable for digging, pouring, weighing, building, or moulding;
- clutter—the sand area becomes an unattractive place to play in or may be avoided because it is too overwhelming;
- mixed messages—for example, that one does not have to put things away;
- loss or destruction of sand materials—smaller items are easily buried and lost when sand is changed, heavier items will cause breakage/splintering of smaller items; and
- dangerous situations—broken items may cause injury; disorganization encourages throwing and dumping of items to find what is wanted.

Although there are many ways that sand equipment may be stored, the methods are dependent on the type of space available, the size of the space, and the types of experiences provided to the children. Irrespective of what storage method is used, the system needs to be clear to all (adults and children), easy to use, and it must be easy to find materials. All systems suggested can be organized by type of materials. Some typical organizations are listed in table 3.3. If there are too many materials in one category, it may be necessary to provide more than one storage unit in each category; that is, for moulding materials, each piece of equipment could be stored in a separate unit—buckets in one unit, specific moulds (sea life, castle, brick) in individual units.

TABLE 3.3

▶ Organization of Sand Materials	
Organization	**Possible Materials**
Digging materials	Scoops, shovels, spoons, tongue depressors, sticks
Moulding materials	Moulds (sea, castle, brick, animal), buckets, natural materials such as shells, cups, plastic containers of various sizes
Smoothing materials	Trowels, heavy cardboard rolls, firm foam, spatulas, scrapers, heavy cardboard pieces, firm plastic pieces
Building materials	Cardboard boxes, plastic blocks, unit blocks, plastic cones
	Large, Lego blocks, Duplo, fences, sticks, logs, shells, pine cones, clear bowls/containers
Gardening materials	Artificial flowers, real plants/flowers (gathered by children on a field trip), rakes, spades, watering cans, pine cones, branches, stones, rocks, resource books
Pouring containers	Measuring cups—one-quarter, one-third, one-half, and full cup; measuring spoons—half teaspoon, teaspoon, half tablespoon, tablespoon; containers of various sized volumes with wide open top, containers of various sized volumes with narrow openings, containers of different shapes but holding the same volume of materials (i.e., a cup that holds 750 mL and a bottle that holds 750 mL)
Filling, emptying containers	Pails of various sizes, plastic containers of various sizes, clear containers of various sizes, plastic cups and mugs, shallow dishes
Problem-solving devices (to aid children in solving problems of pouring, stabilizing, and creating)	Funnels of various sizes; tubes (heavy cardboard and plastic pipes of various thickness and length); plastic and cardboard cone spools
Sifting	Slotted spoons, sifters, plastic open-weave baskets, heavy pieces of screen with edges taped, colanders
Vehicles	Big construction vehicles that children can sit on to operate (graders, cement mixers, diggers, cranes, dump trucks); small construction vehicles as outlined above; variety of small cars; farm machinery (tractors, mowers, diggers, harvesters)
Materials to bury	Plastic gems, stones of various shapes and sizes; large pieces of jewellery (check to make sure that there are no pins or sharp edges); rocks painted gold and silver; large coins; sand- and water-washed pieces of glass; small pieces of driftwood; fossils; colourful stones; shells
Accessories	Variety of small people that are jointed to sit or stand (to represent various cultures, diversity, jobs); animals (zoo, farm, wild, domestic); insects (representative of local region); reptiles (representative of local region: frogs, snakes, turtles); fish; dinosaurs

STORAGE IDEAS FOR SMALL SPACES

- hanging baskets—allows for organization by type (i.e., digging utensils, small vehicles, animals). Advantages: works well for various age groups, as items for older children can be in higher baskets; utilizes vertical space. Disadvantages: baskets need to be anchored, it is easy to swing or bump into baskets, they are more difficult to clean, the floor below needs to be cleaned regularly, it may be hard for children to find a particular item.

- clear plastic containers in a cart (if the cart is on wheels this unit becomes more mobile, to be used in more than one location)—allows for organization by type (i.e., one category item per drawer).
- shelf or small table—outlines of objects on shelf to identify placement of objects.
- "parking lots"—large construction vehicles returned to parking space when play in sand is finished; can be placed under a shelf or under a table.
- clear shoe bags hung on wall—easy to see items placed within bag.

OTHER STORAGE IDEAS

- row of sturdy hooks to attach all digging utensils;
- peg boards hung on wall with hooks—easy to arrange and hang any item by category;
- shelves wide enough to hold large vehicles—attach detachable ramps to drive vehicles into appropriate spot; and
- multi-shelf unit that allows placement of items per category.

▶ Effective Labelling Systems

Labelling systems in the sand area are more problematic than in other areas. Sand is gritty. This makes it hard on labels created. The surface of the label will easily become scratched. Sticking labels onto the storage surface with tape is ineffective. The sand tends to stick to the tape, making the tape progressively less effective. Also, since materials are rotated periodically, labels need to change as well. Many of the items in the sand area are hard to represent by a diagram. The less realistic the diagram, the harder it will be for children to recognize the label. Many of the storage containers are curved, therefore hard to attach labels to. See table 3.4 for some labelling suggestions.

▶ Considerations for Setting Up a Sand Area

1. Safety

- use only sterilized sand;
- change sand regularly;
- clean sand daily after children have used it—children can help sift through and throw out any unwanted pieces;
- dry sand used causes dust particles to fly in the air—keep a spray bottle of water handy and spray the air to attract dust particles and settle them, and spray the top layer of sand periodically;
- keep outside sandboxes covered when not in use to prevent animal excreta—check often;
- shade outside sandboxes; and
- keep broom, dust pan, and garbage can in sand area—children love to help maintain floor, could become part of routine.

TABLE 3.4

▶ Labelling Suggestions

Problem	Possible Solutions
Scratching	Prepare labels in the normal way. Attach a clear sheet of heavy commercial plastic, cut to the size of the labelled area, and place over labels. Works well on shelves, tables, or floors. Easy to exchange labels under the surface, easy to replace plastic.
Rotation	Create clear pockets that labels can be slipped into. Pockets are easily made by using clear Mactac. Cut the Mactac to desired size. Place glued sides together to create a clear plastic sheet. Attach strips around three sides, pasting down and overlapping strip on one side, then turning piece over to glue on other side. Make sure you slit glued side pieces of the open end. It's easy to exchange labels or to place pocket in a new location. Pockets can be attached together to hang on wall or place on any flat surface.
Representation	Take photographs of all items. Keep the photographs as originals; photocopy or scan photos. This way you will have spares to use in other areas, and will find it easy to replace the labels. Cut appropriate pictures out of catalogues, sale flyers, and newspapers. Send a list home to involve families to help collect items.

2. Location
Sand play tends to be messy and should therefore be located on a tiled surface. It is also easier to keep the area clean if the area is confined by two walls or dividers; this keeps the sand from spilling out into all directions. It also has the advantage of removing the sand from a high-traffic area. Sand play is a noisy, enthusiastic activity. It needs to be separated from quiet areas and from the main traffic flow. Otherwise, the activity may attract children's attention away from other activities that they are engaged in.

Outdoor sand activities should be in a shaded area. The ideal sandbox would have a bench-like barrier around it, which keeps the sand confined to one area, gives children a place to sit and watch, provides an easy way to cover the sandbox when not in use, and prevents children using riding toys from bumping into children playing in the sand. The sandbox, both indoors and outdoors, would be best placed near a water source.

3. Types of Areas
Sand can be confined to the standard raised sandboxes indoors; however, the disadvantage is that raised boxes confine the sand play to the waist up. Children will not get the benefit of the full sensory experience or a full range of muscle control. These boxes further confine children's activity to the space immediately in front of them. Small arms cannot reach across the box.

Sand could be put on the floor in a corner, either on a tarp or within a small plastic swimming pool. If the sand is put on a tarp, the tarp must be securely taped down. For either tarp or pool, place small benches or low storage shelves or small tables on one of the other sides, to provide a more secluded and natural setting in which children can enjoy a full sensory experience with full control.

Another consideration would be to decide what other learning areas should be located near sand. Some to consider are:
- water—Sand and water is a natural association that is very familiar to children. There is another great advantage—sand and water together lead to interesting experiences:
  i) What happens to sand when you drop sand into water?
  ii) How long does it take sand to dry out on a hot day?
  iii) How do you get the water out of a mixture of sand and water? Out of a puddle after the rain?
  iv) What happens to the water in a container when you add sand to it?
- blocks—Sand is a good medium to help children learn about different ways to create stable structures. Mackenzie and Reghan had created a structure in the sand (photo 3.24). To stabilize the structure they dug holes first, put in the base pieces, and then covered the holes. Again, it is also a familiar scenario for children. Many of the construction sites use sand; this makes the play more realistic.
- creative art—Sand is used as a medium to create beautiful pictures in many cultures. Pictures of the Navajo sand paintings or examples of sand clay sculptures may provide encouragement to use sand in different ways, especially if it is located near the other art supplies.

4. Guidelines for Using Sand
Children should have few guidelines. Guidelines should refer to safety: sand stays in the sand area, and if sand is spilled it needs to be swept up and thrown in the garbage. Other guidelines might be needed concerning the number of children. It is far more advantageous to encourage children to solve their own problems than to impose an arbitrary limit. If a number of children are playing appropriately together, it is counterproductive to ask one child to leave because there are too many children there. If there is a problem—children are arguing over a piece of equipment, children are pushing each other to gain more space—then it would be more appropriate for the facilitator to intervene to try to have the children solve the problem. For example, three children were playing in the sand area. A fourth child joined the group. The

PHOTO 3.24

children were engaged in creating interconnecting moulds. However, only three moulds were available. Sarah said to the children, "We seem to have a problem." Benjamin said, "I want to play too, but they won't let me." Liesl answered, "There are only three moulds. We don't have enough moulds." Sarah answered, "Well, I see your problem. You only have three moulds, but you need four. What do you think we could do about this?" Jamie thought that perhaps they could go look in the storage room for more moulds. All four children agreed and went to look for moulds with Sarah. They could not find any more moulds, but they found a variety of containers of different sizes and shapes that they could use. All four children continued to create a system of interconnecting moulds.

In this scenario, the children solved their own problem, their play was actually expanded as there was greater diversity of materials, and the structures became much more innovative. When the children had finished their activity, they asked Sarah to take pictures of what they had created. They summed up their effort in one expressive word—"Cool!"—showing their pride in their accomplishment.

5. Alternatives to Sand

Many alternatives can be found to sand tables. Some are food substitutes—rice, corn, and cereal. There is an ethical consideration that each of us must ponder. Do we use food products for play purposes? Does this give a conflicting message to children? (i.e., food can be played with). Can younger children understand that this food is for playing but the food we serve is to eat? Toddlers especially have a problem with this concept, since the props in front of them direct their play. Should children be allowed to play with food when so many children are starving in the world?

These are not easy questions to answer. Each of us must decide where we draw the line. It may help to think about the following points to make the decision easier:

- Are there children and families in your program who are struggling financially? If so, consider the impact of seeing their children play with food that they might not be able to afford to buy to feed them.
- If you have infants and toddlers in the program, it might be advisable to use alternatives to food. Young children will be tempted to eat the food products provided. Play with food is discouraged in most homes.
- What food products do you and your families feel comfortable in using? This is an ideal situation to

involve family members in program planning and making decisions. It has the added advantage that conflicts around sensitive issues can be avoided.

Other alternatives that can be used:

- shredded paper—most printing companies give shredded paper away free;
- paper circles from hole punches—printing companies may collect these for centres;
- material scraps cut into small pieces—these can be reused, as they can be washed;
- dried, crushed egg shells—egg shells *must* be boiled before using and the inner membrane *must* be removed; shells can be coloured; and
- small yarn/ribbon pieces.

6. Display

Since sand is intrinsically motivating to children, especially if the sand area is appropriately set up, it is not as important to add motivational materials to the environment. The best motivation will come from documentation of children's creations by a display of photographs. A display of related books—such as books on flowers, or machinery used in construction—may encourage children to look up information or get new ideas.

▶ Observation and Documentation Techniques

It is important to observe the type of sand play children are engaged in to:

- build on the children's interests—Michael hid magnetic items in the sand when he noticed children separating the magnetic grains of sand from the sandbox with a magnet;
- provide appropriate materials to expand play—plastic jugs were added to the sand area when it was noticed that children were pouring using a variety of containers in water;
- acknowledge children's developmental levels—large and small containers and shovels were provided in the sand storage area to encourage filling and emptying based on coordination differences of the toddlers and older preschoolers in the program;
- make adjustments or changes as needed—if some children wish to do pouring activities (dry sand) and other children are interested in moulding activities (wet sand), the two sections could be divided by a log. The same strategy can be used outside;
- recognize the emergent skills of children—Dillon's efforts to compare the quantity of the two

containers filled with sand by counting was acknowledged by the facilitator, who created a graph that showed how many scoops of sand were put into each container; and

- share the accomplishments of the children with the families and other professionals—For example, photographs of the children at play were enlarged and displayed in the hall of the facility with descriptions of the value of the activities; families and children spent time reading and looking at the display as they came into the centre.

Documentation of sand play was primarily through individual pictures of the children with descriptions of what they were engaged in. These displays were created either by the facilitator or by a combined effort of child and facilitator. When Emily had completed her flower garden (photo 3.13), the picture of her garden was posted along with the following story that she had dictated: "This is my garden. I planted roses and white daisies and other flowers. I found the names in a book. Poppies. Those were the red ones. I watered my garden."

A sand play **portfolio** was developed that showed all the levels of sand play that children were engaged in. This portfolio contained photos of all the children, descriptions of the activity, and an explanation of the value of sand play as it related to various domains— social, emotional, language, cognitive, and physical.

The children could take this book home to show their parents. Additionally, the children used the book to reproduce some of these structures using small blocks for a showcase in the entrance of the curriculum lab preschool.

Some more formal methods of observational documentation are included with samples in the following sections.

CHECKLISTS/CHARTS

Checklists to observe sand play may be used in several ways. They are useful to identify general interest in sand play, specific interest in sand activities, skill levels used, and developmental levels.

Sample Checklists/Charts

These types of tools are easy to use and take very little time to complete. All levels of sand play could be put on the chart, but it is more functional to add levels of play as you see them occurring. This gives the advantage of being more developmentally appropriate and more individualized. For example, you will probably expect to see much more functional play with Dillon and can therefore add this information as it occurs. Figures 3.1 through 3.4 show sample checklists and provide suggestions on how to interpret and use the information gathered.

The chart in Figure 3.3 gives an overview of all the children and of the variety of levels of sand play children are engaged in.

FIGURE 3.1

▶ Levels of Sand Play Chart

Name: Dillon

Level	Date	Type of Play	Evidence
Functional play	05/10	Sensory, solitary	Alone; repeatedly covered/hid hands in sand
Functional play	05/11	Sensory, parallel	Beside Jamie; hid car, scooped sand over car with hands repeatedly

How to Use Information

- provide other materials to expand learning (shovels, scoops, small toys) and treasures to bury (colourful rocks, plastic gems);
- refer children to each other—refer to Jamie's actions when speaking to Dillon and vice versa: "Look, Dillon, Jamie's car disappear**ed**";
- provide alternate experiences—set up a large bin with cloth **scraps** to hide things in; and
- encourage vocabulary development—*disappear, re-appear, vanish, appear.*

FIGURE 3.2

▶ Symbolic Play Chart

Name	Solitary	Parallel	Associative
Aaron	05/11: Digger (hands)		05/11 Benjamin: Digger (hands) and grader (pink foam)
Benjamin			05/11 Aaron: Grader (pink foam) and digger (hands)
Liam		05/11 Benjamin/ Aaron: Grader (trowel)	

How to Use Information

- build vocabulary—smooth, smoother, level, flat, even, uneven;
- provide alternate materials—spatulas, construction vehicle graders, stiff cardboard, windshield scrapers, trowels, hoes, rakes;
- refer children to each other—refer to Benjamin's actions when speaking to Aaron and Liam, and vice versa, "Look how wide Benjamin's track is, Liam and Aaron"; and
- extend play outside in the sandbox or in the snow in the winter.

FIGURE 3.3

▶ **Levels of Sand Play Chart**

Date(s): 05/11, 05/13

LEVELS OF SAND PLAY

Name	Functional, Sensory	Functional, with Tools	Symbolic	Representational
Kai		I		
Benjamin	I		I	
Emily				I

How to Use Information
- provide developmentally appropriate experiences for diversity of interests and abilities; and
- provide developmentally appropriate materials for diversity of interests and abilities.

FIGURE 3.4

▶ **Skills Used Chart**

Name	Skill	Evidence/Dates
Kai	Creating mould with bucket	05/10: At beach, created 15 bucket moulds
Dillon	Covered left hand with sand, pushing sand over hand with right hand	04/15: In sandbox, listened to Deanna describe his actions of hiding hand and responding by hiding or making hand reappear

How to Use Information
- provide variety of moulding materials;
- provide moulding opportunities inside—sandbox, kitchen (to mould play dough into cakes, cookies); and
- expand hiding game—hide small toys in sand or under sand alternatives such as in a bin full of material scraps.

Notice that the information gathered can be used in a variety of ways and in a variety of areas. Some of the skills can be applied in other learning centres. This gives opportunities for children to **transfer skills** gained in one area to another area.

▶ International Considerations

Sand is plentiful in most parts of our world. In areas where sand is abundant or where sand substitutes like snow can be used, various activities occur. Drawing and creating sand sculptures are international activities. Some Native cultures also engage in creating beautiful sand paintings.

Children in Africa have long used sand as their first creative art board (Onyefulu, 1994). Children of the Navajo are exposed to a long tradition of sand painting. Sand paintings are created from pulverized stones and natural pigments. Colours of white, yellow, red, and black occur naturally within the environment; other colours such as pink, blue, and brown are created by mixing the basic colours. The sand paintings are created by carefully sprinkling the coloured sand on the ground. Sand pictures are part of a spiritual ceremony that includes sand painting and chanting (Furst and Furst, 1982).

Children surrounded by this tradition learn very early how to created coloured sand from existing materials. When sand is pulverized, children learn something about how sand is formed. Children also learn how sand paintings are created. It takes years of practice and learning to create the intricate sand art.

Children living in the desert also learn to read tracks in the sand. In Alice Springs, Australia, this technique is used in a natural park, Desert Park. Children are encouraged to learn to read the tracks in the sand and also to try to make their own tracks. This activity uses hands and fingers to create the tracks (photo 3.25 and figure 3.5).

In Mali (Erlbach and Holm, 1997, pp. 40–41), children play a game called *sey*. The object of the game is to find a small pebble, which is called *tibi*. Two circles are drawn in the sand. The bigger circle is about 51 cm (20 in.) in diameter. The inside circle is about 46 cm (18 in.) in diameter. Each player makes three holes in the outside circle (see figure 3.6). The first player hides his or her *tibi* in one of his or her three holes. Player two tries to guess in which hole the *tibi* is hidden. If the player guesses correctly, he or she may hide the *tibi* in one of his or her three holes. If the player does not guess correctly, player 1 makes a hole next to the holes he or she first made. This can con-

PHOTO 3.25

FIGURE 3.5

► Directions and Diagrams on How to Make Footprints with Your Hands

1. Clench your hand into a fist, as shown, and then press it down into the dirt.

2. Use your thumb to make the big toe impression and the tip of one finger to make the rest of the toe marks.

3. Repeat to make another foot.

Source: Desert Park, 2001

tinue until the holes go all around the circle. This game could be adapted easily to a variety of ages and numbers of children.

► Sand Materials

Sand-play materials are diverse and should include both commercially purchased materials and natural materials. (For a listing of materials refer to table 3.3.)

Many materials can be made from recycled items:

- scoops—cut the bottom off any plastic bottle; leaving the bottle top on as a handle, cut a semi-circle around the length of the bottle from the

FIGURE 3.6

► Diagram of Tibi Holes

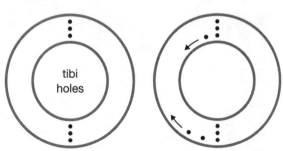

tibi holes

Source: Erlbach, Holm, 1997, pp. 40–41.

bottom to the neck of the bottle back down to the bottom;

- containers—any plastic container will work: margarine tubs, ice cream tubs (the logos can easily be removed using SOS pads);
- sieves—bend firm pieces of wire screen inward on all sides, press with pliers, finish with strong tape (book binding tape) around all sides; plastic fruit baskets also make effective sieves; and
- plastic clear tops from pie dishes, salad containers—useful to create ponds and lakes.

Natural materials add realism to sand play, especially if children can be involved in the collecting process (make careful note of any allergies before collecting items):

- dried flowers, grasses, weeds, vines from the fields in the spring and winter; weeds, grasses, wild flowers during the growing season;
- stones, pebbles, rocks, gravel, shells;
- twigs, branches, small logs, bark; and
- pinecones, chestnuts, acorn caps, and pods.

► Ages and Stages of Sand Play

The stages of sand play can be related to stages of development. It is important to know what the child is able to accomplish at various ages in order to provide a safe and healthy environment that encourages active exploration (see table 3.5).

TABLE 3.5

► Ages and Stages of Sand Play

Stage	Age/Level	Considerations	Behaviours
Functional, sensory	Unsupported sitting, crawl, walk 12 months and up	Sit within sand Large area to allow free movement Ensure safe materials to avoid cuts; with increased age provide both open and raised sand experiences	Wiggle feet in sand; move hands through sand; put sand in mouth*; Pick up objects and put in mouth; sift sand through fingers; cover hands/feet Children of all ages love to sift through sand with fingers, bury body parts, bury and find items; becomes therapeutic activity
Functional play, with tools	12 months and up	Younger children need to be right in sand; play prop-dependent Older children need both open and raised sandbox experiences	Digging, poking, carrying, filling, emptying, repeating actions, burying, finding, patting, pouring, imitating Same behaviours as above: tunnelling, smoothing, experimenting, comparing
Symbolic play	18 months and up	Younger children need experiences to encourage symbolized play—visits to construction sites, road building, farms, gardens Older children need writing materials and books to support play	Actions to represent objects, people, events, along with appropriate verbalizations; start to use one object to represent another (represent machinery to dig, hoe, build) Become increasingly sophisticated in symbolized play—less reliant on actual props; inventive to use other materials
Representational	Older preschoolers and school-aged children	Involve planning, organizing, and role designation Use maps, plans, scripts, written dialogue	Creating, building, dramatization of events, symbolized actions, recognizable structures, creating charts, scripts, maps

*Note: Sand play offers rich sensory experiences for infants, but because infants tend to eat the sand, this becomes a debatable issue for families and early childhood educators. The early childhood educator must weigh the risks and benefits and again decide individually what he or she feels is appropriate. The next step is then to involve families to gain a consensus on this issue.

► KEY POINTS

Learning through Sand Play

- non-threatening;
- enjoyable;
- exploratory;
- developmentally appropriate;
- sensory; and

- supportive of all types of development—social, emotional, cognitive, physical, and language.

Levels of Sand Play

1. **Functional Sensory**—explore aspects of sand without an end product in mind; repetitive action; using hands, fingers, feet, toes.
2. **Functional with Tools**—explore aspects of sand without an end product in mind; repetitive action; using tools, shovels, sticks, boards, foam.

▶ KEY POINTS (continued)

3. **Symbolic**—using one item to represent another, often accompanied by sounds the object makes (e.g., a hand or shovel becomes a digger as the child makes a "brrrrm" sound).
4. **Representational**—play has defined purpose, defined characteristics; structures are recognizable and named.

Properties of Sand

- wet/dry;
- has textures;
- can be manipulated;
- can be formed;
- is sensory;
- encourages all development types: language, social, physical, emotional, cognitive; and
- encourages development of observation skills.

Values of Sand Play

- is a therapeutic activity;
- perform simple experiments;
- develop math and science skills such as measuring, comparing, and problem solving;
- play creatively;
- develop new vocabulary; and
- demonstrate new concepts.

Facilitator's Role

- observe and document children's play and learning;
- set up the sand area both indoors and outdoors;
- provide developmentally appropriate materials—natural, commercial, recycled;
- provide developmentally appropriate experiences—field trips;
- clarify problems, new learning;
- take cues from children;
- give credibility to sand area by supporting children's efforts; and
- model appropriate behaviours.

Organization

- store in containers that are categorized by type of activity; and
- utilize hanging baskets, clear containers, parking lots for construction vehicles, clear shoe bags, hooks, pegboards, and multi-unit shelves.

Labelling

- picture and word;
- compensate for grittiness of sand;
- develop system for rotation; and
- ensure that representations or symbols used are clear.

Safety

- on appropriate surface—easy to clean;
- use sterilized sand, clean daily to rid sand of unwanted items;
- change sand regularly;
- have water spray bottle handy for dry sand—dust is dangerous for children with asthma;
- outdoor sand—covered and shaded; and
- keep broom, dustpan, and garbage can near area to sweep up sand on floor.

Location

- easy-to-clean surface;
- enclosed by two corners to keep area confined;
- away from high traffic area; and
- outside area protected from riding toys.

Alternatives

- moral issue of using food substitutes; and
- use of non-food items—confetti, material scraps, egg shells.

Student Activities

1. For the sensory functional stage of sand play, what types of activities could you set up to encourage exploration using the senses? Think both in terms of indoor and outdoor experiences. Consider that sensory experiences need to involve as many senses as possible.

2. Damon is sitting in the sandbox. He has a rake in his hand. He is pulling the sand toward him, creating a straight line. He then puts the rake next to the line and makes another line. As he is doing this, he is making the following sounds, "Chug, chug, chug. Rmm, rmm, rmm." What stage of sand play is this? Explain your answer. How might you extend Damon's play? What other materials might you supply?

3. Develop a list of language terms that could be used to enhance a child's knowledge of sand.

4. Discuss at least five observation skills that children could develop through sand play. Explain why each skill is important.

5. One of the values of sand is that it is a therapeutic activity. Explain what this means. How could you set up the sand area to encourage children to use it for this purpose? How could you ensure that other children could still continue with their activity also?

6. There is a raised sandbox in the room. It is the appropriate size and has enough materials for four children to use. Six children are around the sandbox. They are pretending it is a bakery and are creating sand pies and cookies. What is the facilitator's role in this activity?

7. Describe how you might set up storage of materials for children who are at the representational stage of sand play. They are particularly interested in construction types of sand play.

8. What are the advantages of a labelling system in sand? What other skills are developed through labelling? How do these skills relate back to child development theory?

9. Discuss what properties of sand can be developed through use of the following materials—crushed coloured egg shells, confetti, and material scraps.

10. Utilize one of the observation charts in a child-care setting. Analyze your results. How could you use this information? What changes would you make?

11. Develop your own portfolio of sand play. You might consider putting in various sections—skills children gain, interesting activities in sand, sand projects, outdoor sand play in various settings, and so on.

12. How could you make tracks in the sand? What materials might you use? Research to find out what kinds of tracks are common in your area. Try to reproduce these.

▶ References

Erlbach, A., & Holm, S. (1997). *Sidewalk Games Around the World*. Brookfield, CT: The Millbrook Press.

Federation of Women Teachers' Association of Ontario. (1986). *Play: Active Learning In The Early Years*. Toronto: Federation of Women Teachers' Association of Ontario.

Federation of Women Teachers' Association of Ontario. (1986). *Learning Through Play*. 87, Number 2. Toronto: Federation of Women Teachers' Association of Ontario.

Furst, F., & Furst, J. (1982). *North American Indian Art*. New York, NY: Rizzoli International Publications Inc.

Hogben, J., & Wasley, D. (1996). *Learning in Early Childhood: What does it mean in practice?* Education Department of South Australia: Hyde Park Press.

Jackman, H. (2001). *Early Education Curriculum: A Child's Connection to the World* (2nd ed.). Scarborough, ON: Delmar Thomson Learning.

Onyefulu, O. (1994). *Chinye: A West African Folktale*. London, UK: Viking Penguin.

▶ Resources

Sand Play

Cole, P., Frankeny, F., & Jonath, L. (1999). *Snowmen*. Vancouver, BC: Raincoast Books.

Mitchell, P. (2000). *Sandcastles*. San Francisco, CA: Chronicle Books.

Stief, K. (Ed.). (1987). *Sand*. City of North York, ON: North York Board of Education.

Wierenga, L., & McDonald, W. (1990). *Sand Castles*. New York, NY: Simon and Schuster.

Garden

Broutin, C., de Bourgoing, P., & Jeunesse, G. (1990). *The Tree*. London, UK: Moonlight Publishing Ltd.

Forey, P. (1994). *Wild Flowers*. Surrey, UK: Dragoon's World Ltd.

Houbre, G., de Bourgoing, P., & Jeunesse, G. (1990). *Vegetables*. London, UK: Moonlight Publishing Ltd.

Ingoglia, G., & Gomboli, M. (1987). *Look Inside a Tree*. New York, NY: The Putman & Grosser Group.

Pope, J. (1994). *Plants and Flowers*. London, UK: Eagle Books.

Quinn, G., & Shillman, L. (1995). *The Garden in Our Yard*. New York, NY: Cartwheel Books.

Valat, P., de Bourgoing, P., and Jeunesse, G. (1989). *Fruit*. London, UK: Moonlight Publishing Ltd.

CHAPTER 4

Water Play

Both children and adults have a natural attraction to water. Not only does it provide such a ready source for problem solving and critical-thinking skills, it also allows for emotional catharsis. It is relaxing, comforting, soothing, pleasing, rhythmic, and calming.

—*Eliason & Jenkins,* A Practical Guide to Early Childhood Curriculum

Chapter Outline

▶ Water Play to Encourage Learning
▶ Child Development: Developmental Skills of Water Play
▶ Value of Water Play
▶ Role of the Facilitator
▶ Effective Storage Systems
▶ Effective Labelling Systems
▶ Considerations for Setting Up a Water Area

▶ Observation and Documentation Techniques
▶ International Considerations
▶ Water Materials
▶ Ages and Stages of Water Play
▶ Key Points
▶ Student Activities
▶ References
▶ Resources

Learning Outcomes

After studying this chapter, the reader will:

1. Identify various levels of water play
2. Explain the value of water play
3. Discuss the role of the facilitator in water play
4. Identify and discuss various aspects of setting up a water play area in indoor and outdoor environments—physical space, storage of materials, labelling
5. Identify and discuss how to observe and record various aspects of water play
6. Discuss how to encourage outdoor water play during various seasons

Interactive Learning Exercises

 Remember, the CD-ROM that came with this text contains interactive exercises that relate to the topics in this chapter, as well as other valuable resources.

▶ Water Play to Encourage Learning

Jenna was having a bad day. She was frustrated because the puzzle she had chosen to do was too hard for her. Her friend Emily had chosen to play with another friend. She wanted to read her favourite book, but another child was already reading it. Jenna wandered around the room. Her lower lip was quivering and her eyes threatened to overflow. As she wandered past the water centre, she heard her teacher, Sarah, talking to Emily. Jenna stopped to listen. As she listened her eyes grew bigger and bigger. She slowly walked over to the water centre. As she watched, Jordan was blowing a bubble (photo 4.1). Emily was standing near Jordan very quietly. She had her hands spread out to catch the bubble as it landed. The bubble broke. Jordan tried again. Again, the bubble broke. Finally, after two more tries, the bubble landed on Emily's hand (photo 4.2). Jenna broke into spontaneous applause. Her face lit up as she called out, "Land one on my hand please!" (photo 4.3).

Water is a magical medium. For centuries water has been used to soothe, relax, teach, enjoy, and sustain. Water play is a wonderful medium to use with children. It is familiar, as children are in contact with water every day. They drink it, freeze it, wash in it, play in it, and cook with it. Water is experienced in a variety of forms: tears; foggy, rainy, or snowy days; rainbows; waterfalls; ice; steam; rivers; lakes; puddles; and dew.

▶ Child Development: Developmental Skills of Water Play

Stages have been developed and categorized based on the predominant developmental milestones within various age categories. These milestones have been adapted from Panikkar and Quinn, 1989.

PHASE 1: FREE EXPLORATION

Bubble play can continue over time and in different locations. Hannah discovered that she could make bubbles while washing her hands. Previously, when asked to wash her hands, she would run to the sink, turn the tap on, and let the water run over her fingers. In order to encourage Hannah to use soap to wash her hands more thoroughly, a soap pump had been provided by the sink. Hannah tried using the pump to put soap on her hands. Her attempt failed; the soap landed in the sink. Instantly, bubbles appeared. Hannah captured the bubbles in her hand (photo 4.4). She put her hands under the water and watched the bubbles disappear. She watched the water and bubbles disappear down the sink. "All gone!" Sarah replied, "Yes, your bubbles are all gone. They disappeared. How did you make the bubbles?" Sarah immediately pumped more soap into the sink. Hannah smiled as she watched the bubbles form.

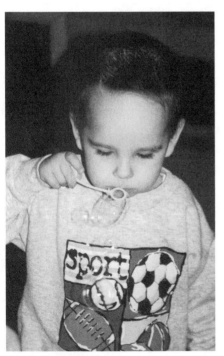
PHOTO 4.1

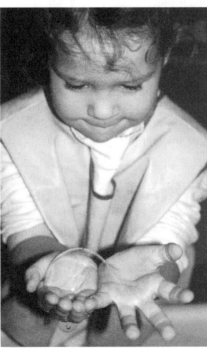
PHOTO 4.2

PHOTO 4.3

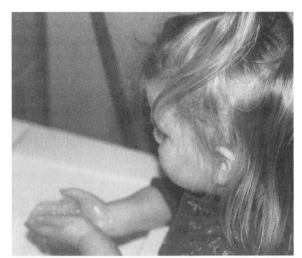

PHOTO 4.4

Hannah was involved in sensory exploration. She enjoyed the feel of the water running over her hands. She enjoyed capturing the bubbles, making them disappear, and reforming them. She continually was involved in a sensory activity as she explored the feeling of the bubbles and the water. During this play, she also learned that bubbles could be made with running water and soap, and could be destroyed by running the water over them.

Alicia (photo 4.5) was also involved in sensory exploration. She discovered that, as she walked through the water, the water around her boots created ripples. She walked through the water several times, carefully watching her boots. Eventually she

PHOTO 4.5

started to stamp her feet gently. When the ripples around her boots got bigger, she smiled.

Callum had been watching Alicia and was also fascinated by the puddles. As the splashes she made got bigger, he stepped back. When Alicia moved elsewhere, Callum pushed his train into the water. He stood at the edge of the puddle and carefully pushed his train as far as he could reach (photo 4.6). He then walked around the puddle and pushed the train back. He watched the wheels partially disappear below the

PHOTO 4.6

PHOTO 4.7

PHOTO 4.8

TABLE 4.1

▶ Possible Concepts to Explore

Concepts	Behaviours	Possible Materials/Scenarios
Temperature (warm, cold, cool)	Hands, fingers: splash, swirl, touch (photo 4.7) Feet: stamp, walk, run Whole body: sit in, jump in, run under, run through, slide into (photo 4.8), walk in rain or snow (photo 4.9)	Water table, small containers, puddles, sink Plastic pools, puddles, wading pools, during rainfall, at the beach, sprinklers, hose
Water is (clear, muddy, bubbly, coloured)	Dropping/throwing things into water (photo 4.10); blowing bubbles (photo 4.11); beating water to make bubbles; finding objects in coloured, muddy, bubbly water; pushing objects into/through water; wading through water (photo 4.12)	Stones, twigs, leaves along rivers, puddles, lakes Water table/large containers (colour with vegetable dye) Objects: plastic fish, shells, colourful stones, plastic gems Push toys, riding toys Soapy water in small individual containers or water table with soapy water (bubble wands, manual beaters, whisks, hands, fly swatters, small branches)
Wet, soapy	Putting hands, fingers, feet into water, puddles Running under sprinklers, water Swimming in pools, at the beach	Discuss feelings (wet, smooth, soapy, slippery (photo 4.13) Observe beading of water, movement of beads down body, raindrops on window pane, raincoat, umbrella

PHOTO 4.9

PHOTO 4.10

PHOTO 4.11

PHOTO 4.12

PHOTO 4.13

water. He discovered that when you push objects through water, parts of the object disappear in it. He learned how to manipulate an object through water without getting wet himself.

The children in these examples were engaged in onlooker and solitary play. Callum needed to become comfortable with the activity before he participated. Each child continued with the exploration of water at his or her own pace. See table 4.1 for more examples of possible concepts to explore.

PHASE 2: EXPERIMENT

Shanleigh had noticed the children blowing bubbles. She got a manual beater from the water shelf, and indicated to Jordan that she could make bubbles too (photo 4.14). Jordan stopped and giggled. Shanleigh said, "I can make lots of bubbles this way. You can only make one." Shanleigh had made the connection between various techniques of making bubbles and had also learned that different techniques give different results. She knew that it was more efficient to create a larger number of bubbles by using a specific tool—a manual beater.

As Shanleigh continued to turn the handle on her beater, she noticed that she got more bubbles when she turned it faster. She got quite excited as the bubbles started to rise from the bottom of the water table. Soon she had a group of children around her trying to create lots of bubbles using a variety of tools—whisks, manual beaters, and hands.

During this stage, the children make the connection between their actions (moving the water by beating, splashing, swirling) and the results (making large quantities of bubbles). They also discovered that the speed at which they used their instruments increased

the quantities of bubbles made. They shared their discoveries either by talking about them, as Shanleigh did, or by showing others how to do it. Jordan showed Jenna how he could make a bubble that would land on

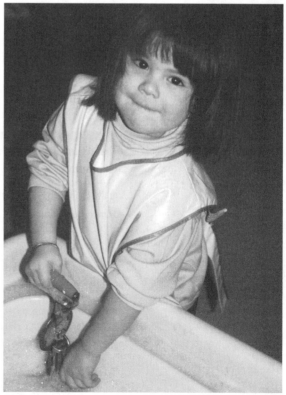

PHOTO 4.14

PHOTO 4.15

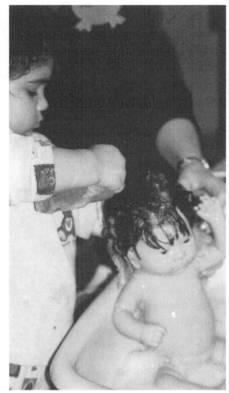

PHOTO 4.16

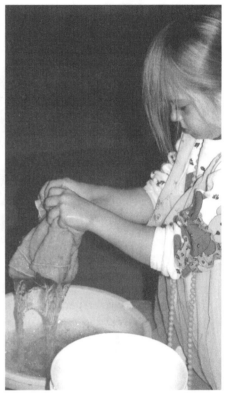

PHOTO 4.17

Emily's hand. As the children continued to make bubbles, they shared their tools. Shanleigh passed her beater to Jordan, as Jordan passed his wand to her.

Kayla was pouring water from one container to another. She had been doing this with various-sized containers before. She finally discovered that the pitcher and the measuring cup held almost the same amount of water (photo 4.15). She is making the connections between the size of the container and the quantity of water each container holds.

TABLE 4.1 (continued)

▶ Possible Concepts to Explore

Concepts	Behaviours	Possible Materials/Scenarios
Cause and effect	Creating bubbles with water	Hands, beaters, whisks, forks in water table
	Washing dolls (photo 4.16), clothes (photo 4.17)	kitchen dramatic play (flour, water, salt, rice, macaroni)
	Creating mixtures: cooking, mixtures to make play dough (photo 4.18), food for dolls (photo 4.19)	Outside, water, sand, soil
		Containers of various sizes, bowls, buckets
		Spoons, shovels, sticks
Comparing quantity	Pouring, transferring water from one container to another, filling and emptying (photo 4.20)	Any containers both in water centre and in kitchen area; in water centre, need a shelf to free hands to pour
Creating movement	Pouring water, squirting water to cause object to move (photo 4.21)	Squirt bottles, paddles, water canals, water wheels, containers with spouts

PHOTO 4.18

PHOTO 4.19

PHASE 3: EXTEND KNOWLEDGE

Braelyn and Makenna decided to create a lake at the beach. First they dug a hole. They carefully patted down the sides of the hole "so that the water won't seep away." Then they filled the hole with water (photo 4.22). Danika joined to help them. The girls decided to make the lake longer and wider. They built a dam around the edge of the lake "to keep the water in." They found that the water still "seeped away." Danika suggested that they should "line the bottom and sides of the lake." An active discussion started. They discussed using rocks, wood chips, and shells. Danika said that they could not put them in close enough, so it wouldn't work. Braelyn said that the

dessert they brought was wrapped in foil. "Excellent!" said Danika. They asked Sarah for the foil, then they lined their lake. When they poured the water in this time, it stayed. "We've created an artificial lake" said Braelyn.

At this level, children solve problems—keeping the water in the lake. Children also interact with each other and with adults to overcome challenges. Braelyn, Makenna, and Danika coordinated their efforts—digging, getting water, and lining the lake. The girls also involved an adult to help them get materials—foil. They clearly understood the language concepts they were using—*seep, artificial lake*. They were able to clarify concepts—what materials would work to prevent seepage. Danika is older than the

PHOTO 4.20

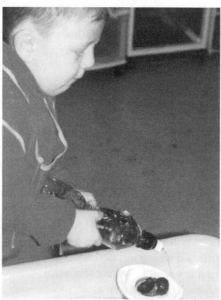

PHOTO 4.21

PHOTO 4.22

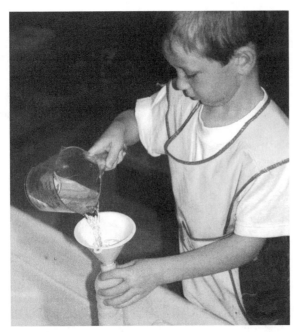

PHOTO 4.23

FIGURE 4.1

▶ Billy's Illustration of How Many Cups Fit into a Bottle

tall bottle   fat bottle   small bottle

other two girls. She was able to clarify that the materials discussed could not work—that is, they could not put materials close enough to prevent seepage.

Billy was trying to find out how much water was contained in the various bottles around the water

centre (photo 4.23). He picked up a two-cup measuring cup. He looked at the first bottle he wanted to fill, but realized that the opening was too small. "Some of the water will spill out. It won't work!" he said. He got a funnel to fill the bottle. He was able to indicate how many cups it took to fill the bottle. Sarah helped Billy graph his results (figure 4.1). At the end of his effort, Billy was able to indicate which bottles held the same amount and which bottles held more. Billy made the connection that bottles may hold the same amount

TABLE 4.1 (continued)

▶ Possible Concepts to Explore

Concepts	Behaviours	Possible Materials
Problem solving	Sarah wanted to make the water fall directly on the water wheel. She looked for materials to help her. She found the plastic tubing. She could not pour water down it. Michael asked her what she could use to make it easier to pour water into the tube. She said "I know, a funnel." She tried various funnels until she found one that fit the tubing (photo 4.24).	Tubing, funnels, waterwheels, measuring cups, plastic pipes, pipes, containers with holes in them, sieves, pumps, tornado makers (photo 4.25), markers, chart paper, scissors, wood, material
Projects	Colin had created a boat in the carpentry centre. The project took several days to complete (photo 4.26). He then tried to sail his boat in the water centre. He found that it did float. Colin tried to blow his boat across the water. He said his sail was too small. He created a newer, bigger sail out of material and dowels. He tried his boat again. He was excited to find that it worked.	Endless number of materials can be used! Materials used depend on the project the children are working on. They should help in the collection of these materials. Colin's materials: packing foam (various sizes), golf tees, glue, wooden dowels, paper, tape, long nails, clamp, saw, hammer

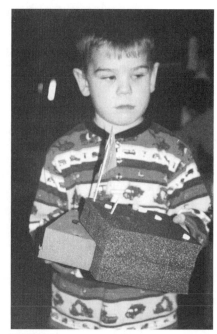

PHOTO 4.24   PHOTO 4.25   PHOTO 4.26

even though they are a different shape (conservation of liquids). He was able to use comparative language—*the same, more, less*.

▶ Value of Water Play

Water is a powerful medium that encourages many skills and can be used in most of the learning areas for young children—drama, carpentry, sand, creative art, music, manipulatives, and math and science. Additionally, it offers children a soothing, therapeutic activity. Children's attention and interest is held for longer periods of time than with any other medium (Eliason and Jenkins, 1999, p. 282). Specifically, water:

- is therapeutic—Jenna (photo 4.3) was immediately soothed by the bubble activity. "Water has always been a therapeutic element, in which children tend to lose themselves to the pleasures of sensory exploration" (Shipley, 2002, p. 367);
- is rich in opportunities to develop new concepts—comparisons (clear water, bubbly water); conservation (Billy with his bottles of the same volume but different shapes); porosity (creating a lake at the beach and watching the water seep away); development of fine motor skills (pouring water from container to container); nature (rain, snow); some objects sink some float (throwing rocks into water, floating a boat); can be formed into mixtures (cooking, making play dough);

- encourages open-ended investigation and experimentation—Callum pushing his train through the muddy water;
- helps develop fine/gross motor control—pouring, filling, measuring;
- promotes emotional growth—sensory, open-ended (Sarah connecting the plastic tube to the funnel, then pouring water into the funnel);
- promotes language development—new vocabulary such as *artificial, swish, splash*;
- encourages creativity—Colin building a boat that he could try out to see if it would float;
- promotes social growth—parallel play (making play dough), associative play (blowing bubbles), and **cooperative play** (creating a lake);
- encourages cognitive growth—problem solving (what materials to use to keep the water in the artificial lake); measuring and counting (to see which container held more water);
- is adaptable to real-life situations—bathing the baby, washing clothes; and
- allows the focus to be on the activity of the child—there is no product at the end.

▶ Role of the Facilitator

"The key to effective water play is the teachers' careful selection of materials that promote specific kinds of learning. Teachers also have a role in facilitating play by thinking through the nature of children's learning at the water table" (Shipley, 2002, p. 368). In order to provide the appropriate materials, the facilitator must:

- carefully observe the children's skills and development to provide meaningful materials—Billy needed help to keep track of the number of cups of water each bottle held. Sarah provided a simple means for Billy to do this himself. She made available a simple graph; Billy could stick on self-adhesive squares for each cup he poured (figure 4.1);
- awareness of the various concepts that can be covered by water—weight, solubility, various forms of water, characteristics of water, and uses of water; awareness of what types of materials can be provided that could lead to concept formation and are open-ended.

Since the nature of water play is both sensory and open-ended, it is critical for the facilitator to:

- know when to step in or when to allow play to continue uninterrupted—As the children were building their lake at the beach, they needed some foil. They asked Sarah for the foil. She got the foil for them and then again left them alone. Her interaction in this play was not needed.
- provide suggestions to expand or continue the play—When Sarah (a student) was trying to direct the flow of water onto the water wheel, she was encouraged to solve the problem by herself. The facilitator simply asked her to think about what she could do to solve the problem.
- expand language—Sarah talked to Hannah about what was happening to her bubbles (they are disappearing). Through their dialogue the play was extended over time.
- facilitate water play in other areas—baby bath, creating play dough, going on field trips (beach, stream, boat building in carpentry). These types of experiences allow children to make connections. Kayla had been pouring water at the water table from container to container (photo 4.15). She later asked if she could pour the water at the snack table. She did so without spilling the water.
- provide materials that ensure success—When Kayla poured the water at the snack table, the facilitator provided a small pitcher to pour from and put a tray under the glasses to minimize the possibility of water spilling.
- provide materials that encourage problem solving—tubing that fits into funnels, bottles of the same size but different shapes, variety of plastic pipes that can fit together in various ways, squirt bottles.
- observe in nature—walks in the rain or snow, trips to flowing water, puddle play, watching rain on different surfaces.

- extend learning—As Shanleigh and Jordan were both creating bubbles, the facilitator could draw attention to the different kinds of bubbles made by the two different methods: blowing causes larger bubbles, whereas using a beater makes smaller, interconnected bubbles.

▶ Effective Storage Systems

As with sand, appropriate storage of water materials becomes critical. When toys are left in the water centre:

- it limits the number of children that can play in that area;
- it limits the type of play that can occur;
- conflicting messages are given to the children—"I don't need to clean up";
- too many concepts may be used—sink and float, pour, throw; children's attention is easily distracted; and
- the area is not aesthetically pleasing—children may not wish to use the area.

Storage is more difficult for water toys, as the toys are wet. The moisture may cause wooden shelves to rot or warp, collect in pools of water that can drip on the floor and become a safety hazard, and destroy labelling systems. Whatever the system, the primary considerations should include accessibility, visibility, and opportunity for the toys to air dry. Some suggestions are to:

- line shelves with a sheet of plastic then an absorbent material—old towels, foam (easy to dry once toys are dry);
- use a small table and dish racks to place wet toys in—centre the lip of the tray over the side of table above a pail to catch drips;
- hang plastic baskets over a pail;
- use open-weave cutlery organizers with protective cover and absorbent surface underneath on shelves or tables;
- use heavier pitchers to hold cutlery;
- hang toys on a peg board using hooks, with painting troughs underneath to catch drips; and
- place plastic storage baskets on a shelf, table, or floor with protective plastic and absorbent material underneath.

Storage of items needs to be clear so that children can easily find the items of choice. If using containers, place like objects together per container (i.e., pails together in one container, measuring cups in another container, tubing coiled and hung on a hook). Too many items in any one container will encourage children to dump materials to find what they want. Items can be placed on a flat surface upside down. Each shelf could hold different items—bottles on one shelf, measuring cups on another shelf, and pitchers on a third shelf. Dish racks could be organized by type—bottles in one, bowls in another.

The system that is ultimately used must make sense to the children and adults. It must be easy to use and easy to clean. When the system becomes too difficult to maintain by any of the participants it is a clear signal that changes must occur.

Additional storage is needed to hang water smocks to protect children's clothing. These are most easily hung on hooks in the water area. The area should also contain a mop and bucket to encourage cleanup of any spills. Children should participate in this effort; child-sized mops and pails need to be provided.

▶ Effective Labelling Systems

Labelling can be problematic in the water area. The water will seep into the labels unless labels are well sealed; a laminator works best for this. Outlines and printing can be done with waterproof markers. Labels can be applied at the side of the shelf or at the front of the shelf or storage unit if size permits. Labels can also be put on the surface itself if materials and protective layers are placed behind the labels. Labelling the sides of baskets, dish racks, or utensil holders is much easier: labels can be directly attached to the front of these units.

Since materials need to be rotated, labels should be prepared ahead of time. Thus attaching additional labels and/or removing labels becomes much easier. Since attachment is difficult to do with tape, use sticky tack or create clear pockets to slide new labels in and out.

Labels can be created by using symbols, outlines, pictures, or photographs. Care must be taken that all individuals can understand the labels. If the picture, outline, or diagram is not clear, it will not be used and the time and effort was wasted. The printed word should always be attached.

▶ Considerations for Setting Up a Water Area

1. Safety
- change water daily;
- disinfect water table and toys at least once a week;
- mop up area if spills occur to prevent children from slipping—rubber, perforated door mats can be put around the water table to prevent slipping;
- ensure children are dressed properly for outdoor water play—bare feet or boots, swimming suits, raincoats, umbrellas;

- locate outdoor water play in a grassy or sandy area—the surface is not as abrasive, in case a child slips and falls;
- check for broken parts—children can be cut if a toy is in water hidden under bubbles; and
- ensure the play area is at an appropriate height—children should be able to easily reach to the bottom and to the middle (children may lose balance and fall in if the area is not an appropriate height).

2. Location
Water, like sand, is a form of messy play and therefore needs to be placed on a tiled surface. There needs to be space around the area to allow the children to move around freely. Care must be taken that the walls around the area are protected against water splashes. Any displays in this area need to have a protective cover (lamination usually works well). Children explore water actively; therefore, this area needs to be separated from quieter areas.

Outdoor water play should be diversified. Children need to be appropriately dressed—raincoats, umbrellas, boots; bathing suits for splashing, jumping, running in water; protection from the sun; towels to dry off (children can get chilled quite quickly); appropriate winter wear for snow and ice play. Since outdoor water play can become quite boisterous, play in pools, under sprinklers or hoses, or at a water table should be on a softer surface like grass or sand. These areas should be away from riding paths and climbing areas to prevent accidents.

3. Types of Areas
Water play indoors can take place in any larger container. Containers or water tables that are clear have the advantage of offering children an additional vantage point: they can actually see things drop and move at the bottom. The size and configuration of the table depends on the space available. Following are some guidelines to consider when setting up water play indoors:
- safety—floor should be easy to clean; it should be safe for children to reach into water or into the centre of the container;
- types of skills to encourage—pouring activities tend to take more room, whereas bubble activities can be done in smaller individual containers on a table;
- types of concepts—sink and float activities should have clear containers so that children can observe what happens to the items when they drop;
- social activities tend to work better around a water table, where more children can participate; and

- play area should be located near a water source—easier to fill and empty.

There are a number of commercially available tables. There are several things to be aware of when purchasing a commercial table. Tables should be sturdy. The actual container should be removable from the frame for easy cleaning. The spout should be replaceable, as it tends to break or leak readily. Other containers that work well are rubber or clear plastic storage bins; these are especially handy as they can also be used for storage purposes and brought out only when needed.

TABLE 4.2

▶ Types of Water Play Areas

Type	Location/Furniture	Materials
Baby bath	Within dramatic house play; change table, baby bath, cribs, dresser for clothing	Dolls of various ethnic groups and gender—should be washable
		Bath supplies—shampoo, soap, powder (substitute corn starch), face cloth, towel, combs, brushes
		Doll clothing for sleeping, playing, outdoors
		Changing—diapers, towels, garbage
Cooking	Kitchen area—sink, counter space, cupboards and drawers for utensils; stove; fridge[1]	Mixing supplies—whisks, beaters, spoons, forks, bowls
		Dry ingredients—flour, salt, drink crystals, spaghetti, noodles, peas, beans[2]
		Water
		Baking/cooking—pots and pans, casserole dishes, baking pans
		Serving/eating—plates, knives, forks, spoons, platters, cups, mugs, saucers[3]
Cleanup activities	Help clean paint easels, tables, floors, dishes; wash doll clothes	Child-sized buckets, sponges, mops, squirt bottles, soap, rags, paper towels
Mud play	Easier outside	Water, soil, items collected from nature, create hole in ground or sandbox, create in containers
Planting	Outside—flower/vegetable bed	Vegetables, flowers, shrubs, beans, grass—fast growing
	Inside—planters, clear containers	

Notes:

1. Consider having a kitchen unit built instead of buying smaller units (photo 4.27). This leads to a more realistic setting and a more aesthetically pleasing area. Dishes and cutlery are organized much as they would be at home.

2. Refer to previous discussion of using food items (pages 16, 63). Realistic items give children more opportunity to practise skills, are more familiar to them, and may be used for real purposes such as making own play dough or preparing own snack.

3. Real dishes offer opportunities to set up a realistic environment that encourages children to handle materials with respect. Materials can usually be bought cheaply at yard sales or flea markets.

PHOTO 4.27

Water is ideally placed beside the sand area. See page 62 in the sand section for a discussion on the value of locating sand and water together. Other areas that can be used for water play are identified in table 4.2 along with appropriate materials.

4. Guidelines for Using Water

Guidelines for using water are similar to the guidelines for sand (refer to p. 62). Emphasis must be placed on safety. For example, Hannah had just started the preschool program. She observed the children in the water area and decided to put on her boots. When the children left the area, Hannah went over to play: she quickly climbed into the raised water table and started to splash with her feet. Children do the unexpected—as caregivers, we must be vigilant and learn to expect the unexpected.

Another safety concern is water on the floor. Children learn very quickly to help mop up spills. Larger spills need the attention of the adults. Telling children that water stays in the water table will work only if the facilitators provide the materials to encourage this behaviour. Is there a platform that one container sits on as water is poured into it? Are the containers the appropriate size for little hands? Do containers have spouts to make pouring easier?

5. Displays

Water is intrinsically motivating. Displays should focus on the documentation of children's efforts through videotaping and/or photographing. Ideas for different water play activities can be set up in an adjacent book area. Water-play books are available with plastic coated surfaces. Books can also be created by taking a book apart, laminating the pages, and then putting it together again in a binder.

▶ Observation and Documentation Techniques

It is important to observe the type of water play that has evolved in order to:

- build upon the interests of the children—extending bubble play to the outside environment, empowering Colin to try out the boat he made in the water centre;
- build upon skills and knowledge of the children—Shanleigh knew how to make bubbles in different ways; provide alternate materials (whisks, beaters, branches);
- provide appropriate materials to expand play—tubing and funnels that the tubing will fit on to encourage experimentation;
- acknowledge the developmental levels of the children—provide a water table that can be reached by all children, provide a clear, removable shelf within the water table to encourage independent pouring; provide containers that have spouts and handles to make pouring easier;
- recognize children's emergent skills—Billy was starting to grasp the concept of conservation. He was provided with an opportunity to test his belief;
- share in the accomplishments of the children with families and other professionals—Colin's efforts to build a boat were recorded through photography and through a description of his actions and comments. His attempts to sail the boat were similarly recorded. A video segment was shot of Colin's efforts to sail the boat. The children thoroughly enjoyed watching the brief excerpt. The documentation of the boat-building scenario was posted outside on the parent board.

Documentation of water play is best accomplished through photography and descriptions of the dialogue and circumstances that evolve during the water play. A water play **portfolio** was developed to document the value of water play and the developmental stages. This is a most useful device to share with families; many families may feel that water play is not a useful activity, as it is messy and children might get too wet. When they look through the booklet and see their children involved in water play activities, many become more open to water play as a learning activity.

OBSERVATION TOOLS

Sample Checklists and Charts

Examples of checklists and charts are provided in figures 4.2 through 4.4.

FIGURE 4.2

▶ Phases of Water Play Chart

Name: Braelyn

Phase	Date	Skills/Concept	Evidence
Free exploration	09/10	Sensory	Made bubbles in sink while washing hands, indicated that the "bubble water" was soapy, slippery, and felt nice on her hands
Discovery	09/15	Creating bubbles of different sizes	Created bubbles by blowing through straw and wand and moving rope loop through air outside, indicated bubble size as small, medium, and large
Extend Knowledge	09/20	Creating bubbles over objects	Used straws to blow bubbles to encase small rubber animals

How to Use Information
- expand handwashing to include other washing activities—doll clothes, table tops, paint easels;
- expand bubble blowing opportunities in other areas—gross motor activities outside to make and catch bubbles;
- use bubble blowing techniques in other areas—music and movement (float like bubbles, burst like a bubble, create bubble songs); creative art (bubble painting); and
- to build vocabulary (*fragile, shimmery, iridescent*).

▶ International Considerations

Water is a scarce resource in many parts of the world, especially arid climates and where water supplies are polluted. In these areas, water play in the traditional sense is not seen. Instead, children learn very early in life how to conserve water and use water appropriately, as this is important to their survival. In the Highlands of Guatemala, children often make games out of work-related activities such as washing clothes in a stream. The girls accompany their mother. The

FIGURE 4.3

▶ Skill/Concept Sample Chart

Name: Billy

Date	Skill	Materials Used	Type of Play
10/09	Conservation	Measuring cup, bottles of same size but different shape, graph to stick on sticky squares to count number of cups per bottle	Solitary

How to Use Information
- provide other mechanisms for identification of equal size—scales, different-sized measuring cups;
- provide more variety of containers with different shape but same size; and
- provide conservation opportunities in sand play.

FIGURE 4.4

▶ Skills Used Chart

Name	Date	Skill	Evidence
Colin	05/16	Floating objects	Put boat he had made in water to see if it would float
		Problem solving	Tried to blow on sail to move boat—said it was too small, made a bigger sail

How to Use Information
- expand to increase knowledge about floating—various types of boats (paper, plastic, wood)
- materials that expand knowledge—boats that can carry loads; materials that can be loaded on boats (rocks, twigs, bottle caps, rubber animals, people); load boats to see how much weight they can carry
- explore projects to see how to create mobile boats—other materials for sails, simple motors

job of washing clothes becomes a game of splashing, giggling, and throwing soap at each other (Johnson, Christie, and Yawkey, 1999).

An activity known as *story knifing* is popular among Inuit girls in Alaska. "The afternoon sun warms the muddy banks of the Kuskowim River as five young Yup'ik Eskimo girls sit quietly talking and working their dull flat knives into the mud in front of them. They are carefully preparing smooth mud palettes to be used for telling stories. After their palettes are ready, the girls begin their storytelling. Each storyteller illustrates her tale by drawing symbols in the mud, which are erased and replaced with new symbols as the story unfolds. When one storyteller finishes, another begins, until they tire of the play or it is time to go home for dinner" (Bennett de Marrais, Nelson, and Baker, 1994, p. 179).

On a trip to Nassau, Bahamas, I observed a family group teaching very young children to dive for items in the shallow waters of the Caribbean. Their siblings practise this skill when cruise ships come into the harbour: the tourists throw coins overboard and watch the children dive to retrieve them.

In many cultures, spontaneous play is valued as a means to socialize the child. "Mothers increasingly initiated pretend play to guide their children toward more socially desirable behaviours" (Haight, Wang, Fung, Williams, and Mintz, 1999, p. 1478). In Taiwan, the approach to teaching children is through "guiding social practices" (Haight, Wang, Fung, Williams, and Mintz, 1999, p. 1486). Thus, water play is not likely to be considered a primary learning experience. This is confirmed by looking through several catalogues that feature educational toys, such as the BATTAT cata-

logue, which is printed in China. Water toys in these catalogues are listed under bath toys. Few of the items in catalogues such as Wintergreen can be found in these catalogues.

In conclusion, it is very important to be aware of the culturally diverse attitudes toward water that are held by the families in each setting. It is important to involve families in the planning and implementation of the learning environment.

▶ Water Materials

Table 4.3 lists water concepts and possible materials. These materials may be provided for open-ended exploration. Some of the concepts, such as boiling, are not appropriate to explore in open-ended activity with children; they may observe these types of concepts when involved in supervised, guided experiences, such as cooking. The type of activity is dependent on age. Preschool children could explore concepts, such as evaporation, through open-ended activities outside with squirt bottles or water-painting activities. School-aged children would be more likely to start measuring or timing the rate of evaporation.

TABLE 4.3

▶ Concepts and Possible Materials		
Concept	**Materials/Activities**	**Associated Vocabulary**
Characteristics of water—weight; colour; state (liquid, steam, solid); temperature (freezing, cold, warm, hot, boiling)	Containers of various sizes with handles to compare weight (buckets, watering cans, plastic containers with handles)	Freezing, cold, cool, lukewarm, warm, hot, boiling
	Squirt bottles or water painting on hot days	Steam, vapour, fog, mist, dew
	Ice cubes or frozen ice shapes in the water table, freezing water in various containers outside in the winter and building with these, thermometers	Rain, sleet, hail, snow, frost
	Guided cooking experiences	Heavy, light, heavier, lighter
	Walks to observe varying weather conditions	
Dissolving	Sugar, drink crystals, salt, Jell-o™, soil, paper scraps	Dissolve, colour, muddy, opaque, clear, suspended
Uses of water	Baby bath, washing, cleaning, planting (see table 4.1 for materials)	Scrub, wash, rinse, clean, polish, sterilize
		Drink, boil, cook
		Shampoo
		Squirt, irrigate, soak
Recreational	Swimming	Speed—fast, slow
	Boating—various boats in water centre outside	Spray, bubbles, wake
	Observe water sports—skiing, surfing, sliding	Tilt, sink, float
	Fishing—magnetized fish/fishing poles, nets, pails	Catch, release, net, fishing bobbers

TABLE 4.3 CONCEPTS AND POSSIBLE MATERIALS (continued)

Concept	Materials/Activities	Associated Vocabulary
Fill and empty	Spoons, scoops, slotted ladles Measuring cups, graduated cylinders Small pitchers, watering cans Film and food containers Squeeze/spray bottles Medicine droppers (share sand toys in water) Basters, milk cartons	Pour, fill, empty, half full, half empty, heavy, light, small stream, large stream, overflow, same, different, more, less, drop-by-drop, spray, squirt, splash
Role play	Firefighter (hose, boots, raincoats) Farmer (irrigate, hose, watering cans, shovels) Cleaner (buckets, mops, soap, squeegees, brushes, rubber gloves, bottle brushes, spray bottles, aprons) Plumber (plastic interconnecting pipes, stoppers, elbows, wrenches)	Spray, squirt, hose, water Irrigate, fill Clean, wipe, scrub, polish, sterilize Fit, attach, fix
Sink and float	Popsicle sticks, spools, corks, styrofoam meat trays (disinfected pre-use), marine life figures, wood scraps, lids, marbles and buttons (older children), foil balls, feathers, tennis and golf balls, rocks, plastic eggs, toy boats	Heavy, light, sink, float, submerged, at the bottom, at the top, in the middle, under, on top of, loaded, sinking
Water flow	All pouring containers and utensils listed previously Water wheels, half pipes, cans with holes punched into them (figure 4.5) Plumbing pipes; pumps	Squirting, flowing, fast, slow, splash, fountain
Absorption	Sponges, foam, material, paper, medicine dropper, food dye, paper towel	Squeeze, drop, splatter, dry, wet, full, dripping, soggy

FIGURE 4.5

▶ **Two Diagrams of Water Jugs and Containers**

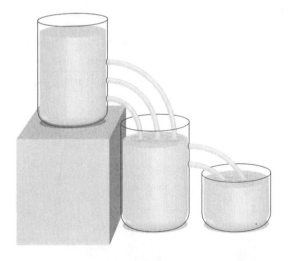
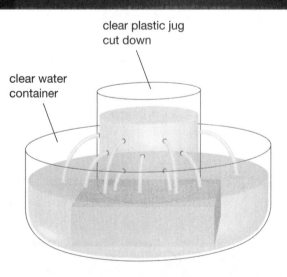

clear plastic jug cut down

clear water container

▶ Ages and Stages of Water Play

The knowledge of ages and stages of water play provides information to the facilitator about not only what are appropriate learning experiences, what possible choices of materials and equipment to use, and what skill levels the children have, but also what safety aspects need to be considered (see table 4.4).

TABLE 4.4

▶ Ages and Stages of Water Play

Phase	Age	Behaviours
Free exploration	Infants	Bath time—splashing with hands and feet when held
		Bath time, sensory water pools—sit in water, grab water toys within reach, put in mouth
		Water pools, hose, sprinklers—drop things in water, put things into floating toys, take them out repeatedly; crawl, run through water sprinklers, climb into pool
		Solitary or parallel play
		Sensory, functional play
Free exploration	Toddlers	Walk, run through puddles, run through sprinklers, jump into water, splash repeatedly
		Water table—drop things; float items; pour water into containers, dump water out repeatedly
		Blow bubbles, chase bubbles, repeatedly
		Bathe "babies," self-care routines—wash hands, brush teeth
		Wash dishes
		Solitary or parallel play, functional play with toys
		Symbolized actions
Experiment to make connections	Preschool, ages 3-5	Solitary, parallel, associative play
		Talk about what is happening, share discoveries with adults, peers, delight in new discoveries
		Drop things into the water, into containers in the water
		Pour, squirt, empty, fill repeatedly
		Wash dolls, clothing, tables, clean floor with mop, clean easels
		Spray sand, create water pictures with spray outside
		Create mixtures—mud pies, play dough
		Cook—soups, cakes, cookies (real and pretend)
		Role-play—firefighter, cook, family member roles
		Explore outside during rain, fog, snow—curious about various weather conditions
Extend knowledge to solve problems	Older preschool and school-aged	Measure amount of rainfall
		Create, rivers, ponds, lakes
		Create changes of state—freeze, melt, create steam
		Create methods to transport a variety of materials of various weights
		Create various methods to make water flow
		Work to create various types of solutions (saturated, supersaturated) to create new products (crystals)

► KEY POINTS

Developmental Stages of Water Play

Phase 1: Free Exploration—open-ended use of materials, hands and fingers, and bodies to find out about various concepts of water.

Phase 2: Experiment—use water and materials in order to make the connections between the child's actions and what happens as a result of that action.

Phase 3: Extend Knowledge—use prior knowledge in order to solve problems, overcome challenges.

Values of Water Play

- encourages skills that extend to most other learning areas;
- encourages creativity;
- develops fine/gross motor control;
- promotes social, emotional, and cognitive growth;
- is therapeutic;
- is rich in opportunities to develop new concepts;
- allows for open-ended investigation and experimentation; and
- is adaptable to real-life situations.

Facilitator's Role

- observe children's skills, interests, developmental levels;
- select materials that ensure success and encourage problem solving;
- be aware of possible concepts to develop;
- be aware of when to become involved and when to observe;
- provide suggestions to extend/expand play/learning;
- provide opportunities to observe water in nature; and
- extend language.

Storage

- lined open shelves;
- containers—dish racks, hanging baskets, cutlery containers;
- peg boards and hooks;
- waterproof smocks, appropriate outdoor clothing; and
- pails, mops, and buckets.

Labelling

- protection against water;
- extra labels for easy rotation; and
- photographs, symbols, outlines, pictures, and words.

Considerations for Setup

- safety—disinfect equipment/toys, change water daily, clean up spills, appropriate protection, appropriate height;
- location—on tile or grassy surface, near water source, out of traffic area; and
- alternative areas—baby bath, cooking, cleanup, mud-play, planting.

Observation

- observation of children's skills, interests, developmental levels—skill charts, developmental stages, concepts formed, interests; and
- selection of materials that ensure success and encourage problem solving.

Student Activities

1. Jennifer is at the water table. She watches the children play at the table. She smiles when Timmy pours water down the rubber tube onto the water wheel and it turns. What would you do in this situation? How would you involve Jennifer without disrupting the play of the other children?

2. Use one of the concepts presented in table 4.1. Develop a list of materials that you would use to explore this concept. What associated vocabulary could be developed?

3. One of the aspects of the experimental phase is for children to make the connection between what they are doing and what is happening. What types of materials would you provide to allow children to explore the concepts of *sinking, submerged,* and *floating*? What system of storage and labelling would you develop to encourage this activity?

4. Describe how you might set up and what materials you would use for a baby bath area that encourages children to:
   i) handle babies appropriately and gently;
   ii) follow the routine of bathing; and
   iii) encourage children to dress and continue the activity into other aspects of caring for babies—feeding, sleeping, taking for a walk.

5. What are some of the ways you could encourage creativity in using the water centre? Consider combinations with other core areas in the room.

6. You have observed Benjamin pouring in the water centre. He needed to use both his hands to fill his pitcher and then pour the water back into the water table. He continued this activity for about two minutes and then left the area.
   i) What additional materials might Benjamin need?
   ii) What adaptations should be made?

7. Observe water play in one of the daycare settings. Identify what strategies the facilitator(s) used. What other interactions do you think might have been used and why?

8. Utilize the observation tool to observe children's developmental levels. Observe children in a child-care setting. Did you observe all developmental levels? Why or why not?

9. Observe children's skills within a daycare setting. Identify how you might use the information gathered in order to expand children's learning.

▶ References

Bennett de Marrais, K., Nelson, P., & Baker, J. Meaning in Mud: Yup'ik Eskimo Girls at Play. In Roopnarine, J., Johnson, J., & Hooper, F. (Eds.). (1994). *Children's play in diverse cultures.* Albany, NY: State University Press, 179–209.

Eliason, C., & Jenkins, L. (1999). *A Practical Guide to Early Childhood Curriculum.* (6th ed.). Upper Saddle River, NJ: Merrill.

Haight, W., Wang, X., Han-tih Fung, H., Williams, K., & Mintz, J. (1999, November). Universal, Developmental, and Variable Aspects of Young Children's Play: A Cross-Cultural Comparison of Pretending at Home. *Child Development.* Volume 70, Number 6, 1477–1488.

Johnson, J., Christie, J., & Yawkey, T. (1999). *Play and Early Childhood Development.* Don Mills, ON: Longman.

Panikkar, B., & Quinn, S. (1989). *Water.* North York, ON: North York Board of Education.

Shipley, D. (2002). *Empowering Children: Play-Based Curriculum for Lifelong Learning.* (3rd ed.). Scarborough, ON: Nelson.

▶ Resources

Water Play

Crosser, S. (1994, July). Making the Most of Water Play. *Young Children.*

Gibson, G. (1995). *Science for Fun: Making Things Float and Sink.* Brookfield, CT: Copper Beech Books.

James, J., Granovetter, R., & Krill, S. (1987). *Waterworks.* Lewisville, NC: Kaplan Press.

Murphy, B. (1991). *Experiment With Water.* Richmond Hill, ON: Scholastic Canada Ltd.

Owl Magazine. (1988). *Kitchen Fun.* Toronto, ON: Greeyde Pencier Books.

Stangl, J. (1986). *Magic Mixtures.* Torrance, CA: Fearon Teacher Aids.

Nature

Cristini, E., & Puricelli, L. (1984). *In The Pond.* New York, NY: Neugebauer Press.

Rinard, J. (1986). *Dolphins: Our Friends in the Sea.* Toronto, ON: National Geographic Society.

Rosen, M., & Leonardo, T. (1995). *All Eyes On the Pond.* New York, NY: Hyperion.

Spier, P. *Rain.* (1984). Toronto, ON: Zephyr Books.

Wood, J., & Dean, K. (1993). *Nature: Hide and Seek Rivers and Lakes.* Toronto, ON: Random House.

CHAPTER 5

Music

Music is universally loved by children. Language, cultural and developmental barriers come tumbling down when children listen to sounds, sing songs, discover rhythms and patterns in nature, make instruments and listen to music. Music is non-judgmental. There is no right or wrong. It is what it is. Everyone can be successful in music.

—Silberg, The I Can't Sing Book: For Grownups Who Can't Carry a Tune in a Paper Bag ... But Want to Do Music with Young Children

Chapter Outline

▶ Music to Encourage Learning
▶ Child Development: Developmental Levels of Music
▶ Value of Music
▶ Role of the Facilitator
▶ Effective Storage Systems
▶ Effective Labelling Systems
▶ Considerations for Setting Up a Music Area

▶ Observation and Documentation Techniques
▶ International Considerations
▶ Music Materials
▶ Ages and Stages of Music
▶ Key Points
▶ Student Activities
▶ References
▶ Resources

Learning Outcomes

After studying this chapter, the reader will:

1. Identify the various developmental stages of music
2. Explain the value of music activities
3. Discuss the role of the facilitator in music activities
4. Identify and discuss various aspects of setting up a music area in indoor and outdoor environments—physical space, storage of materials, labelling
5. Identify and discuss how to observe and record various aspects of music activities
6. Discuss how music activities could be encouraged outdoors

Interactive Learning Exercises

 Remember, the CD-ROM that came with this text contains interactive exercises that relate to the topics in this chapter, as well as other valuable resources.

▶ Music to Encourage Learning

It had been a particularly wet autumn. The children had been walking in the rain, splashing in puddles, and watching the raindrops run down their raincoats, down their umbrellas, and on the windowpane. The children decided to create a rain environment indoors. (See also Chapter 9, on creative art.)

A simple rain song was created that

- had a simple melody;
- simulated the rain falling;
- had a steady beat;
- could be adapted to include body movement; and
- had simple repetitive words.

See figure 5.1 for the simple song.

The children participated enthusiastically over a long period of time. The song was sung at least five or six times per morning with as many as ten repetitions. Often children would initiate the activity. The older children would sing and participate in the actions of the song, or use rhythm instruments to keep the beat (photo 5.1), while the younger children would often observe and participate in only the large muscle movements (photo 5.2).

Through these activities children learned about patterns of sounds, melody, moving their bodies in space, keeping the beat to a simple melody, moving rhythmically, and communicating through music. "As a child learns to clap to the beat of the music, or as he uses triangle, blocks, and sticks to beat out the rhythms or as he marches to different cadences, his physical coordination, his timing, and his thinking develops.... He will also gain memory skills as he learns to sing a variety of songs with different rhythms. Aural, or listening skills will be developed as he listens to the varying pitch, rhythm, and harmony of a multitude of songs and various pieces of music" (Habermeyer, 1999, p. 43).

PHOTO 5.1

PHOTO 5.2

Music is one of the essential learning areas that should be in every early childhood program. Music is a soothing activity that can bring balance and beauty into any environment.

▶ Child Development: Developmental Levels of Music

Stages have been developed and categorized based on predominant developmental milestones within various age categories. These milestones have been adapted from Jalongo and Collins, 1985; Henniger, 1999; Haines and Gerber, 2000; and Pica, 2000. It is important to remember that although stages may arise in a partic-

---

FIGURE 5.1

▶ **Music Bars with Song "Rain Is Falling Down..."**

Rain is f a l l i n g down splash pit ter pat ter pit ter pat ter
(jump into puddle) (rhythm with hands on legs)

Rain is f a l l i n g down splash pit ter pat ter pit ter pat ter
(jump into puddle) (rhythm with hands on legs)

ular order, each stage becomes more sophisticated over time and aspects of each stage may be used selectively by individuals of any age. Adults will attend concerts or listen to specific music on a radio station or CD. When learning a new piece of music, we often imitate others. For example, I once attended a Native drumming session. I watched very carefully how the leader held the drum and used the drumstick and listened for the rhythm of his drumming before I participated. Any band or rock group goes through an experimental stage. They try various combinations until they find one that is satisfying. We discover new concepts every time we hear an instrument that is new to us—new sounds, new ways of producing sounds. The last stage, application, is present when we sing a song, play a song, or listen to an orchestra or singer perform.

PRENATAL STAGE

Numerous studies have tried to identify the effects of early stimulation on the fetus. Early stimulation includes talking, reading, singing, humming, and playing music to the fetus (Begly, 1996; Hepper, 1991; Hoffman, 1999; Shelter, 1990). "Although musical studies on babies in utero are continuing, these early studies suggest that by singing, talking, and reading to the unborn child parents can give a significant advantage in early language, memorization and music development" (Habermeyer, 1999, p. 36).

The ears start to develop in the fourth week of gestation and are further formed during the second month. According to Campbell (1995, p. 20), the ears are the first organs to develop, and the auditory system is functional by three to four months. The fetus starts to react to sounds outside of the womb, as shown by changes in heart rate.

If the fetus is exposed to sounds such as specific pieces of music and the voices of its mother and father, it may develop a memory of and preference for these sounds. After birth, these sounds may be remembered and/or preferred. In the video *What Every Baby Knows* (1984), Dr. T. Berry Brazelton clearly demonstrates this memory. Dr. Brazelton holds a newborn. He speaks to the infant, with no apparent reaction. He then encourages the mother to speak. The neonate immediately turns his head toward the source of the sound. Similarly, the neonate turns toward the source of his father's voice.

LISTENING STAGE

Jennifer sat in the rocking chair holding a sleepy Jeremy in her arms. Jennifer was gently rocking and singing "Hush Little Baby." Jeremy watched Jennifer's

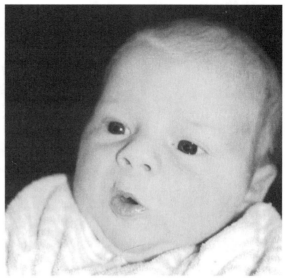

PHOTO 5.3

face intently (photo 5.3). Jennifer looked down at the child and softly continued to sing the song. Jeremy's eyelids slowly closed. Suddenly he would force his eyes open again and look at Jennifer. Jennifer continued to sing and gently rock. Jeremy's body began to relax and his eyes closed. Soon the child was asleep. Jennifer got up and gently put the child into his crib. She turned on a CD of a variety of music that also contained the sound of a heartbeat (Walker, 2000).

Jeremy was soothed by the close comfortable touch of Jennifer, the sound of Jennifer's voice, and the song that Jennifer gently sang. Jeremy clearly listened to Jennifer's voice. He closely looked at Jennifer's face and eventually fell asleep. Providing the music with the heartbeat continued to offer Jeremy a comfortable environment to relax in.

IMITATIVE STAGE

One of the activities of particular interest to the children was the electronic keyboard. At times, Suzette, the facilitator of the infant program, would take the infants to visit the preschoolers and play requests for the children (photo 5.4).

The infants would watch and listen. Jamie observed that some of the children were using instruments to keep the beat and others were singing along. He got very excited. He started to hum in a loud voice. He moved both arms and legs. His hand hit his attached crib toy, which made a noise. He then grasped the crib toy and started to shake it as he hummed along (photo 5.5). He continued to hum and shake his toy until the music stopped.

PHOTO 5.4

PHOTO 5.5

Jamie was showing his enjoyment of the activity. He participated in "singing" along and by moving his crib toy. He knew when the music had stopped, because he too stopped at that point. He discovered that he could also make "music" with his crib toy by shaking it. He was imitating by humming along and by eventually shaking his crib toy.

Lilly had watched the children quietly. One of the children requested the song "If You're Happy and You Know It." A small group of children actively participated. As the children started to clap their hands, a big smile appeared on Lilly's face. She also started to clap along (photo 5.6). When the verse was over, the children stopped clapping and so did Lilly.

Lilly also enjoyed the music by listening and watching. When she recognized a familiar action, clapping, she joined in. When the other children stopped clapping, she stopped too. She watched in order to imitate clapping and stopping.

The activity, which involved a mixed age group, clearly showed the advantages of bringing children of various ages together for some activities. The preschoolers looked forward to the infants coming. The infants were able to observe and imitate some of the behaviours of the preschoolers. The preschoolers also observed the infants and helped to facilitate their learning.

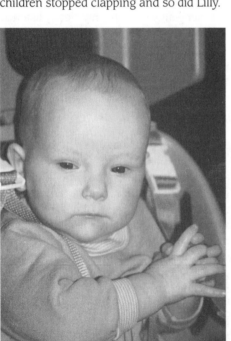

PHOTO 5.6

PHOTO 5.7

Nicholas enjoyed music. When he heard the music play, he would bounce up and down as he was sitting. His arms would shake and his whole body quivered. Billy observed Nicholas' actions. He ran over to the music shelf and got two maracas, giving one to Nicholas. Nicholas took the maraca in his hand. He started to bounce up and down. He stopped and looked at the maraca. He shook his hand. A big smile appeared. Nicholas repeatedly shook the maraca (photo 5.7). Billy smiled and shook his maraca. Nicholas stopped and watched Billy. When Billy stopped, Nicholas started.

Billy had learned to observe and follow through on what he had observed. He saw that Nicholas was enjoying moving to the music. He gave Nicholas an instrument that was an appropriate one to use. Nicholas learned how to use a sound-making instrument. He had not known what this instrument was, but soon learned how to use it. Billy and Nicholas watched and imitated each other.

Lindsay would stop whatever she was doing and come to the music area if she heard the song "Twinkle, Twinkle, Little Star." She would sing along to some of the words and also use a rhythm instrument (the tone block) to keep the beat to the music (photo 5.8). She could do this if the music was slow enough. When the song was finished, she would request it again. Repetitions could be as many as six or seven times.

Lindsay is developing a sense of pitch. She was able to sing phrases of the song in the correct pitch.

She also has developed a definite interest in certain sounds—rain sticks, tone blocks, rhythm sticks, or songs.

EXPERIMENTAL STAGE

Connor had been watching the children engaged in the rain activity. He was in the drama centre helping to set up the fire station. At one point he stopped and sang the song with the children in the music area (photo 5.9). He did not do any of the actions but just sang the words. When he had finished singing, he giggled and started to sing again. "Rain is falling down, on the fire truck, pitter patter pitter patter, on the fire truck." Sarah heard him and said, "You have created a new song! Would you like to sing it again?" Colin smiled and shook his head.

At this stage, children not only learn the words of songs, but also make up and create new songs. The songs they create are usually focused on what they are doing at the present time. It is interesting to note that Colin was engaged in dramatic play. He was seemingly involved in his activity but was obviously listening to and attracted to the music he heard. Children do not always need to be in the music area to participate in an activity. Colin participated in his own way from a distance.

Timmy also heard the song. He was in the creative area. He stopped what he was doing and quickly moved to the music area. He did not sing the words to the song but rather participated in the physical

PHOTO 5.8

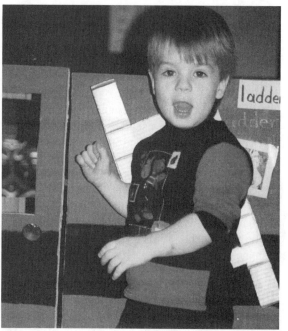

PHOTO 5.9

PHOTO 5.10

PHOTO 5.11

activity of jumping in the puddles to the beat of the music (photo 5.10). He jumped into various puddles, trying to jump as each word was sung. Sarah noticed his attempt and said, "Let's try this one more time, but a little more slowly." This time Timmy managed to jump to most of the beat of the song.

Timmy is a toddler. He participates more at a physical level. He is experimenting following the beat using his whole body. Notice that he could much more readily accomplish the task when the music was paced more appropriately to his ability. The other children also learned that a song can be sung in different ways—fast or slow.

DISCOVERY STAGE

Yasmine enjoyed dancing to music, especially with props. She liked to use a scarf as she twirled around on the spot (photo 5.11). She would manage to use the scarf to follow the speed of the music, fast and slow. She particularly liked the version of "Too Ra Loo Ra Loo Ra" (Musical Reflections, 1999).

Yasmine is combining her interest in music with her preference for active participation. She is creative in her ability to make her scarf flow in time to the music. Yasmine seemed to sense the mood of the music as she brought the scarf up high and let it flutter down as the tone of the music descended. She has grasped some of the basic musical concepts, such as tempo and pitch.

Jenna and Jamie often were in the music area together. Both girls liked to sing, and both girls liked to create their own songs. They would often start with a known favourite song, such as "Hickory Dickory Dock" (Countdown Kids, 1998). They knew both the words of the song and the melody. They would play the CD, sing along, and play musical instruments to support their efforts (photo 5.12). Often they would then use the tune of the song to which they had just listened and invent their own words to the melody. For example, "Dockety, dockety, dock. I ran up the clock. I fell down. Dickety, dickety, dock."

All of the children loved to listen to and sing "Twinkle, Twinkle, Little Star" (Madacy, 1998). The words of the second verse of the song are as follows: "Twinkle, twinkle, little bat. How I wonder what you're at. Up above the world you fly. Like a tea tray in the sky. Twinkle, twinkle little bat. How I wonder what you're at."

Children at this developmental level love nonsense or silly songs, which appeal to their sense of humour and may encourage them to create their own.

APPLICATION STAGE

Billy particularly liked to experiment with rhythm (photo 5.13). He would create a rhythm, then ask Sarah to duplicate it. He loved to have her create a rhythm that he would try to duplicate. The rhythms varied in volume, length of sound, and number. For

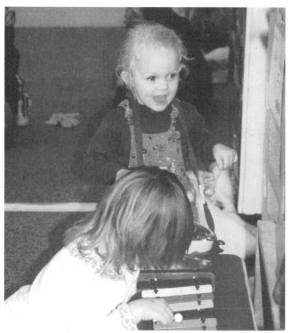

PHOTO 5.12

example, a typical rhythm might be long, long, short, short, long; soft, soft, soft, loud. He has learned to use, remember, and reproduce rhythm patterns of volume and length.

Often, spontaneous music activities would be initiated by the children. Braelyn and Yasmine decided that they would like to create a band. They went around the room inviting children and adults to participate. Often the band would involve favourite songs either sung or played on a CD (photo 5.14). One of the favourite songs children liked to sing or listen to was "Baby Beluga" (Raffi, 1980). Braelyn and Yasmine

PHOTO 5.14

PHOTO 5.13

knew all the words and could sing along. Both girls could also keep the beat to the song.

Children at this level of development like to participate in singing in a group. They have an established musical preference and can reproduce a melody.

Stephanie and Braelyn decided to change the "sitting band" into a "marching band." The two girls marched around the room keeping their own beat—slow, slow, slow, slow. They decided that this activity was too easy. They built an obstacle course to march around (photo 5.15). They also picked the African drum music to march to from the *All the Best from Africa* CD. This clearly shows their ability to coordinate more than one thing at a time—marching, keeping the beat, and walking around, in and out of the obstacles. It is also an example of how children will incorporate cultural values different from their own into their play.

Dillon noticed that the small piano xylophone had colour-coded keys that matched the colours of the notes on the sheet music. He got very excited. He tried to play the music and was successful. He then decided to try this on the electronic keyboard, and found that it did not work. He asked Allianna to help him. She asked him, "How can I help you?" He responded, "We need to colour the keys on the keyboard." They brought over the xylophone piano and compared it to the keyboard. Dillon thought he could stick pieces of coloured paper on the keyboard to match the colours on the xylophone keyboard.

PHOTO 5.15

PHOTO 5.16

Alliana showed him middle C and suggested that this would be a good starting point. They then attached coloured strips to the keys. Dillon tried to play his piece (photo 5.16). He was most excited that he could do this. "Hey, you guys, come and listen to me." Most of the children came to listen to him play his piece again. He asked the children what song he had played. They were able to answer correctly: "Row, Row, Row, Your Boat."

Dillon is starting to reproduce melodies in different ways. He was able to match notes on two different keyboards, recognize that notes have different positions on the keyboard, and follow the pattern of coloured notes to produce a recognizable melody.

I observed a group of grade five students perform in a talent contest. The students had picked a piece of music: "Yellow Submarine," by the Beatles. They played the drums, an electric guitar, and an electric keyboard. A fourth child was designated as the singer. The group played their piece and managed to coordinate a variety of synchronized steps into their act.

These children have clearly learned to play music and read lyrics (they had song sheets to practise from), and were able to synchronize their movements to each other and to the music they were playing.

▶ Value of Music

Music is not only important to young children, it is essential. "Music meets all of the criteria to be called an intelligence, but there's more to be considered than its intellectual qualifications. Music carries emotion and spirit. There's a chance to be sure, that a young child will grow up to be a concert master or violinist. But music can be a great gift to give to all children, a gift they can turn to for soothing relaxation, solving problems, and expressing emotions. Music can be the key that unlocks children's creativity and learning" (Black, 1998, p. 42). See table 5.1 for a listing of specific values of music.

▶ Role of the Facilitator

- provide materials and experiences to motivate children to participate—electric keyboard, CDs of various types of music; rain songs outdoors during rain; Jennifer's father demonstrating Native drums (see Chapter 1); gross motor activities to encourage movement to music;
- model—Suzette playing music the children wished to hear, Jennifer singing to Jeremy, Michael participating in the band and marching band (photo 5.15);
- create an atmosphere that encourages musical activities (photo 5.17);
- provide opportunities for singing—the rain song was introduced outside as children were walking in the rain and jumping in the puddles;
- provide opportunities to move to rhythm—jumping in puddles, clapping rhythm of rain;
- provide opportunities to become creative—provide notes, a musical staff, sheet music; write down

TABLE 5.1

▶ Specific Values

Source	Value	Behaviour
Isenberg and Jalongo, 2001, pp. 163-167	**Psychomotor skills**—use of small and large muscles to build **kinesthetic/bodily intelligence**	Hannah and Timmy jumping in the puddles, Jamie shaking the crib toy, Lilly clapping her hands, Nicholas shaking the maraca, Lindsay playing the tone block, Yasmine twirling the scarf, Jenna beating the drum, Jamie playing the xylophone, Billy tapping a beat on the bamboo drum, Dillon playing the keyboard
	Perceptual skills—recognition of sounds, songs, reacting to music	Jeremy listening to the lullaby, children requesting songs for Suzette to play, Jamie humming and shaking his crib toy, Colin singing along from a distance, Timmy leaving his activity to join into the rain song, Billy creating and following a rhythm, Dillon playing song on the keyboard
	Affective skills—evoking emotional responses	Many repetitions of the rain song, soothing lullaby to encourage Jeremy to sleep, Jamie's expression of joy as he hums along, Nicholas' body movement and facial expression as he moves to the music, Connor's wholehearted joy at singing the rain song, Timmy's enthusiastic response to come and participate when he heard the rain song, Billy's pride when he copied a rhythm, Dillon's excitement when he could play the song
	Social skills	Group participation in rain song, Suzette playing the keyboard, the formation of the band and marching band, Dillon asking the group to listen to his song, Jenna and Jamie creating music together
	Cognitive skills—memory of words of song, process tone and rhythm of melodies, interpret symbols, "can develop all higher-level thinking skills of application, analysis, synthesis, and evaluation" (p. 166)	Hannah being able to listen to the words of the song and jump in time (photo 5.2), Lilly imitating the clapping behaviour of the other children, Connor able to sing all the words of the song and create new words that fit into the melody; Yasmine recognizing that the music had ascending and descending notes demonstrated by moving her scarf up and down, Jenna and Jamie creating new songs, Dillon making the connection between the xylophone piano and the electric keyboard, Billy composing rhythm patterns
	Cultural skills	Jennifer's father playing the Native drums for the children and providing Native drums to play (see Chapter 1, p.10); utilizing instruments from different cultures (e.g., bamboo drum); marching to an African drum beat
Pica, 2000, pp. 28-30	Motivation to communicate	Dillon wanted to communicate his song to the whole group, Connor communicated that the rain was falling on his fire truck, Yasmine expressed herself by moving a scarf to music
	First exposure to own culture	Familiar songs and music—lullabies, nursery rhymes Variety of music—classical, popular, and children's music Native drums, representation of music from various language groups—French and Jewish folksongs, Native songs

TABLE 5.1 SPECIFIC VALUES (continued)

Source	Value	Behaviour
	Improve attention span	Repetition of rain song; creation of band and marching band
	Develop listening skills	Jeremy listening to lullaby, the group of children listening to Dillon play, Yasmine listening to the music and reacting to her feeling to it
	Set mood	Yasmine chose a quiet, slow-moving song; the band group chose an invigourating beat to march to; the "happy" song ("If You're Happy and You Know It")
Rauscher, 1996	Increase **spatial intelligence**	Leads to later improvement of skills in math and science
Coulter, 1995, p. 22	Use of music as a neurological exercise	Combining rhythmic movement with songs and language helps to develop children's minds, leading to social and language development and self-management skills
Honig, 1995, p. 2	Aesthetic development	Develop sensitivity to the feelings and imagery of music
Wendell, 2000, p. 100	Healing power	"The healing power of musical play in the preschool can be used to help children with special needs progress through the developmental stages of early childhood. The connection between music and emotion may help these children communicate feelings and understanding of the world around them. Songs and musical activities about familiar events and open-ended musical play can provide symbols to help children act out various roles that could provide needed therapy" (p. 100)

PHOTO 5.17

children's songs (for example, Dillon creating his own coloured system to play a song);

- provide opportunities to let children listen to facilitator sing and play selections of music;
- use simple instruments—keyboard, drums, rhythm sticks;
- talk to children about aspects of music—how it makes them feel, why they like a piece;
- observe children—active participation outside to a rain song led to the facilitation of the same activity indoors; Billy creating rhythm patterns led to the facilitator playing rhythm pattern games with him;
- adapt/enhance music area—as rain changed to snow and ice, the children helped to adapt the indoor rain activity to an indoor ice surface; provide additional music to complement children's activity (for example, the facilitator added a CD player and lullabies to the infant bathing and sleeping area);
- be enthusiastic about music—sing songs with meaning, show enjoyment in children's musical attempts, use music spontaneously in a variety of

activities (adapt everyday activities to songs about what is happening in the room);

- provide simple instruments that children can use—Billy and the drum, Lindsay and the tone block;
- ensure that the cultural diversity of the children in the program is met—Native drums, French songs;
- provide a balance between individual, small-group, and large-group activity—Billy one-to-one with adult, small band with Michael, Suzette with a large group selecting and participating in "If You're Happy and You Know It"; and
- encourage musical activities both indoors and outdoors.

▶ Effective Storage Systems

Children need to learn to respect musical instruments in terms of how they handle them and the care they give them. This serves as a good model from the real world: musicians take great care of their instruments.

Therefore, it is critical to develop an appropriate storage system. An open shelf can be used for larger instruments, such as drums and xylophones. Rhythm sticks can be stored in open, clear, plastic containers. Containers should be aesthetically pleasing. This can be done not only through the labelling system, but also by taking care not to put out containers that have commercial logos on them. Most of these items are thrown out in family homes, which gives a message to the child that what is in the container is not valuable; therefore, appropriate care may not occur.

Some instruments, such as tambourines, can be hung on hooks. Single kitchen-drawer organizers can be used to store tone blocks along with their stick. Smaller instruments, such as bells and small shakers, may be stored in small baskets or plastic containers. The container should be shallow and large enough to allow each instrument to have a spot of its own.

In order to avoid confusion, instruments should be stored together by type—all the drums together, all the rhythm sticks together. Children need to be encouraged to return instruments to their spots when finished.

Some of the instruments are curved and therefore easily roll off the shelf. Shelves could be lined with material (felt or terry towel work very well) to prevent the instruments from slipping and falling onto the floor.

Musical instruments should be rotated regularly. Make sure that rotation acknowledges the children's interests. If children are interested in and continue to use a certain instrument, that instrument should not be removed; rather, add some instruments that com-

plement the favourites. For example, Lindsay liked the tone block. The tone block was left out, but wooden spoons, musical spoons, and tone bars were added.

▶ Effective Labelling Systems

As with other areas, instruments should have clear labels—picture and word—to encourage all individuals to return items to where they belong. Larger instruments should also have outlines to designate their placement on the shelf. Individual containers should itemize all things within that container by picture and word—bells, cymbals, and castanets.

▶ Considerations for Setting Up a Music Area

The music area needs to have a spill-out area so that children can extend their musical activities to drama and movement. Music needs to be separated from quieter activities, since playing instruments can become quite noisy. Children need to be free to experiment with one aspect of music—volume. Since children also like to sit to play or sing, a rugged area is well-advised. Creating soft comfortable spots with pillows or blankets may encourage sustained activity for listening or playing an instrument (photo 5.18).

Adults need to be in the area, participating either by playing a simple instrument or singing to children.

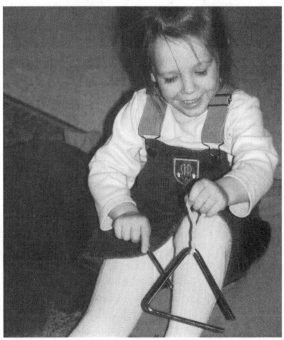

PHOTO 5.18

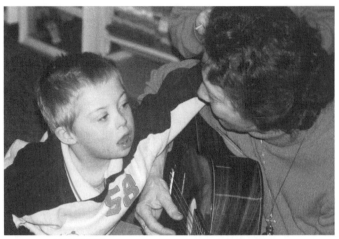

PHOTO 5.19

PHOTO 5.20

Children need to have music modelled. They need to see that adults also value these experiences (photo 5.19).

I remember one profound incident in my life. I was teaching in a primary open area. Children ages 5 to 10 were in this area. We had had a particularly hectic morning. At lunch, I sat in a corner of the room and put on one of my favourite records—the Bielefelder Children's Choir. As I sat listening, engrossed in the music, I suddenly realized I was not alone. About 30 children had heard the music in their lunch room and had quietly come in and sat around me, listening with me. Not a word was spoken. When the music was over the children quietly left.

Musical instruments and a selection of CDs should be available for children's use. Many favourite songs can also be purchased with a sing-along book. This gives an added dimension to the music area as it encourages listening and reading. Examples of such CDs and books are *Baby Beluga, Hush Little Baby,* and, for older children, classical musical stories such as *Peter and the Wolf.* It is important that children learn to use the CD player and CDs themselves to gain greater independence. Even very young children can learn to operate the system if empowered (photo 5.20). Consider covering the control buttons with green and red tape to give children a visual clue for start and stop.

Additionally, this area can be used for watching short excerpts from videos. The *Kidsongs* video (1985) shows a field trip to the farm. When the children on the video sing "Old MacDonald Had a Farm," the actual animals are present and the actual animal sounds are also heard. This allows children who do not have an opportunity to visit a farm to get not only a visual picture of the animals, but also an accurate idea of what the animals actually sound like.

Videos such as *Cats* and *Fantasia* give children an idea of other people's interpretations of music and movement. It is not the intent to subject children to the whole video, but rather to find a small segment that captures their imaginations. Both videos lend themselves to showing just one piece of music.

The video *Stomp* is a wonderful example for both adults and children to see how music—especially beats and rhythm—can be created with almost any materials. This video again lends itself to showing short pieces that will empower children and adults to use natural materials in their environment.

The music area needs to be aesthetically pleasing. For example, when the children were engaged in the rain song a large umbrella was placed in the corner of the area with cushions underneath. Songbooks were added under the umbrella (see the resource list for songbooks at the end of this chapter). A garland of iridescent teardrop shapes was cut apart and the teardrops were hung from the ceiling on fishing line. Children made puddles and put them under the hanging "raindrops."

▶ Observation and Documentation Techniques

Documenting children's activities is extremely important. It gives the facilitator information about:

- the types of music enjoyed by the children;
- how children respond to music, songs, movement activities;

- what types of activities lead to spontaneous singing activities;
- what instruments are being used;
- how the instruments are being used;
- what skills the children are gaining; and
- what cultural interests are being expressed.

Figures 5.2, 5.3, and 5.4 show some appropriate charts that might be used to document children's musical activities.

Possible skills to observe:

- do the children demonstrate their understanding of the following musical elements? (Haines and Gerber, 2000; Pica, 2000; Isenberg and Jalongo, 2001);
- listening—discriminate among various sounds; sequence the rhythm of a song or phrase; sing a simple song or part of a song; length of time engaged in activity;
- **tempo**—the speed of the music (fast and slow);
- **pitch**—how high or low musical tones are;
- volume—how loud or soft a piece of music is or the variations of volume within a piece of music;
- **mood**—"a combination of musical elements that causes an emotional or affective response in listeners or performers" (Haines and Gerber, 2000, p. 14);

- **legato**—smooth flowing with no interruptions (most lullabies);
- **staccato**—punctuated music, choppy, interrupted (*Syncopated Clock*);
- **melody**—tones put together in a sequence, or repetition;

FIGURE 5.3

► List of Children's Favourite Songs and Activities

Favourite Songs/Pieces of Music	Child/Activity
Baby Beluga	Braelyn-book and Raffi song
	Reghan-listen to adult sing and show book
"Too Ra Loo Ra Loo Ra" (Musical Reflections)	Yasmine-moved scarf while listening to music

How to Use Information
- give families ideas of what their children enjoy—good gift ideas for birthdays and holidays, support music activities at home;
- research to provide alternative pieces that have similar elements;
- provide appropriate instruments to use with music; and
- provide appropriate props to use with music.

FIGURE 5.2

► Chart for Observation of Children's Interests

Name	Date	Interest	Evidence
Timmy	02/14 02/15	Do things himself	Took CD out of case, could not put it in player Opened CD player, put CD in, pushed start button
Josh	02/5	Rhythm instruments	Used rhythm sticks—tapping sticks together, walked while tapping sticks

Note: Keep space within the table to be able to add information on subsequent days.

How to Use Information
- adapt activities—the facilitator added a yellow sticker to the button to open the CD player, a green sticker to the start button, and a red sticker to stop the music, and explained the strategy individually to children; Timmy could operate the CD player himself;
- add materials to sustain activity—added tone blocks and small drums to music area; and
- incorporate activities into daily routines—clap to activity children are engaged in, clapping to each syllable: we are wal-king we are wal-king we are wal-king out-side.

FIGURE 5.4

► Skill Sample Chart

Name: Billy

Date	Skill	Evidence
04/22	Keeping steady beat	Used rhythm sticks to keep beat to "Listen to the Horses" from Raffi CD
04/24	March and keep beat	African drum CD-kept beat on drum and could march in time
04/25	Create rhythm patterns	Made up own pattern on bamboo drum, asked adult to listen and copy it
	Repeat rhythm pattern	Listened to and repeated rhythm pattern of slow, slow, fast, fast, slow

How to Use Information
- identify skills used in order to plan next step—copy beat from a simple song; clap rhythm of song to see if Billy can identify it; and
- play rhythm games—see figure 5.5.

FIGURE 5.5

▶ Rhythm Games

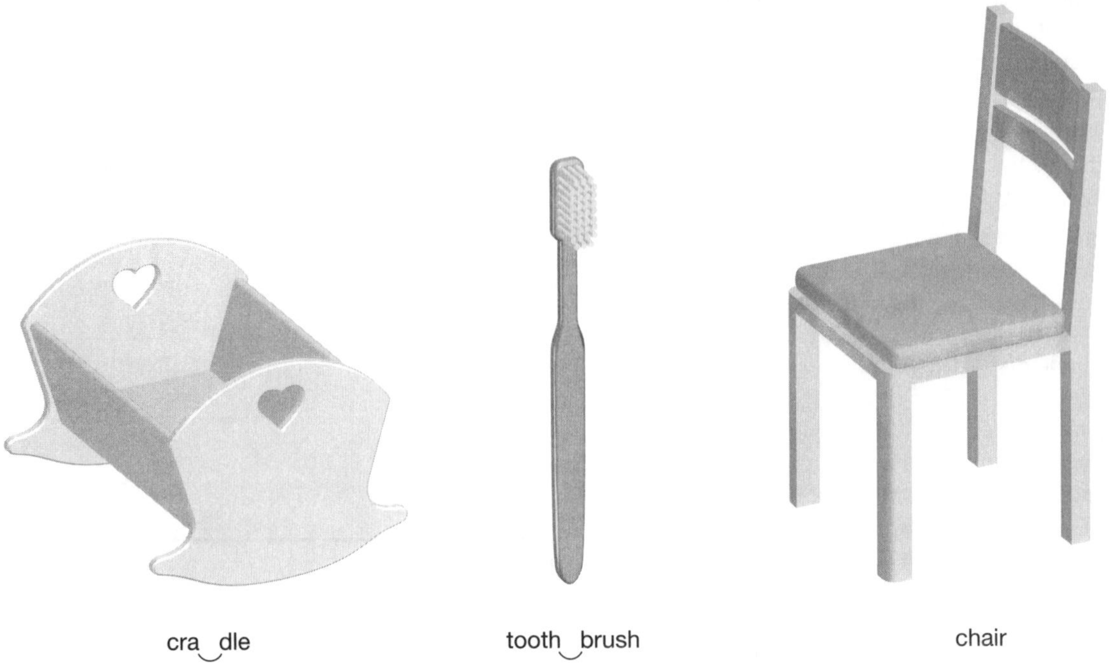

cra dle   tooth brush   chair

- phrases—breaking a song or musical piece into divisions to represent musical ideas;
- **rhythm**—grouping sounds, silences, and patterns together;
- **timbre**—unique quality of a musical instrument or voice;
- **harmony**—"a sequence of one or more changing or repeated tones added to the predominant melody line, to enrich or elaborate it" (Haines and Gerber, 2000, p. 15);
- dynamics—accent on tones and changes in volume—both gradual and sudden; and
- **form**—organization of song or piece of music into an overall design.

ATTENTION SPAN

Attention span is best measured by a **duration count,** how long a certain behaviour lasts. Using a graph is the easiest method (see figure 5.6). The *y*-axis of the graph records the time in minutes. The *x*-axis records the specific behaviour/activity observed. It is wise to record the behaviour as you see it. Additionally, you can record the type of play in the bar created. This gives you two pieces of information: new behaviours can be added above the first behaviour. For example, if you look at Braelyn's behaviour of

listening to "Baby Beluga," you will notice two bargraph indications, indicating that she first listened by herself for 25 minutes and then came back to the activity for a second time and listened in a small group for 10 minutes. When you have completed one day's observation, simply draw a vertical line and date it. This way, the tool can be used over time.

How to Use Information
- extend activities over longer time period; and
- choose longer pieces of music, songs.

▶ International Considerations

Music gives us a rare opportunity to encompass all aspects of diversity. Music exists in some form in every culture within our world. Children are naturally curious about the world around them: music gives them the opportunity to learn about different cultures, ideas, and values. "The malleable nature of the young child makes them particularly open to the development of attitudes and disposition of tolerance and understanding. Opportunities for these qualities to grow and flourish are found in music; music is a part of every world culture and a universal means of communication between individuals" (Haines and Gerber, 2000, p. 26).

FIGURE 5.6

▶ Attention Span, Type of Play

Name: Braelyn

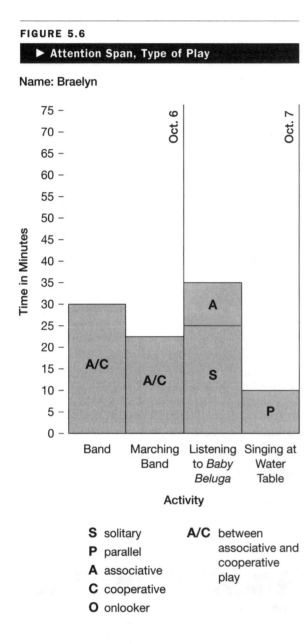

S solitary
P parallel
A associative
C cooperative
O onlooker

A/C between
associative and
cooperative
play

The Association for Prenatal and Perinatal Psychology and Health (AYRAM) encourages prenatal stimulation programs for expecting families. One such program in Mexico has been in operation for six years. The program offers stimulation through music. Long-term benefits have been ascribed through this type of intervention. "The AYRAM prenatal stimulation program is running since 6 years ago and the babies born in 1994, now in preschool (4 and 5 years old), distinguish themselves from others due to their easy way to socialize with other children, better understanding in some subjects, they learned to read and write without difficulty, their comprehension level is high. Their vocabulary is extensive and they

speak with the correct articulation, they can express themselves fluently" (De Leon, 2000, p. 80).

Aboriginals in the Alice Springs area of Australia use a rhythmic activity to increase their children's coordination and speed of response. The piece requires that the participants keep a steady beat with both hands on their knees. Once a steady beat has been established, the word *saba* is called out. This means that the beat changes to:

- a steady beat of three taps on the knees with both hands,
- a movement of both hands to the right in one beat,
- back to a steady beat of three taps on the knees with both hands,
- a movement of both hands to the left in one beat,
- a steady beat of three taps on the knees with both hands,
- back to a movement of the hands to the centre,
- a steady beat of three taps on the knees with both hands,
- movement of hands upward,
- a steady beat of three taps on the knees with both hands,
- clap three times to the steady beat,
- back to a steady beat on the knees.

At the next *saba* call, the beat changes to a faster beat with the same rhythm.

African American music also uses beat and rhythm. "A strong sense of beat and rhythm patterns, syncopations and call-response singing/canting, and work songs are characteristic of African American music appropriate to the music education of young children" (Haines and Gerber, 2000, p. 26). This is appropriate because the music is repetitive and rhythmic.

Table 5.2 summarizes some aspects of music from around the world. The listing is not complete, but does give an overview of the variety and usefulness of including music from other cultures.

▶ Music Materials

See table 5.3 for a discussion of some music-related skills, along with suggestions for possible music or instruments.

▶ Ages and Stages of Music

In table 5.4, stages are presented as they appear developmentally. However, all stages will be present throughout development. Adapted from Pica (2000, pp. 33–34) and Haines and Gerber (2000, pp. 5–8).

TABLE 5.2

▶ Music from around the World (Challis, 1985)

Origin	Example	Musical Aspects
West Indian	"Sweet Potatoes," p. 120	Repetitive, extends knowledge of agricultural society, different ways other cultures make animal sounds
Puerto Rican	"El Coqui" (The Tree Frog), p. 118	Simple words, soft melodic tune, knowledge of different animal life in other parts of the world
African American	"Who Did?", p. 85	Response song, repetitive, chant-like
Venezuelan	"With Twenty Pennies," p. 83	Repetitive, gain knowledge of names of animals and different types of animals
Canadian Native	"Land of The Silver Birch," p. 80	Melodic, learn about animals and plant life in Canada, easy to accompany refrain on drum
Jamaican	"Tingle Lay O," p. 58	Repetitive, easy melody, learn about a donkey
France	"Frère Jacques"	Simple tune, repetitive words, learn another language, can be sung in a round
Germany	"Susie Liebe Susie" from the opera Hansel and Gretel	Teaches empathy, easy melody
Colombian	"Dona Ana," p. 34	Utilizes simple dance, response song; awareness of what grows in a garden
English	"I'm a Little Teapot," p. 17	Descriptive of an object, easy melody, can be acted out
Irish	"This Old Man," p. 14	Combines easy rhythm with actions to support rhythm, easy words, humorous

TABLE 5.3

▶ Skills and Possible Materials

Skills	Possible Musical Instruments/Possible Music
Listening, timbre	Music used in Mexico to stimulate fetus—Vivaldi, Mozart, Handel, Teleman, Bach (De Leon, 2000, pp. 80–81);
	Infant—relax and soothe: *Heartbeat Pacifier*, lullabies; stimulate: *Baby Needs Mozart, Baby Needs Baroque, The Mozart Effect Music for Babies*, songs from around the world
	Toddlers—Countdown Kids, Raffi, singing nursery rhymes, simple songs about everyday routines, listening to adults play simple rhythms, *Mozart Effect Music for Children*, listening to individual instruments (guitar, flute, piano, saxophone, balalaika, zither, drums)
	Preschoolers—all of the above; musical books—*Peter and the Wolf, Baby Beluga*, "Little Fox," "Rain," "Itsy Bitsy Spider"; music of choice
	School-aged—music of choice, introduce to greater variety of types of music (opera, ballet, orchestral, pop, jazz, rap, country)

TABLE 5.3 SKILLS AND POSSIBLE MATERIALS (continued)

Skills	Possible Musical Instruments/Possible Music
Pitch, melody, harmony, form	Xylophones, pianos, keyboards, bells, tone blocks, boomwhackers, zither, recorders, chime bars, variety of songs—simple for younger children, increasing in complexity for older children; school-aged sing in harmony, rounds
Tempo, legato, staccato	Drums, shakers, triangles, tambourines, cymbals, wrist/ankle bells, rhythm sticks, castanets, tone blocks, sand blocks, rain sticks; various types of music, both instrumental and songs demonstrating tempo, legato, and staccato
Volume, dynamics, mood	All of the instruments and music above; Beethoven, *Pastoral Symphony, Reflections in Nature—Native Flutes, Fantasia, Peter and the Wolf*

TABLE 5.4

▶ Ages and Stages of Music

Stage	Age	Possible Behaviours
Prenatal		Detectable movement—kicking, poking, relaxing
Listening stage	Infants	Comforted by music
		Preference for melodic sounds
		Like soothing music to fall asleep to
		Listen to songs about everyday routines—diapering, feeding, bathing
		Find steady rhythms soothing, such as heartbeat, clock
		Turn eyes or head toward sound
		Turn body toward sound, wave hands, feet
Imitative	Infants/toddlers	Initiate or imitate body to respond to music
		Initiate or imitate voice to respond—hum, croon, single words, phrases, simple songs
		Respond to rhythmic movement initiated by self or adult—bounces, claps
		Imitate rhythms
		Have favourite songs, ask for many repetitions
		Can discriminate among different songs
		Enjoy making sounds with musical instruments or other objects in the environment
Experimental	Toddlers/preschoolers	Enjoy experimenting with sound—instruments and sound-making objects
		Regular beat established
		Sing familiar tunes—alone or in groups, not always in same pitch
		Create own words to songs or own melodies
		Use whole body to music—jump, run, tiptoe, walk
		Dramatize songs

TABLE 5.4 AGES AND STAGES OF MUSIC (continued)

Stage	Age	Possible Behaviours
Discovery	Preschool, school-aged	Reproduce sounds, tones, rhythmic patterns
		Greater vocal range
		Create new words to known songs
		Demonstrate understanding of tempo, volume, and pitch in singing and playing instruments
		Prefer active participation
		Enjoy silly or nonsense songs
		Reproduce melody
		Play instruments accurately
		Write and read music
		Enjoy greater variety of songs—group songs, response songs, silly songs
		Definite musical preference
		Coordinate two movements at same time—marching and keeping beat on instrument
Application	School-aged	Read music and lyrics
		Enjoy simple dances
		Harmonize—rounds, canons, simple two-part harmony
		Play an instrument
		Desire to study dance or a musical instrument
		Compare more than two sounds

▶ KEY POINTS

Developmental Levels of Music

Listening—react through eye contact, body movement;

Imitative—participates by imitating, sounds, rhythms, simple songs, and actions to music/songs;

Experimental—uses instruments to create various rhythms, uses whole body to respond to rhythm, tries new words, tones, and rhythms;

Discovery—uses learned concepts in new ways; learns new concepts (humour in music); and

Application—uses learned concepts to create music, play instruments, read music, use concepts for effect, sing in harmony.

Value of Music

- develop psychometric skills, kinesthetic/bodily skills, and perceptual skills;
- motivate to communicate;
- evoke emotional skills;
- encourage development of whole child—social, cognitive, emotional, language, physical;
- set mood;
- increase spatial intelligence;
- improve attention span, listening skills;
- develop aesthetic awareness; and
- is therapeutic.

Role of the Facilitator

- provide experiences and materials;
- model—singing, respect, playing instruments, listening;

► KEY POINTS (continued)

Role of the Facilitator (continued)

- create atmosphere to encourage musical activities;
- provide opportunity for active participation—singing, movement activities, creative activities;
- talk with children about aspects of music;
- observe and document children's interests and abilities;
- adapt and enhance music area as needed;
- be enthusiastic;
- provide balance of self-exploration and group exploration;
- ensure that cultural diversity is represented; and
- ensure musical activities occur inside and outside.

Storage of Musical Instruments

- model respect;
- aesthetically pleasing;
- match system of storage to type of instrument—all rhythm instruments together; and
- provide safe storage for instruments to prevent instruments from falling off shelf.

Labelling

- clear labels—pictures, photographs, and printed word.

Considerations for Setting Up a Music Area

- need for spill-out area;
- separation from quiet area;
- encourage independence;
- use of appropriate, selective portions of videos; and
- aesthetically pleasing.

Observational Techniques

- document in order to learn about—musical preferences, children's responses and activities, what instruments are used and how; skills acquired and cultural interests;
- charts, checklists, lists, duration counts; and
- skills to observe—listening, tempo, pitch, volume, mood, legato, staccato, melody, rhythm, timbre, harmony, dynamics, and form.

Student Activities

1. Observe a caregiver and infant under four months interacting in a musical activity. Describe the caregiver's techniques and the child's responses to those techniques.

2. What signals indicate that an individual is listening to music? Include a description of a non-verbal child and a verbal child.

3. What types of activities could you encourage for imitative play with musical instruments or singing?

4. Jeremy is sitting on the floor in the kitchen. He is watching his mother cook. She is mashing potatoes in a metal bowl. Jeremy crawls to the cupboard. He gets out a pan. He starts to bang the pan on the floor. His mother quickly takes the pan away, saying that this is too noisy. Jeremy starts to cry. How might you have handled this situation differently? What strategies and materials would you use?

5. Children are playing outside. Judy picks up a stick and starts to bang the fence. Jonathan notices her activity. He finds another stick and joins Judy. As the children play they notice that they can make different sounds when they hit different parts of the fence. What stage is this? Justify your answer. What other materials or experiences could you provide to encourage the children to continue with this activity?

6. What types of activity could you set up to encourage appreciation of different forms of music? In your discussion focus on cultural aspects, classical music, and singing.

7. Take any three of the musical skills listed in this chapter. Describe how you might set up the environment to encourage children at the application stage of development. Be sure to discuss setup, materials, storage, and labelling.

8. Observe three different ages of children involved in a similar music activity. Using a duration count, compare their attention spans. Were the attention spans what you would have expected? Why or why not?

9. Observe a group of preschoolers during a musical activity. What musical skills did you observe? Why do you think these skills were observed? What additional skills might have been included in the activity?

► References

Begly, S. (1996). Your Child's Brain. *Newsweek.* February 19, 1998.

Black, S. (1998, November/December). How Minds Grow with Music. *Early Childhood News.*

Campbell, D. (1995). *The Mozart Effect for Children.* New York, NY: HarperCollins Publishers Inc.

Challis, E. (1985). *Jumping, Laughing, & Resting.* New York, NY: Amsco Publications.

De Leon, Arcila M. (2000). AYRAM Prenatal Music Stimulation Program. In *Music within Every Child Conference Papers.* Kingston, ON: Queen's University, pp. 79–82.

Haines, J., & Gerber, L. (2000). *Leading Young Children to Music.* (6th ed.). Toronto, ON: Prentice Hall Canada.

Habermeyer, S. (1999). *Good Music, Brighter Children.* Rocklin, CA: Prima Publishing.

Henniger, M. (1999). *Teaching Young Children: An Introduction.* Upper Saddle River, NJ: Prentice Hall.

Hepper, P. (1991). The Musical Infant. *Irish Journal of Psychology.* Volume 12, 95–107.

Hoffman, S. (1999, May). Take Note. *Homemaker's.*

Honig, A. (1995, July). Singing with Infants and Toddlers. *Young Children.*

Isenberg, J., & Jalongo, M. (2001). *Creative Expression and Play in Early Childhood.* (3rd ed.). Toronto, ON: Prentice Hall Canada.

Jalongo, M., & Collins, M. (1985, January). Singing with Young Children: Folk Singing for Nonmusicians. *Young Children.*

Pica, R. (2000). *Experiences in Movement with Music, Activities, and Theory.* (2nd ed.). Scarborough, ON: Thomson Learning.

Rauscher, F. (1996, Sept./Oct.). The Power of Music. *Early Childhood News.*

Red Centre Dreaming. (2001). *Aboriginal Cultural Show.* Red Centre Resort, Alice Springs: Northern Territory, Australia. http://www.aurora-resorts.com.au.

Shelter, D. (1990). The Inquiry into Prenatal Musical Experience: A Report of the Eastman Project 1980–1987. In *Music and Child Development.* Wilson, F., & Roehmann, F. (Eds.). St. Louis, MO: MMB Music Inc.

Shipley, D. (2002). *Empowering Children: Play-Based Curriculum for Lifelong Learning.* (3rd ed.). Scarborough, ON: Nelson.

Silberg, J. (1990). *The I Can't Sing Book: For Grownups Who Can't Carry a Tune in a Paper Bag...But Want to Do Music with Young Children.* Beltsville, MD: Gryphon House.

Wendell, H. (2000). The Healing Power of Musical Play in Preschool. In *Music within Every Child Conference Papers.* pp. 79–82. Kingston, ON: Queen's University.

► Resources

CD Music

Baby's First Songs from around the World. (2000). St. Laurent, QC: Clair Entertainment Group Inc.

Baby Needs Baroque. (1998). Hollywood, CA: Delos International, Inc.

Baby Needs Mozart. (1998). Hollywood, CA: Delos International, Inc.

Campbell, D. (1997). *The Mozart Effect Music for Children* Volume 1. Pickering, ON: The Children's Group Inc.

Campbell, D. (1997). *The Mozart Effect Music for Children* Volume 2. Pickering, ON: The Children's Group Inc.

Campbell, D. (1998). *The Mozart Effect Music for Babies.* Pickering, ON: The Children's Group Inc.

Countdown Kids. (1998). *Twinkle Twinkle Little Star.* St. Laurent, QC: Madacy Entertainment Group, Inc.

Madacy. (1998). *All the best from Africa.* St. Laurent, QC: Madacy Entertainment Group, Inc.

Musical Reflections. (1999). *Lullabies Cherished Bedtime Classics.* Don Mills, ON: Musical Reflections.

Newbourne, A. (1992). *Native Flutes.* Don Mills, ON: Reflections of Nature.

Raffi. (1980). *Baby Beluga.* Willowdale, ON: Troubadour Records Limited.

Walker, T. (2000). *Heartbeat Pacifier.* Don Mills, ON.: Baby Reflections.

Songbooks

Frazee, M. (1999). *Hush Little Baby.* New York, NY: Harcourt Brace & Company.

Siomades, L. (1999). Honesdale, PA: Bell Books.

Spier, P. (1961). *The Fox.* New York, NY: Bantam Doubleday Dell Books for Young Readers.

Tyrrell, F. (1990). *The Huron Carol.* Toronto, ON: Key Porter Kids.

Warlow, A., & Chesterman, J. (1991). Aylesbury, Bucks: Ginn and Company Ltd.

Videos

Brazelton, T. (1985). *What Every Baby Knows.* Montreal, QC: Screencraft Video Inc.

Kidsongs. (1985). *A Day at Old MacDonald's Farm.* Warner Bros. Records.

Stomp. (1997). *Stomp Out Loud.* New York, NY: Yes/No Production Ltd.

Walt Disney. (1998). *Fantasia.* Burbank, CA: Buena Vista Home Video.

Webber, Andrew Lloyd. (1998). *Cats.* Markham, ON: Polygram Canada.

For the Facilitator

Warren, J., & Hopping Ekberg, M. (1985). *Piggyback Songs for Infant and Toddlers.* Everett, WA: Totline Press.

Warren, J., & Hopping Ekberg, M. (1984). *More Piggyback Songs.* Everett, WA: Totline Press.

Warren, J., and Hopping Ekberg, M. (1995). *More Piggyback Songs for School.* Everett, WA: Totline Press.

Weikart, P. (1997). *Movement Plus Rhymes, Songs & Singing Games.* (2nd ed.). Ypsilanti, MI: High/Scope Press.

Weikart, P. (1990). *Movement in Steady Beat.* Ypsilanti, MI: High/Scope Press.

CHAPTER 6

Block Play

For centuries blocks have been one of the best early learning materials for young children. The variety of shapes, colours, and textures of blocks are perfectly suited to young children who thrive on learning through their senses.

—Stephens, Block Adventures Build Creativity and Concepts through Block Play

Chapter Outline

▶ Block Play to Encourage Learning
▶ Child Development: Developmental Levels of Block Play
▶ Value of Block Play
▶ Role of the Facilitator
▶ Effective Storage Systems
▶ Effective Labelling Systems
▶ Considerations for Setting Up a Block Area

▶ Observation and Documentation Techniques
▶ International Considerations
▶ Block Materials
▶ Ages and Stages of Block Play
▶ Key Points
▶ Student Activities
▶ References

Learning Outcomes

After studying this chapter, the reader will:

1. Identify various levels of block play
2. Explain the value of block play
3. Discuss the role of the adult in the facilitation of block play
4. Identify and discuss various aspects of setting up a block area in indoor and outdoor environments—physical space, storage of blocks for children's use, and labelling
5. Identify and discuss how to observe and record various aspects of block play
6. Identify how to encourage block play outside

Interactive Learning Exercises

 Remember, the CD-ROM that came with this text contains interactive exercises that relate to the topics in this chapter, as well as other valuable resources.

► Block Play to Encourage Learning

Damon was working on building a dinosaur park with blocks. "I like blocks 'cause I can make lots of things. I can build a dinosaur park. I'm making the walls really, really high so the dinosaurs can't get out. Dinosaurs could eat us" (photo 6.1).

As Damon continued to build his dinosaur park, he was soon joined by other enthusiastic children offering varying degrees of help. The park continued to grow and change as the children increased the height of the walls "so's they can't get out and eat us"; added mountains and platforms inside the park "so the dinosaurs have something to do"; and provided hiding places for the smaller dinosaurs "so that they could hide from the Tyrannosaurus Rex" (photo 6.2).

Blocks are a wonderful medium to develop:

- social skills—Damon's play changed from solitary to associative play;
- language skills—spatial terms: *on, on top of,* children described actions and events;
- pre-measurement skills—using appropriate terminology: *height, higher*; and
- symbolic play—constructive play to make the park and dramatic play to act out animal roles.

Blocks are a wonderful medium to experiment with in order to create:

- patterns—making walls by placing blocks end to end;
- pretend settings—creation of the dinosaur park;
- structures using various types of blocks—unit blocks, cardboard bricks, hobbyhorses, planks, cardboard boxes;
- duplicates of existing structures—re-creation of walls and fences; and

- balanced structures—walls, platforms, mountains using blocks and accessories.

Blocks are a wonderful medium to provide opportunities to:

- practise building balanced structures, practise animal roles, cooperate with each other to build and role-play;
- see the results of one's actions—see the final creation, the dinosaur park; and
- observe cause and effect relationships—several children would build a structure that fell down. This built a realization of what needed to be done in order to build a more stable structure: If I place a block squarely on top of another block, I can build a higher structure. If I balance the blocks on top of each other in a haphazard way, the structure will fall.

► Child Development: Developmental Levels of Block Play

Children engaged in block play go through a variety of stages, which seem to be related to spatial relations (Reifel, 1984). "As children mature they make use of a wider range of spatial forms to represent their impressions of spatial configurations" (p. 62). These stages seem to be representative of various ages, but children will repeatedly use the skills of each stage to improve their ability to construct and build during

PHOTO 6.1

PHOTO 6.2

PHOTO 6.3

PHOTO 6.4

PHOTO 6.5

subsequent stages. This allows children to refine their skills, increase their ability to problem solve, and use the knowledge from each stage of development.

STAGE 1: CARRYING AND STACKING

Before children start to build with blocks, they tend to carry blocks around with them (photo 6.3). This stage usually occurs before the children are two years old. Children learn about the texture of the blocks, the weight of blocks, how many they can carry at one time, and how best to carry them (photos 6.4 and 6.5). As children get older, they will use these skills to transport blocks in more efficient ways.

STAGE 2: ROWS AND TOWERS

Children at this stage will start to either stack blocks vertically or build rows horizontally. Stacking blocks vertically is often accompanied by the pleasure of knocking these blocks down, only to build them up again. The child seems to delight in creating a stack of blocks, knocking it down, and repeating this action over and over again. Associated spatial terms that are learned during this type of play are *on* and *on top of*. The child also learns to position blocks more precisely to ensure that blocks either fall or are stable and to realize which size of block will be a better fit (photos 6.6 and 6.7).

PHOTO 6.6

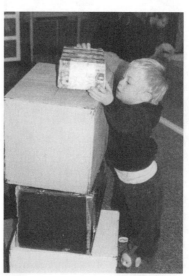

PHOTO 6.7

PHOTO 6.8

Horizontal rows may occur in long straight lines or in multiples of lines. Some associated spatial terms that are learned during this type of play are *beside, next to,* and *by.* The child also learns to position blocks precisely to create a pattern of appropriately sized and shaped blocks, which match to fit end to end or side by side (photo 6.8).

As children progress, these structures become much more elaborate and may involve intricate problem-solving techniques (photo 6.9).

The vertical structure shown in photo 6.9 was created in several steps. First, the children decided to use a table to create height for their structure. The table was too slippery, so it had to be covered. The children

PHOTO 6.9

started to stack various blocks on top of the table. They soon realized that they could no longer reach high enough to pile up more blocks. An active dialogue ensued; the children discussed various ideas. They decided to use blocks to stand on. The largest blocks available were painted cardboard boxes. One of the adults asked the children what might be a problem if these blocks were used. Another child identified that these blocks could break because they were "too flimsy." Eventually it was decided to use the hollow blocks to step on in order to reach. At this point the activity attracted more children. The suggestion was made to build a staircase to reach the top of the vertical stack. The children continued to build the structure. As the structure grew higher, the children were encouraged to discuss how their staircase might be better stabilized. It was decided to build a broader base. When the children again could not reach the top of the structure, they asked if they could get a ladder to reach the top. More adults had to be brought in to help. One adult supervised the child on the ladder; another adult handed the desired block to the child when the child was on the ladder to put it on top.

Since children in this program shared the space with other programs each day, the blocks could not be left out. As a result, the children asked to take a picture of their structure, so that they could build it again the next day. This play extended over many days.

The products of block play can be left standing over a period of time. This gives the children opportunities to:

- add on to their structures;
- change their structures;
- extend the play over longer periods of time;
- evolve to a project;
- respect the creations of other individuals; and
- become involved in dramatic play.

Before the children could be involved in this type of play, they needed to have a lot of experiences building rows and towers. They had to learn:

- how to create stable structures;
- that in order to build higher structures, they needed adults present to supervise;
- that higher structures were dangerous to knock down and this was not allowed;
- what types of blocks were safer to use in constructing higher structures; and
- how to cooperate with each other.

Children experiment with a variety of building techniques if the materials are available and if they are allowed to explore freely. In this kind of environment, vertical structures were built on a variety of surfaces, including narrow spots on tabletops, within

PHOTO 6.10

PHOTO 6.11

other block structures, and with a variety of objects. Liesl tried to balance a marker on top of a vertical stack of small blocks she had created and eventually succeeded (photo 6.10). She learned how to build within a confined space, how to create a balanced structure, and how to balance difficult objects. Liesl experienced self-satisfaction and increased self-confidence in her abilities.

Ashley built two vertical stacks simultaneously with both hands. She continued to repeat this type of play many times. Each time, she tried to build higher stacks. This type of building encourages the child to coordi-nate two actions at the same time (photo 6.11). As she practised, the height of her stacks steadily grew.

Stacking is not confined to blocks only. Children also experiment with other materials. They use other mate-rials to stack (photo 6.12) and to balance (photo 6.13).

Children also extended block play using rows and low towers to build and use obstacle courses (photo 6.14).

PHOTO 6.12

PHOTO 6.13

PHOTO 6.14

PHOTO 6.15

PHOTO 6.16

Children start to build structures that experiment with balancing various blocks on top of each other. Often this is more of a social situation. The two girls shown in photo 6.15 are involved in associative play, sharing ideas and materials but with each girl adding her own idea to the structure.

STAGE 3: WALLS AND BRIDGES

At this stage, children start to create structures that could be duplications of structures that they have seen. Structures may represent roadways or tracks. Accessories may be used, such as vehicles to travel over the created roadways or tracks and under the bridges. Various materials may be used (photos 6.16 and 6.17). As children progress in their skill, techniques become more refined. Many other materials may be used to create bridges (photo 6.18).

PHOTO 6.17

STAGE 4: ENCLOSURES AND PATTERNS

Enclosures have definite shapes and are often used as part of dramatic play. Children may build small enclosures for a specific purpose, such as areas that they can use to confine themselves in a space or to enclose some of the toys they are playing with. With practice, children become very skilled in creating stable structures (photo 6.19).

STAGE 5: REPRESENTATIONS AND REPRODUCTIONS

At this stage, the children use all of their skills and experiences from previous levels to create structures that represent real structures. Children name the structures that they have created.

PHOTO 6.18

PHOTO 6.19

PHOTO 6.20

Billy has created a structure that is a jail. He had made this structure previously, and asked the teacher to reproduce the structure on a plan. The following day he recreated the structure from the plan. He asked for help from the adults to identify that the structure was long enough. "It has to be longer than you." After an adult was lying on the ground beside the structure, he walked around carefully to make sure that the structure was long enough. This is a pre-measurement skill (photo 6.20).

This play extended into a dramatic play episode. Billy named his structure a jail. He crawled into the jail and asked to have the front of the jail blocked by two cardboard ladders. "They look like bars." He then proceeded to break out of jail. This play continued over several days. The structures built became more elaborate, and more children joined the activity both to help build the jail and to break out of the jail. Jails were built that were too tight for some people and collapsed when children tried to break out. This caused much hilarity among the children and had them build more jails repeatedly (photo 6.21).

Other Examples of Representational Building

As they build representational structures, children often become more involved in large group play. They learn to cooperate with each other, to listen to other ideas and viewpoints, to represent the real world through symbolic, often recognizable structures (see the church depicted in photo 6.22), and to use these representations to dramatize situations. Often structures start as one thing but change and become something else.

PHOTO 6.21

PHOTO 6.22

PHOTO 6.23

PHOTO 6.24

Tilli and Alexandria decided to build something. They helped each other gather the materials, deciding to use the long blocks. The girls discovered that these blocks were heavy: they needed two people to carry more than one block. They discovered that if they placed the blocks on the hobbyhorses, the blocks fit.

As their excitement about their discovery mounted, other children noticed the activity and joined in. The girls built a platform to sit on (photos 6.23 and 6.24).

When they had completed the structure, they decided that this structure was a bus. Most of the children joined the activity at this point. Everyone wanted to get on the bus and travel to McDonald's to buy a "Great Big Mac" (photo 6.25).

Although additional props might encourage dramatic play, they are not always necessary. Children represent actions and materials through gestures and sound (photo 6.26).

PHOTO 6.25

PHOTO 6.26

PHOTO 6.27

PHOTO 6.28

PHOTO 6.29

Presenting children with accessories and additional materials may encourage alternative activities and challenges. Providing string and yarn encouraged a group of children to build a spider's web around the hobbyhorses (photo 6.27). A simple box and construction hat encouraged another child to use these items as a truck. The child made the driving motions and sounds of a truck (photo 6.28). Placing tires and larger boards in the block area encouraged this child to try to balance first the two tires and then the long board. He was successful in his attempt (photo 6.29).

Blocks may be used in other areas. For example, some children were building a marble maze. They had created the structure on top of a table. As the structure grew in height, it became difficult for most of the children to reach the top. Children were asked to solve the problem of how to reach the top level. Suggestions were to ask an adult to drop the marble for them, or to ask an adult to lift them up to reach. Both solutions did not satisfy the children for long. One child suggested that they could stand on a chair, and another child suggested that they could use blocks. The children cooperated to build steps with the hollow blocks so that they could reach. Children continued to build an elaborate platform that reached from the block storage area to the marble structure (photo 6.30).

▶ Value of Block Play

Block play provides children with many varied experiences. They learn to:

- problem solve—Tilli and Alexandria found that the blocks were too heavy to carry; they solved the problem by carrying the blocks together;
- develop awareness of spatial terminology and perception of space—*under, over, on, on top of, beside, in*;

PHOTO 6.30

- develop concepts of size—*large, small, long, short, tall*;
- match and sort according to size, shape, colour, weight, type;
- use language associated with block play—as the children built the dinosaur zoo, they used terms such as *making walls, fences, platforms*, and *mountains*;
- socialize with peers—during the "jail break," Billy entertained the other children by talking about what he was doing and by acting out his jail break; and
- cooperate with peers—when the children built the bus, they shared materials and ideas; they helped each other build the structures and they participated in role-playing their trip to McDonald's.

Children also practise skills of:

- balancing and stabilizing—the platforms of the bus so they could sit on it, the staircase to climb on to build higher; and
- recall, to remember and recreate structures—dinosaur park, jail, bus.

Children become involved in **symbolic play** by:

- creating structures with materials provided that represent real structures—jail, bus, park; and
- using objects to represent other objects—Billy used the cardboard ladder as the door of his jail.

▶ Role of the Facilitator

The facilitator continually struggles with knowing when to step in and when to let the play continue without interference. The following are some guidelines that help the facilitator make that decision.

The facilitator should observe and always step in when:

- the play becomes harmful either to the child or to other children—Guidance was needed to ensure the safety of the children as they built their high structure. The children needed the adult to identify that sturdier blocks were needed to support their weight as they built steps to climb to extend the height of their structure.
- the play becomes destructive of the materials or equipment—Since the block play was within an environment that included children with developmental delays and toddlers, the adults in the program had to ensure that children's structures were respected. Adults need to become involved in the block play either at a passive level (positioning themselves within the block play area and using appropriate facial expressions and body language

to indicate an interest in what the children are doing) or by more active participation (offering comments and suggestions, becoming involved in the block play, labelling actions, feelings, and block types). In this way, it is easy for the adult to anticipate and redirect actions of children.

- the children ask for help, or it seems evident that they need help—When the children could no longer reach the top of the structure they had created, an adult helped to solve the problem by providing a ladder and supervision of children using the ladder. A second adult was also needed to ensure the safety of the children.
- arguments among children erupt—When the children were actively involved in discussing how to build their structure higher, the adult realized that this discussion should be monitored. She quietly offered a suggestion by directing the children's attention to a potential problem—"What might happen if you use the cardboard block?" In this way she prevented a possible dangerous situation, helped children solve their own problem, and defused a possible argument.
- the noise level starts to escalate—A technique that often is very effective is to play soft background music to mask abrasive sounds (lights, heating). It was found in the curriculum lab that the noise level dropped almost immediately after the music was played. (See table 5.2 for a listing of appropriate music.) A second technique that works very well is to walk over to the noisy area and start to interact with the children in a soft voice. This forces the children to listen to what the adult is saying and therefore the noise level automatically drops.
- children exhibit signs of stress—raised voices, tense body language, tears. For example, when Billy realized that he had to take down his "jail," he burst into tears. The adult suggested drawing a blueprint of his jail so that he could build it again. This calmed him immediately.
- opportunities to extend the play occur—extending play over more than one day (by drawing a blueprint of the jail), extending play by providing alternate materials (a ladder), extending play by offering suggestions (how to reach the top of the marble structure), becoming involved in the play (lying down beside the structure to be measured), and by providing alternative materials (tires, planks).
- children interfere with each other's creativity—Providing close supervision of children of various ages and abilities and by ensuring that the block area is large enough to accommodate the needs of

the children and has enough materials to support their creative efforts.

- children seem to flit from activity to activity—Observing the children to see if anyone needs to be directed into the activity or away from the activity. Jenna would often be attracted to what was happening in the block area. Sometimes she would be quite content to just watch. Other times she would join in. It is important for the facilitator to allow the child to decide. If Jenna continued to move from area to area, then the facilitator might try to redirect her.

The facilitator should observe without interference when:

- children are gainfully employed—dinosaur park, platform;
- children are interacting with each other and the materials and equipment provided—cooperation between Tilli and Alexandria in carrying the blocks and starting the platform;
- children are solving their own problems—Ashley using both hands to build with, Liesl stacking small blocks vertically;
- play extends over a longer period of time—"jail break"; and
- when materials and equipment are used appropriately—dinosaur park, stacking activities.

Facilitators should focus on making the learning experience and environment positive for all children. Careful observation and documentation of children's interactions, the types of materials used, the type of play occurring, and the skills children are using help the facilitator expand the children's play.

1. Using Open-ended Questions

When the children used the marble game to create structures that eventually they could not reach, the facilitator noticed the problem and led the children through a process of guided questions:

Christopher: "I noticed that you have a problem."

Dakota: "Mmm, I can't bend high enough."

Christopher: "What could I do to help you reach?"

Dakota: "You could drop it."

Christopher complied. Dakota continued with this strategy for a few trials and then indicated that he could not see the marble move down the ramps. Hannah asked if the facilitator could lift Dakota up to reach and watch the marble. This strategy was also tried. Benjamin joined the activity. He thought that he could stand on a chair to reach. This proved to be unsuccessful; the chair was not tall enough. Jonathon

had joined the activity—he suggested that a block might work. Each of the children went to get a hollow block. They placed them in front of the table in a horizontal row. This strategy again failed: the children realized that it still was not high enough. Christopher asked, "How could you make the structure higher so that you can reach?" "We could stack the blocks on top of each other." The children stacked the three blocks on top of each other. A new problem presented itself: now the children found that they could not climb on top of the structure, as it was too high to step up on. Jeremy joined the group and said, "We could build steps." All four children built steps. This strategy worked. The children could climb the steps and reach the top of the structure to drop their marbles.

2. Providing Dialogue to Encourage Spatial Awareness

Blocks are a natural medium for spatial exploration. Facilitators need to be aware of what the children are doing in order to help them become aware of the space around them and of where they are within that space. One technique that can be used involves descriptive dialogue: describe the child's actions, structures made, how the structure is changing, the types of materials used, and the skills developed. For example, Colin used two tires and a two-by-four to build with. He worked on trying to balance the two tires so that they would be "tall." As he was struggling with the weight of the tire, the facilitator, Sarah, offered her help. "The tire seems to be very heavy. Do you need some help?" Colin declined. As Sarah observed, she continued to comment on what Colin was doing. She offered new vocabulary to him. "You have balanced one tire within the other tire. The tire is standing, without falling." As Colin tried to move the tire within the other tire, she said, "That tire seems to be very stable. It is hard to make it fall." Next Colin placed the two-by-four on top of the tire. This was a more difficult task, and it took many trials. When he was successful, Sarah commented "The two-by-four was centred on the tire. One end is as long as the other end and it is in the middle of the tire." Colin walked around the structure looking at it from each end. Finally he nodded.

3. Increasing Awareness of Size

As the children were building steps to help them reach the top of the marble structure, they gained an understanding of size. They discussed terms such as *too high, too low, not high enough,* and *not wide enough.* Christopher was there to model the correct terms and to clarify meaning. For example, one of the children tried to tell the other child that the steps needed to be wider. She kept repeating, "No, no, we have to do this," stretching out her arms to indicate width. Christopher asked her if she meant that the steps had to be wider. She nodded her head.

4. Providing Materials that Allow for Matching and Sorting

As Josh was building a horizontal structure, he carefully found and used only the shoeboxes that had been covered in white paper. He sorted through the pile of blocks and used only these blocks from a variety of other blocks. When he could not reach the blocks he wanted, he used a wooden block to step on.

Sarah and Jessica searched through the blocks until they found four matching arches. They held the arches against each other to see if they were the same. Then they built an enclosure for their dinosaurs.

5. Modelling Appropriate Language

As Chelsea and Nikki are building an enclosure large enough for the two of them to fit into, Nikki is providing such words as *upright, on its side, side by side,* and *on top of.* Eventually the walls became so high that Chelsea could stand up inside and not be seen. Phrases such as *you disappeared, the wall is taller than you,* and *you are shorter than the wall* were used.

6. Providing Opportunities for Socialization

Sarah noticed that Damon was sitting by himself, looking around at the other children. This was unusual behaviour for Damon. Sarah walked over to Damon, smiling at him. As she got closer, Damon smiled and asked Sarah to help him make a dinosaur park. The facilitator helped Damon by following his lead. As the block structure grew larger, more children joined in the play. Sarah stepped back and continued to observe the play.

Damon was initially involved in solitary play (play by himself) building his dinosaur park. As the structure grew in size, other children were attracted. Jason started to add on to the structure at one end. He used similar materials, but did not exchange materials or ideas with Damon. He was involved in parallel play (play beside one another without interaction). Shanleigh and Autumn joined the play. They asked Damon what he was doing. He said, "Making a dinosaur park. You want to help?" The girls nodded. They helped make the walls higher, bring new dinosaurs to the area, and eventually act out the roles of the dinosaurs. During this time, an active dialogue continued.

Shanleigh said, "Look how high my wall is." Autumn glanced over toward Shanleigh and said, as she continued to build a wall, "Mine too!" Damon said, "My dinosaur is climbing the mountain." Autumn looked over and said, "I'm going to jump over the wall." As each child offered his or her ideas, the others may have looked over and shared ideas or comments, but each child continued to do his or her own thing. This is associative play.

7. Providing Opportunities to Cooperate with Others

Alexandria and Tilli were creating a platform to make a bus. The girls worked together to solve problems of

- length—which blocks would be long enough to fit across the central beam of the hobbyhorse;
- thickness—how thick to make the platform;
- stability—how to make it stable so that you can sit on it; and
- increasing length—how to make it longer, so that more children could sit on it.

Sarah watched the play and offered comments as needed. She also provided language to support the building: "I notice that the long rectangular blocks seem to fit."

8. Providing Materials/Ideas to Extend Learning

Billy was building a jail. He had spent more than an hour creating his structure. When it was time for him to leave to go home, he was very upset that the structure would be put away. Sarah asked Billy what could be done to help him remember his structure. He thought it over and replied, "You could make a map like you did of the flower garden for Danielle in the sand. Then I could use the map to make my jail again next week." Sarah asked Billy to get the necessary items to make the map. As she drew a picture of the structure, Billy counted the blocks so that she could make it accurate. He also added some colour to his map to help him remember the blocks he had used. When Billy returned the next week, he asked for his map and proceeded to build his jail again from the plan in his hand.

9. Providing a Variety of Materials

Creativity is enhanced when children are encouraged to use materials in a variety of ways. Blocks do not need to always be made of wood. The long tubes found in the centre of carpet rolls can become smoke stacks, telescopes, or tunnels for cars. Cardboard boxes of various sizes may be used as building blocks or become a vehicle to drive. Blankets and sheets may be used to create ceilings or provide non-slip surfaces. By providing children with a variety of materials to build with one is increasing their desire to build—

both boys and girls play actively in the block area, increasing their creativity and their ability to solve problems together.

10. Providing Opportunities to Recognize the Value of Block Play

Sarah provided many opportunities to show children the value of what they are doing. This was done through:

- showing approval at various stages of the play—Sarah describing Colin's efforts and recognizing his need to solve the problem by himself;
- offering opportunities to share experiences—Tilli and Alexandria needed more space in the block area to build their bus and to accommodate a greater number of children. Sarah quickly moved some of the small tables to create more room;
- taking photographs of the various stages of the play;
- creating displays of children's efforts—photographs and blueprints are attractively mounted and displayed in the block area at the child's level;
- encouraging the process, not the product—responding to what the children were doing (Damon told Sarah what to build in the dinosaur park);
- providing help and support when needed—Sarah noticing that Damon seemed to need attention;
- providing opportunities to extend learning—jail break, building steps to create higher structures;
- knowing when to intervene and when to leave children alone—building with Damon until other children joined him and then stepping back; and
- sharing in the excitement of children's accomplishments, labelling the efforts—Colin's balancing efforts.

▶ Effective Storage Systems

Blocks should be stored together by type; for example, wooden blocks, cardboard blocks, foam blocks. A second level of organization could be by size, shape, colour, or combination of size, shape, or colour. Examples of this might be placing all the ramps together, or placing coloured cardboard brick blocks together by size and colour (for example, the long red cardboard bricks together and the short red cardboard bricks together).

It is important to place blocks together to:

- encourage children to find the block needed;
- encourage development of visual figure–ground skills;
- encourage children to recognize similarities and differences;
- encourage children to visualize various ways to organize information;
- provide children with opportunities to organize their thoughts; and
- provide skill in matching and sorting.

1. **Encourage children to find the block needed.** Small foam blocks of various sizes and shapes were stored in five different-sized wooden containers. Jordan took one of the containers and dumped it on the floor. He started to stack the red foam blocks horizontally. When he had stacked five red rectangular blocks, he could not find any more red blocks. He got another container and dumped it on the ground. He searched through the blocks, but failed to find another block of the same size and shape. Jordan decided to leave the area.

A valuable learning experience for Jordan was lost and less valuable learning has occurred. He had started the process of **matching** and **sorting** by size and by shape. When he could not find any more items, he left all the blocks he had dumped on the floor. He missed an opportunity to continue to build a structure that would become progressively more challenging to balance and that would sustain his interest over a longer period of time. He missed the opportunity to further refine his matching/sorting skills by returning the blocks into a defined storage system. Additionally, Jordan has learned that it is appropriate to dump items and to leave a learning area before putting his materials away. These conclusions were reinforced by Jordan's later actions: he went to the sand area, took out all the pails, and used the last pail he found to fill and empty. Then he left the area.

How might these blocks have been stored more effectively? The same wooden containers could have been used to store the blocks. Each container should have been labelled, by picture and by word, with what the child could expect to find in it. The following systems of organization could be used:

- by same size, shape, and colour; for example, all the red rectangular blocks in one container—This is the easiest organization for a group of children who are at various stages of development. This type of organization is appropriate if children are building structures that use a variety of sizes, shapes, and colours. It encourages children to quickly find the particular block they need to use next. It encourages children who are at stage two (rows and towers) to concentrate on the skill needed (stacking). Cleanup reinforces the skills of sorting and matching. Children are more likely to pattern using this type of organization: for example, structures with a pattern of red, blue, red, blue

- by shape or colour or size; for example, all the rectangular or red or small shapes in one container—This type of organization is appropriate for children who have mastered the skills of matching and sorting and are more than likely at the representational stage of block building. These children are more likely to search for a particular size or shape to complete their structure.

2. **Encourage development of visual figure-ground skills.** "The **figure–ground** relationship is the principle by which we organize the perceptual field into stimuli that stand out (figure) and those that are left over (ground)" (Santrock, 1994, p. E–25). By arranging blocks appropriately, it encourages the child to visualize different components of the perceptual field. Each organization used encourages the child to pick out the relevant stimuli—colour, size, or shape. For example, organizing blocks by shape encourages the child to pick out the specific shape (figure) from a variety of other shapes (ground). Organizing the blocks by colour encourages the child to pick out red (figure) from a variety of other colours (ground).

3. **Encourage children to recognize similarities and differences.** Children match and sort by using distinctive features. Distinctive features "are characteristics of a set of similar things ... that make that set different from other sets" (Schickedanz et al., 1993, p. 356). Distinctive features of blocks contain the following: roundness, squareness, corners, straight lines (diagonal, horizontal, vertical), curved lines, open curves, closed curves, and flatness. "A lot of learning requires that we form categories of things that are similar. We can't cope with a world full of separate and unrelated things; we make the world more manageable by lumping similar things together and responding to them as group" (Schickedanz et al., 1993, p. 357).

By organizing the blocks by similar distinctive features, we help the child to make the connections. We allow the child to associate like groupings. This, according to Piaget, allows for a process of learning that includes *assimilation* and *accommodation*. The young child matches and sorts blocks based on his or her experiences with blocks. As the child uses a greater variety of blocks, he or she assimilates new knowledge about these blocks. For example, the child has used the small unit blocks (cubed and rectangular) to create rows and towers. New blocks have been added, cylindrical blocks. The child has already formed knowledge about blocks—blocks have straight lines and corners, can be stacked, and are long or short. By adding new blocks, the child has to add new knowledge about blocks: blocks may also have curved sides and can be stacked in only one way. This process is called **assimilation**. The child will start to recognize that blocks include items that may have both curves and straight lines. This process is called **accommodation**. By storing blocks by type or similarity, we provide the child with visual organizations that help the child make the connections—assimilate and accommodate new learning.

4. **Encourage children to visualize various ways to organize information.** Blocks may be stored in various ways:
   - according to size and shape—for example, on shelves; all the long rectangular blocks could be stacked together;
   - by weight and shape—all the rectangular hollow blocks stacked together;
   - by colour—for example, all the red cardboard blocks together;
   - by type—all cylindrical blocks in one container.

   This allows the child to assimilate and accommodate various systems of organizing information.

5. **Provide children with opportunities to organize their thoughts.** As children see and use various organizations of blocks, it allows them to form mental representations. Mental representations may be defined as mental pictures that allow children to make sense of their world by thinking about it but without actual interactions. In other words, children will start to make the connections among various types of blocks and between the similarities and differences among blocks. They will be able to use this information to build, without the need to experiment with the materials at hand. The child can build various types of towers using various materials—cubed, cylindrical, or rectangular—based on past experiences. In an appropriate storage system, the child can find the block readily. Children who need to search for particular pieces may easily forget what they had been doing or become frustrated and switch to another activity.

6. Provide skill in matching and sorting. Matching and sorting skills lead to classification skills. Matching involves the ability to identify that one object matches with another object that is the same. In the initial stages, the young child learns to match individual blocks when stacking blocks. Blocks that are exactly the same tend to be easier and more effective to stack or line up. As the child gets older, the ability to recognize that objects may be both similar and different emerges. The child can now recognize not only that the rectangular long block is the same as the rectangular short block because each block has six surfaces, eight corners, and 12 straight lines, but also that it is different because the two blocks are different lengths. This later concept starts in the preschool years, but is not perfected until the child has mastered other skills such as counting and comparison.

Blocks need to be organized to provide children with opportunities to practise the skills of matching and sorting during retrieval and return of blocks. As the child is involved in any stage of construction with blocks, there are a variety of specific blocks that will best meet the particular needs of that moment. It may be that the block needs to be of the appropriate size and shape to fit into a current structure, or that the block or blocks may be the right size and weight to be transported physically or with physical aid from one place to another, or that a specific colour or shape is most desirable for the completion of a particular idea or project. Whatever the need, the primary consideration needs to be that the child is able to find or return the item. Children who are searching quickly lose the concept of what they are doing and change to a different concept. This not only disrupts the thought process, but also it leads to a shortened attention span as the child flits from one concept to another. For example, Taylor was building fences in the sandbox to enclose the zoo animals. She ran out of the rectangular blocks she had been using. Subsequently, she switched to cylindrical blocks. After placing three blocks in a fence-like pattern, she started to place the cylindrical blocks on top of each other. She quickly switched from building an enclosure for animals to building towers. As she ran out of cylindrical blocks, she switched to creating a circle with the semi-circular blocks. Although each activity has merit, the end result was that there was a continual refocusing of energy. Rather than encouraging sustained focus on one task, there was encour-agement to shift attention from one task to another.

Sorting is the same skill as matching but uses a greater number of objects. The child may match two objects that are exactly the same, but will sort when the child continues to match objects that are the same to stack blocks in a tower. Storing blocks by type or similarity is a sorting activity.

▶ Effective Labelling Systems

Any storage system will be effective only if all members—adults and children—know where blocks need to be stored. Additionally, providing appropriate labelling systems encourages children to:

- become more independent, find and return materials more readily;
- use the cleanup activity as a learning activity; and
- recognize the connections between symbols and the real thing, blocks.

Various methods may be used. Any method is effective as long as the system clearly identifies where the blocks belong and block cleanup does not become more involved than block play. If cleanup activities last longer than the actual block play, the system needs to be revised. All types of labelling should include pictures/outlines and words. Words allow children to make the connections between the written label, picture, and real object and model the importance of reading and writing.

APPROPRIATE LABELLING SYSTEMS

- provide a shadow of the outline of each of the various types of blocks;
- provide a picture and word association of each of the types of blocks;
- utilize pictures of the children involved with the block type in building activities; and/or
- provide photographs of the various blocks.

APPROPRIATE STORAGE SYSTEMS

1. Large Blocks
- provide open shelves to store blocks; or
- stack these blocks within a clearly marked area on the floor. This area should provide information on how high the blocks may be stacked and where on the floor they may be placed. This can easily be done using tape. Create a taped area on the floor and on the wall to indicate where blocks might be placed.

2. Small Blocks

As these blocks are not as heavy, more variety in storage can be used. Each method also needs to have a label and a picture in the area that these are stored in. Because the blocks tend to be small, it is easier to store these in containers that can be transported to various locations, and cleanup activities become less tedious:

- small bags with outlines and words of the block types per bag—these bags can then be hung on hooks and children can carry these bags to the location needed;
- small containers labelled with outlines, pictures, or photographs and words—these containers may easily be created from large plastic bottles that have been cut down and the cut edge sanded.

▶ Considerations for Setting Up a Block Area

1. Location

Consideration for setting up the block area follows the same principles whether or not block play occurs inside or outside:

- Effective block play needs to have a large area with room for spill-out. Children's block play often extends to very large areas, especially when they are creating horizontal structures.
- The area should have an absorbent surface to reduce the noise of the blocks. Rugs with a low pile and foam floorings could be used. It is important that the flooring be firm, to allow for better stability of the structures built. Outside, it is not as critical to be concerned about noise. Any paved or smooth area is ideal for block play.
- The block area should be out of the main traffic area, to avoid accidents.
- It is helpful to confine the block area on at least two sides. Corners of a room are excellent spots. Outside this could be accomplished by using walls or fences.
- Blocks should be easily accessible (see storage section previously discussed).

2. Number of Blocks

- The number of blocks that should be available for children varies with the age and the experiences that the child has had with block play.
- Clear guidelines for the number of blocks that need to be available for children vary. According to

Warren (1987), it is suggested that the number of blocks should be dependent on the experience children have with blocks and should be more concerned with sets of various blocks. The recommendations developed for the Board of Education for the City of North York (p. 8) were as follows:

a) Early Experiences—1 set of large hollow blocks, 1 set of unit blocks, and 1 set of **table-top blocks** (plastic cubes, coloured building blocks, integrated block systems) and **poleidoblocks**—cubes, cuboids, cylinders, triangles, prisms, cones, pyramids—in red, green, blue, yellow

b) Later Experiences—1 set of large hollow blocks, 1 set of unit blocks, and 3 sets of table-top blocks.

3. Display

Two factors become important in the display of children's block play—inspiration for the children to become involved in block play, and display of their efforts.

- **Inspiration**—A variety of techniques may be used. These may include photographs of real structures within the children's environments, such as churches and other known buildings; pictures of various structures that children have expressed an interest in, such as traffic ramps, barns, marinas; field trips to construction sites; display of related books; architectural drawings; drawings created by children; and pictures of various building stages such as fenced-in areas for enclosures, or bridges in the community. These might be displayed on a low bulletin board or wall in the block play area.
- **Display of Children's Work**—It is often a problem to display block play as it takes up a great deal of room or may be in a space that is shared by other children. Some suggestions are photographing or videotaping the various stages of block play; making symbolic representations of the play, such as diagrams created by the children or the facilitator; graphing the height or length of the structures; compiling verbal descriptions that the children dictate to a **scribe** and then may wish to illustrate; creating models using smaller blocks to recreate what has been done; leaving the block play up and allowing children both in the same group or different groups to add on to the structure or change it over time.

4. Accessories

Block play also needs to include a number of accessories to augment not only block play but also play with the structures that have been built. Some suggestions for accessories include:

- types of accessories—vehicles (community helpers, transportation, leisure); figures of multi-ethnic family life; animals (dinosaurs, zoo, domestic, farm, wild); community helper figures and vehicles; trains and train tracks; interlocking road systems; plant life (trees, shrubs, flowers); writing materials (crayons, markers, paper, scissors, masking tape to create own accessories); related signs (traffic signs, building signs); found materials (branches, pine cones, pebbles, stones); dress-up clothes (hats, work clothes); and
- storage of accessories—should be by type in clearly labelled containers, by pictures and words for smaller pieces and logical storage for larger pieces (for example, construction vehicles in parking lots outlined on the floor).

5. Respect for Safety

Rules should be few and concerned only with the safety of the children. Often rules are developed for the convenience of the adults for cleanup purposes or convenience and have nothing to do with the child's ability. For example, rules that limit the play to a set number of children do not take into account that a primary learning activity in block play is social play. By limiting the number of children, one automatically limits the types of social play possible and the real opportunities to encourage larger groups of children to play together and to solve their own problems. Some appropriate rules that might be set are that:

- blocks we do not need are put away;
- a "Do Not Disturb" sign can be used to discourage destruction of structures;
- building beyond a certain height requires supervision;
- buildings that are "taller than myself" need to use stable structures (a skill that very young children can learn); and
- tall structures must be limited to certain types of blocks—cardboard blocks, foam blocks, small unit blocks.

▶ Observation and Documentation Techniques

Observation and documentation of block play is most important in order to:

- build on the children's interests;
- provide appropriate materials to expand play;

- acknowledge developmental levels of individual children;
- make adjustments and/or changes as needed;
- recognize emergent skills of children; and
- share the accomplishments of the children with families and other professionals.

Documentation of block play can take on a variety of methods:

1. **Photographs**—This is an excellent way to document the various structures the child has built and to interpret the various skills used (photo 6.31). Interpretation: Emily started to use the quarter-circle wooden blocks. She discovered that two pieces fit together. She called it "half-a-circle." She went to the block shelf and found the other two quarter pieces to complete her circle. She indicated that she had "a whole circle." Emily created what she called "a-half-a-stand-up-circle" using the cylindrical blocks. Emily has mastered the concepts of part and whole and seems to have an understanding of part and whole relationships—half and whole. This type of documentation not only provides valuable clues to the child's abilities, but also can be used effectively to create displays for families and children.

2. **Block Play Portfolios** that use diagrams, photographs, and verbal descriptions of the children's block play could be developed for individual children or as a group book of the variety of play children are involved with. The section on levels of block play (see pp. 114–121) was part of our block play portfolio in the Loyalist College Curriculum Lab Preschool, which is a licensed preschool program that facilitates the

PHOTO 6.31

curriculum training for early childhood educators. Children and families could borrow this portfolio at any time. It was a very popular venture. An example of a diagram and an example of a child's descriptions of building structures (which are also part of the portfolio) are provided below.

Ben's Description of His Insect Tower

I used 15 large cardboard boxes to make steps. I put the horses around the steps to keep others out! I had to use the wooden blocks to make steps to make the tower high. I put the insects on the blocks. I asked Ingrid to make a diagram, so I could make it again next week.

3. **Checklists** may be used to identify levels of block play and/or skills children have used.

SAMPLE CHECKLISTS

Figures 6.1 through 6.4 provide examples of completed block play checklists. Note that the checklist shown in figure 6.1 could also be used to gather information for a group of children, and the checklist shown in figure 6.3 could also be used to develop an idea of the variety of levels of block play children engage in.

FIGURE 6.1

▶ Levels of Block Play Checklist

Name: Jacob

Level	Evidence	Date	Interpretation
Level 2– Rows and Towers	Stacked up to five cuboids blue and pink blocks, knocked them down, repeated activity six times	04/22 repeated same of activity 04/23	Age appropriate Repetitive stage play

How to Use Information
- provide facilitation of the activity with Jacob to see if the height of the structure could be increased;
- facilitate a small-group activity to build and knock down with Jacob, Jason, and Jordan, who are at similar stages of block play;
- to provide alternate materials that may be stacked and knocked down; and
- to share information with Jacob's mother, who has indicated an interest in expanding similar learning activities at home.

FIGURE 6.2

▶ Levels of Block Play Checklist for Multiple Children

Levels of Block Play, Dates, and Evidence

Names	Carrying Blocks	Rows and Towers	Walls and Bridging	Enclosures and Patterns	Representations and Reproductions
Jamie			05/03 Two rectangular blocks to make bridge to drive small car under		
Lindsay	05/03 Transported small unit blocks in wheel-barrow to build with Jamie	05/03 Created road of small rectangular blocks for Jamie to drive cars on			

How to Use Information
- identify age and/or developmental appropriateness of each activity with each child;
- expand the two children's play by providing alternative materials to transport blocks and build bridges and roadways;
- add pictures and books that involve transporting building materials and constructing bridges and roads;
- plan a field trip to a local construction site; and
- increase spatial awareness to add detail to structures—windows, doors.

FIGURE 6.3

▶ Variety of Block Play Checklist

Dates: 05/05, 05/06, 05/07

Names	Carrying Blocks	Rows and Towers	Walls and Bridging	Enclosures and Patterns	Representations and Reproductions
Jamie	I		III		
Lindsay	I	I			
Braelyn					III

FIGURE 6.4

▶ Skills Used Chart

Name	Skills Used	Evidence
Jerome	Pattern of long, short rectangular blocks—20 blocks	05/05 Created long line of blocks end-to-end in long/short pattern
Autumn	Stacked rectangular unit blocks	05/07 Blocks stacked in varying order of sizes. When block fell she tried to put block back on the stack

How to Use Information
- developmental level of each child;
- skill levels used;
- materials to expand to;
- type of facilitation that could be used to expand play; and
- other play areas that could be set up to transfer skills developed.

Information gleaned from this type of activity allows the facilitator to plan for the variety of materials needed to encourage the different levels of block play in the learning environment.

It is important to realize that any information gathered in one area should be coordinated with skills that have been developed in other areas. For example, information about dramatic play in the block area should be compared and interpreted with information from the dramatic play area. Ultimately, the information about a child will be compiled and shared. Sharing can be done through:

- individual portfolios—a book that has a section on block play in it and documents information about the child's block play development over a period of time;
- documentation panels—photographs and written dialogue about a particular interest of a group of children concerning block play projects; and
- booklets that share information about the specific interests of individual children or a group of children.

▶ International Considerations

Block play is a form of play that exists in virtually every culture in the world in one form or another. In areas where wood is scarce, alternatives to wood are used.

In the far north, wood is scarce. Inuit people use stones to build structures called *inukshuk*. They are built to look like a person to frighten the caribou to run toward the waiting hunters. These stone structures are also used as markers to guide travellers (Francis, 2000). Children exposed to these types of cultural customs and the scarcity of building materials will also create structures using stones.

In Japan, in the rainforest, wood is something to be admired and revered. This area is also rich in stones. Children outside were observed creating structures with rocks (photo 6.32).

Some cultures value the aspect of cooperative play. The Japanese will present children with blocks that are heavy; this type of block play encourages children to cooperate, as it takes two children to lift the block to build.

Other cultures value the realism of the block play. In these cultures, blocks represent the real world. Blocks have detail on them that are representative of real structures—windows, doors, shingles, shutters, and so on. Blocks constructed in Europe show this type of variety.

This type of play leads to observation of detail. Children need to look at the structures carefully to

PHOTO 6.32

identify how they fit together; for example, a door needs to be at the ground level, not in the middle of a wall in the upper storey. To be able to do this, children need to remember what a house looks like in order to replicate it. Children also need to solve the problem of how to fit the pieces together—fitting windows, doors, and shutters all on one side of the wall.

Philosophical approaches, such as Waldorf, tend to appreciate the simplicity and beauty of wood. In these programs, blocks will be made of natural wood. Children need to represent their play in a symbolic way. They need to imagine where the doors and windows are or create these by leaving openings. Both of the last two approaches have merit. The differences are philosophical and culturally based.

Brio, Swedish products, are made of natural wood. They require children to put items together in meaningful ways. Tracks can be fitted together to form straight lines, curves, or circles, or can ascend or descend to form hills. Vehicles, such as trains and automobiles, are in colour and are representative of real trains and vehicles. These vehicles can be connected magnetically and can reach any length, dependent on the number of materials available. The vehicles can be loaded with toy logs or other small items. Small accessories include people, trees, animals, related buildings, staircases, bridges, tunnels, cranes, and other functional items. All parts are operational. Bridges, gates, cranes, and railway crossings are functional.

The child involved in this type of play learns about cause and effect and safety features and gains knowledge about different types of operations needed to move items (turn a pulley, rotate a switch, raise a gate). Many of the basic science principles can be explored through this type of activity. These types of actions are not possible with standard sets of blocks.

In summary, differences expressed are either limited by resources, dictated by a particular philosophical viewpoint, or imbedded in the belief of what young children can or should learn.

▶ Block Materials

Table 6.1 lists examples of various types of blocks; figure 6.5 provides examples of common unit blocks.

TABLE 6.1

▶ Examples of Various Block Types

Types of Blocks	Use
Foam blocks—can be purchased in sets containing rectangular, bridge, semi-circular, cylindrical, and triangular blocks in blue, red, yellow, or green, in both large and smaller sizes	Excellent for infant or toddler as easy to grasp Easy to stack, as surfaces are less sticky Excellent to use for patterning skills
Blocks created from various-sized pieces of branches and twigs of trees	Increased skill in stacking Adds creative dimension
Cardboard—brick shaped in squared, small, and large rectangular shapes	Easy to handle, light Relatively safe to build in height Excellent for patterning
Cubes—interlocking various colours	Excellent to develop skill in patterning; comparison; creating sets of equal, more and less; counting; charting
Foam, material covered—commercially available and home-made—may be patterned or plain	Easy to grasp Safe to build in height
Hollow blocks	Building stable structures Use blocks as dramatic props—sturdy enough for children to sit/stand on Encourage cooperation, as blocks may need more than one person to build Encourage problem solving—how to use the blocks for other purposes

TABLE 6.1 EXAMPLES OF VARIOUS BLOCK TYPES (continued)

Types of Blocks	Use
Unit blocks	Skills in pre-measurement, ordering, comparison, counting, balancing, sequencing, patterning, matching, sorting
Boxes—liquor boxes are particularly good, as the dividers for the bottles make them much stronger. Tape the sides shut with duct tape and paint the boxes.	Skill in carrying, transporting Excellent for creating relatively safe high structures Creating balance Matching size
Numeric/alphabet block sets (8-inch cubes)—each side has a different letter/number	Stacking vertically or horizontally; ordering, patterning
Brick city blocks—rectangular, large	Note detail to build windows, doors, storefronts
Paper rolls (paper towel, wrapping paper, carpet)—may be reinforced with recycled paper, taped at ends and painted or covered with Mactac. Care must be taken to make sure that the taping of the ends is straight and smooth so that the block can stand up.	Skill in using cylindrical shapes to build with
Large carpet rolls—may be left plain or painted. These rolls may also be cut in half with a saw to create a tunnel.	Excellent accessory to use as tunnels, to drive or roll materials down or through
Building boards—plastic panels that interlock to build domes	Build covered enclosures Match, interconnect Develop sense of curved covers
Structure sticks—sticks that connect to build	Match, sort Pattern Build open structures
Coloured blocks—various sizes, shapes	Match, sort Pattern
Village, castle blocks—windows, doors, roofs, turrets	Observe detail Create realistic replicas

FIGURE 6.5

▶ **Diagrams of Block Units**

cuboid (square) – 1/2 unit		1/2 circular	
rectangular – single unit – double unit – quadruple unit		roof boards – small – large	
cylindrical – small – large		switch (y-switch) – large – small	
intersection		switch – small	
elliptical		triangular – small – large	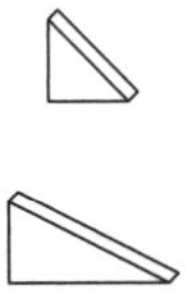
curve		ramp	
1/4 circular		pillar	
small buttress		1/2 pillar	
large buttress			
1/2 arch			

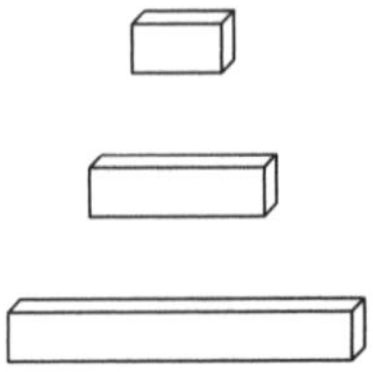

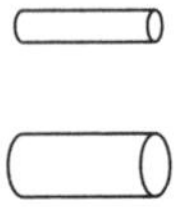

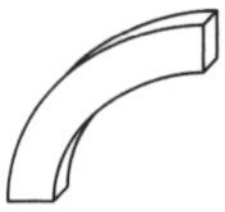

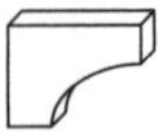

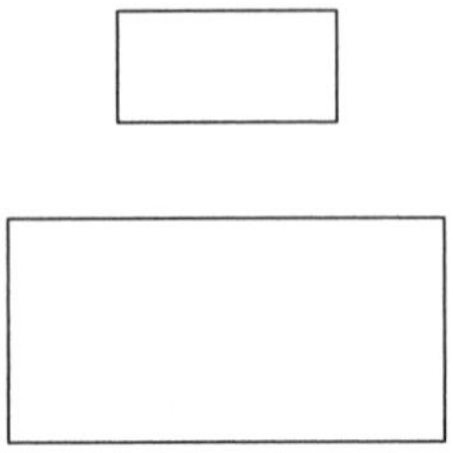

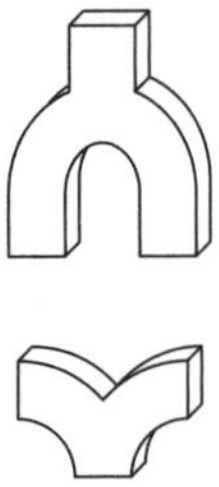

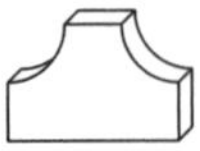

(adapted from Wellhouse and Kieff, 2001, p. 39)

▶ Ages and Stages of Block Play

Table 6.2 provides a summary of the ages and stages
of block play.

TABLE 6.2

▶ Ages and Stages of Block Play

Age	Skills	Types of Blocks
Infants—8 to 12 months	Manipulate blocks Transfer block from hand to hand Stack, pile blocks Drop, throw blocks	Soft foam blocks covered with material Small wooden blocks suitable for small hands Hard foam blocks Care must be taken to ensure that blocks are sturdy and will not shred or break if mouthed or thrown
12 to 24 months	Transport, carry blocks from one location to another Stack two to four objects Push or pull objects	Soft foam blocks covered with material Small wooden blocks suitable for small hands Hard foam blocks Cardboard boxes described previously Wagons, baskets, carts
2 years old	Carry, transport blocks Simple rows and towers	Unit blocks, hollow blocks Blocks from previous ages
3 years old	Easily distracted Enclosures, bridges, may start to name structures Limit choices	Provide greater variety of blocks All types
4 years old	Combinations—towers, rows, enclosures, bridges Use blocks with accessories to engage in dramatic play Use patterns to build Sharing ideas with others Building with others	Large number and variety of blocks to offer opportunities to build in small groups Related books and pictures Large areas to extend play
5 years old	Plan building alone or with others Build realistic structures Add detail to structures—ramps, doors, etc. Use other materials to create signs, roadways Extend building over several days by adapting, adding to structures Engage in dramatic play	Large variety of blocks Crayons, markers, paper, scissors, play dough to create signs and other accessories Related books and pictures Dedicated space to leave blocks out to extend play over several days

▶ KEY POINTS

Stages

Stage 1: Carrying and Stacking.

Stage 2: Rows and Towers—building of horizontal and vertical structures.

Stage 3: Walls and Bridges—build horizontally and vertically to create walls; use three blocks (two for support and one across the support) to create a bridge.

Stage 4: Enclosures and Patterns—build to create a space that is surrounded on all sides by blocks; create a pattern of blocks (a wall that contains a pattern of red, green, red, green, or two walls that use all long rectangular blocks and two walls that use all short rectangular blocks in order to complete an enclosure).

Stage 5: Representations and Reproductions—build recognizable structures that the child names, copy structures from previous ideas (may use plans, pictures to do this).

Value of Block Play

- problem solve;
- develop spatial awareness;
- develop concepts of size, shape, colour;
- develop related language skills;
- develop skills in matching, sorting, balancing, stabilizing;
- engage in symbolic play; and
- socialize with peers.

Role of Facilitator

- guide;
- question;
- dialogue;
- label;
- model language;
- provide materials;
- extend play; and
- value play.

Storage

- organized by type; and
- labelled by pictures and words.

Setting up Block Area

- spill-out space;
- sound absorbing surface;
- smooth surface;
- out of traffic area;
- confined by two sides; and
- accessible.

Display

- photographs;
- drawings;
- replicated displays; and
- leave block play up over time.

Observation

- photographs;
- portfolios;
- checklists; and
- diagrams.

Student Activities

1. From photo 6.32, identify the following:
   a) the stage of block play
   b) an explanation of why you believe this is the appropriate stage
   c) what materials you might provide to extend this play
   d) what language you might model

2. Develop a series of questions about the value of block play that could be used to interview a professional working with young children. Distribute the questionnaire among a small team of students. Each team member interviews one professional. Compare the results by comparing the following:
   a) most common value held
   b) values not identified
   c) why you think you got the results that you did.

3. Observe an adult interacting with children during block play. Identify what techniques the adult used to:
   a) model appropriate language
   b) encourage block play
   c) expand the play

4. In a small group, design an appropriate block play area that considers the following aspects:
   a) physical space
   b) types of blocks
   c) organization of space
   d) labelling system used

5. Select one of the observation tools provided, and implement the tool at least twice in a childcare setting. Interpret and discuss your results.

▶ References

Francis. (2000). *Discovering first peoples and first contacts.* Don Mills, ON: Oxford University Press.

Reifel, S. (1984, November). Block Construction: Children's Developmental Landmarks in Representation of Space. *Young Children.*

Santrock, J.W. (1994). *Psychology.* Dubuque, IA: WCB Brown & Benchmark.

Schickedanz, A., Schickedanz, I., Hansen, K., & Forsythe, P. (1993). *Understanding Children.* (2nd ed.). Mountain View, CA: Mayfield Publishing Company.

Stephens, K. (1991). *Block Adventures: Build Creativity and Concepts through Block Play.* Bridgeport, CT: First Teacher Press.

Warren, A. (1987). *Blocks.* North York, ON: The Board of Education for the City of North York.

Wellhouse, K., & Kieff, J. (2001). *A Constructivist Approach to Block Play in Early Childhood.* Toronto, ON: Delmar Thomson Learning.

CHAPTER 7

Quiet Play

Childcare programs, which some children attend for as many as 10 hours a day, 5 days a week, and sometimes 50 weeks a year, constitute a major part of young children's lives. Being expected to maintain a consistent and sometimes rigorous daily routine is tiring for teachers and can be stifling for children. When children remain in groups for most of these long periods, it is no wonder that they sometimes become competitive, manipulative, anxious, aggressive, or resentful.

Planning spaces where children can be alone for a while during the day, where they can enjoy some privacy and relief from the mainstream, is essential for their mental health. Scandinavian childcare programs ensure that small nooks with covered foam mattresses or beanbag chairs are built into the environment to provide cozy spaces for children when they need a break from the group. A healthy climate for children in group care respects their need for some privacy, provides for some "down time" during the day, when not much is expected of them, and allows them frequent opportunities to remove themselves from the presence of other children.

—Shipley, Empowering Children: Play-Based Curriculum for Lifelong Learning

Chapter Outline

- ▶ What Is the Quiet Area?
- ▶ Quiet Play to Encourage Learning
- ▶ Child Development: Developmental Considerations of Quiet Play
- ▶ Value of a Quiet Area
- ▶ Role of the Facilitator
- ▶ Effective Storage Systems
- ▶ Effective Labelling Systems
- ▶ Considerations for Setting Up a Quiet Area
- ▶ Observation and Documentation Techniques
- ▶ International Considerations
- ▶ Quiet Area Materials
- ▶ Ages and Stages of Quiet Play
- ▶ Key Points
- ▶ Student Activities
- ▶ References

Learning Outcomes

After studying this chapter, the reader will:

1. Define the purpose of the quiet areas
2. Identify the milestones of self-control
3. Discuss the relationship between self-control and the quiet areas
4. Identify the value of the quiet area
5. Identify the role of the facilitator
6. Discuss effective storage techniques
7. Identify an appropriate labelling system
8. Discuss considerations for setting up quiet areas in indoor and outdoor environments
9. Identify appropriate materials
10. Identify developmental guidelines for choosing materials—reading, writing, puzzles, and sewing
11. Identify various documentation techniques in order to observe children

Interactive Learning Exercises

 Remember, the CD-ROM that came with this text contains interactive exercises that relate to the topics in this chapter, as well as other valuable resources.

▶ What Is the Quiet Area?

A quiet area is an area that a child or a small group of children can withdraw to. The area should be inviting, with soft areas for sitting, and be protected from visual and as much as possible auditory distractions. Materials in this area should focus on activities that encourage quiet participation, relaxation, concentration, and privacy. This area needs to be an inviting, cozy area to relax in.

▶ Quiet Play to Encourage Learning

Logan had never been in a setting with so many children. He was reluctant to let go of his mother. He watched the room from the safety of her arms. In one corner of the room was a quiet area, surrounded by a white parachute with a tent-like opening at the front of it. This area contained a variety of books. Logan's mother took him to the area and read him a book. Soon Logan responded with a cheery grin to children entering this area (photo 7.1). It was not long after this that he started to explore the room by himself.

Kayla had been playing in the block area. As more children came to the area to help build, she stood back and watched for a while. Finally she got a book, sat down in a box that had been placed upright for storage of blocks, and looked at her book (photo 7.2).

Ian and Devon had been actively participating all morning. When their mother came to pick them up, they were not yet ready to leave. She took them to the quiet area and read a story to them (photo 7.3). The boys settled down to listen to the story. After she had finished the story, both boys got up and started to get ready to go home.

PHOTO 7.2

Dillon had had a busy morning. He started to wander around. Jennifer noticed him wandering. She asked if he wanted to have his snack. He shook his head and looked into the quiet area. No one was there. He picked up a book and sat on the rocking chair to look at it (photo 7.4). He looked at three books. Then he left the quiet area to get his snack.

On a field trip to a conservation area, quiet restful times were provided throughout the day. Picnic tables were separated and creative writing materials were placed on them. Blankets were provided and a bag of books had been brought. One of the parents had discussed how his Native ancestors had used birch bark to write on. The children immediately looked for pieces of birch bark and placed these in a basket on the table. Jacob found a spot beside an adult and

PHOTO 7.1

PHOTO 7.3

PHOTO 7.4

PHOTO 7.5

When Alicia arrived in the morning, she clung to her caregiver. The caregiver wandered around the room with her. There were no children in the quiet area. Alicia immediately went into the quiet area, got out some puzzles, and quietly played by herself (photo 7.9).

started to write a message for his mother on a piece of wood (photo 7.5).

Hannah had been creating a scenario using a variety of dinosaurs. Many of the children were interested in dinosaur play. Hannah was soon surrounded by six children. A more active type of play emerged. Hannah got up and it seemed that she was going to do something else. She went to the central storage area, got some more dinosaurs, and took them to the corner of the block area. This corner had been set up with a brown blanket placed over soft plastic cushions. She continued to play with her dinosaurs, using the blanket and cushions as a backdrop for her play (photo 7.6).

In the music area, Stephanie had been listening to the "Itsy Bitsy Spider" song and looking at the book at the same time. Emily joined her in the area. She lay down on the pillows under the umbrella and listened to the song (photo 7.7). When it was finished, she asked Stephanie to play it again. Eventually, the two girls lay down side by side, listened to the song, and looked at the book together.

Autumn was often found in the sewing area. The sewing was protected from intrusion by three sides—the parachute of the quiet area, a creative section of the painting area, and a wall to display their work at the back. Autumn used ribbon to sew around the outside of a bear shape that she had previously cut out with the die cutter (photo 7.8).

PHOTO 7.6

PHOTO 7.7

PHOTO 7.8

Jordan had been in the manipulatives area trying to string beads. The children in the area had discovered that you could pour the beads. Subsequently, a very active, noisy activity evolved. Jordan watched for a few minutes. Finally, he gathered two containers of animal beads and his gimp and took them to the quiet area. There he was able to string his beads (photo 7.10).

Haley often liked to be by herself. She particularly liked to draw and write in a quiet place. The dramatic playhouse has two doors that can be opened and closed. The children had learned to knock on the door

if they wanted to join someone and also that entry might be refused. The house had two windows with sheer curtains, which could be closed. One window

PHOTO 7.9

PHOTO 7.10

PHOTO 7.11

also had a counter that Haley liked to use to create her projects (photo 7.11).

In each of the above scenarios, the children had opportunities to pace themselves. Each could find an appropriate setting for a few minutes of quiet. For Logan, Ian, and Devon there was an opportunity to create a smoother transition from one activity to another. For Logan, this created an opportunity to ease more readily into a new situation. Dillon could sit and relax in order to re-energize himself. Kayla and Jordan could find a sheltered area to avoid a situation that they were uncomfortable in. For Haley and Alicia, it was simply an opportunity to do something by themselves.

▶ Child Development: Developmental Considerations of Quiet Play

A quiet area encourages children to learn to recognize their own feelings and react appropriately to those feelings. Children who have choices can make meaningful decisions. Just as a child needs to have a choice of the types of materials to use, a child needs to learn to make choices that directly influence the way he or she interacts with others and the materials

in the environment. This leads to self-awareness and to self- control.

The development of self-control begins very early in life. It begins when there is mutual regulation between the caregiver and child. It begins when the caregiver recognizes the signals the infant gives and responds immediately. It begins with the trust that develops that the infant's signals will be responded to and appropriately handled. Jeremy learned to trust Jennifer to respond to him as needed (refer to photo 5.3). Jennifer recognized the need to soothe and calm Jeremy. She watched his expressions to gauge what to do. She quietly sang to him. He in turn listened to her. She did not rush him off to bed until he had fallen asleep. She saw that he was trying to keep his eyes open and continued to look at her for comfort.

Jocelyn was lying on the floor in front of her mother. She smiled and gurgled. She waved her little hands and said "Baaabaababaaa." Her mother smiled and replied "Baaabaababaaa." This is another aspect of learning self-control: learning the rules for reciprocal interactions and learning to take turns.

Before self-control can develop, children must be aware of themselves as separate beings. They must be able to direct their actions independently and remember past consequences of their actions (Berk, 1998).

When Logan spent his first morning in the centre with his mother (photo 7.1), he listened to her reading a story. During this time, he tried to turn a page. His mother said, "Stop, I am not finished with this page yet. You can turn the page when I am finished." Logan stopped and continued to listen. Logan must have remembered a past experience in order for him to stop and continue to listen. When his mother had finished reading the page, she invited him to turn the page, thus reinforcing his compliant behaviour. This is a first step in self-control. He listened to a directive, and responded to it. His actions also show that he is aware of his ability to make things happen by himself. He is starting to establish himself as a separate individual.

Kayla (see photo 7.2) was often in the block area. On past occasions when other children came into the area, she would try to protect her blocks by shouting, "No!" At this age, Kayla's self-concept is very much part of the concrete possessions around. She spends a lot of time defending her right to control the materials within her possession (Berk, 1998, p. 247). She took a real step forward when she made a different choice: she decided to sit down and quietly read a book by herself. She took control over her own situation and found an activity that was satisfying to her.

Jennifer noted Kayla's actions. When Kayla had finished reading her book, Jennifer said, "Good for you. You found something quiet to do after your hard work with the blocks."

Dillon often wandered when he became tired. Usually, Jennifer would take him to the quiet area and read a book to him. He had also noticed that other children often sat in the quiet area reading a book. This was the first time that he initiated the action (photo 7.4). It shows that Dillon is beginning to recognize how he feels—when he feels tired, he is able to find a quiet activity to help him relax.

Jacob (photo 7.5) had been running around actively—collecting items to take back to the classroom, climbing trees, and running from one area to the next. When he heard that he could write on birch bark, he picked up the largest piece he could find—it was a thin layer of wood. He sat down near an adult, away from the children, and started to write. He was able to find a quiet activity to relax.

Alicia was very shy. When she first entered the preschool in the morning, she needed to find a space where she could relax and get reacquainted with the setting and the individuals in the setting. One of the activities that Alicia enjoyed in the quiet area was working with puzzles (photo 7.9). After working a few puzzles, Alicia would emerge ready to interact with the other children.

Some children, like Haley (photo 7.11), Hannah (photo 7.6), and Emily and Stephanie (photo 7.7), have already learned that there are some activities they prefer to do alone or in a small group.

▶ Value of a Quiet Area

- demonstrate respect for cultural activities—Autumn loves to sew (photo 7.8); sewing and needlework is valued by the Mohawk culture. Autumn has seen her relatives engaged in these activities. She has seen the projects created by her relatives and friends displayed and sold at festivals and stores.
- encourage observational learning—Quiet activities were encouraged as alternative activities to relax and re-energize. These activities were modelled by all adults (facilitators and family members): reading to children as a transitional activity (Ian, Devon, Dillon, and Logan) and acknowledging children who selected a quiet activity: (Jennifer's comments to Kayla reading after the block play).
- provide opportunities for concentration—It is hard to continue to work on a task with so many distractions in a child-care setting: activities of other

children, auditory distractions of other children and adults talking, music, visual distractions of children's movements and activities. In each case the child found an area that minimized either one or all of the distracting elements.
- learn to recognize the need to work alone—Jordan realized that he could not create the string of beads he wanted to create in the manipulatives area. He took his beads to the quiet area and was able to create his string of beads there (photo 7.10). Jordan was still learning to bead. He needed to focus all of his attention on the task to thread the gimp through the bead and transfer his hands to slide the bead down the gimp.
- provide a variety of activities that foster concentration—reading, writing, drawing, sewing, beading, puzzles, listening, dramatic play.
- encourage opportunities for relaxation—Emily (photo 7.7) lying on the pillow under the umbrella listening to the song.
- empower children to pace themselves, learn to recognize their needs, and thus start to establish self-control—Alicia knowing that she needed time to adjust to the new setting (photo 7.9).
- provide a safe setting to practise skills—Sewing requires attention to what one is doing; minor injury could occur when trying to thread a needle or manipulate it through the material. By decreasing the level of distractions, it helps the children concentrate on the task.

▶ Role of the Facilitator

- model the value of quiet time—Jennifer acknowledged Kayla's quiet reading activity, she read to Dillon when he was tired;
- document activities and learning of children;
- provide settings—playhouse, quiet area under the parachute, corner with pillows and blankets, umbrella with pillows under it;
- provide an aesthetically pleasing setting to invite children to enter—parachute hung from ceiling, lacy curtains in playhouse, cushioned area covered with a brown blanket;
- provide opportunities to engage in activities both indoors and outdoors;
- provide settings outdoors that encourage relaxation—blankets and cushions to sit on, bags of books to take outside, writing materials to draw or write, puzzles on a table;
- provide cozy areas that invite relaxation—soft couch, pillows on floor, covered pillows in corner, pillow under umbrella;

- adapt and change as needed—for example, the box that Kayla sat in was converted into a quiet spot near the block area with the addition of pillows and a small shelf of books blocking visibility to the block area; red and green tape was placed on a CD player to encourage independent use;
- negotiate a "do not disturb" routine—children had to knock to enter playhouse if the doors were closed and go away if the child asked to be alone;
- rotate materials as needed based on observations of children's interests and needs;
- provide appropriate materials that promote relaxation and concentration—music, books, puzzles, sewing, props for quiet dramatic play (photo 7.6); and
- develop an atmosphere that encourages all participants to use the quiet area—Logan, Ian, and Devon's mothers helped them during transition; Jennifer helped Dillon when he got tired.

▶ Effective Storage Systems

Storage is critical, as quiet relaxing areas need to be in more than one part of the room. Since the areas need to be cozy and relaxing it is important to avoid clutter and/or a messy appearance. Small bookshelves and small open shelves (for puzzles, sewing materials, writing materials) are ideal within the area itself. Centralized storage that allows children to retrieve items for themselves and take these materials to the quiet area is an excellent technique. Provide small baskets, trays, or small totes to allow children to collect materials to take to the quiet area. Notice that Hannah made effective use of this strategy when she collected the dinosaurs she wanted to use.

Books are often used in other areas to support play. The books should be displayed so that they are highly visible and easy to access. These may be displayed in the following manner:

- on top of a shelf or small table standing up (photo 7.12);
- on a small shelf;
- within an open sturdy decorated box or within an open plastic container, both placed with open side out;
- on book racks mounted in wall or on shelves; and
- on ledges or windowsills.

Sewing materials can be stored on a small open shelf in clear containers. Consider using clear water bottles: take off the label and cut the bottle down to the appropriate size. Punch a hole in the bottom of the bottle. Put the yarn, thread, or ribbon in the bottle. Thread the yarn through the hole. This prevents the

PHOTO 7.12

yarn from becoming tangled and keeps each item separate, ready to use. Push needles into foam pieces. Other items can be stored in appropriate-sized plastic containers or covered boxes (templates, variety of sewing materials in cardboard, plastic, fabric).

Similarly, the materials for the writing area need to be stored appropriately. Consider small plastic containers with hinged tops. These can have all the needed writing materials in them—sets of crayons, pencils, pencil sharpener, eraser, ruler, scissors, glue, set of markers, and tape. These can be stored in the creative area and the child can get them as needed. This saves space and encourages children to use these materials wherever they may be needed. Paper and books for writing could also be stored with the paper supplies—again leading to greater independence for the children and less setup time for the adults.

Another idea is to set up writing suitcases. Hard plastic suitcases are available fairly cheaply. Load these with the supplies listed above. Add a picture dictionary, some books, and perhaps some pictures of current interest. Presto: the children have a travelling writing centre that can be used anywhere (Rich, 1985).

▶ Effective Labelling Systems

In order to facilitate the various developmental levels of the types of books and puzzles children might wish to use, it is necessary to develop a scheme that children recognize and will use. A colour scheme works very well. Shelves could be coded to indicate easiest to hardest skill level; for example, cover the bottom bookshelf with yellow. The colour yellow could denote that the easiest books are stored there. Similarly, paint or cover the bottoms of puzzles with yellow. Children can then put the yellow puzzle back on the yellow shelf. Additionally, put a small clear container on each shelf: if the child cannot complete the puzzle because it is too hard, pieces can be put in the container and then back on the shelf. This encourages appropriate cleanup and respect for the environment.

This system encourages children to make realistic choices. Children like to be able to succeed at tasks. They can learn to judge the level of difficulty they are comfortable with and choose the appropriate activity. This also leads to the development of a positive self-concept: "I can do it by myself."

▶ Considerations for Setting Up a Quiet Area

Harms, Clifford, and Cryer (1998) have developed a scale (Early Childhood Environmental Rating Scale) to evaluate the early childhood environment. One of the items in the scale addresses the need for privacy. In order for a centre to score well on this scale on this item, more than one privacy area is required.

> The intent of space for privacy is to give children relief from the pressures of group life. A place where one or two children can play protected from intrusion by other children, yet supervised by staff, is considered space for privacy. Privacy space can be created by using physical barriers such as bookshelves; by enforcing the rule that children may not interrupt one another; by limiting the number of children working at a table placed out of the traffic area. Examples of space for privacy are a small loft area; activity centers where the use is limited to one or two children; a large cardboard box with cutout windows, and a cushion inside; a small outdoor playhouse. (Harms, Clifford, and Cryer, 1998, p. 13)

Outdoor spaces equally need to be created. Children spend a great deal of time running in large open spaces, riding toys on paths, or climbing and sliding. There must be spots that can become quiet relaxing corners similar to the indoor environment—pillows and blankets under a tree, soft furniture in a playhouse, a tent in one corner of the yard. The quiet spaces need to have similar activities to reinforce the value of quiet time—reading, writing, and activities that foster concentration such as listening to music, working puzzles, or sewing.

1. Aesthetically Pleasing

The **quiet areas** should give an immediate signal to children that "I want to go there." They should also signal that this is a place to relax and feel comfortable in. Think about a place where you as an adult like to relax. Usually it includes soft furniture, a relaxing colour scheme, soft music, and soft or natural lighting. The same atmosphere must be created for young children.

If possible, one of the areas should be near natural light. This is linked to better productivity and a decrease in stress levels (see the section on light in Chapter 2). Explore using alternative lighting for these areas—either full-spectrum fluorescent lighting or incandescent lighting. Remember that these areas need to be well lit so that children can engage in reading and other concentration activities. The need for natural light is an excellent incentive to provide opportunities for quiet activities outdoors.

Use soft shades that have a calming effect in this area—green, turquoise, blue, purple, brown (refer to table 2.5 in Chapter 2). If walls have been painted in neutral colours, warm soft colours can be added to the area through furnishings, material, rugs, pictures, and wallhangings. Outdoors, soft colours can be provided in the pillows, blankets, or tent-like structures that are created. Weaving soft-coloured fabric scraps into fences is one alternative way to add appropriate and attractive colour to the quiet area outside.

The furniture in the area should emphasize comfort (photos 7.1 and 7.3). A small adult-sized couch encourages interactions between adults and children. Cushions (with covers that can be taken off for easy cleaning and/or for changing the atmosphere) can be placed on the floor or ground and against a wall or fence (photo 7.6).

Pictures should emphasize children's artwork and should be appropriately framed and mounted. Pictures of children engaged in activities could also be mounted and hung on the wall. As in many living rooms, artwork from famous artists could also be used (see Chapter 9). Artwork should be displayed outside as well; it can be hung on the fence or propped up on an easel.

These areas, whether they are small or large, should clearly create an atmosphere that encourages relaxation, concentration, and quiet enjoyment.

2. Importance of Modelling

Facilitators must take care to model using quiet areas appropriately. If they are used as time-out areas, the children will quickly get the message that "this is a place I *do not* want to go to." For quiet areas to be truly effective, children must have the choice to control their own behaviour. They need to have the right to choose just as they do in any other area.

Facilitators need to reinforce this positive behaviour as readily as they reinforce positive behaviours in other activities.

3. Placement of Areas

Since the primary consideration is to create small, cozy, comfortable areas around the room to encourage quiet activities that children can withdraw to, the following points should be considered:

- locate areas away from noisy activities;
- locate areas away from main traffic flow;
- make sure areas are protected from visual and auditory distractions; and
- provide more than one area, as more than one child may need to use the area at any one time.

Since most child-care centres do not have unlimited budgets, consider some of the following suggestions:

- decorate cardboard refrigerator boxes (or any other large box)—cut out windows and doors, put cushions inside, put curtains on the windows;
- construct a simple playhouse (see figure 7.1)— these can be constructed cheaply and can be fashioned to fit into existing spaces;
- use corners—cushions against the wall or fence and on the floor or ground can make a cozy place, add book shelves to act as dividers;
- hang a parachute, or hang fabric from the ceiling or the branches of a tree—creates a soft, tent-like area that children can relax in;
- consider adding a system of clothesline wire either vertically or horizontally across the room, just below the ceiling, to suspend items safely;
- suspend sheer curtains or fabric from the ceiling or a tree to act as dividers;
- set up large umbrellas with cushions underneath them as cozy areas; and
- set up boxes turned sideways with cushions or perhaps sheer curtains in front of them to provide quiet nooks.

4. Ensuring Privacy

Since children have a right to—and a need for— privacy during the day, some guidelines need to be established. There are many ways to do this. If the system is to work, all participants must understand it and agree to use it. Therefore, the guidelines should be as simple and as natural as possible. Consider mechanisms that children are already familiar with— closed doors, knocking on doors, ringing a doorbell, and asking permission. Some mechanisms that can be used are:

- doors that open and close;
- curtains that can be open or closed;
- small gates (baby gates) between walls and shelving units;
- a stop sign that can be hung or placed in front of an entry; and
- a low structure such as a bench that can act as a barrier.

5. Types of Activities

Reading

Reading is an activity that needs to clearly reflect aesthetic qualities. There are a large number of books on the market that are of very poor quality. Pictures are unclear and poorly presented, with poor quality artwork and often equally poor content. Remember the first time you held a book in your hand that you were almost afraid to hold because it was *so* beautiful? You gingerly turned each page, anticipating new delights. You carefully stroked the pictures—they were the most lovely that you had ever seen. Such a book will last a long time, because the child treasures it. When you treasure something, you tend to take care of it.

Aesthetics is something that develops over time. When you present books to children that are aesthetically pleasing, you are also developing a sense of what is beautiful. Books such as the books illustrated by Graeme Base and Philippa-Alys Browne not only give the child a sense of beauty, but also develop appreciation of the various styles that an artist might use.

Reading is a natural quiet activity. Children need to engage in reading activities daily. Adults need to read to children individually and in small groups. Reading is another way to gain independence and to become more self-reliant. Reading also gives children many opportunities to gain additional skills.

- research: picture dictionaries, science books, theme books—Children learn to look up and find things for themselves (look up pictures, words; match objects to pictures; identify names; find out how to do something; Billy looking for ideas for creating a house in carpentry (photo 7.13); Jacob finding an animal he had been playing with (photo 7.14);
- increase vocabulary: picture books, picture, dictionaries, concept books;
- learn about opposites; labelling (objects, feelings, actions, events); associating meaning to pictures and words;
- sing a book: learn to associate words to pictures; provide a soothing activity;

FIGURE 7.1

▶ **Construction of a Simple Playhouse**

Side 1—window with counter
• 1/2-inch pressboard

Side II—window (open)
• Add curtain rod inside and curtains

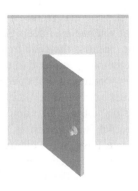

Sides III and IV
• Each with door that opens

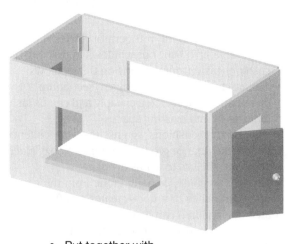

• Put together with door hinges on each side
• Possible to create other panels and interchange

• read easy-reading books: repetitive, predictable text—learn the association of the printed word; word recognition; read alone;
• identify feelings: stories about various events, picture books—establish self-identity; recognize feelings; label feelings; preparation of events;
• learn to count—count objects on a page;
• look for detail: figure–ground—finding detail within a busy background;
• recognize parts and wholes: only part of a picture is shown, child needs to make the association to the whole;
• predict sequence: predictable, everyday occurrences; life cycles, seasons, routines;
• increase awareness of colour, size, and objects;

• appreciate classic stories from different viewpoints: stories that have been told for generations, often in many cultures;
• introduce cultural perspectives: introduce children to various different cultures;
• enjoy poetry: children enjoy the natural rhythm;
• recognize and respond to humour: flip and match books, funny stories, jokes—Braelyn (photo 7.15) created her own funny book about feelings. She would ask to have her picture taken, then she would dictate the words to go under her picture. The words were typed under the pictures and the book was laminated and bound. This became one of the children's favourite books;

PHOTO 7.13

PHOTO 7.14

- learn about different family types—books that represent single families, blended families, families from various cultures, and family members involved in diverse roles; and
- learn to appreciate various languages—present familiar books in different languages.

Writing

Positively reinforcing children's early writing attempts will encourage them to gradually develop their future skills as writers and will emphasize writing as an important life skill.

> "Children begin to use writing long before they can control the mechanics of writing.... Children ask teachers [adults] to write signs, messages, letters and stories. So teachers [adults] supply demonstrations of different forms of writing and children gradually try out successive approximations of the adult forms. Children's ability to differentiate between drawing and writing develops gradually between the ages of 3 years and 6 years. Both drawing and writing are ways of using symbols to represent experience. Both are preceded by scribbling and appear to develop in a parallel manner (Connell, 1985, p. 19)" (Hogben and Wasley, 1996, p. 74)

Writing is an activity that requires concentration and an environment that allows for creativity.

Children should be able to write by choice, and therefore meaningful opportunities must be created. The area should:

- be aesthetically pleasing—a neat place to work, working utensils in well organized, labelled containers (sharp pencils, charcoal, coloured pencils, pens, crayons, markers, erasers, chalk and chalkboard, rulers, dictionaries, letters to copy, books for motivation, stories of children posted); writing tools from various cultures;

PHOTO 7.15

- have small table and chairs to work at;
- have accessible materials;
- have a scribe handy—someone who can write down the words the child wishes to write;
- publish books or stories that children have written;
- have neat paper—lined, unlined, folded;
- have a wide variety of paper and envelopes;
- contain small neat books to decorate and write in;
- show examples of various ways of writing—shopping lists, letters, stories, poems;
- have colours that encourage creativity, such as pale yellow or orange (refer to table 2.5); and
- natural lighting, if possible, or alternatives (see Chapter 2, p. 32).

Consider using sand or flour as an alternative writing medium. This can be put on a coloured tabletop or within coloured cookie sheets. Use old cookie sheets. Clean them, then paint with enamel paint. Thus when the child makes his letters or words, they are in colour. Consider painting the tray different colours; this leads to a greater surprise. Children can perform this task with fingers, brushes, and sticks. When they are finished, the message can be erased and redone (photo 7.16).

Computers are a wonderful tool in this area. Haley had dictated a story that she wanted to include in her writing book. She asked to type it on the computer herself. She copied what she had written. She then pasted her story into her book and illustrated her story.

Josh found it difficult to write his name. However, he could use the electric typewriter or the computer to type his name (photo 7.17). He was very proud of his name when it appeared. Our children are growing up in an age of technology. They need to learn to use this technology just like any other tool. "Today, adolescents must be able to read, write, and converse, and also use pagers, cell phones, video games, computers, software, electronic mail, and the Internet" (Schickedanz, Schickedanz, Forsyth, and Forsyth, 2001, p. 626).

Puzzles

Puzzles also encourage concentration and quiet activities. Some puzzles lend themselves to individual activity and some to small group work, such as larger floor puzzles. Puzzles are a valuable activity, as they require the child to look at detail (the shape of the piece, the images on the piece), practise matching parts to wholes, and demonstrate the fine motor control to fit pieces together.

Puzzles also should be chosen for their aesthetic qualities. Again, the puzzle should inspire a sense of beauty. Is the picture clearly recognizable; are the colours realistic or imaginative; is the background appropriate; do the colours blend together in a pleasing way; are the individual pieces distinct; and is the picture presented attractive?

Sewing

I once took part in a sewing circle. We were making a friendship quilt to hang on the wall of a new children's pioneer museum. The project involved the following participants:

- children—3 to 14 years of age: involved in drawing the design with crayon on pieces of quilting material; sewing the pieces together; putting an edge around the outside; ironing pieces to absorb colour from the wax; adding detail with embroidery floss; and

PHOTO 7.16

PHOTO 7.17

- adults—teachers and family members (various ethnic backgrounds: Dutch, German, Italian, Native, Ukrainian): helping to iron the pieces, sewing pieces together on sewing machines, embroidering, and adding edging.

The project was set up in a large room. The room had various areas for measuring, cutting, drawing, ironing, sewing, and embroidery. The children decided on what they wished to represent about themselves or their community and drew these concepts on the fabric scraps. All age groups were encouraged to use the sewing machine and the iron under close supervision.

The embroidery areas were set up in comfortable corners, with quilts hanging both on the walls and from the ceiling to detract from the rest of the room. This area tended to be much quieter; individuals in it were intent on their projects. Conversation was muted. In this area, children were initially given pieces of material—plastic squares with large holes, burlap, and heavy cotton—to practise various stitches. Preschool children generally went around the squares with various types of yarn. Older children displayed various skill levels to finish squares with inside designs and bordering techniques.

These skills were directly applied to the quilt. The adults sewed a plastic strip around the outside of the quilt. Younger children were able to use skills they had learned to finish the border. Older children decorated each square by going around the crayon design and adding detail.

This activity truly helped the children gain many skills—independence, fine muscle control, working together as a team, creating a product that was displayed and admired by the community, pride in accomplishment, and understanding of cultural values.

The adults modelled appropriate techniques from their cultural perspectives. Different squares took on a variety of cultural dimensions in terms of colour and embroidery design. The value of an aesthetically pleasing quiet area was also clearly modelled. The whole exercise modelled and reinforced aesthetic and creative efforts using a different medium.

Felt Boards

Felt boards, or a low bulletin board covered with felt, can be another relaxing activity for children. Favourite characters from stories, sequence items (dressing and other routines), open-ended materials (animals, familiar objects, vehicles, people) can be presented in clear pockets hanging beside the felt board. These materials may encourage children to recreate a story or create a new one. Activities such as matching and sorting can

also be used. Again, pieces should be carefully selected or carefully made to respect aesthetic qualities.

6. Display

The quiet areas are excellent places to display some of the children's efforts. Much of the work that is done in this area tends to be either work that is put away when completed (puzzles) or something the child may wish to take home (Billy's bag). The picture of Billy (photo 7.18) could be enlarged, framed, and placed on the wall in the sewing area. This gives a dual purpose: it encourages other children to create their own projects, and it gives Billy satisfaction that his efforts have been noticed.

Other efforts, such as beading, should be displayed. Good beads are expensive to purchase and children need to realize that beads, just like any other materials used within the centre, need to stay in the centre. Displaying framed photographs of children's efforts helps them in two ways: they have a personal record of what they have accomplished, and they may look at the photo on another day to see if they would like to continue the activity. Shanleigh often used the beads. She would come in and look at her picture; at times, she actually replicated what she had done on a previous day by looking at her picture.

PHOTO 7.18

Another way to display beads is to use a piece of dowelling or a firm cardboard tube that has been painted. Put some hooks in regular intervals in the dowelling/tube. This can hang over the centre of the table (provided that the children can reach it) or near a wall to hang their work. This way the children can continue with their efforts another day.

Writing projects that need to be completed can be placed in shopping bags with the children's names on them, in individualized stacked boxes, within large envelopes, or hung on a string with a round clasp. This models respect of privacy for each child and indicates that some work can be completed over time.

▶ Observation and Documentation Techniques

One important consideration to observe is the self-control that children are developing. One way that this can be done is through a combination of tools: attention span (how long the child is engaged in the activity), location of the activity, and types of skills used (see figure 7.2 and photo 7.18). This information is useful as it allows you to add other sewing materials to continue this project (material, leather, and different types of yarn, plastic, canvas). The information is valuable as you can give an accurate picture of the child's fine motor skills, creative efforts, and ability to work independently as you interact with his or her parents. Taking a picture of his efforts reinforces the observations and interpretations made.

For a good overall gauge of how your quiet areas are working, you can take a frequency count of the areas and how often children are in those areas (see figure 7.3).

FIGURE 7.3

▶ Use of Quiet Areas Chart

Name	Date	Playhouse	Open Box	Reading	Sewing	Puzzles
Billy	10.02 10.03				II	
Kayla	10.05		I			
Alicia	10.03					III

This tool helps the facilitator to identify:
- how often the children use the areas;
- what materials are most popular;
- if the children developing self-control;
- who is using the areas most; and
- the overall effectiveness of areas set up.

To provide information about the types of books or puzzles that children use most, compile lists of books and puzzles and track how often they are used. These lists could be posted in the area to provide excellent information on what materials need to be rotated and which ones should remain within the area.

▶ International Considerations

Not all cultures value quiet time for children or individual time in the same way. In any setting that has large numbers of children, quiet time tends to be valued as a working time for the children. The child is

FIGURE 7.2

▶ Observation of Quiet Area

Name: Billy

Time: 5 10 15 20 25 30 35 40 45 50 55 60
X X X X X X X X X X X X

Activity: Sewing   Oct.22

Skill: Created own pouch—cut out shape, punched holes, sewed together, put flowers into it, created handle

Type of Play: Solitary

assigned a task, works on this task alone, and often remains quiet until the task has been completed. One does not have to travel too far to see these types of programs—one need only look at many pre-kindergarten and senior kindergarten classes. Each teacher could be responsible for as many as 30 children by herself or himself. The issue in a class this size becomes that of control. The teacher needs to be aware of where the children are at all times and what they are doing. Group activity that is teacher-directed is usually the norm in such settings.

Reading is an activity that is not necessarily valued by some cultures. Cultures that have a rich heritage of storytelling tend not to rely on reading. Many aboriginal cultures around the world fall into this category. These children are rarely exposed to books or the written word before they come to school or preschool. Special attempts must be made to continue the rich heritage of storytelling. Providing books of some of these stories may help to bridge the gap. Additionally, inviting the elders in to the classroom may provide opportunities for storytelling and for recording the stories for the children. Children can be encouraged to illustrate the story after it has been written. Alternatively, children's stories can be documented and illustrated and used within the book corners.

Many of the world's children live in miserable poverty. Even in our Western cultures the poverty rate is abysmal. "Child poverty in Canada is increasing. The number of children living in poverty grew from 1.36 million in 1994 to 1.5 million in 1996, rising from 19.5% to 21% percent of the child population (Canadian Council on Social Development, 1998)" (Watson, Watson, Wilson, and Crowther, 2000, p. 14).

Children living in poverty do not have enough food to eat, let alone appropriate living quarters or books to read. Many of these children live in homes where the adults themselves are illiterate. These conditions lead to a lack of personal space, a lack of resources to learn from, and a lack of motivation to learn due to poor nutrition. "Poor children suffer the most from unhealthy environments" (Canadian Council on Social Development, 1998, p. 21).

Children in these conditions need to be nurtured in all ways. First, their basic needs must be met—good nutrition, breakfast at arrival, clean clothes. At the same time, understanding and empathetic caregivers must nurture the child and the family's emotional needs. It is through building trust that these children will learn to initiate activities in order to grow socially, emotionally, and cognitively.

Aesthetic beauty of materials is another cultural difference. Look in any catalogue of children's toys. Puzzles in our culture often lack aesthetic beauty. Compare puzzles in any catalogue to puzzles produced in Germany, for example. The Ravensburger puzzles have beautiful pictures, are realistic representations, present various viewpoints, and are developmentally appropriate for various levels. The Waldorf school of thought provides children with natural materials that blend in a pleasing way within the environment—natural wood, soft shades.

▶ Quiet Area Materials

Materials are listed in tables 7.1 through 7.4. Additionally, appropriate materials can be found in other chapters of the book.

TABLE 7.1

▶ Ages, Stages, and Books

Listing includes diversity in race, gender, and culture

Age	Skill	Behaviour	Examples
Infant up to 6 months	Listen and look	Facial expression, body movement—arms and legs to show excitement, eye-contact with book	Simple picture books that have bright contrast, single image, and are familiar to the child—easy to create yourself Simple nursery rhymes—especially to do with body parts
Infant 6-12 months	Listen, look by myself, identify pictures	Turn pages, get own book, indicate preference through body language, babbling, and first words Point to pictures to identify	Board books, simple bright pictures, familiar topics, simple stories, simple nursery rhymes Dyer, J. (1986). *Moo, Moo, Peekaboo!* New York, NY: Random House. Argueta, B., & Lousada, S. (1998). *Baby Faces.* New York, NY: Dutton Children's Books.

TABLE 7.1 AGES, STAGES, AND BOOKS (continued)

Age	Skill	Behaviour	Examples
Infant 12–18 months	Identify pictures Recognize books/stories	Identify through pointing Increased ability to verbally identify Repeated requests for same story Chooses and brings book to be read	Board books, picture books; simple story lines; expanded content; simple language; lots of repetition; simple nursery rhymes Argueta, B. & Lousada, S. (1998). *Playing with Pets*. New York, NY: Dutton Children's Books. Butler, J. (2001). *Whose Baby Am I*. New York, NY: Penguin Putman Books for Young Readers. Yoon, S. (1999). *Foil Fun Colors*. Santa Monica, CA: Piggy Toes Press.
Toddler	Follow story Read by self Established preference	Independent choice Repetitive—same story over and over again; enjoys stories about things evolving around him/her—new baby in the family, daddy's/mommy's work Intensely curious about things, animals, vehicles	Picture books with detail; simple stories with lots of action; repetitive; rhyming elements Volkmann, R. (2001). *Curious Kitten*. New York, NY: Random House Children's Books. Martin & Carle. (1991). *Polar Bear, Polar Bear, What Do You Hear?* New York, NY: Henry Holdt and Company, LLC. Kopper, L. (1994). *I'm a baby you're a baby*. London, UK: Penguin Books Ltd.
Preschool and school-aged	Research—look up information Level of search more sophisticated with age Increase vocabulary	Look for pictures Look for words to spell Look for identifying features—shape, colour, size Look for ideas Use dictionaries; ask meanings of words; learn meaning of words from picture clues and from context of story	Realistic pictures to help identify words; dictionaries Valat, Perols, Jeunesse, & Bourgoing. (1989). *Colours*. London, UK: Moonlight Publishing Ltd. Watts, B. (1991). *See How They Grow: Duck*. Richmond Hill, ON: Scholastic Ltd. Evans, D., & Williams, C. (1992). *How Things Work*. New York, NY: Dorling Kindersley Ltd. Ardley, N. (1995). *How Things Work*. New York, NY: Dorling Kindersley Ltd. Browne, P. (1996). *A Gaggle of Geese*. New York, NY: Simon and Schuster Books for Young Readers.
Preschool and school-aged	Sing a book	Follow words in book as listening to song	Adams, P. (1973). *There Was an Old Lady Who Swallowed a Fly*. Singapore: Child's Play International. Rodgers, R., Hammerstein, O., & Warhola, J. (1994). *My Favorite Things*. New York, NY: Simon and Schuster Books for Young Readers.
Preschool and school-aged	Look for detail	Look for items hidden in a busy background	Picture books with a lot of detail; find hidden object books Fowler, R. (1995). *There It Is*. London, UK: Campbell Books.

TABLE 7.1 AGES, STAGES, AND BOOKS (continued)

Age	Skill	Behaviour	Examples
Beginning reader	Read easy-reading books Repetitive, predictable text Predict sequence	Read some words, memorize story and read, sound out words, put in words through context, look at pictures to recognize words	Repetitive books with pictures to illustrate story; simple words Druce, A., & Ludlow, P. (1998). *Witch, Witch come to my party.* Auburn, ME: Child's Play International. Cater, D. *In a Dark, Dark Wood.* New York, NY: Simon and Schuster Books for Young Readers. Brown, R. (1988). *A Dark, Dark Tale.* Toronto, ON: Stoddart Publishing Co. Ltd. Charlip, R. (1964). *Fortunately.* New York, NY: Macmillan Pub. Co. Cheyette Lewison, W., & Wijngaard, J. (1999). *Going To Sleep On The Farm.* New York, NY: Dial Books for Young Readers.
Preschool and school-aged	Identify feelings	Label feelings from picture Empathize with character, event Relate feelings to own feelings Read and discuss feelings	Short stories with related pictures; stories with moral dilemmas Dijs, C. (1996). *Daddy Would You Love Me If...?* New York, NY: Simon and Schuster Books for Young Readers. Joosse, B., & Lavallee, B. (1991). *Mama, Do You Love Me?* Vancouver, BC: Raincoast Books. Harris, P. *Looking at Opposites Got Cold Shy Bold.* Toronto, ON: Kids Can Press Ltd. Gilmore, R., & Sauve, G. (1999). *A Screaming Kind of Day.* Markham, ON: Fitzhenry & Whiteside Ltd.
Preschool and school-aged	Learn alphabet Counting; comparisons	Count objects Recite alphabet Identify colours, objects, shapes	Selsam, M. & Donnelly M. (1995). *Big Tracks, Little Tracks: Following Animal Prints.* New York, NY: HarperCollins. Brown, R. (2001). *Ten Seeds.* London, UK: Anderson Press Ltd. Jeunesse, G. and de Bourgoing, P. *Colours.* London, UK: Moonlight Publishing Ltd. Base, G. (2001). *The Water Hole.* Toronto, ON: Doubleday Canada. Johnson, S. (1995). *Alphabet City.* Toronto, ON: Penguin Books Canada Ltd.
Preschool and early school-aged	Recognize opposites, differences—appreciate classic stories from different viewpoints	Recognize opposites—first gross differences, leading to minute differences in the school-aged years	Picture books with clear opposites Thompson, M., & Newland, G. (1999). *Make a Change Opposites.* Brookfield, CT: Millbrook Press, Inc. Opposite approaches in known stories—*Goldilocks and the Three Bears* Two opposite approaches: 1. Turkle, B. (1976). *Deep In The Woods.* New York, NY: Dutton Children's Books. 2. Brett, J. (1990). *Goldilocks and the Three Bears.* New York, NY: Dover Publications.

TABLE 7.1 AGES, STAGES, AND BOOKS (continued)

Age	Skill	Behaviour	Examples
Preschool and school-aged	Introduce cultural perspectives	Curious about other cultures; perhaps some prejudice about how other cultures live	Realistic books and stories about other cultures Kindersley, A., & Kindersley, B. (1995). *Children Just Like Me*. Bolton, ON: Fenn Publishing Company. Rattigan, J., & Hsu-Flanders, L. *Dumpling Soup*. (1993). New York, NY: Little, Brown and Company. Waters, K., & Slovenz-Low, M. (1990). *Lion Dancer Ernie Wan's Chinese New Year*. New York, NY: Scholastic Inc. Palazzo-Craig, J., & Nagano, M. (2001). *The Magic Peach: A Story From Japan*. Memphis TN: Troll.
Preschool and school-aged	Enjoy poetry Listening to rhyme, different forms of writing	Enjoy listening to poetry, rhyme Can recite simple to more complex poetry rhyme with increased age	Variety of poetry—nursery rhymes Moxley, S. (1995). *Skip Across the Ocean: Nursery Rhymes from Around the World*. London, UK: Frances Lincoln Ltd. De Coteau Orie, & Canyon, C. (1995). *Did You Hear Wind Sing Your Name? An Oneida Song of Spring*. New York, NY: Walker and Company. McConnell, R. (1978). *Norbert Nipkin*. Toronto, ON: Cerebrus Publishing Company Ltd.

TABLE 7.2

▶ Puzzles

Age	Materials
6 months–12 months	Toys that encourage infants to put things into slots—sorting wheel, sorting cub; fitting small toys (watch for sharp edges, must be large enough to prevent choking) into jars, bottles These activities give familiarity with shape, size, and fit
12–18 months	Continue with slot-type toys, small puzzles—single pieces with knobs to aid handling—initially four pieces, increase as child gains skill
Toddler	Continue with single pieces with knobs; add simple puzzles, inlay puzzles, and expand to interlocking puzzles with few pieces; increase number of pieced puzzles as child is ready
Preschool	Increase number of pieces within interlocking puzzles as child is ready; floor puzzles; multipurpose puzzles—magnetic, pieces used for other purposes such as add wheels to cars to drive; sequence puzzles—life cycles, dressing, seasons; underlying structures under pieces
School-aged	All of the above—increase the complexity and subject matter with age

TABLE 7.3

▶ Sewing Materials

Age	Materials
Preschool and school-aged	Plastic needles with large eyes and blunt end; scissors; hole punch; yarn (taped end), ribbon, thread, embroidery floss; material, cardboard; templates; plastic lids with edges cut off; plastic canvas; burlap; felt; cotton; buttons; decorative items—flowers, beads, loops; embroidery frames; sewing machine; crochet hooks; knitting needles
	Books—simple pattern books such as Sabine Lohf. (1989). *Things I Make with Cloth.* London, UK: Victor Gollancz

TABLE 7.4

▶ Writing Materials

Materials are cumulative. Each stage adds new materials to existing ones.

Age	Materials
12 to 18 months	Crayons, paper (taped down), non-toxic markers, chalk, chalkboard; non-toxic finger paint; finger paint paper, Plexiglas, table tops
Toddler	Pencils, pencil crayons, erasers, rulers, writing booklets
Preschooler	Lined paper, picture dictionaries, alphabet letters, numbers, picture word cards, phonic cards, computer
School-aged	Dictionaries, lined workbooks, cursive alphabet, software for writing stories

▶ Ages and Stages of Quiet Play

Milestones in developing self-control are outlined in table 7.5.

TABLE 7.5

▶ Milestones in Developing Self-Control

Age	Milestones
Birth to six months	Mutual regulation of attachment between infant and caregiver—child gives signal, caregiver responds immediately; builds trust in ability to get a response
	Reciprocal relationships—turn-taking: infant initiates, caregiver listens and responds or vice versa
Six months to 12 months	Mobility gives infant opportunity to separate self from mother—builds awareness of self as a separate individual
	Social referencing—begin to understand feelings of others around them by reading facial expressions
	Providing positive interactions with infants helps to start to develop emotional self-regulation

TABLE 7.5 MILESTONES IN DEVELOPING SELF-CONTROL (continued)

Age	Milestones
12 months to 18 months	Compliance—first indicator of self-control; aware of caregiver's wishes and expectations
Toddler	Self-control appears—very fragile; need reminders and continuous prompts
Preschool	Steady gain in self-control; linked to ability to understand and communicate language; self-control evident in various types of approaches—avoiding situations, asking for attention, selecting activities; how materials are used; how to interact with various individuals
School-age	Need practice to self-regulate—monitor own actions, check results of actions, and have someone redirect or guide as needed

▶ KEY POINTS

Quiet Area—space to withdraw, either individually or in a small group, for relaxation and concentration.

Milestones in Development of Self-Control

- mutual regulation of attachment to build trust;
- reciprocal relationship—turn-taking;
- building of self as separate individual;
- start to develop emotional self-control;
- establishment of compliance;
- fragile self-control; and
- building self-control.

Value

- demonstrate respect for cultural activities;
- encourage observational learning;
- provide opportunities and activities for concentration;
- learn to recognize need to be alone;
- encourage opportunities for relaxation;
- empower children to pace themselves; and
- provide a safe setting to practise skills.

Role of the Facilitator

- model value of quiet time;
- provide aesthetically pleasing setting;
- provide indoor and outdoor quiet time/setting;
- provide cozy areas to encourage relaxation;
- adapt and change;
- negotiate right to privacy;
- rotate materials;
- provide appropriate materials for concentration and relaxation; and
- develop atmosphere that encourages participation in quiet activities.

Storage

- avoid clutter;
- centralized storage;
- portable units to help gather needed materials;
- small book shelves and open shelves;
- display books—on shelves, ledges, window sills, wall racks, open containers;
- clear units for easy visibility;
- safety—blunt plastic needles stuck in foam; and
- portable writing containers, writing suitcase.

Labelling Systems

- colour scheme to denote level of difficulty.

Considerations for Setting Up the Quiet Area

- aesthetically pleasing;
- importance of modelling;
- placement of areas;
- ensuring privacy;
- types of activities—reading, writing, puzzles, sewing, felt boards; and
- display.

Observation and Documentation Techniques

- observation of self-control;
- combination of tools;
- use of quiet area; and
- lists.

Student Activities

1. Discuss how the quiet area can help to develop self-control.

2. What strategies might the facilitator use to help children use the quiet area?

3. You are in an area that has a high density of Chinese and East Indian families. How might you adapt the quiet area to reflect their cultural values?

4. You are working in a setting that has a diverse population of individuals. One of the children comes from a large family. This child, Naomi, is always near or with other children. By mid-morning, Naomi becomes very cranky and tired. She follows the other children or an adult and cries if they ignore her. You talk to Naomi's mother. She indicates that someone is always with Naomi. If she is tired someone will lie down with her to tell her a story. What strategies might you try to help Naomi?

5. Develop a mini floor plan along with a list of materials you would include for a quiet area.

6. How might you set up a quiet area outside? Your setting has mainly concrete (sand under the climbers only) no shade trees or plants of any kind, building walls on two sides, and a chain-link fence on the other two sides.

7. What types of portable storage can you provide to encourage children to use materials in the quiet area?

8. For a group of children ages 2–5, in an environment that includes Native children, African Canadian children, Danish children, and Italian children, what types of books would you provide? List the books specifically by title and indicate why you included each one.

9. You have a parent who expresses concern because you have a sewing centre set up. This parent feels that the needles are dangerous, as they might poke out someone's eye. How would you respond?

10. Work in a small group. Each member of the group chooses one puzzle and one book that they find aesthetically pleasing. Present your book and puzzle to the group and indicate why you found each one particularly pleasing. Compare your results. How were your group members' preferences similar or different? Discuss why you feel this way.

11. For each of the reading skills listed, find one book that can be used for that purpose. Indicate the reason for your choice.

12. Develop two writing books for two different age groups. Have another individual evaluate your effort. Consider aesthetics, developmental ability, purpose, and interest of the children.

13. Evaluate a display area in any child-related setting. Consider aesthetics, placement, child-directedness, and interest level.

14. Observe children in any setting. Utilize one of the tools developed. Compare your results with your classmates. What overall conclusions can you make individually and for the whole group?

▶ References

Berk, L. (1998). *Development Through Lifespan.* Toronto, ON: Allyn and Bacon.

Canadian Council on Social Development. (1988). *The Progress of Canada's Children 1998.* Ottawa, ON: Canadian Council on Social Development Publications.

Harms, T., Clifford, R., & Cryer, D. (1998). *Early Childhood Environment Rating Scale: Revised Edition.* New York, NY: Teachers College Press.

Hogben, J., & Wasley, D. (1996). *Learning in Early Childhood: What Does It Mean in Practice?* Education Department of South Australia: Hyde Park Press.

Rich, S. (1985, July). The Writing Suitcase. *Young Children.*

Schickedanz, J., Schickedanz, D., Forsyth, P., & Forsyth, G. (2001). *Understanding Children and Adolescents.* (4th ed.). Toronto, ON: Allyn and Bacon.

Shipley, D. (2002). *Empowering Children: Play-Based Curriculum for Lifelong Learning.* (3rd ed.). Scarborough, ON: Nelson.

Watson, L., Watson, M., Wilson, L., & Crowther, I. (2000). *Infants and Toddlers.* Scarborough, ON: Nelson Thomson Learning.

CHAPTER 8

Dramatic Play

Dramatic play opens up doors of wonder, enchantment, courage, and fun for young children. Yet it is far from simply an imaginative experience. While creative development is enhanced through pretend play, so are social, emotional, physical, and cognitive development. Literally every aspect of development is enhanced when children engage in dramatic play.

—Hereford and Schall, Learning through Play: Dramatic Play

Chapter Outline

▶ Dramatic Play to Encourage Learning
▶ Child Development: Developmental Stages of Dramatic Play
▶ Value of Dramatic Play
▶ Role of the Facilitator
▶ Effective Storage Systems
▶ Effective Labelling Systems
▶ Considerations for Setting Up a Dramatic Play Area

▶ Observation and Documentation Techniques
▶ International Considerations
▶ Dramatic Play Materials
▶ Ages and Stages of Dramatic Play
▶ Key Points
▶ Student Activities
▶ References
▶ Resources

Learning Outcomes

After studying this chapter, the reader will:

1. Identify the stages of dramatic play
2. Identify the value of the dramatic area
3. Identify the role of the facilitator
4. Discuss effective storage techniques
5. Identify an appropriate labelling system
6. Discuss considerations for setting up the dramatic area both indoors and outdoors
7. Identify appropriate materials
8. Identify various documentation techniques in order to observe children

Interactive Learning Exercises

 Remember, the CD-ROM that came with this text contains interactive exercises that relate to the topics in this chapter, as well as other valuable resources.

▶ Dramatic Play to Encourage Learning

It had been raining steadily for a week. The children had watched the raindrops run down the windowsill, had walked outside with umbrellas, had splashed in the puddles, and had decided that this was all so much fun they could do this type of play inside. They also had been singing and doing the actions to the rain song (see Chapter 5, p. 92).

Jordan got the umbrella from the dramatic area. He walked around the room, quietly singing to "Pitter, patter, pitter, patter." Jordan laughed and said, "Pitter, patter on my umbrella." Jordan continued to walk around with his umbrella, as Billy continued to play and say, "Pitter, patter." Lindsay heard the boys and ran over to watch Jordan and Billy for a few minutes. Finally, she got a drum. She started to play the drum and say, "Pitter, pitter, pitter" (photo 8.1).

Often, dramatic play emerges out of everyday actions and events. As children observe what is going on around them—rain, musical activity—they become very creative to adapt and create new situations and events.

▶ Child Development: Developmental Stages of Dramatic Play

The level of dramatic play that Jordan, Billy, and Lindsay were involved in is stage one: prop dependent, imitative play. Jordan used a real prop, the umbrella, to imitate pretend rain indoors. Billy had been playing a bamboo drum in the music area

PHOTO 8.1

(photo 5.13). The sound of this drum closely imitates the sound pattern of rain. His interest was sparked by Jordan's activity and he immediately started to play the rhythm of the rain according to the song that they had learned. Lindsay was involved in imitative play. She had listened to and watched the boys. She then copied Billy on the drum.

It is interesting to note how the play changed from solitary play to parallel play to associative play within a short time. Jordan had initially been involved in solitary play. When he wanted more interaction, he tried to attract attention to what he was doing by raising his voice and walking closer to other children engaged in play. Billy picked up on what Jordan said and added the sound of rain to Jordan's pretend rain play activity. The two boys were engaged in associative play. Each continued to be involved in his own activity, walking around with the umbrella and playing the drum but also sharing ideas and comments—the sound of the rain. Lindsay's play changed from onlooker play to parallel play when she decided to get a drum and imitate Billy's drumming. Each of these children were using their own instruments and playing their own rhythm.

The indoor rain activity continued over several days. Billy and Emily decided that they needed a big umbrella. Billy helped to create a note on the computer:

We need a great, big, huge umbrella, PLEASE.

He posted the note on the door of the preschool. One of the parents brought in a patio umbrella the next day. Billy and Emily noticed the umbrella immediately when they came in. They put up the umbrella in the music area, because this is where they had been singing and acting out the rain song. The two wanted the umbrella in this area as it would provide a dry spot to rest, out of the rain. Each child independently decided what was needed to go under the umbrella. Billy wanted a place to lie down. He brought in a pillow and a blanket. Emily decided to get a bed that looked like a bench to sit on. They jointly decided where they could put the materials (photo 8.2). Billy lay down because he needed a rest. Emily arranged her materials on the bench and eventually sat down with her doll. She talked to her doll, explaining to her that they would be nice and dry under their big umbrella.

Autumn had noticed Billy and Emily setting up the area. She ran back to the dress-up area and put on a raincoat. As she started back to the music area, she noticed that Yasmine was washing one of the dolls' hair (photo 8.3). "Autumn, come and help me," said

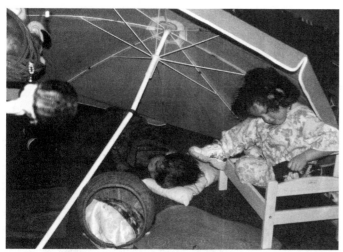

PHOTO 8.2

Yasmine. "The other baby needs to be washed too." Autumn went over to the cradle to pick up the doll that Yasmine was pointing to. After washing the doll, she brushed her hair (photo 8.4). Then both girls dressed their dolls with underpants, a sweater, and slacks. They picked up their dolls and walked toward the umbrella. "I am getting wet," said Yasmine. "Not me," said Autumn. "Come under the umbrella," called Billy. "You can put your babies on the bench," offered Emily. "They won't get wet here." Yasmine put her doll on the bench. Autumn said that her baby was too young to sit. Billy moved over and said that she could sit beside him. Autumn sat beside Billy with the doll on her lap.

The type of dramatic play these children were engaged in is stage two: familiar routines and roles. Each child was acting out roles that were familiar. Emily and Billy often participated in outdoor events with their parents. Each was able to recreate an outdoor environment indoors. Yasmine and Autumn were able to follow the routine and sequence of bathing and dressing babies. Yasmine and Autumn were aware of their babies' abilities. Yasmine realized that her baby was already able to sit by herself, whereas Autumn knew her baby still needed to be held. They were engaged in a parenting role. All children were able to maintain their roles through appropriate social interactions.

It is again interesting to note how the children influenced and expanded on their play. Autumn was initially interested in the rain play scenario. She showed her interest by putting on a raincoat. She was distracted by Yasmine's activity and encouragement to help in the bathing routine. Although Yasmine did not seem to notice the rain activities in another part of the room, she obviously had. Both girls extended

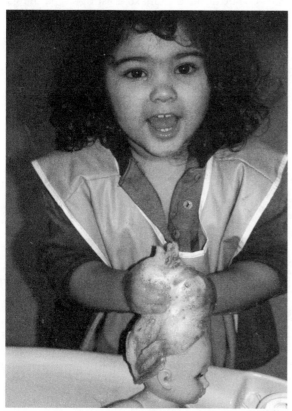

PHOTO 8.3

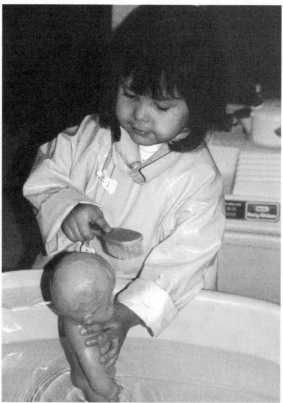

PHOTO 8.4

their role-play to accommodate the outdoor rain play situation.

Ted and his teacher, Michael, had been discussing driving cars. Ted suggested to Michael that they could both drive a car. Both sat on the floor to drive, making the sounds and motions of steering a car. Benjamin noticed the activity and asked if he could play. Ted said, "Sure." Michael stepped away to observe the two boys. Benjamin suggested that they could use a beanbag as a car. Ted agreed and the two boys took turns driving the car (photo 8.5). Benjamin looked over to the group under the umbrella and shouted, "We'll be the taxi. Come and take a taxi." Billy promptly got up, ran over to the taxi, and sat down behind Benjamin and Ted. Benjamin was the driver. "Where do you want to go?" asked Ted. "McDonald's!" answered Billy. Benjamin started his taxi by pretending to turn a key. He turned the wheel as they drove. All the boys made a car sound. On their way to McDonald's, the boys actively talked to each other. Billy told Benjamin to stop for a red light. Benjamin made a screeching sound and pumped his foot up and down. Billy pretended to fall into the door.

Billy shouted, "We're at McDonald's, let's go through the drive through." They called out to Iorahkote, who was using a toy telephone, "We need a hamburger and a Coke." Iorahkote immediately responded, "Okay." Iorahkote ran over to the kitchen area and picked up a tray. He placed two glasses on the tray and picked up two pieces of play dough. He ran back to the boys and handed them the drinks and hamburgers. "Hey, what about me?" shouted Benjamin. Iorahkote ran back to the kitchen. He could not find another glass, so he took a cup and some play dough. He gave these to Benjamin. "I wanted Coke, not coffee," said Benjamin. Iorahkote shrugged his shoulders. "That's okay," said Benjamin.

These boys were engaged in stage three of dramatic play: diverse routines and roles. The boys started with familiar routines—driving a car—and were able to switch to routines and roles within their community—taxi driver and eating at McDonald's. Ted started out in a prop-dependent, imitative role. He copied the actions of his teacher, Michael. When Benjamin joined the activity, the dramatic play changed from prop-dependent, imitative play to acting out familiar roles, and became less prop-dependent. The boys were able to symbolically represent the taxi using a beanbag chair. As the dramatic play continued, the play changed to diverse roles. Benjamin became a taxi driver, Billy and Ted became passengers, and they included Iorahkote as a service provider. Each boy had to be familiar with these roles within their community, and was able to add to the play by offering suggestions and acting out scenarios to make the play more realistic—stopping at the red light. The older boys, Benjamin and Billy, acted as leaders to facilitate and expand the play. The younger boys, Ted and Iorahkote, accepted and followed through on the suggestions. Benjamin initiated the taxi routine and Billy the McDonald's routine.

Olivia, Mackenzie, and Haley decided that they were going to create a bakery. Olivia said that her mother always made a list, so that she wouldn't forget things. They decided to make a list of all the things

PHOTO 8.5

PHOTO 8.6

PHOTO 8.7

PHOTO 8.8

they needed and asked Jennifer to write it down. They decided that they needed a recipe; cookie cutters; flour; salt; water; brown, green, and yellow drink crystals; bowls; a cash register; and some money. The girls went around to collect the things and checked off each item when they had found it with Jennifer's help.

When they had found all the things, they set up the "selling part" in the playhouse. They discovered that the playhouse was too far away from the kitchen. They tried to move the house, but needed more help. Finally all the girls and Jennifer moved the house closer to the kitchen. Sarah asked if she could help. The girls asked her if she would like to make some play dough. Sarah agreed that she could (photo 8.6).

The other girls set up the playhouse as a bakeshop. Haley decided to follow a recipe to make cookies. Mackenzie decided to make the birthday cake (photo 8.7). Olivia decided that she would be the "sales lady." As she was starting to sell the baked goods, Reghan came to buy something. She wanted to buy some animals. Olivia explained that this was a bakeshop. Reghan suggested it could be both. Olivia agreed and went to get some animals (photo 8.8).

The activity attracted other children. Iorahkote came over and tried to take one of the "muffins" (photo 8.9). He was quickly told that he had to wait until it was in the store and then he could buy it. He promptly brought the muffin tin to the store. He again tried to take one. Sarah said, "You have to pay first!"

Jennifer asked Iorahkote to ask how much the muffin cost. "About ten dollars," said Sarah. Mackenzie gave him some money. He handed it to Olivia, who then said, "Now you can have a muffin." Iorahkote tried to put it in his mouth. Olivia said, "Stop. It's only pretend, you really can't eat it." Iorahkote gave the play dough back.

During this scenario, the children were able to work together to plan their play, by creating a list of things they needed. They discussed what they needed and who would do what. It involved several children. They created their own props. This is stage four of dramatic play: communicative cooperative play.

PHOTO 8.9

► Value of Dramatic Play

- develop self-confidence in own ability to act—Sarah was confident in her ability to make play dough; she had made it before and was able to create a usable play dough.
- develop self-control—When Iorahkote took some play dough, Sarah was able to tell him verbally that he had to buy it. He did bring it over to the "bakeshop." As a toddler, his self-control is still fragile. Jennifer realized this and guided him to help solve the problem.
- distinguish fantasy from reality—Olivia had a clear sense that the muffins they had made were not real. She was able to help Iorahkote realize this.
- practise fine motor skills—The children practised kneading, rolling, shaping, and decorating the dough.
- imitate actions and behaviours in a safe way—All materials were realistic. The children could form the dough into the desired shapes. Even if Iorahkote had eaten the dough, it would not have harmed him as natural products were used.
- learn to take another's perspective—Olivia was able to listen to the suggestion made by Reghan and offer both animals and baked goods to sell.
- share ideas and materials—Benjamin and Ted were able to share the steering wheel and were able to agree to become taxi drivers.
- learn to negotiate—Sarah tried to negotiate with Iorahkote. Jennifer helped by modelling a strategy that worked.
- learn to compromise—Mackenzie had wanted to use real candles on her cake. She asked Jennifer if there were some available. Jennifer said that they did not have any candles. Mackenzie was upset and said that then she could not make a birthday cake. Jennifer asked her to think about what else to use. Mackenzie said "Nothing!" and walked away. She came back a few minutes later and said that she could use pretend candles—toothpicks.
- learn about similarities and differences—Billy was able to create a rhythm that sounded like rain. Sarah was able to create the play dough by adding more flour to make it drier and adding more colour to make it redder.
- think about situations and materials in new ways—Benjamin was able to create a car out of a beanbag. Iorahkote was able to substitute a cup for a glass when he couldn't find one. Billy and Emily were able to create an outdoor area to stay out of the rain.
- learn to understand symbols—Haley could follow the picture in the cookie recipe to form her cookie.
- solve problems—The girls worked together to move the playhouse closer to the kitchen. The girls were able to list the materials and find the materials they needed with minimal help.
- expand communication skills—In all scenarios, children had to listen to each other's ideas and respond to them appropriately.
- express emotions in a safe way—When Mackenzie was upset, she was able to leave the area. Jennifer realized she needed some time alone. Mackenzie did come back and continued to make her birthday cake using alternative materials.
- work through stressful situations—If children are upset, or are in a stressful situation at home, they may try to act out the stressful situation in the drama centre. Rather than jumping to conclusions, the facilitator needs to listen carefully to what is going on and support the child in working through the situation. Melanie had just had a new baby brother. She was rather quiet and withdrawn in the morning and Jennifer asked her what was the matter. Melanie said that perhaps her mother should take the new brother back to the hospital. Jennifer asked her if she would like to learn to bathe a baby so she could help her mother. Melanie brightened up and carefully listened to Jennifer as she explained how to test the water, hold the baby, and bathe the baby. The next day, Melanie came back and very proudly said that she had helped to bathe her new brother: her mother let her test the water.

► Role of the Facilitator

- document children's learning and activities;
- encourage children to express emotions—Jennifer encouraged Mackenzie to express herself. She also offered a suggestion, then left Mackenzie alone to work through her problem;
- learn to "read" children—Melanie's behaviour was different when she came in. Jennifer immediately asked what the problem was and understood what to do about it;
- listen for emotions—Jennifer realized that Sarah was getting frustrated with Iorahkote's behaviour. She quickly stepped in to help solve the problem;
- let children take the lead—The girls could manage most of their bakery shop scenario themselves. Jennifer stepped in only when asked (to write the

list and help check it off) and when she anticipated a problem (moving the playhouse);

- provide appropriate props—All the props for all scenarios were available: umbrellas, steering wheel, ingredients for play dough;
- accept children's ideas—Jennifer helped to create the indoor rain area, helped set up the baby bath area;
- get involved in the play—Jennifer was involved in helping scribe and check off items;
- know when to step in and when to leave children alone—Jennifer knew to step in to help move the playhouse, as it was potentially dangerous for the children to do it by themselves. She listened to Sarah's voice and realized she was getting frustrated and therefore stepped in. She encouraged the children to continue the activities without her;
- ensure a variety and appropriate number of materials—In each case, children were able to find what they needed;
- collect a variety of props—Jennifer helped Billy write a note to post to get a large umbrella;
- encourage discussion—Iorahkote was encouraged to ask his playmates how much an item cost. The children readily responded to his request;
- encourage problem solving—Mackenzie was encouraged to think about alternatives to candles;
- encourage children to share feelings, ideas—Melanie was asked to tell how she felt. Children were encouraged to share their ideas in writing to create a list of what they needed;
- encourage reading—Haley was given a recipe to follow. Books on the bakery and about the rain were left within the areas. Jennifer read the list of words back to the children so that they could find the items and check them off;
- refer children to each other—Iorahkote was referred to Sarah;
- brainstorm with children—Jennifer created a list of items with the children;
- incorporate a variety of methods—drawing, reading, writing (puddle raindrops, books, recipes, creating lists); utilize chants, finger plays, music (the rain song);
- utilize children's interests—helped to set up an indoor rain scenario; and
- encourage dramatic play both indoors and outdoors—The car-driving episode continued to be popular during outdoor play. Children took turns driving the truck, this time from the top of the climber (photo 8.10).

▶ Effective Storage Systems

1. Storage for Realistic Types of Play

Some types of play, for example practising routines such as dressing, washing dishes, and bathing babies, should be as realistic as possible. Children need to learn how to do these things properly—foods that belong in the fridge should be placed in the fridge, foods that belong in the freezer should be placed in the freezer, cutlery and dishes should be organized just as they are in a real kitchen; a baby bathing scenario should include all items that would be included in a real setting; and dress-up clothes should be hung on hooks or hangers. The real setting should be emulated closely so that the child learns the appropriate skills of organizing, the appropriate sequence of steps, and gentle handling where appropriate.

2. Imaginary Play with Props

The second kind of storage needed is for the props that children use to imagine with. These include things like steering wheels, magic wands, scarves, hats, capes, blankets, and so on. For the child to use these items he or she must be able to see them.

PHOTO 8.10

Follow a natural sense of how to store these: hats can be placed on top of shelves, scarves are easily hung on hooks. Prop boxes can be created that include magical items—magic wands, magic rings, stars (figure 8.1). Children will enjoy the mystery of what is hidden in the box. Blankets can be hung on blanket frames. Follow the rule that materials must be easily accessible, the organization must be logical, and it must look attractive. No one likes to get dressed in wrinkly clothes.

FIGURE 8.1

▶ Magic Prop Box

- Hinged box
- Could pick up on magical moments of the year
- Props inside: magical, not necessarily Hallowe'en-related

▶ Effective Labelling Systems

Labelling in the drama area needs to use common sense. Remember that the purpose of labelling is to make things easy to find. It makes little sense to label the fridge or stove; children can find these items. If the purpose is to teach the child the word, then perhaps a picture dictionary would be of more use. If the storage is logically organized—dishes in cupboards, cutlery in drawers, clothes folded in drawers—children will know where to put things or where to find them.

Other things such as props should be labelled. Label the shelves with pictures and words to indicate where things should go—hats and scarves on hooks, and so on.

▶ Considerations for Setting Up a Dramatic Play Area

Dramatic play offers a unique opportunity to learn about other cultures and also about individuals with a disability. Children can learn to:

- use different types of eating utensils;
- do different types of work—such as pulling a rickshaw (made from a box); making igloos in the winter or straw huts in the summer;
- create buildings out of cardboard boxes to represent different architectural designs;
- try on realistic clothes from other cultures;
- act out stories from other cultures;
- represent diversity in dolls, books, and display materials;
- represent props from various cultures—Japanese fans, Indian scarves, jewellery from various cultures, and books indicating how children live in various cultures (e.g., Kindersley, Barnabas and Anabel. (1995). *Children Just Like Me.* Bolton, ON: Fenn Publishing Company; Rattigan, J., and Hsu-Flanders, L. (1993). *Dumpling Soup.* New York, NY: Little, Brown and Company);
- use props to gain familiarity with disabilities—small wheelchair (may be borrowed from various agencies for a short time), crutches, leg braces; and
- use these materials in indoor and outdoor environments.

Drama should not be confined to just daily living experiences. Dramatic play must also be encouraged in other areas. For a centre to score at an excellent level on the Early Childhood Environment Rating Scale (ECERS), more than one area of dramatic play must be available: "Props for at least two different themes accessible daily (Ex. housekeeping and work)" (Harms, Clifford, and Cryer, 1998, p. 32).

1. Housekeeping or Daily Living Centre

The housekeeping area is an essential area to encourage children to practise everyday living skills. You should try to make this area as realistic as possible. Consider creating a dramatic area that has the following components:

- kitchen area—Children should have real materials to work with. When children can create real mixtures they learn about **quantity, measurement,** consistency, **viscosity,** and number (math and

PHOTO 8.11

science skills). They learn to use the tools of cooking appropriately—measuring with spoons or measuring cups, adding quantity by measuring as opposed to dumping (photo 8.11). They learn to use this information to transfer it to a different situation—serving food, pretending to feed dolls, pretending to eat (photo 8.12). They learn the routines of cooking, setting the table, cleaning the table, washing the dishes, drying the dishes. They learn to respect materials in their environment—handling objects with respect, taking care of objects and the environment, and cleaning up when they have finished a job.

- baby bath—Children should have all the materials and equipment available to give them experiences that encourage them to learn about safety in water, for example keeping the baby's face out of the water, not leaving the baby unattended, dressing the baby appropriately for the weather conditions, going out with a baby; and the routines of washing, for example undressing, washing, using shampoo and soap, drying, powdering, diapering, dressing appropriately for the next step (sleeping, playing, going outside) (photo 8.13).

- bedrooms—These could be in one of the quiet areas. Children are then aware that babies are sleeping and one needs to do quiet activities when someone is sleeping. Beds, cribs, or cradles need to be realistic: they should have a mattress, sheet, pillows (depending on supposed age of baby), pillowcases, cover sheet, and blanket. Children can learn the routine of making the bed, putting the baby to bed, reading to the baby, singing the baby to sleep, or playing soothing music. If sheets and blankets are aesthetically pleasing and there are a

PHOTO 8.12

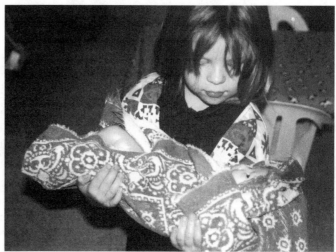

PHOTO 8.13

variety of choices, children will wish to change the beds according to their individual tastes and preferences.

- cleaning—Cleaning routines are a natural part of daily living: washing clothes, hanging them to dry; cleaning floors: sweeping, vacuuming, mopping, polishing; cleaning tables and windows with squirt bottles, rags, paper towels.

2. Puppets

A puppet theatre is easily constructed using plywood, hinges, material, and paint (figure 8.2). Children will often act out familiar stories, personal adventures, poetry, or stressful situations when they are hidden behind a screen. Puppets should be attractive and clean. When purchasing or making puppets, try to stick to puppets that can be used for more than one purpose; for example, animal puppets (a dog could be a wolf or a dog; a cat could become a lion if a mane is attached, a fish could become a shark or a whale) and people puppets (girl, boy, male, female could become Little Red Riding Hood if a red hood is available; mother, grandmother).

3. Interest-Related

Children often become interested in particular ideas or scenarios—indoor rain activity, driving activity. If the props are readily available or if children are encouraged to express their ideas and help in collecting materials (Billy's note to parents to obtain the large umbrella), children will be encouraged to become creative. A hat can change the play from a construction worker to a baseball player (photo 8.14). Even objects around the classroom can encourage

FIGURE 8.2

▶ **Puppet Theatre**

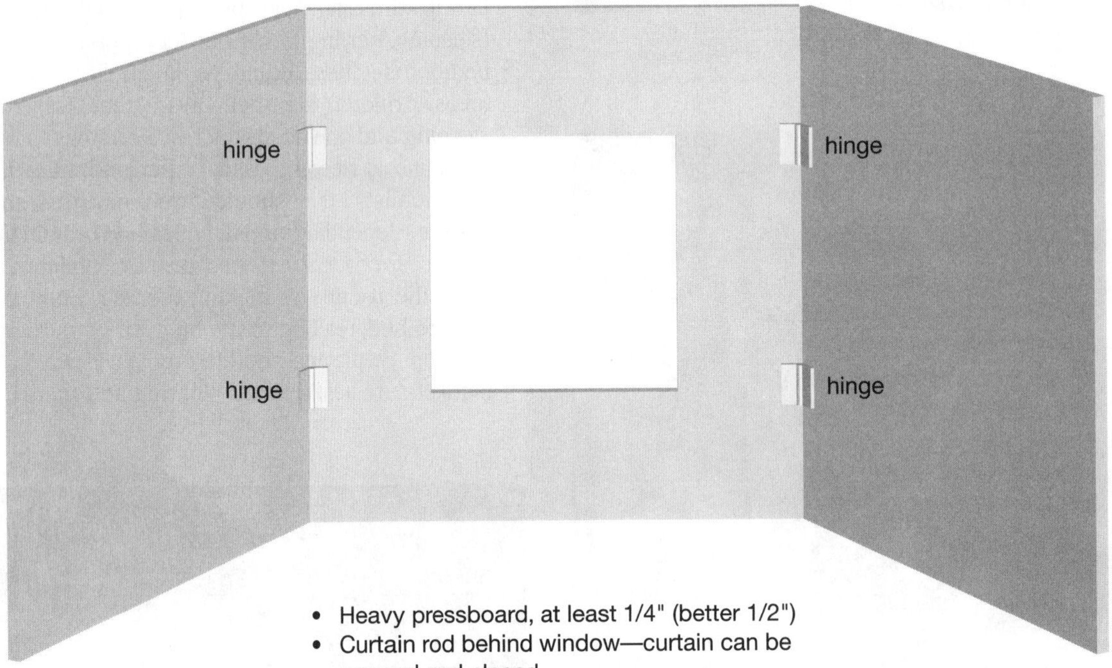

- Heavy pressboard, at least 1/4" (better 1/2")
- Curtain rod behind window—curtain can be opened and closed
- Height – either on table, small for finger puppets, or child sized
  – 2–3 children fit behind

Alternatives:
- Heavy cardboard boxes—cut one end off and cut sides down, cut in window, table top
- Fridge or stove boxes—cut one side off and cut window in opposite side, floor
- Decorate, attach curtains

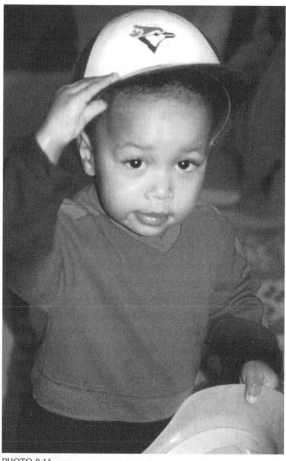

PHOTO 8.14

PHOTO 8.15

and entice children's imaginations. Ben had built a robot at home; now he became a robot at preschool (photo 8.15). A large box can turn into a cave for animals to hibernate in (photo 8.16).

These activities can occur anywhere in the room:

- sand play dinosaur zoo (see Chapter 1, pp. 5–8);
- creative art activities—play dough; dinosaurs stuck in the mud (see photo 1.1);
- water play—washing clothes (see photo 4.7);
- music—creating a marching band (see photo 5.15);
- blocks—dinosaur park (see photo 6.1);
- quiet area—flannel board, acting out a story using flannel board pieces;
- manipulatives—creating a pond to play with small animals (see photo 10.3); and
- carpentry—creating items that can be used in dramatic play—building fences for animals at the farm, houses for a train scene, signs for traffic locations.

4. Prop Boxes

One way to utilize children's interests in a variety of ways and to engage their curiosity is to develop prop

boxes. These boxes should be aesthetically designed (figure 8.1) and should contain materials that will support and enhance children's dramatic play. Children can take the boxes anywhere—including outside. Materials in the box should support the play, not direct the play; therefore, children should brainstorm what kinds of boxes they might wish to have

PHOTO 8.16

and what should go into the boxes. Children should help to collect the items. Some ideas for prop boxes are as follows (adapted from Myhre, 1997):

- jewellery and accessory prop box—ideal to support role play and therefore should include male and female items of each: watches, bracelets, necklaces (make sure that jewellery is sturdy and has no sharp edges or loose parts), ladies' gloves, sunglasses, glasses frames, rings, jewellery boxes, small shatterproof mirror, earrings;
- writing suitcase—small plastic suitcase with a variety of paper (both lined and unlined), alternate writing tools (pencil crayons, markers, feathers, chalk, pens, crayons, pencils), ruler, eraser, small notebook, dictionary, glue stick, scissors, tape;
- work-related prop boxes—dentist, mechanic, firefighter (should contain pertinent tools and clothing); and
- decorating box—variety of small scrap materials, paper, string, yarn, foil, lace, variety of scissors and shears, glue, markers, crayons, oil pastels, chalk.

Storage of these boxes should be in a central location for easy access. Children should be able to take these boxes to any location. Boxes should be clearly labelled by picture and word so that children know what is in the box and where to return items.

5. Safety Considerations

- breakable items—ensure mirrors are shatterproof; ensure breakable dishes or other glassware are used in carpeted areas; ensure jewellery is sturdy (check frequently);
- remove drawstrings on clothing that could lead to choking;
- ensure props are age-appropriate—dress-up clothes should follow ability level of child to dress and undress self; avoid small items (jewellery) for children who are still mouthing items;
- discuss safety guidelines with children—climbing with trailing scarves; using breakable objects; using sharp objects such as knives;
- clothing that fits—hem clothing to avoid trailing clothing that children can trip on; use shoes that *fit* (high-heeled shoes are dangerous and inappropriate for the developing foot);
- disinfect clothing—choose hats that can be easily cleaned;
- ensure cleanliness—all clothing items need to be washed regularly; and
- design safe storage—hooks that are protected from bumping into; sturdy containers that do not fall apart when transported.

▶ Observation and Documentation Techniques

One of the techniques to gather information pertinent for children's dramatic play is to survey the children's families. A variety of methods could be used, but irrespective of what the method is the facilitator needs to do some basic research first to ensure that the right questions are asked. The facilitator needs to know:

- the diversity of the group;
- specific cultural heritages celebrated by the group;
- what some cultural considerations might be; and
- what conflicting practices might be evident.

For example, a 20-month-old child started the daycare experience. He came from an immigrant family. This child had never been left anywhere without his parents or grandparents. He had never slept anywhere but in his mother's bed. He had no siblings. His grandparents had not immigrated. He was used to a vegetarian, spicy diet.

By mid-morning he was sobbing uncontrollably. He refused to let go of the adult who had first greeted him. He refused to eat, drink, or sleep. Finally, the mother was called to pick him up. After two weeks of similar situations, the daycare finally suggested that the parents needed to look elsewhere.

Although we can put strategies in place, the above incident could have been mitigated or perhaps prevented. This is pertinent not only to dramatic play but also to all other types of play within the environment. When a child is put into an environment that is totally strange—group time versus individual time, many children versus one child, shared attention versus individual attention, strange foods, and unknown routines, it is not surprising that the child will find the transition uncomfortable. Prior to enrolling children, you might use the following techniques:

- have an intake interview that allows you to discuss the philosophy of your centre, discuss how the family member feels about that philosophy, and discuss adaptations you both are comfortable with; and
- give out a handbook that clearly explains the program; ask the family to read it and come back to discuss the information.

It is important to discuss information with families. It is easier to gauge their reaction, to compromise on some points, to come to agreement about the child, to make the family feel that they are immediately a part of the program, and to help you make informed decisions about what kind of adaptations you and the program may need to make.

After children are enrolled in the program, ask families to participate in a family night to discuss the program for their children. When families feel their input is valuable and listened to participation will be high. If families cannot come during the evening, set alternative times—a weekend picnic with children's activities may give time for smaller group discussions. This also gives you an opportunity to observe the children and families interact.

OBSERVATION OF THE ENVIRONMENT

The following questions should guide you to make decisions on when changes or adaptation should be made:

1. Are all ethnic groups within the room represented?
2. Have you represented a diversity in pictures, books, props, materials, and equipment?
3. Do dress-up clothes represent various cultures and both genders?
4. Are gender roles open-ended?
5. Are families invited to participate through planning and evaluation of experiences?

Figures 8.3 and 8.4 are examples of observation checklists.

FIGURE 8.3

▶ Observation of Dramatic Play Stages Chart

Name: Lindsay

Stage	Date	Evidence
Imitative	09/10	Watched Billy play drum. Used left hand to play one side of the bongo drum and right hand with drum stick
Prop-dependent	09/15	Wrapped doll in a blanket. Put doll in buggy and went for a walk

This information can be used to provide more opportunities for Lindsay to imitate actions. As she is walking with her doll, imitation of gestures could be made—for example, goodbye. A sidewalk could be created indoors or outdoors with a crossing guard to increase awareness of road safety. Other props could be provided to continue role-play of caring for babies—front or back packs to carry baby, car seats in vehicles.

FIGURE 8.4

▶ Interests of Children Chart

Name: Billy

Dates	Description
09/11	Rain play—creating indoor rain area
09/12	Collected materials for area with sister Emily—developed note, used computer to print, posted note for parents to help gather materials
09/13	Expanding area to include sheltered spot

This type of tool not only tells you what kind of activities children are engaged in, but also gives some information about how long the interest continues and some idea of their skill levels. This will help to facilitate future experiences—have a computer available, involve the child in a brainstorming process.

▶ International Considerations

International perspectives on play vary. Some of the variation is based on belief, some on economics, and others on the view of the child. The differences can be summarized in the points below.

1. **Types of pretend play vary from culture to culture and are dependent on the interactions of the children and caregivers.** Fung (1994) identified that pretend play between the Chinese caregiver and child focused on teaching the child culturally appropriate forms of social behaviour. In Irish American families (Mintz, 1998), the focus of pretend play was to establish self-esteem and independence from caregivers. Not surprisingly, Chinese caregivers initiated more play activities, whereas Irish American children initiated more pretend play activities.

These two viewpoints clearly indicate a cultural value that is quite different. On one hand the adult directs the play; on the other hand, play is directed away from the adult. Clearly, these cultural differences need to be discussed and clarified with families prior to imposing one or another system upon the child.

2. **Types of play materials are dependent on culture and on economic resources.** "Empirical evidence indicates that the spontaneous pretend play of European American, middle class children typically occurs in relation to objects, particularly toy miniatures such as dolls, cars and phones (e.g. Haight & Miller, 1993; Pulaski, 1973). In cultural groups where toy miniatures are scarce (Heath, 1983) or nonexistent (Gaskins, 1990) children enjoy active play lives (Schwartzman, 1986) constructing props from the materials at hand" (Haight et al., 1999, p. 1477).

3. **Pretend play varies from social routines to fantasy play around children's movies, books, and related play materials.** In cultures where toy miniatures were related to current themes from movies or books, there tended to be more emphasis on fantasy play (Haight et al., 1999).

4. **Areas with a lack of economic resources show more work-related play.** Children in many parts of the world live in societies that have no child-care systems. In these societies, children work or play alongside the adults (see Chapter 4 for an example from Guatemala, p. 84).

5. **The value a society places on play as a means of learning gives rise to different types of pretend play interactions.** "When interacting with their children across a variety of contexts, Chinese caregivers generally were highly didactic, directive, and demanding mature behaviour relative to Irish American caregivers. They generally expected children to listen attentively to their elders, understand what was said, and behave accordingly (see Fung, 1994; Miller et al., 1966). Overall, Irish American caregivers were relatively more focused on meeting their children's perceived individual needs, and supporting their individual interests. They often allowed their children to initiate and lead interactions around topics of the children's own choosing" (Haight et al., 1999, p. 1483).

6. **Societal pressures are placed on children to prepare children for the next stage of education.** "Today, there are tax-supported kindergartens in every state, and some twenty-three states are considering programs for four-year-olds. In too many schools kindergartens have become 'one-size-smaller' first grades and children are tested, taught from workbooks, given homework, and take home a report card. The result of this educational hurrying is that 10 to 20% of kindergarten children are being 'retained' or put in 'transition' classes to prepare them for the academic rigors of first grade!" (Elkind, 1988, p. 7).

▶ Dramatic Play Materials

Table 8.1 lists suggested dramatic play materials along with the types of areas where each would be appropriate.

TABLE 8.1

▶ Dramatic Play Materials

Type of Area	Possible Materials
Kitchen	Stove, fridge (a real bar fridge works well), kitchen cabinets, sink, table, chairs, highchair
	Cutlery—knives, spoons, forks, serving spoons, serving forks, cutlery drawer organizers (use adult dessert-sized flatware, butter knives)
	Dishes—small plates, middle sized plates, small bowls, small mugs, small juice glasses, demi-cups and saucers (Corel-type dishes are safe)
	Cooking—small frying pan, spatula, small whisk, small pots and pans, cutting board, small wooden spoons (easy to purchase at flea markets)
	Baking—small muffin trays, baking pans, baking forms
	Storage—small canister set, small pitchers, small sugar bowl, small serving platters and bowls
	Measuring—measuring cups, measuring spoons

TABLE 8.1 DRAMATIC PLAY MATERIALS (continued)

Type of Area	Possible Materials
	Washing dishes—dish pan/sink, dish soap, dishcloth, dish towel, towel rack
	Cleaning—child-sized dust pan, dust brush, broom, mop
	Decorative—tablecloth, placemats, vases, flowers, plants
	Other—oven mitts, pot holders, serving trays, aprons, ice cube trays, table protectors, garbage can
	Mixture materials—flour, salt, sugar, water, spaghetti, macaroni, drink crystals (see discussion Chapter 3, p. 63)
Baby bath	Low chest of drawers—doll clothes, diapers, bedding
	Low table as change and bath table—baby bath, shampoo, powder (cornstarch), comb, brush, face cloth, towels, towel rack, bath toys, mirror, dirty clothes hamper, garbage can
	Cleanup—mop, broom, dustpan, dust brush
Sleeping area	Cribs, cradles, beds
	Fitted mattress, sheets, pillows, pillowcases, and blankets per bed
	Story books; sleep-time music (Chapter 5, p. 100); CD player
Puppets	Finger puppets, stick puppets, puppets on a string, hand puppets
	Puppet theatre
	Props for puppets—kerchiefs, small brooms, wands, colourful material
Props	Sheets, blankets, pillows
	Blocks from block area, planks, foam blocks
	Boxes of various sizes to turn into cars, other vehicles, caves, houses
	Wagons, shopping carts
	Steering wheels, umbrellas
	Small rugs and carpets
	Music (see Chapter 5 for more on music)
	Brainstorm with the children and families to add other items
Dress-up clothes	Involve families to obtain culturally related clothes
	All clothing should be child-sized to prevent accidents
	Obtainable at second-hand clothing stores
	Pajamas, dressing gowns, bath robes, night gowns
	Capes, colourful scarves
	Suits, ties, shirts (long sleeved and short sleeved, vests, sweaters)
	Dresses, skirts, tops, blouses, sweaters, jackets
	Hats: dress hats, sport hats, construction hats (should be washable)
	Gloves: work gloves, fancy gloves, driving gloves
	Costumes: fairy, prince, ballerina, doctor, police officer
	Shoes: boots, sandals, running shoes
	Shatterproof, child-height mirror
Kits	Magic kit (see p. 168); doctor's kit

TABLE 8.1 DRAMATIC PLAY MATERIALS (continued)

Type of Area	Possible Materials
Props	Blankets, sheets, pillows, curtains, small carpets or rugs
	Multi-cultural (see p. 168)
	Boxes of various sizes—turn into caves, vehicles, homes
	Blocks from block area and supplies as listed on pp. 132–133
	Seasonal additions or cultural decorations—lights; skating rink;
	Real plants and flowers (see table 2.2), artificial flowers, watering can
	Steering wheels, riding toys
	Hoses, nozzles, small ladders

▶ Ages and Stages of Dramatic Play

Table 8.2 summarizes the ages and stages of dramatic play.

TABLE 8.2

▶ Ages and Stages of Dramatic Play

Stage	Age	Behaviours
Stage 1: prop-dependent, imitative	1-year-olds 2-year-olds	Imitate facial expressions and simple actions
		Use props as intended, play directed by props
		Solitary play
		Play parallel to others
		Imitate actions of peers or familiar adults
		Influenced by props—the prop will dictate the play
		Repeat actions or routines
		Use sound effects in their play
		Communicate through gestures, body language, and single words or phrases
Stage 2: familiar roles	3-year-olds	Engage in role-play by taking on roles of significant adults in their lives
		Interact with peers during role-play through actions and words
		May start to plan play by gathering props, and by identifying what they will do verbally
		Favourite themes include housekeeping, father and mother roles
		May have imaginary friends
		Dress-up

TABLE 8.2 AGES AND STAGES OF DRAMATIC PLAY (continued)

Stage	Age	Behaviours
Stage 3: diverse roles	4-year-olds	Take on roles of non-familiar adults
		Take on adventurous roles such as firefighter, police officer, pilot, construction worker
		State that this is a pretend activity
		Use a variety of items to represent props—symbolic representations
		Repeat favourite dramatic experiences
		Re-enact activities or events
		Increased time spent on dramatic activity
		Use variety of voice tones during play
Stage 4: communicative, cooperative	5-year-olds and older	Create own characters
		Draw on characters from books and television
		Extensive discussions about play
		Increased attention to detail
		Start to use mime
		Extend play activity over more than one day
		Involve several children
		Create own props
		Create own episodes in writing
		Create extensive plots

▶ KEY POINTS

Stages of Dramatic Play

Stage 1: prop-dependent, imitative—imitate, use props as intended, play influenced by props.
Stage 2: familiar roles—act out roles of familiar adults.
Stage 3: diverse roles—act out roles of non-familiar adults.
Stage 4: communicative, cooperative—create own characters, scripts, and props.

Value of Dramatic Play

- develop self-confidence in own ability to act;
- develop self-control;
- distinguish fantasy from reality;
- practise fine motor skills;
- imitate actions and behaviours;
- take another's perspective;
- share ideas and materials;
- learn to negotiate;
- learn to compromise;
- learn about similarities and differences;
- think about materials and situations in new ways;
- learn to understand symbols;
- solve problems;
- expand communication skills;
- express emotions in a safe way; and
- work through stressful situations.

Role of the Facilitator

- encourage children to express emotions;
- learn to "read" children and document your observations;
- listen for emotions;
- let children take the lead;
- provide appropriate props;
- accept children's ideas;
- get involved in play;
- know when to step in and when to leave children alone;

▶ KEY POINTS (continued)

Role of the Facilitator (continued)

- collect a variety of props;
- encourage discussion;
- encourage problem solving;
- encourage children to share ideas and materials;
- encourage reading;
- refer children to each other;
- brainstorm with children;
- incorporate various methods;
- utilize children's interests; and
- encourage dramatic play indoors and outdoors.

Storage Systems

- storage for realistic dramatic play; and
- storage of imaginary props.

Labelling Systems

- model after realistic settings; and
- common sense.

Considerations for Setting Up a Dramatic Play Area

- multi-cultural considerations;
- housekeeping or daily living centre—kitchen, bathing babies, bedrooms, cleaning;
- use puppets; and
- provide interest-related props.

Observation of Documentation Techniques

- parent surveys;
- environment;
- stages of dramatic play; and
- interests of children.

Student Activities

1. You have a new family that is going to enter your preschool program. The parents of these two children have died tragically. They have come to live with their uncle and aunt and two cousins who are already in school. The girls are twins, aged four. The girls do not speak any English; they have arrived from Cuba. What information might you wish to gather from the family? What changes might you consider making in your dramatic area?
2. How might you continue to expand the dramatic play of Billy and Emily? What other materials might you need?
3. Discuss the importance of providing real, aesthetically pleasing materials.
4. Why is a theme-based curriculum that changes every week not particularly valid for dramatic play?
5. Discuss ways that you could involve families in the program.
6. Choose one culture that you know relatively little about. Research that culture and indicate some of the resources you might wish to include within the environment.
7. If all of your children come from a middle-class white background, why is it still essential to include experiences about other cultures in your program?
8. Pick one of the areas in the housekeeping area. Develop a floor plan, list of materials, and storage of materials for that area.
9. Using the tool on observation of dramatic play, observe two children of different ages. Compare the results. How were they similar or different? Were all the differences due to age?

▶ References

Elkind, D. (1988). *The Hurried Child.* Don Mills, ON: Addison-Wesley Publishing Company, Inc.

Fung, H. (1994). *The socialization of shame in young Chinese children.* Unpublished doctoral dissertation, University of Chicago.

Haight, W., & Miller, P. (1993). *Pretending at Home: Early Development in a Sociocultural Context.* Albany, NY: State University of New York Press.

Haight, W., Wang, X., Han-tih Fung, H., Williams, K., & Mintz, J. (1999, December). Universal, Developmental, and Variable Aspects of Young Children's Play: A Cross-Cultural Comparison of Pretending at Home. *Child Development.* Volume 70, Number 6, 1477–1488.

Harms, T., Clifford, R., & Cryer, D. (1998). *Early Childhood Environment Rating Scale: Revised Edition.* New York, NY: Teachers College Press.

Heath, S. (1983). Ways with words: Language, life and work in communities and classrooms. Cambridge, UK: Cambridge University Press.

Hereford, N., & Schall, J. (1991). *Learning through Play: Dramatic Play.* New York, NY: Scholastic Inc.

Mintz, P. (1998). The socialization of self in middle-class, Irish American families. Unpublished doctoral dissertation, University of Chicago.

Myhre, S. (1997, Spring). Enhancing dramatic play with prop boxes. *Texas Child Care.* 2–10.

Pulaski, M. (1973). Toys and imaginative play. In J.L. Singer (Ed.). *The child's world of make-believe.* New York, NY: Academic Press.

Schwartzman, H. (1986). A cross-cultural perspective on child-structured play activities and materials. In A.W. Gottfried & C.C. Brown (Eds.). *Play interactions: the contribution of play materials and parental involvement to children's development.* Lexington, MA: Lexington Books.

▶ Resources

Books/Poetry for Dramatization

Brown, M. (1985). *Hand Rhymes.* New York, NY: Puffin Unicorn Books.

Davis, A., & Petricic, D. (1998). *The Enormous Potato.* Toronto, ON: Kids Can Press Ltd.

Inkpen, M. (1993). *Lullabyhullaballoo!* London, ON: Hodder Children's Books.

Moxley, S. (1995). *Skip Across the Ocean.* London, UK: Frances Lincoln Limited.

Roddie, S., & Cony, F. (1991). *Hatch, Egg, Hatch.* Toronto, ON: Little, Brown and Company.

Rounds, G. (1993). *The Three Billy Goats Gruff.* New York, NY: Random House.

White Carlstrom, N., & Alley, R. (1999). *Who Said Boo?* New York, NY: Aladdin Paperbacks.

Winch, J. *The old man who loved to sing.* (1993). Sydney, Australia: Scholastic Australia Pty Limited.

CHAPTER 9

Creative Arts

Young children, art, and creativity are very compatible. Young children are often noisy, active, and messy. Art too can be noisy, active, and messy. Art can also be quiet and meticulous like a child who sits motionless while small fingers try to glue together pieces of paper, yarn, and ribbon. Art allows children to experiment and explore, to see what they can create. It is fun even though the finished product might not resemble anything in the real world.

—Schirrmacher, Art and Creative Development for Young Children

Chapter Outline

- ▶ What Is Creativity?
- ▶ Creative Arts to Encourage Learning
- ▶ Child Development: Developmental Levels of the Creative Arts
- ▶ Value of Creative Arts
- ▶ Role of the Facilitator
- ▶ Effective Storage Systems
- ▶ Effective Labelling Systems
- ▶ Considerations for Setting Up a Creative Arts Area

- ▶ Observation and Documentation Techniques
- ▶ International Considerations
- ▶ Creative Arts Materials
- ▶ Ages and Stages of Creative Arts
- ▶ Key Points
- ▶ Student Activities
- ▶ References
- ▶ Resources

Learning Outcomes

After studying this chapter, the reader will:

1. Identify the creative process
2. Identify the stages of creative arts
3. Identify the value of the creative arts area
4. Identify the role of the facilitator
5. Discuss effective storage techniques
6. Identify an appropriate labelling system
7. Discuss considerations for setting up the creative arts area in indoor and outdoor environments
8. Identify appropriate materials for painting, sculpting, drawing/writing, paste and cut, print making, and weaving—both indoors and outdoors
9. Identify various documentation techniques in order to observe children

Interactive Learning Exercises

 Remember, the CD-ROM that came with this text contains interactive exercises that relate to the topics in this chapter, as well as other valuable resources.

▶ What Is Creativity?

Creativity is often linked with art or music. However, creativity is not limited to either art or music. Creativity is a process that encompasses all we do—our actions, our thoughts, and our responses. "Creativity is a special and different way of viewing the world in ways in which there are no right or wrong answers, only possibilities. Think of creativity as an attitude rather than an aptitude" (Schirrmacher, 1998, p. 6).

The children's behaviours described in this book demonstrate creativity in many ways. Schirrmacher (1998, p. 6) identifies specific aspects of the creative process. The aspects are listed below, with examples of how the children demonstrate these aspects in the activities they are involved in:

- try out new ideas and different ways of doing things—Mikel (see photo 1.1), as he used the play dough to create a scenario for his dinosaurs;
- push boundaries and explore possibilities—Haley (see photo 12.1), as she created something in carpentry, something she previously thought girls could not do;
- manipulate and transform ideas and materials—Mackenzie (see photo 8.7), as she created a birthday cake;
- take things apart and put them together in different ways—Benjamin (see photo 12.5), as he used the Brio parts to create a structure;
- physically play with objects—Timmy (see photo 10.5), as he shook his rattle;
- imagine, engage in fantasy, or just daydream—Braelyn (see photo 5.17), as she became a ballerina on the "frozen pond";
- solve problems or try to figure things out—Jacob, Benjamin, and Liesl (see photo 11.2), as they tried to figure out if it was ice or glass; and
- ask questions or challenge accepted ways of thinking of acting.

▶ Creative Arts to Encourage Learning

It had rained solidly for a week. When the children came in one morning, most of them talked about how wet they were and that they could not play outside. It was decided to go outside and play in the rain. The children put on their raincoats, splash suits, and boots and went for a walk in the rain. They splashed in puddles, watching the raindrops run down their raincoats and umbrellas and trying to catch the raindrops with their open mouths. When the children returned indoors, they decided that this was so much fun that they would create rain indoors.

A group of children sat down with Jennifer to discuss what they could do and what they needed. Since it was near the end of the day, the topic was dropped. The adults decided to start the rain theme. They cut up a Christmas garland that had iridescent tear-shaped drops in it. These were strung from the ceiling, along with some umbrellas. A few puddles were created out of blue paper, laminated, and placed on the floor.

When the children came the next morning, they immediately went over to the rain area. They gently touched the "raindrops." They giggled and laughed as they stood under the umbrellas. They jumped in the puddles.

When they started to sing the song and jump in the puddles), they noticed that there were not enough puddles for the number of children involved. Jennifer asked the children how they could solve the problem. Liesl suggested that they could make some more puddles. Soon there was a buzz of activity in the creative art area as children started to make puddles (photo 9.1).

PHOTO 9.1

The power of the creative art area is that children can be encouraged to look at art as a way of integrating all activities within the room. When children start to relate and link activities, they are truly maximizing their learning potential. They discover that they can:

- control what is happening in the environment;
- accomplish tasks by themselves;
- work together on a common goal; and
- derive satisfaction from their efforts.

▶ Child Development: Developmental Levels of the Creative Arts

1. Painting and Drawing

Benjamin had discovered finger painting. He was working on a large sheet of paper, spreading paint over the paper with his hands and fingers. He covered the whole paper with paint. As he was spreading the paint, he noticed that he could make marks on the paper with his fingers. He drew lines and circles repeatedly (photo 9.2). He would erase the lines or circles by smoothing the paint with his fingers. When the paint was "not sticky enough," he added more paint to his paper. Jennifer noticed his efforts. She commented about how he was making the circle or line appear or disappear. When Benjamin recreated the circle, he whispered, "Appear!"

Benjamin is at the **scribbling** stage. He was involved in a kinesthetic experience. He was using his whole body—bending over to reach the top and sides of his paper, moving his arms, hands, and fingers over the whole page. This will help him to build memory about what the finger paint felt like, how he had to move to create, and how he had to move his body to get different effects (bending over to reach the top or sides).

He is manipulating the medium (paint) with his hands and fingers in order to cover the page, create circles and lines, and cover the designs made.

Brooke went to the shelf to choose a brush. She brought it to the paint easel and started to paint (photo 9.3). She alternates between using one hand or two hands to paint. She holds the brush in a whole-hand grip. Whenever someone walks by, Brooke looks up. She watches to see what the person is doing, but continues to paint. She forms lines and dots. Each line created is made in one movement. There is little wrist action or finger action. Occasionally she looks at her paper and smiles.

PHOTO 9.2

PHOTO 9.3

Brooke is at the first substage—**disordered and random scribbling**. She is enjoying the activity. She is making random haphazard marks, sometimes without looking at what she is doing. She is also involved in a pleasurable, kinesthetic experience. She is learning to understand that by moving her arms and hands in certain ways she can make a number of different marks on the paper. At this stage, she is involved in the process only. There is no end product or labelling of her scribbles.

Jordan has chosen two different brushes to work with (photo 9.4). He is making much more controlled marks than Brooke (photo 9.3) was. He uses a whole-hand grasp, but is starting to move his wrist to control his work. His marks are much more varied and he is covering the whole page. Jordan's scribbles are starting to show more intricate swirls and loops. He repeats motions—large arm movements with wrist movement—as he creates curves and types marks. Jordan painted three similar paintings.

Jordan is at the **controlled scribbling** stage. He has more control over his hand movements and can therefore create more intricate patterns. Note the variety of marks made—curved and straight lines, looped lines, horizontal and vertical alignments, and thick lines and thin lines.

Jenna spends a lot of time in the art area creating intricate designs. She indicates that she is making a fish (photo 9.5). She is grasping the marker or crayon with her fingers and looks over her creations before she starts to put new marks in. She carefully colours in small segments of her design.

Jenna is at the **named scribbling** stage—fish. She has much more control over her scribbles. Note the intricate pattern created and the diversity of the marks created—tight swirls, horizontal and vertical marks, circles, straight and curved lines. She deliberately picks a space to colour—more intentional placement of marks and colours. When someone walks past Jenna, she continues to concentrate on what she is doing.

A few weeks later Jenna has refined her skills to a greater degree. She now creates recognizable figures (photo 9.6). When Jordan asked her whether that was her mommy, she answered, "Yes!" Later she indicated to Jennifer that this was her baby brother.

Jenna now uses recognizable geometric shapes to complete her drawing—circles for the head, nose, and eyes and straight lines for arms, legs, and hair. The colours that Jenna uses are colours that she likes rather than realistic colours—a blue head, yellow hair, red eyes, nose, and mouth, and purple arms and legs.

PHOTO 9.4

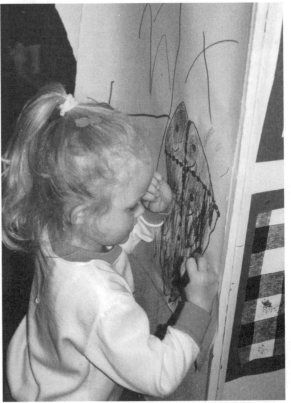

PHOTO 9.5

PHOTO 9.6

PHOTO 9.7

On an early-spring field trip, the children took drawing materials outside. A large clipboard had been created—a large stiff plastic sheet, the size of the newsprint, with a large clip at the top. Olivia and Danika started to draw signs of spring—running water and the sun. They quickly decided to draw what they soon would see—flowers, butterflies, and grass (photo 9.7).

Haley decided to draw two dogs. She placed the dogs on one side of the paper so that her story could appear on the other side (photo 9.8). She dictated the story to Jennifer. "The dog is going for a walk with his friend another dog. They are going for a walk in the park and they are going up the slide up the ladder and then down the slide."

Jenna, Danika, Olivia, and Haley are all at the **preschematic** stage. Notice the different levels of abilities at this stage. Jenna draws symbols to represent people. She generalizes her symbols—sometimes the symbol is her mom, sometimes her baby brother. Her symbolized form is recognizable with facial details, but is distorted in size—the head is the largest part of her drawing. The drawing has meaning to her—it represents her family.

Olivia and Danika are symbolizing water and grass by colour—blue for water and green for grass. Both girls are drawing representations of flowers and butterflies. They draw on their experiences of what flowers look like. Haley is drawing representations of dogs. She started out with the large dog. She ran out of space, so she drew a small dog on the right-hand side. Her story emerged, but has little relationship to her drawing. All three girls have increased their use of detail in drawing—stems, petals, decorated wings, leaves, centres to flowers, ears, facial features, a body, and four legs.

PHOTO 9.8

PHOTO 9.9

Taylor is drawing what she sees outside (photo 9.9). She is drawing the waterfront. She has filled in the base of her picture with water, followed by a pebbly beach and then the grass. She is just finishing her drawing of the playhouse from the playground.

Billy had asked Jennifer to trace him. He then drew an x-ray picture of himself (photo 9.10). He included all his bones, including the break he had in his leg the previous year: it shows up very faintly on the left leg by a dotted line. He drew in his lungs, coloured in blue; his stomach, with the carrot, cheese, and banana he had eaten in the morning; his skull; and his brain. He said, "My brain is active. That's why it is red and yellow" (photo 9.11).

Taylor and Billy are at the **schematic achievement of a concept** stage. Taylor's drawing is a flat, vibrantly coloured representation of what she sees. The colours are representational of the colours of the things in front of her. She has portrayed a baseline, is providing detail, and is starting to represent the drawings as they should be. Billy has produced a drawing that includes both interior and exterior detail. He has taken time and effort to include a great deal of detail. He has used symbolized form through colour—active brain (yellow and red), blue lungs to represent air, and realistic colours for the foods he ate. The drawing clearly shows Billy's extensive knowledge about his own body.

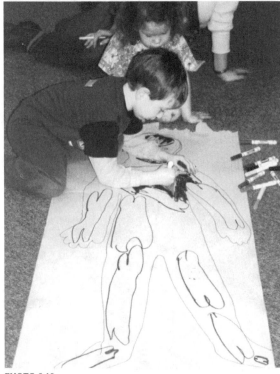

PHOTO 9.10

PHOTO 9.11

2. Aesthetic Criteria

The aesthetic criteria of art are made up of various elements, including **line,** colour, **shape, mass and volume, design and composition, pattern, space, balance,** and **texture.** Children need to learn and experiment with these elements in various ways:

Line: Yasmine created a picture of the water behind her (photo 9.12). She said the water was dancing. Note how her lines represent the swirls and eddies in the water. The darker lines represent the water flowing over the rocks. Jordan enjoyed the feeling of creating flowing lines (photo 9.4). He also learned to use thick and thin lines depending on the brush he used.

"Lines can be used in many different ways. Lines have their own dimensions, including size, directions, length width and weight. They also have their own personality" (Schirrmacher, 1998, pp. 152–153).

Colour: Benjamin (photo 9.2) and Jordan (photo 9.4) were attracted by the bright warm colours. Benjamin usually picked red to work with. There is good research to show that colour makes us feel. "Colors have thermal qualities that have a psychological impact on the viewer. Colours can make us feel" (Schirrmacher, 1998, p. 155). Both Benjamin and Jordan spent a long time painting—40 min-

utes. Both boys were totally absorbed in the activity.

Shape: Chelsea wanted to sew. She could not find a shape that she wanted to use. She wanted the shape of a "big teddy bear." Her brother heard her talking to Jennifer. He came and said, "I can make one for her. What colour do you want, Chelsea?" She decided on yellow. He took one of the small bear outlines and placed it on the light table. The light from the projector reflected the bear shape onto the paper. Jennifer held the yellow paper in front of the projection. Jeremy traced the paper. Liesl watched and said, "I can cut it cut for you." Chelsea punched the holes and then used red ribbon to sew around the outside of the bear (photo 9.13).

All of these activities enhance the children's concept of shape—enlarging a shape, tracing around a shape, cutting around a shape, and drawing shapes (Liesl's puddle) (photo 9.1).

Mass and volume: Jacob shaped and re-shaped the play dough. He rolled it out, flattened it with his hands, and reformed it into a ball. Eventually he rolled it into a long sausage shape (photo 9.14). "A big snake," he said. He brought it over to show

PHOTO 9.12

PHOTO 9.13

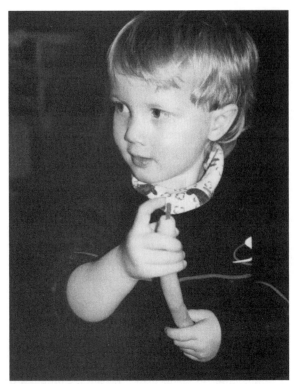

PHOTO 9.14

PHOTO 9.15

Jennifer. On his way he passed the sewing centre. He saw some small pieces of red straw. He stuck one into the top of his "snake." "Ssssss," he said as he showed it to Jennifer. Jacob worked and reworked the dough. Through this activity he saw that the dough changed. Sometimes it looked bigger and sometimes it looked smaller.

Design and composition: Hannah painted the head of a cat. She carefully chose the colours that she wanted to use. She cut out the head of the cat. She noticed that it was difficult to cut out the whiskers, so she left a border around the whiskers. She looked at the various pieces of construction paper. She picked one that fit the cat's head "perfectly." She then pasted the cat's head onto the paper (photo 9.15). Hannah used all aspects of aesthetic design—lines (curved and straight), colour, shape (triangular, round), mass, and volume (how the cat could fit onto a single sheet) in order to create a pleasing composition.

Pattern: Liesl represented the pattern of the rain in the creation of her puddle (photo 9.1). She has represented the rain falling into the puddle with small coloured-in circles. She has represented the ripples with open and closed circles surrounding her small coloured-in circles. "Pattern surrounds

us. Fence posts, steps, rungs of a ladder, railway tracks, and spokes on a wheel all suggest a repetitive pattern" (Schirrmacher, 1998, p. 161).

Space: Emily has utilized the space on the box to paste leaves on it (photo 9.16). She has used both the inside and the outside surfaces. She has attached one leaf to each side. "Within the overall space, the artist must deal with the problem of arranging elements. How many shapes or symbols will be used? Where will they be placed? How much space will remain?" (Schirrmacher, 1998, pp. 161–162).

Balance: Billy (photos 9.10 and 9.11) has created formal balance of placing his internal structures within his body frame in the correct proportions. "When the forms appear to be in proportion to each other, the picture is said to have balance, equilibrium or harmony" (Schirrmacher, 1998, p. 62).

Texture: Danika had been outside collecting materials to create her picture. She had created a frame of wood, wallpaper, and string (photo 9.17). She next created a picture of the wild flowers and grasses she had found outside to attach inside her frame. Danika used a variety of textures to complete her project—smooth, fuzzy, stiff, soft.

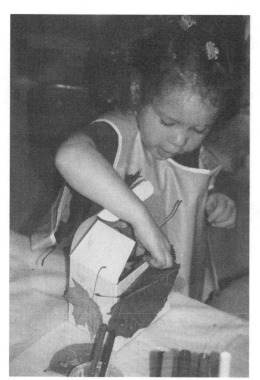

PHOTO 9.16

PHOTO 9.17

▶ Value of Creative Arts

1. Enhances Communication Skills

- express feelings and ideas in alternate ways—Hannah and Jenna represented their pictures with happy faces (photos 9.6 and 9.15); Yasmine's picture of the "dancing water" (photo 9.12);
- communicate universally—children draw in every part of the world (photos 9.23 and 9.24);
- enhance ability to interpret symbols—Jacob pointed to Danika's and Braelyn's picture and identified the flowers and butterflies;
- dictate stories about their artwork—Haley's story (photo 9.8); and
- develop fine motor control for later writing skills—note changes in grasp with age from full hand grasp (photo 9.3) to the **tripod grasp** (photo 9.4).

2. Enhances Thinking Skills

- develop critical thinking skills (recognition, comparison, prediction)—Benjamin moved from finger painting into painting other objects with his hands. It had been one of the children's birthday. The mother had brought in balloons to hang. Benjamin picked a pink balloon and started to cover it with yellow paint. Then he switched to red. He was surprised when the red mixed with the yellow gave him orange. He said, "I made orange." Jennifer asked how he had done it. "Watch!" he said and proceeded to mix red and yellow. He then decided he wanted to change the pink balloon into a red balloon. "I'll make all the colours disappear by using lots of red," he predicted. When he had finished he had succeeded (photo 9.18). Jennifer told him that what he had predicted had indeed happened.
- increase understanding of science and math concepts in more meaningful ways—explore missing principles: mix to make play dough, wash hands in sink and watch the colour of water change, count to make sure that there are enough items (Haley's two dogs).
- solve problems—how to represent items: Billy's bones (photo 9.10), how and where to attach leaves to the box (photo 9.16).

3. Enhances all Curriculum and Development Areas

- providing connections and patterns across curriculum—using art to make puddles for music and movement; collecting weeds and grasses from a nature walk and using these in creative picture making;

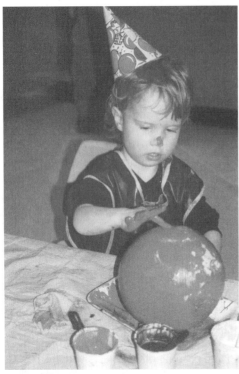

PHOTO 9.18

PHOTO 9.19

- using active participation and sensory experience—open-ended activities, process-oriented; finger painting, drawing with markers, painting with brushes;
- enhancing aesthetic development—through talking and reflecting with children about their creative artwork;
- enhancing observation skills—observing outside to draw: Yasmine and the water (photo 9.12), Taylor at the waterfront (photo 9.9);
- increasing task persistence—Jordan completing three paintings; and
- understanding of cultural values—Several dream catchers were hung in the sewing area. Several of the children created a dream catcher. The children discussed with Jennifer what a dream catcher is and where one should hang it. The children decided to hang the dream catcher over the doll beds. "The art of any cultural or ethnic group often reveals values held by that group" (Hurwitz and Day, 2001, p. 13) and taking pride in accomplishment. For example, Katie had finished a painting. It was framed and hung in the art gallery. She wanted to have her picture taken with it (photo 9.19).

▶ Role of the Facilitator

- document children's learning and activities;
- provide a variety of developmentally appropriate materials (see listing of materials at the end of this chapter);
- value children's creativity;
- comment on what children are doing—describing Benjamin's efforts to make the symbols appear and disappear;
- demonstrate techniques or ways of using tools— Jennifer modelled using the brush to stipple, similar to the technique used by Monet;
- avoid models, emphasize process—no pre-cut or prepared models available, emphasis on children's process;
- talk about art—talk about the elements of aesthetics (photo 9.4): long lines, short lines, red lines, intersecting lines, horizontal lines (photo 9.16); one leaf per side, all maple leaves, small leaves, large leaf is overlapping;
- encourage cleanup (photo 9.20);
- provide opportunities to use art in a variety of settings—outdoors, indoors, in music area;
- research to become more informed about art. "Before using these elements when you discuss art with young children, you will want to become familiar with them yourself. Do some reading or take a course in art appreciation, visit museums, study art work in an art history book, or engage in art projects yourself" (Schirrmacher, 1986, p. 5);
- encourage children to experiment—experiment with different media to learn to use them (photo 9.21);

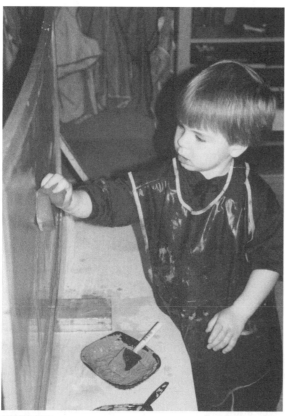

PHOTO 9.20

PHOTO 9.21

- display art—framed, aesthetically pleasing (photo 9.22); and
- encourage reflections—Jacob (photo 9.14) adding a tongue to his snake to make it more realistic; Yasmine asking Jennifer to paint with her. A print

PHOTO 9.22

of Monet's *Woman and Child in the Garden* hung over the paint easel. Yasmine painted using similar colours and techniques—pale pink, pale blue; dots; and short strokes. Jennifer painted a similar scene. Every once in a while, Yasmine would ask to look at Jennifer's painting. She would step back and say "Cool!" When they were both finished, an active dialogue started.

Yasmine (pointing to the woman): "Who is that in your picture?"

Jennifer: "I hadn't thought about it. Who do you think it is?"

Yasmine (shrugging her shoulders): "I don't have a person in mine. I have lots of flowers."

Jennifer: "No you don't. I have flowers in my picture too. Some of them are the same colour as yours."

Yasmine: "Yes. I wonder who she is?"

Jennifer: "She has brown hair. Maybe it could be you?"

Yasmine (looking at it for a moment): "No, she is too big. It's my mom."

▶ Effective Storage Systems

Art can become messy very quickly. When the art area is left in a mess, it becomes unappealing for children to use the area. It lacks aesthetic value. Therefore, it is most important to develop a system that allows children to find and return things appropriately.

1. Appropriate Modelling

Paintbrushes should be left standing stem up or put in containers lying flat. If paintbrushes are left bristles down, the bristles very quickly get ruined; the bristles either turn out or get broken. This makes the brush an ineffective tool to work with. Any painter will always make sure that the brushes are appropriately cared for.

Water should be available to clean the brushes or create different techniques, such as a wash. Water needs to be cleaned after the child is finished. Dirty water affects the quality of the paint and the vibrancy of the colours on the paper. Children can change their own water if they are given small plastic containers to use.

Protective coverings should be worn to protect clothing from spills. It is helpful if adults too wear a smock or apron to protect their clothing.

2. Cleanup

Children enjoy cleanup. They can clean up their paintbrushes, paint easel, finger paint table, and glue marks, and put their scraps in the garbage. Squirt bottles and rags or sponges are easy tools for children to use to clean up the area (photo 9.20). The advantage of using a squirt bottle is that the children will not be able to create a flood. A sponge is easy to wring out and is very absorbent. Provide a pail to wring out the sponge.

Children who become involved in maintaining the environment become more independent and responsible for their actions.

3. Types of Storage

Centralized Storage

A centralized system of storage encourages children to think about what they want to do and what materials they need. Consider creating open shelves that will encourage children to easily find the materials they need. Items on the bottom shelves could be items readily available to the children. The higher shelves could be used for materials for rotation, or extra supplies and materials that are donated.

- paper—on an open shelf, sorted by size and colour;
- cut down clear bottles for things such as straws, twigs, popsicle sticks;
- stackable plastic bins—buttons, wood scraps, material scraps;
- paintbrushes—stem down in large foam pieces, sorted by size of bristle;
- materials for print-making—organized by type within small clear plastic containers;
- decorative materials—small items such as glitter, and sand (in plastic shakers, with larger items in small containers with lids that can easily be refilled);
- gluing materials—tape, glue bottles, glue sticks, glue paddles in small plastic containers;
- writing utensils such as markers, pencil crayons, pencils—pencil and/or marker holders, pencil cases, small plastic boxes with lids;
- paint—in paint easel;
- yarn, ribbon, and so on—see Chapter 7, p. 145;
- items for mixing, cutting, shaping—sorted by type in individual containers or within small plastic drawer unit;
- containers for mixing, holding paint—stacked on shelf; and
- cleaning supplies—bucket, squirt bottle, sponges or rags under sink.

Mobile Storage Units

- caddies that can hold brushes, paint, markers;
- writing boxes—small hinged boxes containing essentials that can be carried from place to place—glue, scissors, set of markers and crayons, pencils; and
- small plastic drawers on wheels that can be pushed to new locations.

▶ Effective Labelling Systems

A good labelling system will cut down the time for everyone. All items should be by picture and by word. Organize the area by function—all the attachment materials together. Observe to see if the system is working. Involve the children in helping to organize the area and to label it.

- photographs of items such as scissors and glue;
- small mats with outlines—red circle with red glitter on it: match container to outline;
- example of what is in a box taped to the box—yarn, ribbon; and
- clear diagrams representing items.

▶ Considerations for Setting Up a Creative Arts Area

1. Location

The creative arts area is a large area, as there are many types of activities that should occur regularly—painting, sculpting, cut and paste. It should be on a tiled surface so that it is easy to clean. A water source—both adult- and child-sized sinks—should be readily available.

The creative art area should be used in many areas. The easiest way to do this is by encouraging children to gather materials in **mobile storage** units and carrying these to other locations. For example—road signs need to be created in the block area, play dough is needed in the kitchen area, or a shopping list needs to be created in dramatic play.

The creative arts area can be effectively combined with any area in the room. Consider natural combinations such as woodworking and art. These two areas can share many of the materials and share some common space. Also consider placing some of the components of creative arts in other areas—writing and drawing with reading, sewing in the quiet area, and dough in the kitchen area.

Creative art should be practised in both indoor and outdoor environments. Nature provides a marvellous incentive to create—the rainbow in the sky, sunlight dancing on the water or on the leaves of a tree, and the realism of colour. Children gain through observational learning.

The creative art should be set up in order to accommodate all individual levels of development, from the child who cannot perform a certain task such as cutting to the child who has mastered that skill. "In a classroom situation, children will exhibit as many different levels of skill and creativity ability as there are children in the room. If there is a child with a particular disability he or she should be considered as just one more child in the room with a different skill level. Everyone's work will be unique because we are all different and each of us creates our own version of how we think things should be. Art is a way of expressing ourselves and we all do that differently. Enjoyment comes from the process of creating, and this method of self-expression builds self-esteem" (Libby, 2000, p. 4).

2. Aesthetic Elements

Children are learning about aesthetic values. An environment that is cluttered, messy, and unattractive will be counterproductive. Children need to be surrounded by beauty in order for them to create beauty. Consider hanging artwork by well-known painters in the area. This will expose children to various styles of art, encourage them to try new techniques (Yasmine and Jennifer looking at the techniques used by Monet) and learn about cultural values, and encourage discussion. See the Resources listing at the end of this chapter for some possible artwork to use. "*Using Art to Make Art* encourages exploration, creativity, and self-expression, while developing basic art skills and concepts" (Libby, 2000, p. 1).

Children's own artwork should dominate the area. However, the artwork needs to be displayed appropriately (see the section on display). Since children's work will have a high use of bright, vibrant colours, the colour scheme in this area should be more neutral. Avoid overstimulation. It is very distracting to paint on a surface that is a bright primary colour; it is equally distracting to work in an area that is busy with colour.

3. Model

Adults need to model appreciation of the creative efforts. The elements of art are ideal to discuss with children—line, colour, mass or volume, pattern, shape, space, texture, and composition: *You have used thick lines and thin lines; I see the pattern of the raindrops.* Use reflective dialogue, similar to that evident in the discussion between Yasmine and Jennifer. Adults should engage in creative art experiences.

4. Display

Children's creative efforts must be displayed. Create an art gallery to display children's work (photo 9.22); this could be in the main entrance as parents come in. Create displays of artwork in store windows of local merchants. This raises the awareness and appreciation in the community of children's work. Above all, create a gallery that is appreciative of the children's efforts. Appropriate framing, mounting, and display of two- and three-dimensional work is essential.

Frames are easily constructed using cardboard, paper, tape, glue, and paint. Encourage families to participate in creating frames (figure 9.1).

5. Furniture

Furniture should be flexible. Children will need opportunities to work on flat surfaces, on slanted surfaces, by themselves, or in groups. Easels that encourage both individual and/or group participation, tables

FIGURE 9.1

▶ Creating a Frame

Step 1   Take size of paper used for painting

Step 2   Cut 4 strips—matching sides of painting, each with additional length to create frame

Step 3   • Attach all four corners with tape
         • Make sure it is secure

Step 4   • Cut 6 small heavy cardboard strips
         • Strips should be half the width of the frame
         • Glue to frame as shown in diagram A – 3 sides
         These will create room to slide painting in

Step 5   Cut out a large piece of cardboard to fit the frame exactly

Step 6   Attach cardboard back to frame—tape 3 sides completely (diagram B)

Step 7   Decorate

Step 8   Slide in picture

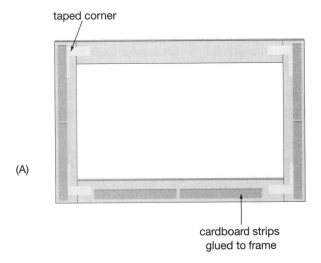

taped corner

cardboard strips glued to frame

(A)

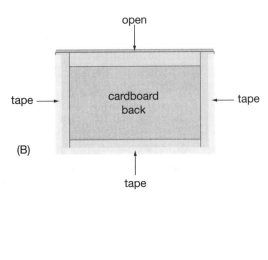

open

tape →   cardboard back   ← tape

(B)

tape

that can be pushed together or separated for individual or group work, and wall or floor spaces that can be used for larger projects encourage a variety of experiences. Drying racks or open shelves could be used to store wet paintings. Additionally, there needs to be a table or shelf that can store projects that will evolve over time.

▶ Observation and Documentation Techniques

In order for the facilitator to provide the appropriate experiences, careful documentation of children's skill levels must be done. Skills such as the type of grasp used influence the type of brushes available (length of handle, size of bristles). If children are mixing colours, provide materials such as small Styrofoam plates to mix on. Instead of providing the colour pink, provide red and white and let the children mix the shade of pink they want. Figures 9.2 through 9.4 show some sample checklists.

SKILL SAMPLE

Portfolio
Collect some of the artwork and keep it in a portfolio. Take pictures of three-dimensional structures and put these into the portfolio. Add pictures over time. Date each picture and record the stage of development on a master list at the front of the portfolio. This gives you an excellent view of progress over time.

FIGURE 9.2

▶ Skill Checklist

Name: Jordan (photo 9.4)   Dates: 10/17

Stage	Element	Action
Controlled scribbling	Lines	Curved, long, smooth, thick, thin, looped, horizontal, vertical
	Grasp	Repeated movement of arm across whole page, picked two brushes—thick/thin, alternated using them
	Colour	Red, yellow, blue, light green
	Concentration	Followed action of marking with his eyes
	Space	Covers whole page

This sample gives important information:
- uses different brush size for different effects;
- enjoys the kinesthetic experience of moving the brush across the page;
- uses the whole page; and
- exhibits total concentration on task.

Some ways that you might use this information to enhance the experience might be to:

- provide background music to paint to;
- provide greater variety of choice in colour or paintbrush size;
- increase surface size of paper—paint on boxes, large mural paper on wall; and
- provide opportunities to finger paint.

FIGURE 9.3

▶ Evaluation of the Creative Art Area Chart

Dates: 10/15, 10/16

Names	Painting	Drawing	Cut/Paste	Sewing	Sculpting
Brooke	I				I
Hannah	I	I	I		I
Katie	I	I			I
Liesl		I	I	I	

This type of tool gives you two types of information. One is to identify what the children's interests are, and the other is to identify areas that need to be adapted or changed. If an area is not used, you might want to look it over and decide why. What changes/adaptations need to be made to encourage children to work in that area?

Questions to Ask Yourself
- Is the area attractive to look at?
- Are the children enjoying themselves?
- Do the children and families look at the display area?
- Is there active discussion among children and between adults and children in the area?
- Are children using art materials in other areas?
- Are the adults modelling appropriate behaviours?
- Are the children cleaning up after themselves?

FIGURE 9.4

▶ Observation of Aesthetic Elements Chart

Name: Jordan (photo 9.4)

Aesthetic Aspect	Date(s)	Evidence
Line	04, 22	Painting with brush—non-stop circular lines covering whole page
Colour	04, 22	Circular painted lines—red, blue, yellow, green
Shape		
Mass and volume		
Design and composition		
Pattern		
Space	04, 22	Covered whole page
Balance	04, 22	Covered page with flowing, circular, distinct lines
Texture	04, 22	Created painted texture by using different sized brushes to apply paint

This kind of tool gives information about the aesthetic qualities that children are using in their artwork. This information can be used to:

- identify what materials to provide—colour, type of brushes, type of paper;
- identify aspects of aesthetic design that can be discussed with individual children;
- identify areas that are missing within the creative arts program;
- provide relevant motivation—field trips, display art work, discussions, art books, and visiting artists; and
- help build individual creative art portfolios.

PHOTO 9.23

▶ International Considerations

"Analyzing the cross-cultural studies of children's art done by anthropologists, as well as research by psychologists on how children learn to perceive visual elements, they argue that all studies of children's art must consider the cultural environment in which it is created. In a culture such as the United States, in which words are valued over images, beliefs about child art will reflect that value system. The emphasis on using art as another form of language is indicative of this" (Koster, 1997, p. 14).

When learning through verbal interactions is stressed, artwork will reflect less detail and will include more symbolized forms that are stereotypical; for example, fingers represented by straight lines, houses represented as square boxes.

In contrast to this, one must look at the creative art produced by the children of Reggio Emilia. These children are encouraged to study art in its various forms. One project, the construction of an amusement park for the birds (Reggio Children USA, 1997), clearly shows the creative power that children can aspire to. The children were involved in a four-month project in which they discussed, researched, drafted, created, and executed an amusement park for the birds. The children created paintings and real working models. "My fountain is made with straws that I made in the tank the other day. I put some pinwheels and straws that the water comes out of. When the water goes down from the straws, after it goes on the pinwheels and they turn around" (Reggio Children USA, 1995, p. 102).

Similarly, children in Japan learn to use their observational powers to create drawings. On a school holiday in Japan, children went to visit one of the historic sites. One child had brought his drawing materials

PHOTO 9.24

with him and was drawing by carefully observing the detail of the carving above him. He was oblivious to the hordes of people around him. Notice the detail used in the formation of his work (photos 9.23 and 9.24).

In contrast, the artwork of aboriginal peoples is much more stylized. Children growing up in these cultures experience very rich verbal communications. Stories are passed down verbally from generation to generation. Storytelling is a recognized art and is highly valued. In Desert Park in Alice Springs, Australia, attempts have been made to expose children of various cultures to aboriginal paintings. One form that is used by the aboriginal tribes is face painting. Symbols of aboriginal face paintings are provided visually (photo 9.25). Materials are provided so that the children can create their own paintings.

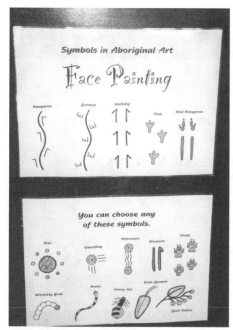

PHOTO 9.25

In summary, art is a universal language. Artwork ranges from:

- the narrative style of early cave drawings—depicting details of a hunt, to
- tapestries telling a story about one episode such as a battle, to
- paintings and sculptures rich in detail, to
- variations in colour and media—silk painting with bright vibrant colours, ink drawing on parchment, to
- abstract visions of pure colour and form.

Each culture places its own value on how to represent the world in art. Each child growing up in that culture will learn to appreciate and respect those values. It is up to us as educators to expose children to this universal language—the creative arts. It is one language that truly has no barriers.

▶ Creative Arts Materials

1. Painting
Table 9.1 provides ideas for possible painting tools and surfaces.

Possible Reproductions to Use
- Mary Cassatt—*Mother Playing with Her Child*
- Claude Monet—*Water Lily Pond*
- Pablo Picasso—*Mother and Child*
- Henri Rousseau—*Equatorial Jungle*
- Salvador Dali—*The Persistence of Memory*
- Vincent van Gogh—*Sunflowers*
- Sculptures—animals, people, from classical pieces such as *The Thinker* to modern pieces of abstract art

2. Sculpting
Table 9.2 provides ideas for possible sculpting materials.

3. Drawing/Writing
Table 9.3 provides examples of possible drawing and writing materials, along with the appropriate media.

4. Paste and Cut
Table 9.4 provides examples of some possible paste and cut materials.

TABLE 9.1

▶ Painting Materials	
Possible Tools	**Possible Surfaces**
Tools—paintbrushes of varying sizes and thicknesses, both for paper painting and house painting; paint rollers; edgers; sponge brushes	Paper—construction, manila, newsprint, wallpaper, cardboard, finger painting, wax, large rolls of paper (brown and white)
Alternative tools—toothbrushes, shaving brushes, weeds; fingers, feet	Wood—sanded, smooth
	Boxes, Styrofoam packing pieces
Liquid paint, dry paint, food colouring, vegetable dyes, finger paint (paint should be washable; add some detergent to it to make it easier to clean)	Plexiglas table tops—take print of finished product
	Fabric

TABLE 9.2

▶ Sculpting Materials

Media	Tools
Play dough (home-made and commercial)	**Open-ended**
Clay	Knives, spatulas, scissors, shears, mallets, rolling pins, garlic press, bowls, spoons, forks
Papier-mâché	
Sand	Creating design—interesting pieces of china or cutlery that have etched designs, ceramic stamps, stones, fossils, shells
Cement	Plants—dried weeds, flowers, twigs, bark
	Directed
	Moulds, cookie cutters, muffin tins

TABLE 9.3

▶ Drawing/Writing Materials

Media	Tools
Paper—lined and unlined, newsprint, construction paper, envelopes, letter	Pencils, crayons, markers, pencil crayons, oil pastels, chalk, pencil sharpeners, rulers, erasers
Make booklets for children to write in	Colours should include skin colours, pastel shades, fluorescent shades, and various shades of colours
Rolls of paper to create lists	
Chalk board	

TABLE 9.4

▶ Paste and Cut Materials

Media	Tools
Paper—tissue, newsprint, construction, cardboard, corrugated, doilies, paper plates	White glue, paste powders, flour and water mixture, glue sticks, glue containers with lids, glue brushes, glue paddles
Specialty papers—animal skins, fabric design, insect, sea life, skin colours, airplane, holograph, photo-sensitive, foil, wallpaper	Masking tape, clear tape, double-edged tape
Fabric—satin, metallic, polyester, canvas, burlap, felt, fleece, corduroy, cotton, netting, sheer	Blunt children's-sized scissors (try scissors before you put them out; it's most frustrating for a child to learn to cut with scissors that are impossible to cut with—better to have no scissors), shears, container to hold scissors, variety of pinking shears (both right handed and left handed)
Boxes—various sizes and shapes (photo 9.16)	
Decorative—buttons, straws, beads, sequins, artificial flowers and leaves, greeting cards, calendars, magazines, wrapping paper, pompoms, cotton balls, feathers, pipe cleaners, glitter, confetti, shredded paper, yarn	Stapler
Wood scraps	Soft wire, yarn, string
Coloured pasta, rice	

5. Print Making

Table 9.5 provides examples of some possible print-making materials.

6. Weaving

Table 9.6 provides examples of some possible weaving materials.

▶ Ages and Stages of Creative Arts

Table 9.7 outlines the stages of artistic development.

TABLE 9.5

▶ Print-Making Materials

Media	Tools
All materials listed previously	Wood with string wrapped around it, sponge shapes, wooden shapes, dried flowers, grasses, weeds, letters, numbers, rubber stamps, shapes the children find, special-effects rollers, patterned corks, leaves, bark, hands, feet, fingers, tools, keys, cut-out shapes, odd shapes

---

TABLE 9.6

▶ Weaving

Media	Tools
Frames—cardboard with centre cut out, wire frames, plastic frames, old picture frames, wooden frames, pipe cleaners or wire to twist into frame, rings, branches, dried vines, hoops	Materials—yarn, wool, paper, fabric, grass, sticks, laces, cord, wallpaper borders

---

TABLE 9.7

▶ Stages of Artistic Development

Age	Stage	Characteristic
2–4 years	Stage 1: Scribbling: Beginnings of Self-Expression	Kinesthetic, manipulative, and expressive behaviours
1½–2½ years	Substage 1A: Disordered and Random Scribbling	Large-muscle, whole-arm movement; kinesthetic pleasure
		Whole-hand grip
		May not look at paper while marking
		Haphazard lines
		May scribble beyond confines of paper
		Exploration—cause and effect—marks made when tools are moved across paper
		Lines made with single movement
		Tight grip with rigid wrist position
		Minimal finger movement

TABLE 9.7 STAGES OF ARTISTIC DEVELOPMENT (continued)

Age	Stage	Characteristic
2–3 years	Substage 1B: Controlled Scribbling	Smaller marks, better control
		Marking motions repeated
		Uses wrist motion to gain more control
		Stays within confines of paper
		Variety of lines and directions appear
		Better visual and motor control of placement of lines
		Watches intently while scribbling
		More intricate loops and swirls appear
		Wider range of scribbles
3½–4 years	Substage 1C: Named Scribbling	Spends more time making markings
		Gives names to scribbles, but name may change during process
		Relates scribbles to things in environment
		Holds marking tools with fingers, better fine motor control
		Greater variety of lines
		Increased concentration
		More intentional placement of marks
		Awareness of intentional use of empty space
		Appearance of scribbles may not match label given except to child artist
		Moves from sheer physical expression to making marks that stand for something else by giving them a name
4–7 years	Stage 2: Preschematic	Symbolic representation built up from other former scribbles that begin to be recognized by others
		Appearance of geometric forms
		Random placement and size and out of proportion
		Random floating spatial arrangement
		May turn or rotate paper while drawing
		Child draws what they feel—leading to distortion and omission of parts of human figure drawing
		Head-feet presentation of human figure
		Over time arms, body, fingers, toes, clothes, hair, and other details appear
		Objects drawn as isolated entities; no relationship
		Very personal idiosyncratic symbols
		Relative size appears at end of stage
		Child learns that he/she can symbolically represent what he/she knows or has experienced
		Colour used randomly
		Draws things important or relevant to self
		Objects are drawn facing forward

TABLE 9.7 STAGES OF ARTISTIC DEVELOPMENT (continued)

Age	Stage	Characteristic
7–9 years	Stage 3: Schematic Achievement of a Concept	Form concept is developed and repeated
		Drawing reflects a child's concept, not perception of an object
		Bold, direct flat representation
		Two-dimensional spatial representation
		Drawing reflects a child's concept, not perception of an object
		Baseline and sky line begins to appear
		Drawing reflects what child knows
		Subjective portrayal of space
		X-ray drawing appears simultaneously, showing exterior and interior view
		Human figure made up of geometric shapes is repeated and refined
		Detailed and decorative
		Move to greater conformity or "stiffness" in drawing things the way they should be
9–12 years	Stage 4: Dawning Realism: The Gang Age	Greater awareness of detail
		May be more self-conscious about their art
		Plane replaces baseline
		Objects drawn are smaller and less distorted

Adapted from Schirrmacher (1998, pp. 125–126)

▶ KEY POINTS

Creativity is:

- trying out new ideas and different ways of doing things;
- pushing boundaries and exploring possibilities;
- manipulating and transforming ideas;
- taking things apart and putting them together in different ways;
- physically playing with objects;
- imagining, engaging in fantasy, or just day-dreaming;
- solving problems; and
- asking questions.

Ages and Stages of Creative Art (Schirrmacher, 1998, pp. 125–126)

- disoriented and random scribbling;
- controlled scribbling;
- named scribbling;
- preschematic;
- schematic—achievement of a concept; and
- dawning of realism: the gang age.

Aesthetic Elements

- line;
- colour;
- shape;
- mass and volume;
- design and composition;
- pattern;
- space;
- balance; and
- texture.

Value of Creative Arts

- **Enhances communications skills**—express feelings and ideas in alternate ways, communicate universally, dictate stories about pictures, develop fine motor skills.
- **Enhances thinking skills**—develop critical thinking skills, increase understanding of math and science skills, solve problems.

▶ KEY POINTS (continued)

Value of Creative Arts (continued)

- **Enhances all curriculum and developmental areas**—providing connections, using active participation involving all senses, enhancing aesthetic development, enhancing observations skills, increasing task persistence, understanding cultural values, taking pride in accomplishments.

Role of Facilitator

- provide developmentally appropriate materials;
- value creativity of children;
- demonstrate techniques;
- avoid models;
- talk about art;
- encourage cleanup;
- use art in a variety of settings;
- research to become more familiar;
- encourage experimentation;
- display art; and
- encourage reflection.

Effective Storage Systems

- appropriate modelling;
- cleanup;
- centralized storage; and
- mobile storage units.

Effective Labelling System

- photographs;
- outlines;
- examples; and
- diagrams.

Considerations for Setup

- location;
- aesthetics;
- model;
- display; and
- furniture.

Observation and Documentation Techniques

- portfolio;
- skill checklist;
- evaluation of creative art area; and
- questions to ask.

Student Activities

1. Compare the art done by Brooke (photo 9.3) and Jordan (photo 9.4). How are they similar? How are they different? What materials might you provide to keep the children's interest?

2. Jenna (photo 9.6), Danika, Olivia, and Haley are all at the same stage. Compare the development of drawings over this stage. Describe the new skills that are emerging.

3. Utilize any one of the photographs of the children involved in creative art. Analyze the picture in terms of the aesthetic elements.

4. You observe three children interacting with play dough. The children have green play dough and six cookie cutters. The children are rolling the dough, breaking it into smaller pieces and re-shaping it. They are talking about how big or small their piece is. What other materials might you provide to enhance the activity? What elements of aesthetics might you talk to the children about?

5. Children have been outside collecting items to use in their creative activities. They have found stones, dried grasses, dried flowers, seedpods, pinecones, and shells. They want to create a picture frame and decorate the frame with these items. What kinds of experiences do the children need before they can create frames? What additional materials will the children need to collect?

6. Develop a portfolio of one child's artwork over a longer period of time. What changes can you identify over time?

7. How might you set up a paste and cut corner in a room? Specifically, discuss what materials you would put out, how these materials would be organized, and what observations you would have to keep.

8. What kinds of materials might you provide to a child who is just learning to cut?

9. Find some information about art appreciation. Jot down five points that you had not considered. How might you incorporate these ideas in working with young children?

10. A parent comes to you and complains about the poor artwork her son is doing. She says that when she was a little girl, art skills were taught. She asks why the children in this program are not taught to draw properly—an apple should look like an apple, after all. How would you respond?

11. Benjamin has painted the balloon. He got distracted and put his hands into the paint jars, took the paint out, and started to finger paint on the table. He has mixed the colours and is very excited because he has made a new colour. Paint is all over the table, the paint jars, Benjamin's arms, face, and hands, and his clothes. What is your reaction? How will you deal with this situation? What learning has occurred for Benjamin?

12. Collect some items outside. Use the items that you have collected to create a masterpiece. Try to incorporate as many of the elements of aesthetics as possible.

▶ References

Hurwitz, A., & Day, M. (2001). *Children and Their Art: Methods for the Elementary School.* Orlando, FL: Harcourt College Publishers.

Koster, J. (1997). *Growing artists teaching art to young children.* Scarborough, ON: Delmar.

Libby, W. (2000). *Using Art to Make Art.* Scarborough, ON: Delmar.

Reggio Children. (1995). *The fountains.* Municipality of Reggio Emilia: Infant–Toddler Centers and Preschools.

Shirrmacher, R. (1998). *Art and Creative Development for Young Children.* Scarborough, ON: Delmar.

Shirrmacher, R. (1986, July). Talking with Young Children about Their Art. *Young Children.* 3–7.

▶ Resources

Painting

Gibson, R. (1997). *I can finger paint.* London, UK: Usborne Publishing Ltd.

Lohf, Sabine. (1989). *Things I make with cloth.* Ravensburger Buchverlag: Federal Republic of Germany.

Maiotti, M., & Marchiori, R. (1982). *Humands.* Florence, Italy: La Nuova Italia.

Ploguin, G. (1998). *Painting on Stones.* Tunbridge Wells, UK: Search Press Limited.

Sculpting

Fernandes, K., & Fernandes, E. *Little Toby and the Big Hair.* Toronto, ON: Doubleday Canada Limited.

Reid, B. (1988). *Playing with Plastecine.* Toronto, ON: Kids Can Press Ltd.

Gibson, R., & Tyler, J. (1989). *Playdough.* London, UK: Usborne Publishing Ltd.

Paste and Cut

Fiarotta, P., & Fiarotta, N. *Cups & Cans & Paper Plate Fans.* New York, NY: Stirling Publishing Co.

Hayes Richmond, M. (1997). *Look What You Can Make With Tubes.* Honesdale, PA: Boyds Press.

Owens, C. (1996). *Beautiful boxes.* Toronto, ON: Quatro Inc.

Print Making

Bartlett, N. (1991). Children's art & crafts. *Australian Women's Weekly Home Library.* North Vancouver, BC: Whitecap Books Ltd.

Bartlett, N. (1996). Children's art & crafts. *Australian Women's Weekly Home Library.* North Vancouver, BC: Whitecap Books Ltd.

Tofts, H. (1989). *The Print Book: Fun Things to Make and Do with Paint.* New York, NY: Scholastic.

CHAPTER 10

Manipulative Experiences

Manipulative materials develop small muscles in children's fingers and hands, basic concepts, and eye–hand coordination. Children's use of manipulative materials provides important opportunities for early literacy and numeracy development; offers concrete experiences with basic attributes of color, size, and shape; provides opportunities for cooperative problem solving; and increased awareness of cultural diversity.

—Isenberg and Jalongo, Creative Expression in Early Childhood

Chapter Outline

- What Is Manipulative Learning?
- Manipulative Experiences to Encourage Learning
- Child Development: Developmental Levels of Fine Motor Control
- Value of Manipulative Experiences
- Role of the Facilitator
- Effective Storage Systems
- Effective Labelling Systems
- Considerations for Setting Up a Manipulative Area

- Observation and Documentation Techniques
- International Considerations
- Manipulative Materials
- Ages and Stages of Development of Fine Motor Skills
- Key Points
- Student Activities
- References

Learning Outcomes

After studying this chapter, the reader will:

1. Identify the stages of fine motor development
2. Define manipulative learning
3. Identify the value of the manipulative area
4. Identify the role of the facilitator
5. Discuss effective storage techniques
6. Identify an appropriate labelling system
7. Discuss considerations for setting up the manipulative area in both indoor and outdoor environments
8. Identify appropriate manipulative materials
9. Identify various documentation techniques in order to observe children

Interactive Learning Exercises

 Remember, the CD-ROM that came with this text contains interactive exercises that relate to the topics in this chapter, as well as other valuable resources.

▶ What Is Manipulative Learning?

Manipulative learning involves learning by using hands and fingers to touch, grasp, carry, twist, take apart, put together, attach things to each other, feel through touching, develop **eye-hand coordination,** operate tools (scissors, wrenches, hammers), expand on self-help skills (buttoning, pouring, eating, dressing), and become more independent and self-confident in one's abilities.

Manipulative skills are enhanced in every area of the learning environment:

- dramatic play—dressing oneself, pretend cooking, missing materials;
- music—playing musical instruments;
- sand—digging, pouring, smoothing, shaping;
- water—pouring, cleaning, mixing;
- creative art—drawing, painting, gluing, sewing;
- quiet area—putting puzzle together, turning pages of a book;
- carpentry—hitting nail on head with hammer, twisting screw into wood; and
- math/science—sorting, weighing.

Manipulative skills and materials have been discussed in previous chapters. Discussion of skills and materials in this section will focus on other materials and equipment that could be included and on the fine motor development that is enhanced through these activities. Although these skills develop in a natural developmental sequence, children of various ages use and practise the skills. This allows children to refine skills and ultimately leads to greater independence.

▶ Manipulative Experiences to Encourage Learning

After our field trip in early spring, the children started to look at books about pond life. They were especially intrigued by the animal life in the pond and by the puzzles that also explored life in the pond and life around the pond. One was a magnetic puzzle about insects. The children enjoyed manipulating the magnetic "net" to catch an insect and then matching it to the insect in the big book (photo 10.1).

This activity expanded into creating an indoor pond. For the water, they decided to put the big blue flannel board on the floor. Next evolved a lively discussion of what was needed.

Alexandria: "Real ponds have mud, rocks, logs, and weeds in them."

PHOTO 10.1

Chelsea: "Animals too—snakes, lizards, and bugs."

Jamie: "I know, turtles, frogs, and fish!"

Alexandria: "Well, let's do it. I know what it looks like so I'll do the pond part."

Jamie: "Can I help?"

Alexandria: "Do you know where the rocks are?"

Jamie shook his head, no.

Alexandria: "I'll show you, come on."

PHOTO 10.2

PHOTO 10.3

Chelsea went to the animal bins and got out some lizards and snakes. She started to move them in the "water" (photo 10.2). Alexandria and Jamie returned. "You have to stop. The pond is not ready yet." The children added rocks, logs, driftwood, and plastic aquatic plants to their pond. Jamie got some of the fish and frogs. Both Chelsea and Jamie started to move their animals. Jamie lined up the fish in the water. He started to put one frog or one snake on a rock (photo 10.3). Chelsea pretended her snake was catching the fish to eat.

Alexandria was not satisfied. She said that the pond needed more things: it needed a stream to flow into it and it needed mud at the side of it. Anne listened and asked, "How could we make the mud and the stream?" Alexandria said, "Let's look in the storage room to see if we can find something." Alexandria found blue corrugated paper and blue construction paper. As she looked around she saw a roll of blue plastic. "This is perfect. We'll use this." She carried the roll over to the pond. She cut off a piece and put it to one end of the pond. She went back to the pond book and looked through it (*All Eyes on the Pond*).

The pond was left out. Jamie and Chelsea immediately went back to their pond and continued to **manipulate** the animals. Alexandria got the brown blanket and said that it could make a bank. She put it between the pond and the stream. She had noticed some dried flowers outside the window. She went out

PHOTO 10.4

with an adult to bring in a few flowers. She put these "on the bank." She thought that she could create mud with a box of sand and water. She then collected the animals she could use. "Take a picture of this, please" (photo 10.4). Pond play continued for more than four weeks.

Throughout this experience, children learned to work together, to solve problems together and independently, to use materials from other areas, to symbolize their play with creative use of props, and to manipulate real objects and materials.

▶ Child Development: Developmental Levels of Fine Motor Control

Timmy came to visit Liesl, his sister, with his father. The children were involved in a musical activity. Timmy sat with support in his father's lap. Liesl brought him a small rattle. Timmy shook it. He looked at it and shook it again (photo 10.5).

Timmy was able to hold the rattle when it was placed in his hand. He was also able to shake it. He watched his hand carefully. This activity is helping Timmy develop eye–hand coordination. His father watched him carefully and encouraged him verbally.

PHOTO 10.5

PHOTO 10.6

When he dropped the rattle, his father gave it back to him.

Justin also came to visit his sister, Olivia. He grasped a fence with his whole hand and immediately put the fence in his mouth (photo 10.6). When he took the wooden fence out of his mouth he banged it on the floor. He immediately banged it on the floor again. A big smile appeared. He continued to smile and bang the fence on the floor and then on a drum that Olivia put in front of him.

Justin is learning about the object by touch and taste. He has learned about the texture of the object—it's smooth, the wood is hard, and it makes noise when banged. Manipulation at this age involves the hands, fingers, and mouth. It is very important to watch that objects are not small enough to choke on and the toy is safe to put into the child's mouth.

Nicholas discovered the maracas (photo 5.7). He had learned to shake these at an earlier stage. He has developed his skill to hit the bongo drums with two drumsticks (photo 10.7). He does not always hit the drum. Eventually he puts down the green drumstick and continues to beat the drum with the shorter drumstick. He hits the drum each time.

Notice not only that Nicholas is holding the stick in his hand but also that he is using his thumb and forefinger. He has learned to be much more accurate in

PHOTO 10.7

PHOTO 10.8

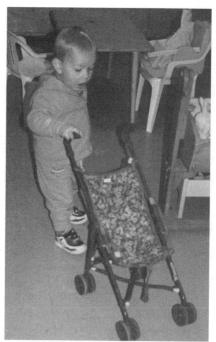

PHOTO 10.9

hitting the drum. His eye–hand coordination has improved tremendously. He is not yet ready to coordinate using both hands effectively.

Nicole loved to pick up the large colourful puzzle blocks (photo 10.8). She would pick them up, bang on them with her hands, and bang them on the floor. Within a month, she was walking. She still played with these blocks but now would pick them up and carry them from one spot to another.

Nicole is developing coordination. She is able to lean forward, pick up the block, and sit up again without falling. As Nicole learned to walk, her balancing skill also improved enabling her to stoop down, pick up the block, and carry it to a new location.

Callum loved to manipulate things that moved—throw balls, push and pull vehicles, push the stroller. One day he pushed the stroller and let it go. He was delighted to see that it moved away from him. He ran after it and repeated the activity. Jennifer noticed his efforts. She gently pushed it back to him. Callum caught it in his hand (photo 10.9). He seemed astonished that the stroller was in his hand. Jennifer and Callum continued with this activity many times.

Callum is learning that he can control his fine and gross muscles to cause movement. He has also improved his grasping ability and eye–hand coordination in order to reach and catch an item that is in motion.

Logan has further developed this skill. He tried to carry the ball up the hill, but it was too difficult. He would drop it and it would roll back down the hill. He finally was able to get it to the top of the hill by pushing it up the hill in front of him (photo 10.10). Logan has coordinated both gross and fine motor skills to manipulate the large ball effectively—walking, pushing, and rolling the ball and stopping the ball at the top of the hill.

The children had created a roadway system outside. The system contained interlocking tracks, both circular and straight. They problem solved to create a hill by using tunnels to fit under the tracks. Logan

PHOTO 10.10

PHOTO 10.11

PHOTO 10.12

used the small cars to push them up the hill (photo 10.11), using his hands to push both cars all the way up the hill in one continuous motion. He then watched as they rolled down the other side.

Logan had refined his skill to work in a continuous motion to steady two cars and move them to the top of the hill. He managed to do this despite the fact that he was disadvantaged by a heavy snowsuit and mittens.

Lindsay was often at the bead area. She would take a container of beads, dump them out on the table, and then pick up the beads one by one and put them back into the container. Eventually she was able to gather more than one bead by sweeping her hand across the table (photo 10.12).

This type of activity gives Lindsay practice with her **pincer grasp** and eye–hand coordination. The beads are difficult to pick up. They are on a slippery surface. She has to refine her grasp to adjust to this situation. This is also a very sensory activity—the beads make a great sound as they clatter onto a hard surface; the beads make a very colourful presentation on the natural wood surface, and the feel of the smooth wood and bumpy beads adds a tactile experience.

Jennifer had noticed that the children were dumping the beads onto the table. The beads would spill onto the floor and the result would be a huge

PHOTO 10.13

mess. She decided to leave out various types of containers that would contain the activity a little more and help the children develop skill in pouring objects (as opposed to pouring water or sand).

Kayla filled the flat dishes with beads. She would grab handfuls of beads and drop them into the plastic dishes. At first she dropped them close to the dish, but as she continued the activity she raised her hand to drop them. At first the beads spilled onto the table. Eventually she adjusted the way she let the beads go and the height, so that she was able to manage to land most of the beads in the dish. She then took each dish that she had filled and poured it into a large bowl (photo 10.13). She would repeat this activity many times.

Kayla was involved in repetitive play. She has learned to grasp more than one object with her hands. She has learned to coordinate her efforts to use both hands simultaneously. She has further learned to transfer skills of pouring from one situation to another—pouring water into a glass, pouring rainbow beads. She has also increased her eye–hand coordination to be more accurate in dropping the beads into the dish from varying heights. Notice that Kayla still needs two hands to control her ability to pour. This is also a very sensory activity. The beads feel quite different when picked up as a group—they're hard, bumpy, and they move within the hand when

picked up. The sounds created by dropping them into a dish are quite different from dropping them into an empty bowl as opposed to a bowl that is almost full. The beads also looked very colourful against different background colours.

The children continued to refine this activity. The sensory aspects of the sounds, textures, and colours attracted even the older children. Yasmine brought a pitcher and a jug over to the manipulative area to pour beads into various containers (photo 10.14). Notice how carefully she is pouring the beads. She has gained much greater control. She managed to pour the beads from the pitcher to the mug with very few beads spilling onto the table. She also managed to coordinate her two hands together—holding one container in one hand as she pours with the other hand.

Katie is using markers outside to create (photo 10.15). She is still using a **palmar grasp** to scribble, but is also using her thumb and forefinger to guide her. There is also some wrist action. Her scribbles are confined to one area before she moves on to another area on her page, thus using less whole-arm action.

Reghan has cut and torn a piece of paper into smaller segments. She is colouring the paper that she has cut (photo 10.16). She has more control of her fingers and wrist. She is using much less whole-arm movement. Notice how she can control her marker in a very small space.

PHOTO 10.14

PHOTO 10.15

PHOTO 10.16

PHOTO 10.17

PHOTO 10.18

Timmy is trying to put the wooden shapes into the matching holes. He tries each piece several times to see if it will fit in the hole. He twists and turns each piece. He tries the piece in each of the holes on the top of the box (photo 10.17). He tries to force it into the hole by pushing it with his hand. At one point, he tried to use the wooden mallet to hammer it into the hole. Jennifer noticed that he was getting frustrated. She asked him if there was somewhere else on the box he could try to fit the piece. Timmy turned the box over. He went through the process again of trying to fit the piece into different holes and was successful.

Timmy is using **trial and error learning**. He has refined his skill—notice that he can handle the piece by using his thumb and forefinger. He can twist and turn the piece to see if it will fit. He has also learned that sometimes force can be used—hand and hammer. He did not think of turning the box. His experience so far has been that he has only one surface to work on.

Emily was at the manipulative area, putting beads into a sorting tray. She would drop the beads from her hands and drop them onto the tray. Her face would light up every time the beads dropped. Suddenly she left the area. She went over to the creative art area and picked up a covered container. She tried to get the lid off. At first she just pulled on the edges (photo 10.18). Next she brought the container up to her eyes and looked at it. She put her fingers at the edge of the lid and managed to pry it open. Emily started to put her beads into the container. She put the lid on and shook them. She took the lid off and poured them from the container into the tray. This activity was repeated many times.

Emily has learned to try various strategies. She tried lifting the lid off. When this did not work she managed to pry the lid off. She has developed much greater control of her fingers. She needed to use all of her fingers to do this. She also needed to control her wrist and arm action in order to put the lid on and take it off. Emily knew that she could make a satisfying sound in another way. She knew where to find a container that would work.

PHOTO 10.19

PHOTO 10.20

PHOTO 10.21

Jacob used two sets of the stackable containers to stack. He was able to balance these in various ways (photo 10.19). He managed to balance the stack with a shorter piece at the bottom. Whenever a piece would fall, he would try it a different way, or try a different piece. Michael noticed his efforts. He said, "Jacob, you have balanced another piece on top."

Jacob is attempting this task through trial and error. As he builds, he is able to control his hand and finger movement. He has gained strength in his fingers. He can pick up heavier pieces with two fingers. He has greater control over his wrist and fingers to balance the structure. He is using less whole-arm movement.

Emily, on the other hand, has refined her skills to be much more precise. She has created balanced structures on the stackable train set. She needed to manipulate the block—twist, turn, place within hole—in order to stack the blocks onto the stackable train set (photo 10.20).

Yasmine created a block structure on a table outside (photo 10.21). She was able to control her hand movements to build balanced structures, despite the fact that she was wearing gloves and a heavy snowsuit. She has developed much greater control of her eye–hand coordination—placed blocks precisely on top of each other so that they balance, controlling her fingers and wrist so that she would not knock other blocks down.

Aaron was attracted by all the activity in the bead area. He stood back and watched the children string the beads. He eventually picked up one bead. He turned it over in his hand. He touched the hole in the

PHOTO 10.22

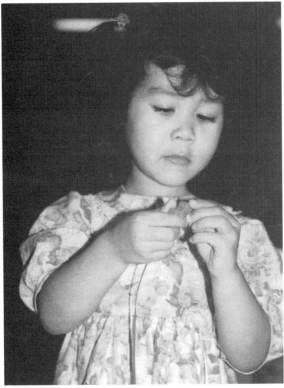

PHOTO 10.23

PHOTO 10.24

bead (photo 10.22). Finally he picked up a handful of beads and dropped them back into the tray.

Aaron used his tactile sense to explore the bead. He carefully looked at it as he also felt it. He has gained sufficient control over his fingers to turn a small item around in his hand and to touch and explore it to learn more about it.

Chelsea creates long strings of beads. She strings beads until her string is full. She is able to coordinate a number of fine motor skills. Notice how carefully she watches what she is doing (photo 10.23). She is able to push the gimp through the small hole, hold the bead with the same hand that pushed the gimp through the hole, pull the gimp out with her other hand, and let the bead slide down the gimp. The skills that she has gained are eye–hand coordination (to push the gimp through the hole), control of individual fingers (to transfer position of hand and wrist), and control (to add slight pressures on the bead to move).

Mandie is connecting the waffle blocks. As she tries to connect the blocks, the edges sometimes overlap. She tries to force the pieces together. Mandie realizes that this does not work. She lifts the piece up and tries again. She manages to connect the first block with the three interconnecting pieces attached. As she connects more blocks, she sometimes has two or three interconnecting pieces lock into place (photo 10.24).

PHOTO 10.25

PHOTO 10.26

PHOTO 10.27

Mandie is connecting her waffle blocks by trial and error. She does use her thumb and forefinger to help, but still uses her whole hand to try to force pieces into place. Her placement is not always exactly in line with the connections. She is still developing her eye–hand coordination and control of her other fingers.

Liesl has constructed a working model out of Brio toys. She placed three wheels on two long screws and connected the wheels by attaching two links on either side of the two screws (photo 10.25). As she tries her model, she is excited to find that it will roll on the carpet. She next tries to roll it down the ramp. It also works!

Liesl constructed her toy by turning the wheels onto the screw. She then had to connect one link to each end of the protruding screw. Her last step was to connect the second link to the screws. She needed good eye–hand coordination to thread the screws, line them up appropriately, and attach them firmly. She found that when she tried to run the "rolling machine" down the ramp one of the links fell off. She added four bolts, one on each end of the screws.

Jacob is connecting a larger puzzle. As he works on the puzzle he puts some pieces in immediately. These are pieces that he recognizes, such as the big wheels. Others he simply tries to fit in where there is a matching connection. When a piece does not fit in immediately or is hard to connect he tries to pound it in with his hand (photo 10.26).

Jacob is starting to look at the pieces to fit them into the appropriate spot in a puzzle. For other items

he simply tries to push the piece into a spot that looks like it might fit. He is still working on his fine motor control to be able to fit the piece exactly into the spot it should fit in. He said to Jennifer, "This is part of the wheel." Jennifer answered, "I see that. I also notice it has some green colour at the top."

In contrast, Cindy and Sarah are working on a long floor puzzle. They discuss which piece is next by looking at the interior detail of the puzzle. Once they have found the piece, they put the piece exactly in the spot and press it into place. They have also created the word *cows* out of the interlocking foam puzzle. They copied the word from the animal dictionary cards at the writing centre. Sarah counted three cows and Cindy promptly found a number 3 and placed it in front of the word *cows*. They are explaining what they are doing to Michael (photo 10.27).

Both Sarah and Cindy have good eye–hand coordination and full control of all fingers and their wrists. They can connect pieces precisely in the correct spot.

▶ Value of Manipulative Experiences

• improve fine motor skills—increased complexity in ability to do puzzles; Alicia doing a one-piece puzzle (photo 7.9), Sarah and Cindy doing a large floor puzzle (photo 10.27);

- improve hand-eye coordination—increased ability to bead; Aaron exploring beads (photo 10.22), and Chelsea beading long string of beads (photo 10.23);
- improve ability to use tools—Reghan using a screwdriver (photo 12.7);
- improve self-help skills—increased ability to pour; Iorahkote (photo 4.20) and Billie (photo 4.23);
- improve problem-solving skills—Chelsea, Jamie, and Alexandria creating an indoor pond (photos 10.2, 10.3, and 10.4);
- improve cutting skills—Jordan snipping the edges of paper (photo 9.21) and Liesl cutting out a puddle (photo 9.1);
- improve observational skills—Aaron noting detail on a bead (photo 10.22), Timmy noting detail of differences in shape (photo 10.17), Jakob noting detail in puzzle (photo 10.26);
- transfer skills from one area to another—Kayla pouring water (photo 4.15), then pouring sand, then pouring beads (photo 10.13);
- support emerging cognitive skills—one-to-one correspondence; Jamie putting one animal on each rock (photo 10.3); matching puzzle insects to pictures of insect (photo 10.1); creating words and counting (photo 10.27);
- support other curricular areas—fine motor skills needed to play drum, pour water/sand, create moulds, manipulate play dough, paint, turn pages, create mixtures, thread a needle, hammer a nail, increase vocabulary;
- provide opportunity to use all of the senses—pouring beads—sound of falling beads, texture of the beads (hard, bumpy, smooth, indented), colour of the beads, use both fine and gross muscles, learn words associated with beads, coordinate skills (eye–hand coordination, transfer and hold bead from one hand to the other, pull gimp out); and
- provide opportunities to engage in various types of play—Jakob in solitary play completing puzzle (photo 10.26); Aaron and Timmy at the bead area (photo 10.22); associative play Jeremy and Autumn discussing insects (photo 10.1).

▶ Role of the Facilitator

- document children's learning and activities;
- provide developmentally appropriate materials—magnetic puzzle of insects and book to match insects to;

- provide experiences that enhance success—gimp to thread beads as the tip is stiff and therefore easier to put through beads;
- provide help as needed—helped Alexandria find materials for pond; pushed stroller back to Callum;
- adapt and change environment as needed—provided dishes and bowls to allow children to pour beads;
- become knowledgeable about developmental milestones—recognized that some children were starting to write, count, match number to number of objects (photo 10.27) and provided related dictionary cards, foam numbers, and puzzle forms;
- support children's efforts—Michael listening to Sarah and Cindy (photo 10.27);
- ensure activities flow from indoor to outdoor activities—manipulative activities (photos 10.11 and 10.21);
- support language development—Michael talking about a balance to Jacob; Jennifer expanding Jakob's statement that he had found part of a wheel by pointing out more detail (green colour);
- know when to leave children alone and when to help—left children to build pond, helped when Alexandria asked for help; and
- provide opportunity to solve own problems—supported Jacob to build using alternate materials, stacking cups instead of asking him to stack them properly.

▶ Effective Storage Systems

Manipulative materials have many small parts. These parts, when lost, make some toys useless (puzzles) and others potentially dangerous (beads; can easily cause slips and falls). With the great variety and number of items, it can also potentially become very messy and time consuming to clean up the area—if all the beads are dumped, it takes a long time to reorganize them.

Materials need to be logically organized in a way that makes sense to children. You can organize by colour, by shape, or by size. For example, all the vehicles could be stored together, all the large beads could be put together, all the big Duplo could be placed together.

Containers appropriate for storage could be both recycled materials and commercially produced materials (see table 10.1).

TABLE 10.1

▶ Storage Containers	
Storage Container	**Possible Materials**
Clear water, juice, or pop bottles—cut to appropriate size	Beads, gimp, small plastic or rubber sorting toys (bears, vehicles), letters, numbers, small blocks, tangram pieces, cubes, Brio parts, Duplo
Stackable plastic containers	Duplo, blocks, gears, fences, connecting toys such as waffle blocks
Centralized storage—clear drawers on wheels	Plastic animals, magnetic or wooden numbers, letters, accessories—rocks, pinecones
Small wooden drawer units	Beads, gimp, small plastic or rubber sorting toys (bears, vehicles), letters, numbers, tangram pieces
Puzzle racks	Puzzles
Open low shelves	All materials organized by type, puzzles stacked
Sorting trays	Any materials that can be matched or sorted, such as beads or small rubber vehicles
	Also could be left empty on shelf to sort into
Plastic-case car organizers	Small cars
Clear drawer set for organizing workbench accessories	Brio toys—organize by type (wheels, connecting bars, screws, tools, nuts, bolts)

▶ Effective Labelling Systems

It is critical that all containers are labelled by picture and by word. Children can sort items into the appropriate storage container. It is an excellent way to have children match and sort. It also prevents unnecessary dumping in order to find the specific items you are looking for. For example, if I wish to find a small bear, I simply look into the container holding small bears, as opposed to dumping out all the bears to find a small bear.

▶ Considerations for Setting Up a Manipulative Area

1. Materials

Materials in this area should be available for a variety of concepts—size, colour, and shape. Children should gain experiences by manipulating materials that provide opportunities to compare, count, match, and sort in a variety of ways—by stringing, by lining up in rows,

or by stacking. Materials should be set out that include the following criteria (Dodge and Colker, 1992):

a) **Self-Correcting Materials**—These are materials that can be put together in only one way. The end product will always be the same. Examples of these types of activities include puzzles and many of the Montessori materials, such as fitting knobbed cylinders into the correct slots. These materials have the advantage of providing children with a known outcome. The process of how to put the puzzle together can change, but the end result is always the same. Many tasks, such as reading and mathematics, have a similar process. How one reads is up to the individual—sounding out words, reading words in context, or recognizing the shape of the word. However the word will always be the same word.

b) **Open-Ended Materials**—These materials can be put together in any way. Both the materials and the product may vary. Examples of these types of materials are Lego, Duplo, Lincoln blocks, bristle blocks, beads, and Tinker Toys. The advantages to these types of materials are that they encourage individual problem solving, imagination, creativity, and persistence. The child can approach the task from any focus and the end result will be totally different. Note how Liesl and Benjamin have used the Brio set in quite different ways (photos 10.25 and 12.5).

c) **Some materials fall into both categories.** The intent is that the activity is to be completed in one certain way. For example stacking rings and stacking cups fall into this category. They are to be stacked in one way, from biggest to smallest. If all pieces are used, there is only one way to do this. However, as you saw with Jacob (photo 10.19), these materials can also be used in a number of different ways. It is critical that the facilitator recognizes the value of both activities and encourages the child to approach the task from his or her perspective.

d) **Collectibles**—These are items that children can collect to work with. Children may collect various different rocks, pieces of washed glass, stickers, or stuffed animals. Usually children initiate this type of activity; however, adults can also bring in and share their collections. Collections can be used in many ways—perception of another individual's viewpoint, looking at similarities and differences, matching and sorting activities, deciding where new items belong, and working over time.

e) **Cooperative Games**—These games encourage children to share materials and toys, take turns, and socialize with each other. Care should be taken that the games chosen encourage a process as opposed to setting up a cycle of winning or losing. Some games in this category are lotto games, dominoes, and memory games.

2. Aesthetics

Materials need to be aesthetically presented. An area that has materials dumped all over will not be attractive to children. In fact, this type of scenario may well encourage children to engage in some less desirable behaviours: walking over the toys on the floor and breaking them, throwing materials, or using laces to whip through the air. A well-organized area will encourage the appropriate behaviour from children with a minimum of re-direction from the adults.

Avoid bright colourful rugs in this area. Manipulative materials tend to have bright vibrant colours. When working with brightly coloured toys it becomes very difficult to find these pieces if they are dropped on a rug that is equally brightly coloured. It is also very difficult to concentrate on an activity if the colour stimulus is so overwhelming.

3. Cleanup

Cleanup activities should become fun learning opportunities. For example, sorting bears by colour into coloured jars or trays is fun and also a learning experience. Children enjoy matching and sorting activities, and this provides opportunity to do so.

4. Levels of Play

Care must be taken to carefully observe the activity the children are involved in. The area needs to be flexible to make changes and adaptations as needed. Various possibilities of level of play should be possible. Large puzzles work well on a rugged surface—they don't tend to slide around as much. Small block play is also better on a rugged surface. There should be a spill-out area so that the child can continue to build, if needed. Some things work better at a small table with chairs—individual puzzles, or sorting trays to sort colours into. Any activity at a table should either have materials that are flat with the minimum number of pieces, or be protected by containers that avoid spilling things all over the floor.

5. Location

The manipulatives can be placed with any number of the other areas because many of the toys are of related concept. The closest linkage is with blocks, as there are already a number of similar materials that can support each other. Additionally, the spill-out area can be shared by both centres.

Math and science concepts are also closely linked to the manipulative area. Concepts such as counting, matching, sorting, comparing, seriation, and patterning are shared among the three areas.

▶ Observation and Documentation Techniques

1. Skills Development

As shown by figure 10.1, Timmy is exploring various types of grasps to develop his fine motor skills. He seems to enjoy manipulative tasks. Provide materials that encourage grasping and refine grasping skills such as various sized sponges and soft balls in the water table, chalk and chalk brushes at the easel.

2. Portfolio

The scenario with Alexandria, Chelsea, and Jamie lends itself well to a **portfolio** development. The discussions and the spontaneous language used should

FIGURE 10.1

▶ **Grasping Skills Chart**

Name: Timmy

Date	Type of Grasp	Evidence
02,05	Four fingers to grasp block	Twisted, turned block to fit into shape sorter
		Prompted to look at other sides of sorter
02,06	Palmar to grasp sponge	Clean Plexiglas divider—got fingers full of paint, squeezed sponge, water ran down his arm and down divider

FIGURE 10.2

▶ **Interest and Attention Span Chart**

Name: Emily

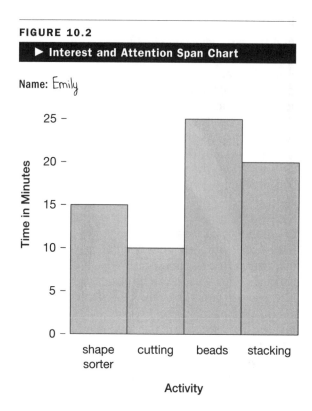

be recorded, along with the activity that the children engaged in. Photographs should be used to support the activities. These panels make a wonderful display in the manipulative area. They encourage children to look over what they have done, reinforce the importance of writing and reading, and serve as motivation to continue with the task. When the activity is finished, the information can be put into booklet form for children to look at in the future.

This type of format gives rich information about the activities the children are involved in and the language and skills used, and gives the facilitator opportunity to conduct personal research in order to guide children—necessary experiences such as going back to the pond to observe, additional books, supportive videos.

3. Combination Tools

This type of information gives detail on what the children are interested in and how long the activity continues. One can easily add additional detail—within the bar write in the type of play (i.e., S for solitary). When the observation is finished, simply draw a vertical line at the end of the graph and date it. This graph can be continued the next day (see figure 10.2).

This type of information gives you some idea about how long the child persists with the task. Children who are practising new skills generally attend to the task longer. A child who flits from activity to activity is either finding the task not challenging enough or too difficult, or has mastered that skill. This will guide the facilitator to adapt or change the materials as needed.

▶ International Considerations

It would appear that all children engage in some type of manipulative play. Manipulative play is defined by the objects that children have available to play with. For example, peer interactions in Polynesia include gathering, sorting, throwing, dropping, and smashing activities with natural elements. Children drop or gather stones, leaves, fruit, and insects. They pound stones together to make sounds, cover rocks with mud, throw stones for dogs to chase, drop items from bridges, and roll items down slopes of hills (Roopnarine, Johnson, and Hooper, 1994, p. 83).

Children in the village of Dene, inland of the western coast of Senegal, were observed in more work-related play. This type of play prepares the children for the expectations that are placed upon them later. Roles tend to be gender-determined. Both girls and boys engage in tasks that they would see their parents engaged in. By the time the girls are five or six years old, they are expected to have learned tasks and are expected to participate in household routines. For example, girls would fetch water from the well and pour it into the drinking containers. They would be involved in washing clothes. Boys, however, spent more time exploring the countryside with other boys. After the age of seven, both girls and boys spent an increasing amount of time on work-related tasks—girls on household chores, boys on agricultural types of activities (Roopnarine, Johnson, and Hooper, 1994, p. 169).

In Sweden, children are exposed to manipulative toys that encourage them to make connections between the toy and other skills. The Brio toys for infants and toddlers include stackable train toys that are magnetic. This makes the task of stacking or connecting trains much easier for little fingers. In addition, the child learns the relationship of cause and effect: When I bring these items in close proximity, they will attach.

Brio toys for older age groups encourage children to build a realistic train set—tracks, trains that can be loaded and unloaded, railway crossings with gates that open and close, and accessories (trees, people, buildings, animals) that can be placed to create a village, town, or farms along the track. The children not only use fine motor control to build, but also need fine motor control to operate the various mechanisms—tilting the railway car to unload, opening and closing gates, and turning a platform to change the direction the train can travel in. In addition, tools are provided that will help children build individualized structures

and vehicles. These tools are either plastic or wooden but work on the equipment or materials provided.

In contrast, many of the carpentry toys that can be bought in North America emphasize pretend play. These toys will make a sound or might move, but are not functional—for example, when the child pushes the button the drill will move and make a sound but cannot drill a hole.

It would seem that the skills valued by a particular culture are represented in the types of activities and play materials presented to the children. Additionally, the types of materials available depend on the economic standard of that particular society. Irrespective, children learn to use fine motor skills that are useful to them and that they need for future success within a particular setting.

▶ Manipulative Materials

Materials are cumulative. Subsequent age groups may use toys of previous age group(s). Complexity of toys changes in detail, size, and number of pieces (see table 10.2).

TABLE 10.2

▶ Manipulative Materials

Age	Possible Materials	Purpose
Birth–4 months	Finger rattles, wrist rattles	Draw attention to fingers, hand
	Mobiles hanging face down or at side of crib so infant can see hanging moving parts	Encourage swatting
	Place bright toys or noisemakers in front of infant	Encourage reaching
	Small rattles, toys with handle to fit in hand—place in hand	Encourage shaking
	Toys with wheels, balls—place in front	Push, pull
4–8 months	Soft balls, small soft toys	Grasp ball with whole hand; release, drop, throw
	Small drums, spoons, lids, sturdy rattles	Bang
	Pail, containers—small (large enough to prevent choking) unbreakable toy items	Drop in pail, dump out
8–12 months	Small toys—dolls, stuffed toys	Poke, pinch, carry
	Blocks, pots/pans, wooden spoons	Bang
	Small toys to put into containers, staking rings	Use thumb and forefinger to pick up and put into container

TABLE 10.2 MANIPULATIVE MATERIALS (continued)

Age	Possible Materials	Purpose
12–18 months	Small toys, crayons, markers	Grasp using thumb and fingers
	Picture books	See result of actions; point to items
	Toys on shelves, in baskets, on table	Reach to grab—lift, carry
	Snaps, buttons, zipper	Undo
	Balls	Roll, catch when rolled back
	Soft unbreakable objects—soft blocks, balls	Throw, put in containers, dump out, stroke, stack
18–24 months	Markers, paint, pencils, crayons	Scribble
	Objects to twist, turn, pound—pounding benches, vehicles that twist apart, put together; jars with lids—take off put on	Take apart, put together; twist, turn
	Shovel, pails, containers, scoops, water/sand wheels	Fill, empty, pour
Toddler	Textured objects—balls of different texture; finger paint; blocks of different texture—wood, foam, cloth	Label texture
	Beads—various sizes, shapes (transportation beads, animal beads, geometric beads, button beads, rainbow gems)	Match, sort, stack
	Duplo, gears; bristle blocks	String, pour from container to container, match, sort
	Puzzles, foam boards—single piece with knobs, simple interlocking	Build, take apart, put together
	Play dough—mallet, plastic knives, rolling pins (see Chapter 9, p. 198)	Dump all pieces, trial-and-error to put together
	Doll clothing—with snaps, zippers	Dressing, undressing dolls
	Shape sorters	Shape, form, reform
	Peg boards with large pegs	Trial-and-error to place shapes into correct slots
	Rubber animals and vehicles—various colours, sizes	Place in, take out; match, sort
Preschooler	Puzzles and form boards—up to 20 pieces for younger age; up to 50 pieces for 5-year-old; floor puzzles	Look at detail to fit, look at edge to fit—some trial-and-error
	Beads	Work together
	Small objects—animals, vehicles, people, plants	Pattern, sort
	Coloured various sizes—cubes, pegs, blocks, numbers, letters, hoops, and sorting containers (trays, baskets)	Match, sort
	Magnetic objects—Brio train, magnets (horseshoe, paddles), letters, numbers, magnetic shapes	Match, sort, form words, attach, pull apart, create designs, pictures
	Construction toys—Brio, Tinker, Lego, waffle blocks, tangrams, pattern blocks	Create objects, designs—pull apart, put together, create designs, objects, pictures
School-age	Coins, cub-o-links, multilinks blocks, unifex blocks, attribute blocks, sequence cards	Classify, count, compare
	Increasingly more complex puzzles	Strategies for completion—all the sky pieces, all the edge pieces sorted out, put together

▶ Ages and Stages of Development of Fine Motor Skills

Table 10.3 summarizes the development of fine motor skills.

TABLE 10.3

▶ Development of Fine Motor Skills

Age	Skills
Birth to 4 months	Grasp reflex—hand closes when something placed in hand Whole hand to grasp objects when placed in hand Eye-hand-coordination—swats at objects, may miss
4–8 months	Whole-hand grasp, fingers against thumb; uses thumb and finger to pick up; passes objects from hand to hand; grasps and deliberately releases; Uses objects to pick up, drop, shake, clap, bang
8–12 months	Uses thumb and forefinger and/or two fingers to pick up; fingers used to poke, pinch; carries objects in hand; clap; bang; imitate actions; use writing tools to create marks; strokes textured objects; takes clothes off—undoes large buttons, snaps, zippers
12–18 months	Thumb used with all fingers, points to objects, pictures; may start to show hand preference, carries objects around room, throws objects, rolls and catches rolled objects; reaches accurately, scribbles, starts to dress self
Toddler	Throw at target; twists, turns objects; pick up items to put into something else—spoons, shovels, scoops
Preschool	Increased finger movement, learn to coordinate movements—start to cut with scissors, dress self, more control of wrist action, change from palmar grasp into tripod grasp, decrease in whole-arm movement to draw, write, paint
School-aged	Increased dexterity—peak improvement between four and eight; Advanced skills—play musical instrument, draw, paint, cut, learn to print, write; greater integration of fine and large motor skills

▶ KEY POINTS

Manipulative learning is: using fingers and hands to explore objects.

Ages and Stages of Fine Motor Development

- **birth–4 months**—reflex grasp, swatting;
- **4–8 months**—whole-hand grasp, thumb and finger to pick up small items, transfer from objects hand to hand, voluntary release;
- **8–12 months**—thumb used with all fingers, pincer grasp, imitate actions, unbutton, unzip, scribble;
- **toddler**—throw, fill, and empty;
- **preschool**—increased finger dexterity, **tripod grasp,** decrease in whole-arm movement; and
- **school-aged**—increased dexterity, advanced skills.

► KEY POINTS (continued)

Value of Manipulative Experiences

- improve fine motor skills;
- improve eye–hand coordination;
- improve ability to use tools;
- improve self-help skills;
- improve problem-solving skills;
- improve cutting skills;
- improve observational learning;
- transfer skills from one area to another;
- support emergent cognitive skills;
- support other curricular areas;
- provide opportunity to use multi-sensory approach; and
- provide opportunity to engage in various types of play.

Role of the Facilitator

- provide developmentally appropriate materials;
- provide experiences that enhance success;
- provide help as needed;
- adapt and change environment as needed;
- become knowledgeable about developmental milestones;
- support children's efforts;
- provide activities indoors and outdoors;
- support language development;
- know when to step in; and
- provide opportunities to solve own problems.

Effective Storage

- organized by type;
- types—recycled clear bottles, cut down; stackable containers;
- centralized storage;
- wooden drawer units;
- puzzle racks;
- open low shelves;
- sorting trays; plastic car organizers; and
- workbench plastic organizers.

Effective Labelling System

- picture and word.

Considerations for Setting Up the Manipulative Area

- Materials—self-correcting, open-ended, dual category, collectibles, cooperative games;
- Aesthetics—well organized, avoid clutter, careful use of colour;
- Cleanup—fun, learning opportunity;
- Levels of play—on the floor, on a table; and
- Location—near blocks or math and science.

Observation and Documentation Techniques

- Skill development;
- Portfolio; and
- Combination tool.

Student Activities

1. Go to a toy store and develop a list of manipulative materials available for the various age groups. Discuss points as outlined in the chart below.

Age	Description of Manipulative Toy	Evaluation of Toy
Infant: first four months		
Infant 4–12 months		
Infant 12–18 months		
Toddler		
Preschooler		
School-aged		

2. Analyze photo 10.1. What three fine motor skills can you identify? What other three skills can you identify? Discuss how the skills you have identified relate to each other.
Use photos 10.2 and 10.3 and the description of the scenarios on p. 207. Develop a mini book for the children as a reference to this activity. Discuss the value of providing beads as a manipulative activity.

3. Try to write your name by:
    a) holding the pencil in a whole-hand grasp without using your thumb, keeping your wrist stiff, and using your whole arm to write;
    b) now, try the same process but you may use your thumb to help you; and
    c) lastly, try the process by using less arm movement and adding some wrist movement.
    Compare your results. What materials and or equipment would have made your task easier? How might you apply this experiment to your work with young children?

4. Jessica is cutting with her scissors. She cannot control her scissors and hold the paper. What strategies might you use to help her with this task?

5. Callum (photo 10.9) is intrigued by rolling items. What other activities and materials might you provide to continue to build Callum's fine motor skills and eye–hand coordination?

6. Observe an infant and a toddler using fine motor materials. Compare their:
    • grasp in using the materials;
    • choice of materials; and
    • overall strategy to accomplish the task.

7. Develop a combination tool to observe a preschooler during various fine motor activities. Observe the preschooler. How could you use this information? What changes and or adaptations might you suggest?

8. You have purchased a large quantity of geometric beads of various sizes, shapes, and colours. Describe the system of organization you would set up.

9. A parent and child bring in their collection of rocks, fossils, shells, and washed glass that they have collected over time at various beaches. They want the collection back when you are finished with it. How might you use this collection? How would you show respect for the time and effort the parent and child had put in? How would you ensure that the collection stays intact?

▶ References

Dodge, D., & Colker, L. (1992). *The creative curriculum* (3rd ed.). Washington, DC: Teaching Strategies, Inc.

Isenberg, J., & Jalongo, M. (2001). *Creative Expression in Early Childhood.* Upper Saddle River, NJ: Prentice-Hall, Inc.

Roopnarine, J., Johnson, J., & Hooper, F. (Eds.). (1994). *Children's play in diverse cultures.* Albany, NY: State University Press.

CHAPTER 11

Math and Science

Math and science are interrelated; fundamental mathematical concepts such as comparing, classifying, and measurement are simply called process skills when applied to science problems. That is, fundamental math concepts are needed to solve problems in science. The other science process skills (observing, communicating, inferring, hypothesizing, and defining controlling variables) are equally important for solving problems in both science and mathematics.

—*Charlesworth and Lind,* Math and Science for Young Children

Chapter Outline

- ▶ Math and Science to Encourage Learning
- ▶ Child Development: Components of the Learning Cycle as Applied to Math and Science
- ▶ Value of Math and Science
- ▶ Role of the Facilitator
- ▶ Effective Storage Systems
- ▶ Effective Labelling Systems
- ▶ Considerations for Setting Up a Math and Science Area

- ▶ Observation and Documentation Techniques
- ▶ International Considerations
- ▶ Math and Science Materials
- ▶ Ages and Stages of Math and Science
- ▶ Key Points
- ▶ Student Activities
- ▶ References
- ▶ Resources

Learning Outcomes

After studying this chapter, the reader will:

1. Identify the stages of the learning cycle as applied to math and science
2. Identify the value of the math and science area
3. Identify the role of the facilitator
4. Discuss effective storage techniques
5. Identify an appropriate labelling system
6. Discuss considerations for setting up the math and science area in both indoor and outdoor environments
7. Identify appropriate math and science materials
8. Identify various documentation techniques in order to observe children

Interactive Learning Exercises

 Remember, the CD-ROM that came with this text contains interactive exercises that relate to the topics in this chapter, as well as other valuable resources.

▶ Math and Science to Encourage Learning

On several field trips, spanning early to late spring, the children gained many insights about their environment and the time of year. Benjamin and Jacob noticed that although it was still cold outside, the ground not covered by the snow was wet. Benjamin had noticed that when he had stepped onto the ground it was "softer" and "squishy." He also noticed that his footstep appeared and that his footstep began to fill with water. He tried to enlarge his footstep and noticed that the water seeped over his boots (photo 11.1). He stamped into the footstep, and when he removed his foot more water appeared. He said, "Maybe the sun is hot and melting the snow into the ground." Rachelle suggested that he try it in other spots. Benjamin and Jacob tried to create footsteps in other spots. Sometimes the ground was "too hard." Benjamin was clearly puzzled. Why would the ground be softer in some spots and hard in other spots? He thought that it might have something to do with the river that flowed close by.

Jacob found a puddle. He found a piece of "pretty glass" right on top of the puddle. He lifted up the "glass" very gently and carefully to show Michael (photo 11.2).

Michael: "It does look like glass."

Some of the other children gathered around to look at Jacob's pretty glass.

Liesl: "I think it might be thin ice."

Michael: "How could we find out what it is?"

PHOTO 11.1

PHOTO 11.2

Benjamin: "Maybe we could lay it on the blanket and see if the sun melts it."

Liesl: "Maybe we could take our gloves off and see if it is icy."

The children quickly took their gloves off and felt it. They decided it did feel icy.

Liesl: "My hand is wet. It must be ice, 'cause my hand's melting it."

Olivia: Maybe we could take it inside and see if it will melt. Then we will know for sure."

All the children agreed to do this.

Yasmine found a flower (photo 11.3). She looked at it very carefully. She said that it had a stick part, a great, big, huge flower part, and a crinkly brown part. Jennifer heard her and said, "You have noticed a lot about the flower. It does have a big flower, and the stick part is called its stem. What do you think the crinkly part was?" Yasmine wasn't sure. "Let's take it inside and look in our book," she suggested.

Logan found a stick (photo 11.4). He carried it with him for a while. He saw a log and began to bang the log. Jennifer thought it sounded like horses clipping, clopping. She began to sing the Raffi song "Listen to the Horses."

PHOTO 11.3

PHOTO 11.4

Several other children found sticks and tried to play the beat on various logs or beat two sticks together. The older children sang the words to the song and could keep the beat. The younger children watched the older children and Jennifer and also tried to keep the beat.

On the way back, the children discovered that the snow banks created by the snow plough were a won-

derful place to roll the ball up and down. Stephanie tried to carry the ball up the slope, but she said that the slope was "too slippery and too gritty" (photo 11.5). Benjamin and Braelyn discovered that they could use the chunky snow to make designs on the wall. The snow stuck to

PHOTO 11.5

PHOTO 11.6

PHOTO 11.7

PHOTO 11.8

the gritty surface (photo 11.6). Anastasia had brought back a stick. She played it on the upside-down pails (photo 11.7). She beamed. "Horsie sound," she said.

When the children came inside, they put the "thin ice, maybe glass" in a bowl. Yasmine got the flower book and a magnifying glass to look at her flower. She decided that maybe the crinkly things could be leaves that had died. She said they were on the "stem." Jacob kept looking at his "pretty glass." He noticed it was now "small." Liesl said, "I knew it was ice. It melted so it can't be glass."

PHOTO 11.9

PHOTO 11.10

PHOTO 11.11

PHOTO 11.12

The children went back out to the environment many times to notice changes. Each time, they discovered and saw new things. Braelyn noticed that the tree had pussy willows on it. She also noticed that it was soft and that the yellow "pollen" came off in her hands (photo 11.8). Jordan discovered that the tree was very tall. He kept looking up to try to see the sky. He stopped at several trees and looked up to see "how tall" they were (photo 11.9). Liesl discovered that she could climb a tree and balance on it (photo 11.10). She noticed that the bark was rough. She also noticed that this tree had no buds or leaves yet.

Taylor found the first flower (photo 11.11). She indicated that it was all right to pick since it was a dandelion. She looked at the flower very carefully. She said there were too many petals to count. When the children saw Taylor's dandelion, they immediately ran to find some. Olivia pointed to the ones near her and counted out eight dandelions. Later in the year, the children enjoyed blowing the dandelion seeds and trying to catch them (photo 11.12)

Children were encouraged to collect items. Before each field trip, they talked about what was appropriate to collect and what was best left. The children created a list of what they could collect and what should not be collected. Reminders had to be given to help them remember.

Collecting items changed from weeds, grasses, leaves, and stones to wading in the water to find

PHOTO 11.13

colourful stones, washed glass, and shells to bring back for their collections (photo 11.13). Riely noticed that there were tiny fish in the water. He tried to catch one, but he said they were too fast.

Through these outdoor experiences the children had opportunities to:

- become aware of the environment by using all their senses;
- observe detail in colour, size, and shape;
- learn about space through **active exploration**—climbing wading, touching, feeling;
- learn about time—returning to the same area over time to observe seasonal changes;
- learn about sequence—water table snow to water to dry grass; winter to spring to summer;
- communicate their ideas and discoveries with others;
- begin to discover relationship of size—tiny, tall, small (pre-measurement concepts);
- predict what will happen (ice or glass?), and validate their predictions (the ice melted);
- make inferences—sun melting the snow and ground being softer near the river;
- gather and use gathered materials to sort into collections;
- count items—flowers, too many to count;
- learn vocabulary associated with math—*too many, different, tall*; and with science—*pollen, parachute seeds*;
- become curious about the world around us—observing detail, questioning, making inferences, looking up information; and
- brainstorm ideas—making lists of what could or could not be collected.

These types of activities lay the foundations of many of the concepts of math: counting, comparing, sorting/matching, developing associated vocabulary, and all of the concepts of science: observing, learning to sort (leads to later classifying skills), communicating, measuring, predicting, and making inferences. Children are exploring the environment to become aware of the world around them, experiment with the materials within their space, start to question and compare their findings, and start to use the information to test their understanding in new situations. The children found the dandelion, they could recognize it by its shape and colour, they could see it as it changed from flower to seed, they could simulate the wind by blowing the seeds, and they could plant the seeds to grow into dandelions.

▶ Child Development: Components of the Learning Cycle as Applied to Math and Science

Rory pulled the rattle in front of him (photo 11.14). The more he pulled, the more the shapes started to dance and shake. They made a soft noise that seemed to delight him. He seemed to keep time to the movement and noise of the rattles with his sucking. The faster the rattles shook, the faster he sucked. This is one way that infants communicate their pleasure—increased speed of sucking.

Rory is becoming aware of the shapes—he can feel them (bumpy, smooth, hard); he can see the bright colours; he is learning about the size (they fit into his hand); he is learning about space (sitting upright to manipulate objects, reaching for things in front of him); and he is learning about cause and effect (when I touch the rattle it moves and makes a noise).

PHOTO 11.14

Jacob (photo 8.2) is becoming aware of new concepts around him. He has several concepts about the ice he found: weight (light to carry); size (melts); discovered relationships (ice gets smaller when it melts); discovered sequence (pick up ice, bring indoors, ice melts); colour (clear colour); and compare (looks like glass).

Logan and Anastasia also developed new awareness of objects within their environment. Logan (photo 11.4) discovered that he could use a stick to create sound (discovering relationships). He learned about personal space—how close he needed to stand to the log to hit it. He became aware of a sequence of actions—find a stick, hit the log, listen, and keep the beat of the song. He observed and imitated behaviours—keeping the beat.

Anastasia applied what she had observed to a new setting (photo 11.7). She found a new stick, created a beat on a new item—pails—and identified the beat as the same as the "horsie sound" (math and science, recognizing similarities and differences).

Hannah (photo 11.15) is imitating behaviours she has observed. She had noticed that the older children had set up the platform to jump from and were jumping. As she jumped, she explored the space around her. Hannah repeatedly jumped in a variety of ways—forward and backward. As she gained confidence, she jumped higher. As she jumped, Ann commented that she was jumping *frontward, higher,*

farther, thus providing appropriate terminology. These are terms needed to help in developing measurement and directional skills. This also gives her an awareness of sequence—climb on the platform, jump off, and land.

Yasmine observed many things about the flower she had found (photo 11.3). She became aware of the colour and shape—crinkly leaves, thin strong stem. Yasmine examined the flower in different ways—with her eyes, through a magnifying glass, and by looking up the information. She matched her flower to another flower in one of the books to infer that the "crinkly part" was a "dead leaf."

Liesl explored space. She could verbalize her experience and draw a conclusion about that experience—she could balance on the tree (photo 11.10). She was able to compare information from one setting to another—there were no leaves or buds on this tree.

Over time, the children were able to compare what had happened and apply this information to a new task. The photographs of the children engaged in different activities—picking the dandelion, a picture of the number of dandelions Olivia had found, blowing the dandelion seeds, chasing and catching the seeds—were used to encourage children to put these experiences in the correct sequence.

The children brought back many items to the indoor environment. The children started a collection

PHOTO 11.15

PHOTO 11.16

of shells. Children collected their own shells and families contributed shells that they had found. The collection was used in many ways:

- match shells that are the same; match shells to their pictures;
- identify shells by name—olive, clam;
- draw shells, use shells to make prints;
- sort shells—same shells, same sizes, same colours;
- compare shells and talk about how they were the same or different;
- sequence shells from smallest to largest or vice versa; sequence shells in accordance to how "loud" they are (photo 11.16);
- weigh shells;
- count shells; and
- display shells.

Collections are a valuable way for children to make the connections between what they know and what new information they are gaining. Hannah applied information from a past experience—listening to shells on a beach in Florida. She was able to identify that she didn't hear the ocean in all the shells in front of her, but that she did hear the lake in the ones the children had found. She was further able to recognize and name some of the shells she had seen at the ocean.

There are a multitude of discoveries that children can make about science and math. Science and math are wonderful activities to evoke curiosity that naturally leads to learning. Some of the other learning activities that children engage in are:

- sorting (photo 11.17)—Jamie and Lindsay sorted the animals into like groups (all the dogs). Further, they lined up the animals in one straight row. This

PHOTO 11.18

is an aspect of one-to-one correspondence (one animal per spot).

- sorting to count—Jordan had created a string of beads of all dogs. He showed it to Dillon. Dillon counted all the beads. Jordan wanted to count them too. Dillon held the string as Jordan counted (photo 11.18). Dillon had correctly counted 18 beads. Jordan counted five beads and then repeated a number. Dillon said "No, that's number six." Jordan corrected himself. Every time Jordan said the wrong number, Dillon told him the correct one (children learning from each other).
- predicting and comparing—Emily thought that cows were heavier than pigs. She weighed them to find out (photo 11.19). She was very surprised when she noticed that the pig was heavier than the cow. "The cow looks heavier," she said. Clearly

PHOTO 11.17

PHOTO 11.19

PHOTO 11.20

PHOTO 11.21

she was not quite sure that what she saw was really true. The pig was heavier on the scale, but the cow looked heavier because it was bigger. This leads to later skills of conservation—realizing that quantity is the same irrespective of the alignment or containment. Two lines of 12 pennies will have the same amount irrespective of how long or short the line is. Two containers of equal size will hold the same amount of water, even though one is tall and skinny and one is short and stout.

- becoming aware of and exploring new concepts— Benjamin had helped find "magnetic sand" in the sandbox. The magnetic kernels had been collected in a clear plastic container that was sealed. Benjamin is moving the magnet around the bottom of the container (photo 11.20). He is excited to discover that "the magnetic sand stands up" and he can make it move.

- **one-to-one-correspondence**—Jordan is using a muffin tin to place one vehicle in each slot (photo 11.21). "One-to-one correspondence is the most fundamental component of number. It is understanding that one group of a number of things has the same number of things as another. For example; each child has a cookie, each foot has a shoe, each person wears a hat. It is preliminary to counting and basic to the understanding of equiv-

alency and to the concept of conservation of number" (Charlesworth and Lind, 1999, p. 92).

▶ Value of Math and Science

- learn through observing—Braelyn (photo 11.8) and Yasmine (photo 11.3);
- make and test predictions—Jacob and Liesl deciding if it was ice or glass;
- make inferences—Benjamin deciding the ground was wetter near the river;
- make logical connections—Jordan (photo 11.21) finding that only one item fits per slot;
- learn by trying things in new ways—keeping the beat with rhythmic instruments and keeping the beat with found items (photo 11.4 and photo 11.17);
- increase awareness of the world around them— field trips to explore environments;
- utilize math and science skills in a variety of ways—one-to-one correspondence in manipulative area (photo 11.21); measuring to create play dough (photo 8.6); counting beads (photo 11.18);
- make connections between the outdoor and indoor environments—collect materials to bring inside to use (shells, flowers, stones);
- conduct simple experiments—bringing ice in to see if it will melt;

PHOTO 11.22

PHOTO 11.23

- follow a scientific process—observe (waterlogged ground around Benjamin) (photo 11.1); experiment (step in hole, watch water seep over boots, make hole bigger); reflect on what has happened (sun made the snow melt); test reflection (other ground was frozen); reflect again (it is close to the river);
- enhance problem-solving skills—how to sort a collection, how to move a ball up the hill (photo 10.10);
- look at things in different ways—Benjamin using a magnet on the "magnetic sand" in a clear container (photo 11.20);
- apply knowledge gained from experiences—Hannah sorting shells by sound (photo 11.16); and
- work with known concepts in different ways—Mario creating a pond for the plastic frogs at the light table, which reflects and enlarges onto the wall (photo 11.22); Dillon creating various ways to create movement of various items with ramps and cardboard tubes (photo 11.23).

▶ Role of the Facilitator

- document children's learning and activities;
- ask alternative questions/make alternative comments—problem solving questions (Michael asking how one could find out whether it is glass or ice; Jennifer making an association with a sound heard and music that had been played previously);
- "focus on the beauty and wonder of nature" (Wilson, 1995, p. 7)—Braelyn looking at buds, Taylor looking at a dandelion;
- "introduce nature-related materials into the different learning centers" (Wilson, 1995, p. 4)—shells in manipulative area; logs in sand area and blocks area;
- provide and read books about nature;
- "model interest in and caring for the natural environment" (Wilson, 1995, p. 9)—discussions with children prior to going out on a collection trip;
- "sharing enthusiasm, curiosity, and wonder" (Dighe, 1993, p. 59)—Michael acknowledging that the ice did look like glass;
- "focus attention" (Dighe, 1993, p. 59)—providing equipment to focus attention (magnifying glasses); point out interesting items;
- take cues from children—took cue from Benjamin and Liesl with regard to the ice;
- provide safety—before any field trip, facilitator checked environment for possible hazards; provide safe materials to use indoors (plastic containers for "magnetic sand");
- extend children's interest—return to locations more than once to look at the changes that occurred;
- provide developmentally appropriate materials—children looked up information on the computer about the insects they saw at a later date; magnets; magnifying glasses; fish tank indoors;
- facilitate investigation—help children by asking questions to guide the process (ice episode);

appropriate resources indoors (books, computer software);

- research—become knowledgeable about science and math to be able to guide children to discover concepts; and
- facilitate discussion—talk about what children are doing, what else they might find; look for similarities, differences.

▶ Effective Storage Systems

Effective storage for all materials has been discussed in the manipulative, sand, water, and quiet areas. One additional consideration should be to set up a curiosity table. This table encourages children to look at either a collection of items or sometimes a single item. The children were fascinated by the insects they had seen outside. The curiosity table had been draped with a green cloth that had boxes placed under it to create focal points for three small walnut shells and several books on insects (see References). Each shell contained a different kind of insect. When jiggled, the legs moved. Josh was fascinated by the ladybug. He carried it very gently and with great pride to show to others (photo 11.24).

Additional equipment, such as magnifying glasses, magnets, scales, measuring units, and weights would be stored similarly to the materials in the manipulative area.

PHOTO 11.24

▶ Effective Labelling Systems

The labelling system would follow the same process as all other areas—specifically, similar to the manipulative area.

▶ Considerations for Setting Up a Math and Science Area

1. Outdoor Experiences

"Experiences in the out-of-doors tend to be rich in opportunities for nurturing growth in all of the developmental domains, including adaptive, aesthetic, cognitive, communicative, sensorimotor, and socioemotional" (Wilson, 1995, p. 4). After any outdoor exploration, the experience should be represented indoors through a documentation and display of children's experiences and through bringing in some of the natural materials indoors. Children should have sturdy containers to collect items. Sturdy plastic baskets work well (photo 9.17).

Once indoors, the items need to be put away—some will go to the creative areas, some could go to the sand or water area, some could be placed in the manipulative area, and some could go to the science and math area to be scrutinized more closely.

2. Aesthetics

"Aesthetics means being sensitive to beauty in nature and arts. Such sensitivity is fostered not by talking about beauty but experiencing it in a variety of forms—the sight of snow on evergreen boughs, the smell of the earth after a spring rain, the sound of a bird singing overhead, and the feel of a kitten's fur or moss on the side of a tree" (Wilson, 1995, p. 4). This beauty must be represented indoors. If children are working with collections, they must have an individual spot to work with them. The Montessori approach offers some unique ideas. Each child has a personal rug. This rug is used to create a personal space on the floor to work on. A similar process could be used with children's collections. They could be kept in individual boxes on a shelf. When the child wishes to add to or use his or her collection, they could get a plain rug or piece of material out to place their display on.

Another suggestion is to create "mini-museums of collections" (Kokoski and Downing-Leffler, 1995, p. 37). These would be displayed at all times, could be added to, or could be changed.

3. Location

Although science and math could be placed anywhere in the room as the skills tend to be—and should be—used in all learning areas, the most logical location would be the manipulative area, as it has the most common materials for math and science. If children are growing plants, these should be near natural light.

▶ Observation and Documentation Techniques

1. Skill Sample

Figures 11.1 through 11.3 provide examples of observation and documentation techniques.

FIGURE 11.1

▶ Skill Sample Chart

Name: Jordan

Date	Skill	Evidence
15/10	Counting	Counted beads to six, repeated numbers after six
15/10	One-to-one correspondence	Filled all parts of muffin tin with rubber cars
18/10	Sorting	From a collection of animals, sorted only the dogs to string

---

The type of tool shown in figure 11.1 can be used for any of the skills in math or science. It gives information about Jordan's skill level and also his interests in this area. It gives the facilitator ideas to help expand concepts—encourage counting beyond six, provide alternative materials to sort (geometric beads to string)—and is useful in reporting information to families.

2. Checklists/Frequency Counts

List all the children's names. You simply date and check off when you have seen that particular skill. You should record it more than once, as the behaviour may not yet be consistent. This gives you a good idea of how to expand experiences and materials to reinforce or enhance these skills.

FIGURE 11.2

▶ Counting Checklist

(Counting objects and identifying how many objects have been counted)

Names	Dates	0-3	0-5	0-7	0-10	Include number
Dillon	10/10					18
Jordan	10/10		I			

---

3. Documentation

Follow a similar process as outlined on pp. 218–219 of Chapter 10, on the manipulative area.

4. Learning Cycle

Information gleaned from the chart shown in figure 11.3 gives an indication of the various approaches that Benjamin uses when he is involved in new or repeated experiences. This allows the facilitator to more carefully set up experiences and materials for the children.

FIGURE 11.3

▶ Learning Cycle Chart

Name: Benjamin   Dates: 11/10, 11/12

Component	Documentation
Awareness	Found magnet in sand centre, noticed that it had "stuff" on it that would not clean off—new learning "magnetic sand"
Explore	Collected "magnetic sand" from sandbox
Inquire	Moved "magnetic sand" in clear container with a magnet, said it "stood up"
Utilize	

▶ International Considerations

It is important to realize that children construct their own knowledge no matter where they live or what activities they are involved with. "This means that children in Alaska will be learning about drying fish, singing, dancing, and playing drums. This means that children in Florida will be learning about what to do in a hurricane watch, how to avoid fire ants, and why to protect turtles. Most children in Alaska and Florida learn how to build houses, whether they be of ice, pine boards, cement, brick, or hollow blocks" (Yinger and Blaszka, 1995, p. 15).

Children learn to use the materials that are available to them to construct knowledge about math and science. They may use different materials to count or have different experiences in classrooms that may be directed or open-ended, but they all learn the required skills. "Children in Alaska count with snowballs, bones, and stones. In Florida they use shells. Children in both areas learn to count, but they learn best when they use things that are readily available" (Yinger and Blaszka, 1995, p. 15).

The environments that children explore and learn about are quite different throughout the world. Those experiences are dictated by the type of climate, the type of vegetation, and societal values and activities. Some of these environments seem harsh and unrealistic to some individuals, just as more permissive practices seem too lax to others. Children in Alaska may learn to go ice fishing, hunting, hiking, and sledding under difficult circumstances. Children in Florida may learn to pick, juice, and taste oranges, grapefruits, and lemons, and also to swing from 10-foot-high palm-tree branches" (Yinger and Blaszka, 1995, p. 15).

Some cultures, such as China and Korea, tend to have higher expectations of their children to excel in math- and science-related activities. In these cultures, the instruction is often very teacher-directed. Children are expected to learn by rote memorization and rote counting. The recent jump in knowledge about brain development and appropriate ways of teaching young children has started a slow revolution in most parts of the world. Most cultures now acknowledge the child's right to learn to play. Sadly, not all cultures have the finances or the expertise to provide appropriate environments for young children.

▶ Math and Science Materials

Many of the materials have been listed in other chapters. Therefore, only more specific additional math and science materials are listed in table 11.1.

TABLE 11.1

▶ Math and Science Materials	
Concept	**Possible Materials**
Compare	Nesting cups, attribute blocks, pattern blocks, tangrams, geometric shapes, geometric solids, graphs
Match, sort, pattern	Shells, stones, beads, miniatures (animals, vehicles, dinosaurs, shapes, insects), sorting box, peg boards, picture dominos Gimp, sorting trays, unifix math cubes
Counting	Dice—numbers, symbols; dominos, counting cubes, abacus, numbers, numbers and matching sets of various numbered objects, money, clocks, sand timers, unifix math cubes
Measure	Weight—scale, weights, clear geometric volume sets, set of graduated cylinders, measuring cups, measuring spoons
Natural materials	Ropes, chains, tubes, polyvinyl pipes, twigs, soil, mud, stones, leaves, grass, blowing seeds, growing plants, logs, log rounds
Animals	Fish, ant farm, earthworm farm

▶ Ages and Stages of Math and Science

Components of the learning cycle (Bredekamp and Rosegrant, 1992; and Charlesworth and Lind, 1999, p. 10) have been adapted to reflect science and mathematical content. Children progress through these cycles as they mature and develop the skills needed—language and physical maturity. Children will repeat cycles when they have developed the maturity and skill base, each time the new skills or knowledge are explored. Table 11.2 provides a summary of the ages and stages of math and science.

TABLE 11.2

▶ Ages and Stages of Math and Science

Age	Component	Possible Behaviours
Infant	Awareness Develop a general understanding/recognition of objects, people, events, concepts—provides basis for future learning	Use senses to learn about shape, size, weight, and colour by looking at objects, touching, picking up, putting in mouth, dropping, manipulating (see photos 10.5 and 10.6) Learn about space by being transported to different environments, placed in different environments; infants visiting siblings in child-care environments—(see photo 10.8) Learn about time—providing predictable routines—eating and sleeping based on infants' needs Learn about sequence—when I am wet, I feel wet. I cry, the caregiver comes, I get changed Mobile infants learn about more spatial terms—crawl under, crawl up or down Mobile infants start to make decisions—where to go, what to get, how to make things happen—throw, roll (see photo 10.7)
Toddler	Awareness—develop a general understanding/recognition of new objects, people, events, and concepts Develop more specific understanding/recognition of known objects, people, events, and concepts Exploration—sensory experiences to construct personal meaning about objects, people, events, and concepts	Learn about weight and size by carrying, stacking, moving objects (see photo 3.1) Learn about shape and colour by examining new objects, observing actions of others (see photo 10.22) Learn about space by walking, running, climbing, riding, jumping (see photos 10.5 and 10.10) Learn about time and sequence through regulated routines—eating, sleeping Stack objects, sort objects by colour, size, shape (photo 10.19) Match objects to pictures, label objects (photo 7.1) Develop sequence in play situations—wash baby, build and knock down towers, empty and fill (photo 8.12) Observe and imitate behaviours (see photo 5.10) Discover relationships—cause and effect: When I push the ball, it rolls (photo 4.6) Create—drawings, paintings, structures (photo 9.3)

TABLE 11.2 AGES AND STAGES OF MATH AND SCIENCE (continued)

Age	Component	Possible Behaviours
Preschooler	Awareness—develop a general understanding/recognition of new objects, people, events, and concepts Develop more specific understanding/recognition of known objects, people, events, and concepts	Learn about concepts through manipulation, asking questions, looking at books, observing others: Weight and size by carrying, constructing, manipulating (photo 6.2) Shape and colour by examining new objects, comparing objects, talking about objects (photo 4.3) Space by walking, running, climbing, riding (photo 11.10) Time and sequence through regulated routines—going to work, going to school, seasonal changes, dressing self, meal time, nap time (photo 5.17)
Preschooler	Explore—active experiences to construct personal meaning about objects, people, events, and concepts	Match—find required objects in pictures, books (photo 10.1) Sort objects—colour, size, shape—easily distracted, may switch sorting criteria mid-stream (yellow bears to yellow cars to red cars) Measure—use rudimentary method (string, body) (photos 6.20, 6.21) Compare—shells according to sound (photos 11.15, 11.16) Match symbols to objects/pictures (photo 10.1) Develop sequence life cycles, seasonal (photos 11.11 and 11.12) Create own interpretations (photo 9.12) Discover relationships—seasonal changes (photo 11.8) Collect information—gather materials, make collections (photo 11.13) Count objects—may count incorrectly (missing numbers or repeating numbers); may not give correct answer when asked how many, even after counting (photo 11.17, 11.18) One-to-one correspondence (photos 11.20, 11.21)
Preschooler	Inquiry—compare own results to others, look for similarities and differences Utilization—apply understanding to new situations	Examine items in different ways—by looking, using magnifying glasses, from different angles (photos 11.19, 11.20) Investigate to see which item is heavier, which line is longer (photo 11.18, 11.19) Give explanations based on personal perspective—jar is larger because it looks larger Use past experiences that worked in new situations—used pitcher to pour water (easier to pour with spout); used pitcher to pour beads (photo 10.14)

TABLE 11.2 AGES AND STAGES OF MATH AND SCIENCE (continued)

Age	Component	Possible Behaviours
School-aged	Awareness—develop a general understanding/recognition of new objects, people, events, and concepts Develop more specific understanding/recognition of known objects, people, events, and concepts Explore—active experiences to construct personal meaning about objects, people, events, and concepts	Learn about concepts through writing, manipulation, asking questions, reading, performing operations and observing: weight and size by measuring with tape, scale, thermometer recording, calculating (photo 12.11) Shape and colour by examining new objects, comparing objects, talking about objects, representing objects (photo 4.3) Space by walking, running, climbing, riding, measuring, drawing, calculating (photo 6.20) Time—telling time, calculating time Classifying—objects, pictures, words (photo 10.1) Measure—use rudimentary method (string, body) (photo 6.21) Pattern—completes simple *abab* patterns, easily distracted to switch to new pattern (i.e., red car, blue car, red car, blue car, blue elephant, red car, yellow car, yellow elephant)
School-aged	Inquiry—compares their results with those of other sources, recognizes commonalities and makes generalizations	Compare—in writing, or representations Develop sequence—increased complexity Interpretations—on experiment/activity Discover relationships—between numbers, sets of numbers, among animals Collect information—gather materials, gather information in writing Count objects—count correctly, form sets of numbers Perform operations—addition, subtraction, division, multiplication, conduct simple experiments Explain results—verbally or in writing Compare results—with peers, in books Use conventional methods—formulas for solving problems, method for experimenting Generalize to new situations—create electric circuit, use to run Lego
School-aged	Utilization—apply understanding to new situations and settings	Write reports, demonstrate principles, prepare presentations, discuss results, evaluate and readjust

► KEY POINTS

Concepts

- math and science share fundamental concepts—counting, comparing, sorting, matching, measuring; and
- math and science share processing skills—observing, predicting, communicating, inferring, and reflecting.

Components of Learning Cycle

- creating a general awareness through active, sensory involvement of objects, people, events and concepts;
- exploring—active experience to construct personal meaning about objects, people, events, and concepts;
- inquiring—compare results, check results, verify results; and
- utilizing—apply knowledge and skills gained to new situations and settings.

Value of Math and Science

- learn through observing;
- make and test predictions;
- make inferences;
- make logical connections;
- learn by trying new things in new ways;
- increase awareness of world;
- utilize math and science skills in a variety of ways;
- make connections between outdoor and indoor environments;
- conduct simple experiments;
- follow scientific process;
- enhance problem-solving skills;
- look at things in different ways;
- apply knowledge gained from experiences; and
- work with concepts in new ways.

Role of the Facilitator

- ask alternative questions;
- focus on aesthetics;
- utilize natural materials;
- provide related books;
- share enthusiasm;
- focus attention;
- follow children's lead;
- provide safe environments;
- provide developmentally appropriate materials;
- extend children's interests;
- facilitate investigation; and
- facilitate discussion.

Effective Storage/Labelling System

- similar to manipulative, sand, water, quiet areas; and
- curiosity table.

Considerations for Setting Up a Math and Science Area

- **outdoor experiences**—coordinate indoor and outdoor experiences;
- **aesthetics**—sensitive to beauty in nature, pleasing display of collections;
- individual working spaces, mini-museums; and
- **location**—suitable in all learning areas, most elements in common with manipulative materials, near natural light.

Observation and Documentation Techniques

- skills charts;
- frequency counts/checklist;
- portfolio; and
- learning cycle chart.

Materials

- compare;
- match;
- sort;
- pattern;
- measure;
- natural; and
- animals.

Student Activities

1. Conduct a field trip in your neighbourhood. Identify the possible dangers. Identify strategies you might use to ensure a group of four- and five-year-olds has a safe field trip.

2. You have just been hired in a daycare program for infants. The only type of science and math activity that you can see happening is going out for walk. The infants usually sleep in their strollers during this time. What strategies might you use to bring more awareness about the environment to your group of children?

3. It has been raining steadily; the children have not been outside for a few days. You encourage the families to bring appropriate clothing to go outside. What might you do with your preschool group to involve them in science and math activities? What additional safeguards do you need to take in these circumstances?

4. You do not have a lot of natural elements within your setting. What might you be able to collect? How might children help in the process? How could you include families?

5. What additional knowledge might you have to research to become more effective in facilitating math and science?

6. Observe the skills of one toddler, one preschooler, and one school-aged child. How are their skills similar? How are they different?

7. Using the learning cycle, describe how you have gone through each of the components of the cycle during your studies in the early childhood field.

8. List some simple experiments that preschoolers could be involved in. Look over your list. Eliminate those that involve teacher-directed activity. Choose one of the remaining experiments. List the experiences that children have to have before they can become involved in this experiment. How would you set up the environment to encourage children to participate?

9. You have been given a budget of $500 to spend on materials for math and science. What would your purchase be? Give reasons for your choice.

► References

Bredekamp, S., & Rosegrant, T. (Eds.). (1992). Reaching Potentials: Appropriate Curriculum and Assessment for Young Children. *Young Children.* Vol.1, p. 33.

Charlesworth, R., & Lind, K. (1999). *Math and Science for Young Children.* (3rd ed.). Albany, NY: Delmar Publishers.

Dighe, J. (1993, March). Children and the Earth. *Young Children.* 58–63.

Kokoski, T., & Downing-Leffler, N. (1995, July). Boosting Your Science and Math Programs in Early Childhood Education: Making the Home-School Connection. *Young Children, 35–39.*

Wilson, R. (1995, September). Nature and Young Children: A Natural Connection. *Young Children.* 4–11.

Yinger, J., & Blaszka, S. (1995, November). A Year of Journaling—A Year of Building with Young Children. *Young Children.* 15–20.

► Resources

Children's Books

Bently, D., & Deesing, J. (1996). *If You Were a Bug...* Santa Monica, CA: Intervisual Books, Inc.

Belz Jenkins, P., & Rockwell, L. (1995). *A Nest Full of Eggs.* New York, NY: HarperCollins Publishers.

Berenstain, M. (1992). *Butterfly Book.* Racine, WI: Western Publishing Company Inc.

Hunt, J. (1992). *Butterflies.* San Luis Opispo, CA: Blake Publishing.

Kuchalla, S., & Britt, G. (1998). *Now I Know Birds.* New York, NY: Troll Associates.

Lovett, S. (1992). *Extremely Weird Insects.* Santa Fe, NM: John Muir Publications.

McDonnell, J., & Connelly, G. (1990). *Wind What Can I Do?* Elgin, IL: Child's World Inc.

Roberts, M. (1996). *World's Weirdest Bats.* New York, NY: Troll Communications L.L.C.

CDs

Encore Software. (2001). *Pets, Food and Telephones.* New York, NY: Sesame Workshop.

Encore Software. (2001). *Shoes, Bugs, and Farms.* New York, NY: Sesame Workshop.

Fisher Price Ready for School. (1997, Winter). David Anderson and Associates. *Newsweek.* p. 41.

Glasklar. (2000). *Birds, Insects, and Spiders.* Duluth, GA: MegaSystems.

Jump Start Preschool. (2000). Torrance, CA: Knowledge Adventure Inc.

Jump Start Toddlers. (2000). Torrance, CA: Knowledge Adventure Inc.

Let's Pretend! Our Backyard Is A Playground. (1977, Winter). *Newsweek.* p. 28.

OmniMedia. (1997, Winter). Treasure Hunt. *Newsweek.* p. 31.

Plums at the Zoo. (2001). Les Jeux, GB: Micro-Tel.

Plums at the Farm. On Track Software. Les Jeux, GB: Micro-Tel.

Preschool Thinking Skills. (2001). Grand Haven, MI: School Zone Publishing Company.

Toddlers Sesame Street Learning Series. (1997). Redwood City, CA: Creative Wonders.

CHAPTER 12

Woodworking

Working with wood is a great adventure! With all the varied attributes–types, textures, weights, colors, and smells–wood offers children a total experience with opportunities to explore, discover, and create. As they hammer, saw, sand, glue, and paint wood, children develop fine and gross-motor skills–improving their coordination and control.... Best of all, woodworking is physical fun that is endlessly challenging!

–Feeney, The Wonders of Working with Wood

Chapter Outline

- ▶ Woodworking to Encourage Learning
- ▶ Child Development: Developmental Levels of Woodworking
- ▶ Value of Woodworking
- ▶ Role of the Facilitator
- ▶ Effective Storage Systems
- ▶ Effective Labelling Systems
- ▶ Considerations for Setting Up a Woodworking Area

- ▶ Observation and Documentation Techniques
- ▶ International Considerations
- ▶ Woodworking Materials
- ▶ Ages and Stages of Woodworking
- ▶ Key Points
- ▶ Student Activities
- ▶ References
- ▶ Resources

Learning Outcomes

After studying this chapter, the reader will:

1. Identify the stages of woodworking
2. Identify pre-woodworking skills
3. Understand woodworking skills
4. Identify the value of the woodworking area
5. Identify the role of the facilitator
6. Discuss effective storage techniques
7. Identify an appropriate labelling system
8. Discuss considerations for setting up the woodworking area in both indoor and outdoor environments
9. Identify critical safety aspects of woodworking
10. Identify appropriate materials
11. Identify various documentation techniques in order to observe children

Interactive Learning Exercises

 Remember, the CD-ROM that came with this text contains interactive exercises that relate to the topics in this chapter, as well as other valuable resources.

▶ Woodworking to Encourage Learning

Haley was watching Billy working at the carpentry bench. Billy had decided to build a house. Finally Haley sighed and left. Deanna heard her sigh. She asked her why she was sighing.

Haley: "I wish carpentry was something I could do."

Deanna: "Why can't you?"

Haley: "Only boys are good at carpentry."

Deanna: "Oh, I don't think so. I'm good at carpentry. I am sure you would be too."

Haley: "What have you made?"

Deanna: "Come with me and I will show you."

Deanna took Haley over to the manipulative area. A small wooden dollhouse was set up in the area. Inside the dollhouse was wooden furniture. Deanna indicated to Haley that she had made the dollhouse and some of the furniture in it. Haley sat down and looked at the dollhouse and started to look at some of the furniture. Deanna smiled and walked away.

A little while later, Deanna saw Haley in the carpentry area. She had nailed two pieces of wood together by attaching a thin fourth strip to the back of the wood with small nails. Deanna walked over and watched Haley. Haley nailed two pieces of brown leather to the top of the wood. She cut out a black piece of fabric and nailed it in the centre. Next she painted a design on her wood (photo 12.1). Haley held it up and said, "I guess girls *can* do carpentry."

PHOTO 12.1

▶ Child Development: Developmental Levels of Woodworking

Before children can actively participate in creating in the woodworking area, they have to develop a number of skills. Some of these skills develop naturally as children grow and mature.

- **eye–hand coordination**—Infants start to develop the ability to look at an object, grasp it, and shake

PHOTO 12.2

PHOTO 12.3

PHOTO 12.4

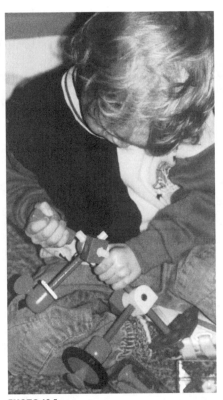

PHOTO 12.5

PHOTO 12.6

it within the first four months of life. As they become more familiar with the objects, they begin to selectively pick one object to manipulate it to cause it to move or make a sound (photo 12.2); and

- push, pull, twist, turn—Many of the toys provided to infants encourage the infant to push a button, turn a knob, or pull a knob out (photo 12.3).

Other skills need to be nurtured by providing children with materials and equipment that will give them the necessary experience and practice.

- hammering—hitting an object on a specific spot to make it move (photo 12.4);
- using tools to attach and take apart objects (photo 12.5); and
- experimenting with wood to build or create structures or designs (photo 12.6).

As children's fine motor control and eye–hand coordination improves, they are ready to participate in woodworking activities.

The toy workbench fascinated Reghan. She loved to take the plastic screwdriver and twist the plastic screws into the workbench. She discovered that there were screws and screwdrivers available in the carpentry area. She experimented with a variety of types of screwdrivers to drive the various types of screws into the board (photo 12.7).

Reghan learned to match the tools to their materials. She developed fine motor skills and coordination skills—placing the screwdriver into the hole or

PHOTO 12.7

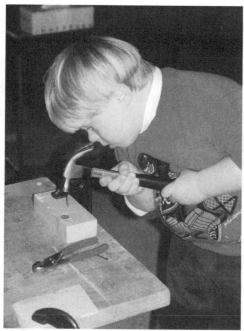

PHOTO 12.8

PHOTO 12.9

slot, turning the screwdriver, and applying pressure to drive the screw into the wood.

Josh loved to hammer. He had practised hammering nails into a board that had already been started by placing nails of various sizes into the board. He decided that he wanted to start his own nail. He found it difficult to start the nail. Deanna noticed his struggles. She asked if she could help. "Yes!" replied Josh. Deanna said, "Maybe if I hold the nail for you can start it." She took a pair of pliers and held the nail on the wood. Josh started to hammer the nail in. When it was far enough into the wood, Deanna removed the pliers and Josh continued to hammer his nail into the board (photo 12.8).

Josh visited the carpentry area almost daily. He often practised sawing pieces of wood into smaller pieces. He tried to clamp the wood onto the workbench. Deanna noticed that he was having difficulties. She went to help. She held the clamp for Josh and Josh screwed it tight. Josh sawed his wood into three pieces (photo 12.9).

Josh improved his eye–hand coordination skills in his ability to hit the nail on the head and drive it into the wood and to saw through the piece of wood. He is still experimenting with different ways of hitting the nails. Notice he is using two hands to accomplish the task. He also knew that he had to clamp the wood to be successful.

Joshua decided to make an airplane. He chose the pieces of wood that he could use. He then clamped his wood into the miter box and cut off a corner. Since the wood was very thick, it took him a long time. He decided to wait to finish it another day. The piece of wood was put on the to-be-completed section of the display shelf in the woodworking area. Joshua returned to his task the next day. He sawed off another piece and again left the task to be finished. On the third day, he immediately went back to the carpentry area. He found a long piece of wood to use as wings. Joshua measured the long piece by holding it over the piece he had already cut. He drew a line across it and then cut the wood near the line. He nailed down the wood onto the cut piece. Joshua continued to work on his plane, adding different details

PHOTO 12.10

PHOTO 12.11

PHOTO 12.12

PHOTO 12.13

with markers. He also used a cylindrical piece of wood to create a pilot (photo 12.10). He finally took his plane home to finish there.

Jakob and Mario decided that they wanted to make a birdhouse. Deanna helped them find a simple pattern in one of the books. Jakob measured the wood to cut it to "same sizes" (photo 12.11). Mario cut the wood in the miter box to give it a "roof shape" (photo 12.12). Jakob's father came in to help the boys with their project over several days. He showed Mario how to clamp the wood so that he could nail the sides of his birdhouse together (photo 12.13). He let the boys watch as he drilled the hole for the door. The boys completed their project over many weeks. The final stage was to paint the birdhouse white.

All three boys were able to sustain attention over a period of time. Each boy knew what task he wanted to accomplish and what tools were needed to accomplish that task. The boys had learned how to use the tools more effectively—cut wood on an angle, choose the appropriate sized nails, and measure the wood to be able to cut it. All three boys worked independently with a minimum of assistance. They knew how to clamp the wood and needed help only to tighten the clamp more securely. They were able to start driving their nails into the wood by themselves. They were able to fit the pieces of wood together to match their expectation. Mario and Jakob were able to follow a pattern to complete their birdhouse.

► Value of Woodworking

- seeing the results of their actions—the look on Haley's face (photo 12.1) is a clear indication of the sense of achievement experienced;
- improve their coordination—Josh as he hammered and sawed the wood; Mario starting and continuing to drive the nails into the wood;
- improve control—Reghan screwing the screws into the wood, Josh hammering the nail into the wood;
- cooperate—Jakob and Mario working together to complete their birdhouses;
- develop self-confidence—Haley, after completing a project that she did not think she could do, developed other projects over time;
- develop perseverance—Mario and Jakob completing their birdhouses, Joshua completing his airplane;
- develop understanding of relationships—cause and effect: clamping wood makes it easier to hammer or saw; wood can be cut into many pieces;
- develop understanding of one-to-one-correspondence—one side of a piece of wood fits one side of another piece of wood to make a birdhouse;
- use math skills such as counting and measuring—Mario counting the number of pieces he needed for his birdhouse, Joshua measuring the length needed to complete his plane;

PHOTO 12.14

- match appropriate tool to job—Reghan matching screwdrivers to heads of screws;
- learn to use tools safely—Josh knew he had to clamp wood to hammer and saw it;
- sustain interest over time—Jakob and Mario building the birdhouses, Joshua creating his plane;
- expand vocabulary—all children learned the names of the tools they were using;
- learn properties about wood—wood can be attached together by nailing it (bird houses); wood can be made smooth by sanding (photo 12.14); wood can be decorated (photo 12.1); wood can be cut in different ways (photos 12.9 and 12.12); and
- solve problems together—When Reghan initially started to use the screwdrivers, she found it difficult. She started out by using two hands. Mackenzie noticed what she was doing and showed her how to do it more effectively (photo 12.15). She said, "You have to push down on the screwdriver like this." At first Reghan ignored her, but when she noticed that Mackenzie's screws were moving down she tried it differently and was successful.

▶ Role of the Facilitator

- document children's skills, learning, and activities;
- become familiar with tools, materials to understand the potential of the woodworking area;

PHOTO 12.15

- provide a safe environment—woodworking area protected on three sides from traffic flow, out of main traffic flow area;
- provide safe materials—soft wood, appropriate sized nails, appropriate sized tools;
- model safe practices—wood clamped before sawing or hammering; tools returned to correct spots when finished; hold nail with pliers;
- monitor children in the area—Deanna stepped in to help when needed; clamp wood, hold nail for hammering;
- model/expand vocabulary—facilitator named tools and actions as they were being used;
- recognize child's ability level—knew that Josh might need help hammering or clamping; offered only as much help as he needed;
- provide developmentally appropriate materials—wood pieces to glue and paint (photo 12.6); peg-board work bench (photo 12.4);
- appreciate children's efforts—provided area for displaying completed work; took photographs of children working on projects and displayed them;
- provide an area to store works in progress—birdhouses, plane;
- ensure tools are safe to use—clamps work, hammer heads are securely fastened, saws are sharp enough to cut wood (dull saws slip and can cause injury); nails are safely stored;

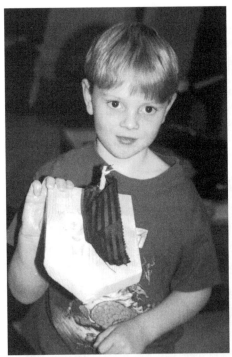

PHOTO 12.16

- provide adequate time—within the day (Haley completed her project in one day) and over time (birdhouse, boat);
- share in pride of accomplishment—Ben created a boat (photo 12.16). Deanna looked at the boat and said that he had worked very hard on the boat. She asked him if it was a sailboat. He proudly nodded yes; and
- recognize children's feelings and provide appropriate feedback—Haley thought girls could not do woodworking. Deanna told her they could and showed what she had done. Haley thought about it and completed a project with wood.

▶ Effective Storage Systems

It is extremely important that tools are stored appropriately. Storage systems that are appropriate should model a real workshop. Following are some suggestions:

- peg-board panel on back of a shelf or wall (hang tools on hooks); hammers, clamps, screwdrivers, pliers, saws;
- small organizer chests with clear fronts to store nails and screws, nuts and bolts;
- organized bins for various types of wood—milk cartons work well, can be stacked in front of a wall on the floor;

- small stackable plastic containers for decorative materials—make sure these materials can be nailed or glued;
- shelf to organize things such as work gloves, measuring tape, rulers, miter boxes, wrenches, glue, sharp pencils, sanders, hand drills;
- wall rack for books with ideas for woodworking;
- display shelf, rack, and/or small table for finished products and for projects in progress;
- visible and accessible; and
- away from active work area (i.e., if a child is sawing, the storage area should not interfere with another child trying to get a hammer or another tool).

▶ Effective Labelling Systems

Labelling becomes critical in woodworking. Children need to know precisely where materials are stored and where to return them. Dumping nails on a table to find the size of nail that is needed is dangerous. Leaving tools dumped on top of each other may result in a cut when trying to pick up a tool or may result in a hammer falling on someone's foot. Labelling in this section is easiest by outlines and words.

Create shadow pictures of the tools to place on the peg board where the tools hang. These can be created with permanent markers. Similarly, items on the shelf can be arranged the same way. Materials in small organizer chests can be labelled with the word and tape the nail or screw right on the front of the drawer ensuring that the nail tip is well covered.

Small stackable bins have a slot for labels at the front. Again it is easiest to tape a sample of the materials at the front so that children know at a glance what is in that bin. Creating small plastic pouches that are securely attached tend to be more secure. For larger wood pieces, save the netting from bottles, vegetables, or fruit and put a sample item in the netting. Hang netting at the front of the milk carton.

For safety's sake, children need to learn to choose the tool and material they need to work with. When they have finished, the tool needs to be returned immediately to the designated spot.

▶ Considerations for Setting Up a Woodworking Area

Safety of children is the first thing that needs to be considered when setting up the woodworking area. Children are very focused on what they are doing. They will not stop to think that they may hit someone if the person is too close while they are hammering. The space needs to be set up to minimize any accidents from occurring.

1. Location

- out of main traffic area—in a corner of a room, in an area that is protected on three sides; use a wall and low shelves or display tables to barricade the other two sides;
- near creative art—children can then take their creations to finish—decorate, paint; wood can be used for three-dimensional activities or projects; and
- on tiled surface—easy to clean; easy to find nails if they drop.

2. Safety

- store items that are needed at workbench or near workbench—hammers and saws within reach of working areas;
- create more than one area within area—one side of worktable used for sawing, other side for hammering; separate table for sanding, gluing, decorating; encourage finishing of projects in creative art area;
- model and reinforce safety expectations—tools picked up by handles and carried facing down, return tools when finished, clamp wood for hammering or sawing, pick up or sweep up immediately or as needed;
- model and reinforce nails left in containers on shelf, not on worktable—hammering causes vibrations, nails move and drop on floor, children may step into them;
- limit the number of children—dependent on size of area, identify how many can safely hammer or saw;
- model and reinforce correct use of tools; and
- monitor area when children are working there.

3. Display

Display items effectively. Create displays that have more than one level. This type of storage tends to work both for work in progress and for items that are completed. This can be created as follows:

- place empty boxes, foam pieces on a table, arrange to have a centre of focus—that is, high to one side or middle of the table, and low on the other side(s);
- drape with material, sheet, blanket—make sure you cover all boxes and that you drape material to create "mountains and valleys" following the contour of the boxes set out;
- make sure display area is at an appropriate height for children—children should be able to retrieve or place items; and
- place items on top of contours created.

Create a photographic display of children's work that identifies the various stages of progress through a project, or the various skill levels children are involved with. This can appear on a documentation wall in the carpentry area. Ongoing projects are ideal to use for this purpose. It acts as a motivation point for other children and as a reminder for children completing the project. Other completed projects can be stored in individual albums that children and families can refer to.

▶ Observation and Documentation Techniques

WOODWORKING SKILLS

Figure 12.1 is an example of a skill chart.

FIGURE 12.1

▶ Skill Sample Chart		

Name: Reghan

Date	Skill	Evidence
10.15	Match	Screwdriver to head of screw
	Coordinate two actions	Twist screw into wood—turn and push

The information gathered can be used in other areas. Reghan is observing detail (the type of head a screw has), and matching this information to what type of tool she needs to use. Matching detail or noting detail is a skill needed for reading (letters or words that are the same), writing (printing a "b" and a "d"), and math (numbers that are the same or sets of numbers that are the same). Activities could be set up in these areas to expand her skills.

DOCUMENTATION OF A PROJECT

Mario and Jakob's project was documented using photographs and written descriptions. At each stage a picture was taken and the details of that scenario were documented. As an example, one documentation panel has been developed using photo 12.12. Mario took a narrow piece of wood. He went over to the worktable. The miter box was already clamped to the table. He got another clamp and attached it to the wood at the end. He tightened the screw. He picked up a saw and started to saw the wood. The wood moved around in the miter box. Mario stopped cutting. He called to another child, "Hey Billy, I need help. It's not tight." Billy walked over and tightened the clamp. Mario started to saw again. He cut the piece of wood. He brought the piece of wood over to the pieces he had already cut. He stood two pieces of wood on their ends and put the narrow piece on top. "It's not big enough." He went over to the wood area and looked for a new piece of wood. The next episode would be his search for a new piece of wood and the interaction with the adults to facilitate the process.

This type of information gives rich detail about what the child is doing, what language is being used, and what the progress of the activity is. It gives the facilitator information about:

- what experiences the child needs—measuring; making pattern for new piece; comparing sizes of wood; brainstorming the process;
- what materials need to be available—pieces of wood that can be easily cut to required size; create template of birdhouse; create birdhouse out of template prior to cutting it out of wood;
- the skills Mario already has—knows who to ask for help; knows how to use various tools; is aware of safety factors and uses them; and
- information about his language skills—uses complete sentences; expresses his problem situation verbally.

Panels that are created can be posted on the wall as they are created. When the project is complete, these can be transferred to booklet format, which can be used as reading material for children and families to refer to.

▶ International Considerations

Very little information is available about children and woodworking in other countries. It is anticipated that in cultures where woodworking is a cultural value, children would be exposed to woodworking and would learn to work with wood early. Woodworking is also a more expensive learning activity. In economically deprived areas or in areas where wood is a scarce commodity woodworking would not be found.

Woodworking materials are similar with respect to tools and how the materials are used in the Western cultures. The wood that is used changes depending on the species that grow in that part of the world. For example, Hogben and Wasley (1996) recommend also using bamboo and cane (Australia).

▶ Woodworking Materials

Table 12.1 lists examples of some woodworking materials and ways to use them.

TABLE 12.1

▶ Woodworking Materials

Material	Examples
Wood	Soft wood—balsa, white pine, poplar, basswood
	Hardwoods such as maple, oak, birch, chestnut—too hard for nailing but can be used for exploring wood, gluing, decorating
	Plywood or fir, hemlock, and spruce—poor choices as these woods splinter easily
	Dowelling of different sizes, Popsicle sticks, tongue depressors
Decorative materials	See creative art materials in Chapter 9
Woodworking bench	Sturdy—should not move when children are sawing, pounding
	Suitable height, width
Tools for safety	Adjustable clamps, work gloves (child-sized)
	Safety glasses—note: most safety glasses that are an appropriate size for children are toys and restrict vision—children cannot see what they are doing. It is safer not to use safety glasses in this case

TABLE 12.1 WOODWORKING MATERIALS (continued)

Material	Examples
Other materials	Tree stumps, log rounds, corks, ribbon, material, leather, vinyl, plastic
	Lids, scissors, shears, dowelling, string, yarn, soft wire, carpet pieces
	Paper, corrugated paper, boxes, wheels, reels, various wood shapes
Tools	Saws—small crosscut saw, point saws, hacksaws
	Hammers—mallets, claw hammer with steel shank
	Shaping tools—files; hand drills; planes; sanders; sandpaper of various grades, rasps
	Screwdrivers—various types
	Holding tools—pliers, vices, pincers
	Attachments—flat-headed nails: various sized heads and lengths
	Various types and sizes of screws, nuts, and bolts
	Pencils, rulers, angles, measuring tape

▶ Ages and Stages of Woodworking

Table 12.2 outlines pre-woodworking skills and ages and stages of woodworking.

TABLE 12.2

▶ Pre-Woodworking Skills and Ages and Stages of Woodworking

Age	Skill	Materials
Infants–8 months and up	Push	Popup toys—push down on a button, a toy pops up or out
	Pull	Tops—push the button and the top spins
		Pull-apart toys—Duplo, ring'o'links
	Pound	Pounding toys—peg and hammer benches, ball maze (hammer ball into maze), pound coloured knobs to pop up toys
	Twist, turn	Turn keys on toy houses to open doors, dials on crib toys
Toddlers	Play with wood pieces (sensory experience)	Wood of different sizes, shapes, weight (well sanded) to build with, paint, decorate
	Pounding toys	Hammers and pounding benches
		Plastic or wooden workbenches—screws, screwdrivers, nuts, bolts, spanner
	Using tools—twist, turn	Take apart, build vehicles—screws drills, nuts, bolts, screwdrivers, spanners
		Nuts and bolts sets
		Brio building set—use plastic tools and various shaped parts to construct creations

TABLE 12.2 PRE-WOODWORKING SKILLS AND AGES AND STAGES OF WOODWORKING (continued)

Age	Skill	Materials
Three-year-olds	Hammer	Golf tees or large-headed nails into Styrofoam, fiberboard
		Nails into soft wood; nail two pieces of wood together
	Screw	Insert screws into wooden board, children screw in and out
	Attach	Various items to a piece of wood—with nails, glue
	Sand wood	Sanders
	Decorate	Paint—rollers, brushes
	Saw	Thin pieces of soft wood clamped to workbench, child-sized saw
Four- and five-year-olds	Combine pieces to create an object	Saw wood to get correct size, measure pieces; use miter box to cut angles; work on projects over time; attach pieces in various ways—glue, different sized nails, screws
		Use clamps to secure wood
	Follow a plan	Look up ideas for projects
	Use right sized materials—nail to size to fit size of wood	
School-aged	Increasingly more skilled	Increasingly complex projects

▶ KEY POINTS

Child Developmental Levels of Woodworking: Pre-Woodworking Skills

- infants—push, pull, pound, twist, turn;
- toddlers—play with wood, pounding toys, using tools;
- 3-year-olds—hammer, screw, attach, sand, decorate, saw;
- 4- and 5-year-olds—combine pieces to make projects, follow a plan, use appropriate materials and tools; and
- school-aged—increased complexity of projects and skill.

Value of Woodworking

- seeing results of actions;
- improve coordination;
- improve control;
- cooperate;
- develop perseverance;
- develop understanding of relationships;
- develop understanding of one-to-one-correspondence;
- use math skills;
- match appropriate tool to job;
- learn to use tools safely;
- sustain interest over time;
- expand vocabulary;
- learn about properties of wood; and
- solve problems together.

Role of the Facilitator

- become familiar with tools and materials;
- provide safe environment;
- model safe practices;
- monitor children;
- model/expand vocabulary;
- recognize child's ability level;
- provide storage for projects;
- ensure tools are safe;
- provide adequate time;
- share pride in accomplishments; and
- recognize children's feelings.

► KEY POINTS (continued)

Effective Storage Systems

- peg boards with hooks;
- organizer chests;
- bins;
- stackable containers;
- shelves;
- wall racks; and
- display shelf.

Effective Labelling Systems

- outline;
- words; and
- attach samples.

Considerations for Setting Up a Woodworking Area

- **Location**—out of traffic flow, near creative art, on tiled surface.
- **Safety**—accessibility of storage, separate pounding, sawing, and finishing areas; model and reinforce safety; limit number of children; model and reinforce correct use of tools; monitor area.

Display

- work in progress and final products; and
- photographic display.

Observation and Documentation Techniques

- skill checklists;
- project documentation; and
- display.

Student Activities

1. Create an item that you could use within a preschool setting—doll house, doll furniture, boat, puzzle. Identify what tools you used, how you used them, and what process was used.
2. Go to a hardware store. Create a list of appropriate tools that would be suitable for a child-care setting. Explain your choices.
3. Go to a toy store. Identify toys that would be suitable for pre-woodworking skills for infants and for toddlers. Explain the value of each toy as it relates to pre-woodworking skills.
4. Jamie was trying to hammer a nail into a piece of wood. He consistently missed the top of the nail. What strategies could you employ to help him become more successful?
5. Observe a three-year-old and a four-year-old at the woodworking area. What skills and what tools were used by each? Compare your results.
6. Many centres for young children do not include woodworking areas. The main reason given is that it is not safe for young children. What strategies could you use to ensure safety?
7. Explain why woodworking is an excellent area to include within a program for young children.
8. For each of photos 12.2, 12.5, and 12.13, describe what the child learned through the activity depicted. Compare the skills of each age group represented by the pictures. How have the skills changed with age?
9. How did Deanna, the facilitator, support the children's learning and accomplishments?

▶ References

Feeney, L. (1991, April). The Wonders of Working with Wood. *Scholastic, Pre-K Today*.

Hogben, J., & Wasley, D. (1996). *Learning in Early Childhood. What does it mean in practice?* Education Department of South Australia: Hyde Park Press: South Australia.

▶ Resources

Shipley, D. (2002). *Empowering Children: Play-Based Curriculum for Lifelong Learning.* (3rd ed.). Scarborough, ON: Nelson.

Skeen, P., Garner, A., & Cartwright, S. (1984). Woodworking for Young Children. Washington, DC: National Association for Young Children.

Glossary

(Numbers in parentheses refer to the chapter(s) containing the main discussion of the term.)

accommodation
The process by which an old idea or concept is changed to fit new ideas or concepts. (1, 6)

active exploration
The child uses all of his senses to interact with the materials and individuals in his or her environment. (11)

active learning
Children learn by negotiating their own learning and exploring the environment by using all of their senses. (2)

activity plan
Written documentation that itemizes all critical components for one learning experience (for example, a plan to make play dough snowmen that is suitable for one or more children). (2)

aesthetics
The appreciation of beauty that develops over time; it is culturally determined and dependent on exposure to various experiences. (2)

aesthetic feeling
Feelings evoked by listening to good literature or music, or walking in nature, or admiring beautiful art or sculptures, or expressing oneself in written format. (2)

aesthetic response
Expression of aesthetic feelings by talking about one's experience, or writing about one's experience, or quietly enjoying the moment, or actively participating by dancing, moving, or singing. (2)

assimilation
The process by which new ideas or concepts are used to fit into existing ideas or concepts. (1, 6)

associative play
Play between two or more children who are using the same or similar materials, are talking about what they are doing, and are sharing materials and ideas, but are engaged in individual activities. (1)

balance
Art work in which all forms are in proportion to each other is considered balanced. (9)

behavioural response
A response that is automatic; that is not determined by sex, age, income, culture, or environment, and that the individual is unaware of making. (2)

blocks (6)

> **carrying and stacking (stage 1)**
> Blocks are transported from one area to another area, either with hands and arms or by loading them into containers and then carrying them. Blocks are stacked or piled in haphazard manner without attention to alignment or placement.

> **rows and towers (stage 2)**
> Blocks are placed precisely end on end with careful consideration of alignment and placement in order to create vertical or horizontal structures.

> **walls and bridges (stage 3)**
> Blocks are placed end to end and on top of each other precisely in order to create a combination of vertical and horizontal alignments to form walls. Gaps are created to form windows, doors, bridges, or gaps in structures are created.

> **enclosures and patterns (stage 4)**
> Walls are extended to create an enclosed space that may be used to confine individuals or materials within that space. Often patterns are created using size, shape, or colour—large rectangular block, small rectangular block, large rectangular block, small rectangular block..., red block, green block, red block, green block....

> **representations and reproductions (stage 5)**
> Children use blocks to build something specifically, such as a house, a field, or a zoo. Children may try to reproduce familiar structures—own home, bridge in neighbourhood, or a garage with ramps.

classifying
Arranging in groups and subgroups or classes considering more than one attribute. For example, classifying food into food groups requires thinking that could involve all or some of the following attributes—shape, colour, size, taste, and knowledge. (2)

cognitive play
The interaction between play and mental growth and development. (1)

collaboration
The process in which two or more individuals share ideas, materials, and space in order to plan an activity and to reach a common goal. (1)

collectibles
Items that children can collect and work with, such as rocks, washed glass, shells, and stickers. (10)

constructive play
Children use materials, space, or objects to create a specific idea or structure. (2)

cooperative games
Games that encourage children to share materials, take turns, and socialize with each other. (10)

cooperative play

One or more children work together toward a common goal. Ideas, space, and materials are shared, the goal is planned, and specific roles are assigned. (4)

creative art (9)

scribbling

Child manipulates art materials to make random marks on a surface. The child enjoys the kinesthetic experience without intending to produce an end product.

disordered and random scribbling

Child uses a whole-hand grip and whole-arm movement to create haphazard marks on a surface. Child may or may not observe own actions.

controlled scribbling

Child produces smaller, less haphazard marks within a confined space with much greater muscle control. Child watches various types of scribbles as they are made.

named scribbling

Child spends more time on process with much greater fine muscle control. Scribbles show greater variety, intentional placement, and are named. Names may change during the process and may not resemble marks made.

preschematic

Child begins to symbolically represent people, objects, and ideas through drawing and painting. Sizes, spatial arrangements, and proportions are distorted with omission in some drawings, such as human figures.

schematic achievement of a concept

Drawings reflect the child's perspective. Drawings are two-dimensional representations with great details and are very decorative.

realism

Over time drawings become increasingly more realistic with greater attention to detail and fewer distortions.

creativity

"Creativity is a special and different way of viewing the world in ways in which there are no right or wrong answers, only possibilities. Think of creativity as an attitude rather than an aptitude." (Schirrmacher, 1998, p. 6) (1, 19)

critical period

A period of time during which growth and development are more optimal. (1)

design and composition

Various aspects of aesthetics are used to create a design or composition—line, colour, space, balance—that is pleasing to the creator. (9)

developmentally appropriate practices

Practices that match strategies and curriculum to children's individual development, learning styles, and experiences within the context of family, culture, and community. (1)

divergent thinking

The ability to think in a variety of ways or solve problems in more than one way. (1)

dramatic play (8)

stage 1—prop-dependent, imitative

Children imitate behaviours, use props as they were intended to be used, and their play is influenced by the models and props available.

stage 2—familiar roles

Children act out familiar roles of adults, animals.

stage 3—diverse roles

Children act out roles of non-familiar adults, animals.

stage 4—communicative, cooperative

Children create own characters, scripts, and props.

duration count

Documenting the length of time involved in an activity, event, or behaviour. (5)

emergent curriculum

The curriculum evolves from the interests and abilities of the child in collaboration with family members and facilitators. Children learn to take responsibility for their learning and adults provide the experiences that foster the learning. (1)

eye–hand coordination

The ability to use both the eyes and the hands together to accomplish a task such as beading, grasping, sewing. (10, 12)

facilitator

A facilitator is an individual who guides learning. This requires continuous observation of the learner, collaboration between the learner and the adult, and continuous adaptation of the learning environment to foster learning. (1)

figure–ground

The ability to distinguish specific details from a background—finding one specific can of Campbell's mushroom soup from all other similar soups; listening to one conversation in a noisy room, or picking out a rough texture from a smooth background. (6)

form

The organization of a song or piece of music into an overall design. (5)

full-spectrum fluorescent lighting
Fluorescent lighting that offers a full spectrum of wavelengths. This type of lighting produces the closest match to sunlight. (2)

functional play
Repeated practise of skills through interactions with objects, people, and communication without a specific product or purpose. (1)

functional space
Aspects of space that dictate how and where to place materials and equipment within an environment in order to maximize the learning experiences of children. (2)

harmony
"A sequence of one or more changing or repeated tones added to the predominant melody line, to enrich or elaborate it." (Haines and Gerber, 2000, p. 15) (5)

inclusive setting
Settings that are inclusive provide opportunities for active participation of all children—irrespective of culture, ability, gender, ethnicity, or socio-economic status. (1)

individual plan
Written documentation itemizing all critical components for one learning activity, such as learning to write one's own name; usually used with children with special needs. (2)

key experiences
Experiences that engage children in ongoing interactions with each other, adults, and materials within the environment in order to promote emotional, physical, language, cognitive, and physical development. (2)

kinesthetic/bodily intelligence
The ability to coordinate fine and gross motor activities with other activities in order to do more than one thing at a time—marching to a beat while keeping the beat with an instrument. (5)

learned response
A response that is made based on past experiences. Knowledge has been gained that is dependent on gender, age, income level, and cultural background. (2)

learning areas/interest centres
Specific areas within a learning environment that are set up to introduce new skills and concepts, build on and reinforce existing skills and concepts, offer opportunities to extend skills and interest, and provide opportunities for active exploration and learning. (2)

legato
Describes a song or piece of music that flows smoothly and continues without any interruptions. (5)

lesson plan
Written documentation that itemizes all components for one directed activity, such as the life cycle of a frog, suitable for a large group of usually school-aged children. (2)

line
"Lines can be used in many ways. Lines have their own dimensions, including size, directions, length, width, and weight." (Schirrmacher, 1998, p. 152–153) (9)

literacy
The ability to learn to read and write. (1)

manipulate
Involves using hands and fingers to touch, grasp, develop eye–hand coordination, operate tools (scissors, hammer, saw), expand on self-help skills (dressing, eating), and become more independent and self-confident in one's abilities. (1, 10)

mass
Most substances have *mass*, a coherent body of matter of a defined or undefined shape. It is important for children to manipulate various types of mass to gain familiarity and experience, such as play dough, rubber balls, clay, and goop. (9)

matching
The ability to pick out two items that are identical in one or more aspects—two spoons that are identical in shape, size, and colour, or two blocks that are identical in colour and shape but are of two different sizes. (1, 6)

measurement
Child may use tools such as string, hands, or their body to measure and compare size. As children gain experience in measurement they will use more formal tools, such as scales, rulers, or thermometers. (3, 8, 11)

melody
Musical tones that are put together in a sequence or repetition of tones. (5)

mobile storage
Storage of children's materials in containers that offer opportunities for individuals or groups of children to physically move materials from one location to another. (2, 9)

mood
"A combination of musical elements that cause an emotional or affective response in listeners or performers." (Haines and Gerber, 2000, p. 14) (5)

multiple intelligences
Howard Gardner proposes that there are seven basic intelligences—linguistic, logical/mathematical, spatial, musical, bodily/kinesthetic, interpersonal, and intrapersonal. An

individual may show intelligence in any or more than one of the seven domains. (1)

music (5)

prenatal stage
Involves the development of the hearing mechanisms and becoming aware of and remembering certain sounds, such as mother's voice.

listening stage
The ability to discriminate between various sounds or sequences of rhythm of a song or phrase in order to sing or beat the rhythm to a simple song or part of a song and to maintain that activity over time.

imitative stage
Active participation by copying sounds, rhythms, simple songs, and actions to music/songs.

experimental stage
Active participation by using musical instruments to create various rhythms, using the whole body to respond to music, or experimenting by creating new words, tones, and rhythms.

discovery stage
The child uses learned concepts in new ways (new words to a known melody) and learns new concepts (humour in music).

application stage
The child uses learned concepts to create music, play instruments, read music, use concepts effectively, and sing in harmony.

nonauditory effect
Noise that does not damage the hearing mechanism but may affect one or all of the children's behaviours physiologically, motivationally, or cognitively. (2)

one-to-one correspondence
The understanding that one group of a number of things has the same number of things as another. (1, 11)

onlooker/observer play
The child is not actively involved in a play activity, but rather stands back to see what is happening. (1)

open-ended materials
Accessories are materials that can be used with any core materials. They are *open-ended* because a child may use them in any way they wish without the requirement of a designated end product. (1, 10)

palmar grasp
Using the whole hand and all fingers as one unit to pick up objects. (10)

parallel play
Children play beside each other, with similar materials, without sharing materials or ideas. (1)

pattern
A repeated sequence of colour, shape, or size such as red beads, green beads, red beads, green beads.... (9)

perceptual
Process by which information is received and made sense of through the five senses. (5)

pincer grasp
Using the forefinger and thumb to pick up objects. (10)

pitch
The range of high to low or low to high of different musical tones. (5)

poleidoblocks
Cubes, cuboids, cylinders, triangular, prisms, cones, pyramids, in red, green, blue, yellow. (6)

portfolio
A collection of information about an individual child that includes photographs, written documentation, and collections of the child's work that covers all aspects of a child's development. (3, 4, 6, 10)

position statement
Written communication that indicates the stand an individual or agency holds on specific issues. (1)

process-oriented
As the child is involved in play, the way in which materials are used, put together, or described are of primary importance. The way in which the final result is constructed is stressed. (1)

project approach
An in-depth study of a particular interest that is initiated by a child or children in order to gain real-life experiences and to apply these experiences to gain greater knowledge, skills, and expand their interests. (2)

protagonist
An individual who initiates or leads actions or ideas. (1)

psychomotor skills
These are skills that use both large and small muscles and thinking skills in order to create actions, scenarios, or projects. For example, independent dancing requires the individual to interpret the music, moving in time to the music through body and hand motions. (5)

quantity
Children learn about "how much" when they compare and use comparative language such as *more than, less than, the*

same as. As they get older they learn to use numbers to identify weight, size, temperature, and volume. (8)

quiet area
An area that a child or a small group of children can withdraw to in order to participate in quiet activities, relax, concentrate, and gain privacy. (2, 7)

repetitive play
Play that involves actions that are repeated over and over again. Through this kind of activity the child practices skills and gains experience. (3)

representational play
The play has a defined purpose, defined characteristics, and recognizable structures that are named. (3)

rhythm
The grouping together of sounds, silences, and patterns. (5)

scaffolding
The adult supports the child's learning by providing experiences at the child's developmental level in order for progress to the next developmental level to occur. (1)

scribe
An individual who writes down exactly what a child dictates. (6)

seasonal affective disorder (SAD)
This disorder is characterized by depression during the fall and winter, when there are shorter days and subsequently individuals have less direct exposure to sunlight. (2)

self-correcting materials
These materials can be put together only one way. The end result will always be the same. Examples are puzzles, stacking toys, and peg numbers. (10)

shape
Shape may be defined by the effect that is created by the outline of the person, place, or thing. (9)

social play
Children explore social interactions between each other and adults in order to learn about social situations—role play, appropriate language, sharing of ideas and materials, working toward common goals, and problem-solving of social situations. (1)

sorting
The ability to pick out two or more items that are identical in one or more aspects—10 red beads from a collection of beads of various colours, or 16 blue square blocks from a collection of blocks that are different shapes, sizes, and colours. (6)

space
This is a limited or unlimited area that may or may not hold objects, symbols, or people. (9)

spatial intelligence
Understanding terms that indicate direction—*in, on, right, left, over, under....* (5)

staccato
Describes music that is punctuated, choppy, or has a number of interruptions. (5)

symbolic play
During symbolic play the child substitutes one thing for another—an action to represent a word, an object to represent another object, or an idea represented in writing or through art. (1, 3, 6)

tabletop blocks
Small blocks such as small unit blocks, coloured blocks, Lego, small cubes that can be used to build on the surface of a table. (6)

tempo
The speed of music—fast to slow, or slow to fast. (5)

texture
Indication of how a surface or a substance feels or looks. (9)

theme-based planning
Thematic planning involves the organization of learning experiences around a central focus. As many aspects of the learning environment as possible are integrated into that focus. (2)

therapeutic
An activity that is soothing or relaxing to an individual. (3)

timbre
The unique quality of a musical instrument or voice. (5)

transfer of skills
The ability to use a skill learned in one situation in a new and different situation, such as pouring water and then pouring sand. (3)

trial and error learning
Successive random attempts to solve a problem until the solution is found, such as trying to put a puzzle piece into various slots until the correct slot has been found. (10)

tripod grasp
Using the thumb, forefinger, and middle finger to write or print. (9, 10)

viscosity
The degree to which a liquid is resistant to flow. (8)

water play (4)
> **free exploration**
> Open-ended use of materials using fingers, hands, and bodies to discover various concepts about water.

experiment

Use of materials and water in order to make the connections between the child's actions and what happens as a result of those actions.

extend knowledge

The use of prior knowledge in order to solve problems and overcome challenges.

web-based planning

This type of planning integrates information from theme-based planning to be represented in a visual format that is flexible to document a large number of learning experiences. (2)

Index